Julia 1.0 Programming
Complete Reference Guide

Discover Julia, a high-performance language
for technical computing

Ivo Balbaert
Adrian Salceanu

BIRMINGHAM - MUMBAI

Julia 1.0 Programming Complete Reference Guide

First published: May 2019

Production reference: 1170519

Published by Packt Publishing Ltd.
Livery Place
35 Livery Street
Birmingham
B3 2PB, UK.

ISBN 978-1-83882-224-8

www.packtpub.com

`mapt.io`

Mapt is an online digital library that gives you full access to over 5,000 books and videos, as well as industry leading tools to help you plan your personal development and advance your career. For more information, please visit our website.

Why subscribe?

- Spend less time learning and more time coding with practical eBooks and Videos from over 4,000 industry professionals

- Improve your learning with Skill Plans built especially for you

- Get a free eBook or video every month

- Mapt is fully searchable

- Copy and paste, print, and bookmark content

Packt.com

Did you know that Packt offers eBook versions of every book published, with PDF and ePub files available? You can upgrade to the eBook version at `www.packt.com` and as a print book customer, you are entitled to a discount on the eBook copy. Get in touch with us at `customercare@packtpub.com` for more details.

At `www.packt.com`, you can also read a collection of free technical articles, sign up for a range of free newsletters, and receive exclusive discounts and offers on Packt books and eBooks.

Contributors

About the authors

Ivo Balbaert has been a lecturer in web programming and databases at CVO Antwerpen, a community college in Belgium. He received a Ph.D. in Applied Physics from the University of Antwerp in 1986. He worked for 20 years in the software industry as a developer and consultant in several companies, and for 10 years as a project manager at the University Hospital of Antwerp. From 2000 onwards, he switched to partly teaching and partly developing software (at KHM Mechelen, CVO Antwerpen). He also wrote an introductory book in Dutch about developing in Ruby and Rails, Programmeren met Ruby en Rails, by Van Duuren Media. In 2012, he authored a book on the Go programming language, The Way To Go, by IUniverse. He wrote a number of introductory books for new programming languages, notably Dart, Julia, Rust, and Red, all published by Packt.

Adrian Salceanu has been a professional software developer for over 15 years. For the last 10, he's been leading agile teams in developing real-time, data-intensive web and mobile products. Adrian is a public speaker and an enthusiastic contributor to the open source community, focusing on high-performance web development. He's the organizer of the Barcelona Julia Users group and the creator of Genie, a high-performance, highly productive Julia web framework. Adrian has a Master's degree in computing and a postgraduate degree in advanced computer science.

Packt is searching for authors like you

If you're interested in becoming an author for Packt, please visit `authors.packtpub.com` and apply today. We have worked with thousands of developers and tech professionals, just like you, to help them share their insight with the global tech community. You can make a general application, apply for a specific hot topic that we are recruiting an author for, or submit your own idea.

Table of Contents

Preface

Julia offers the high productivity and ease of use of Python and R with the lightning-fast speed of C++. There's never been a better time to learn this language, thanks to its large-scale adoption across a wide range of domains, including fintech, biotech and artificial intelligence (AI).

You will begin by learning how to set up a running Julia platform, before exploring its various built-in types. This Learning Path walks you through two important collection types: arrays and matrices. You'll be taken through how type conversions and promotions work, and in further chapters you'll study how Julia interacts with operating systems and other languages. You'll also learn about the use of macros, what makes Julia suitable for numerical and scientific computing, and how to run external programs.

Once you have grasped the basics, this Learning Path goes on to how to analyze the Iris dataset using DataFrames. While building a web scraper and a web app, you'll explore the use of functions, methods, and multiple dispatches. In the final chapters, you'll delve into machine learning, where you'll build a book recommender system.

By the end of this Learning Path, you'll be well versed with Julia and have the skills you need to leverage its high speed and efficiency for your applications.

This Learning Path includes content from the following Packt products:

- Julia 1.0 Programming - Second Edition by Ivo Balbaert
- Julia Programming Projects by Adrian Salceanu

Who this book is for

This Learning Path is ideal for you if you are a statistician or data scientist who wants a crash course in the Julia programming language while building big data applications. Basic knowledge of mathematics and programming are needed to understand the various methods that are used or created during the course of this Learning Path.

What this book covers

Chapter 1, Installing the Julia Platform, explains how to install all the necessary components for a Julia environment. It teaches you how to work with Julia's console (the REPL) and discusses some of the more elaborate development editors you can use.

Chapter 2, Variables, Types, and Operations, discusses the elementary built-in types in Julia and the operations that can be performed on them so that you are prepared to start writing code with them.

Chapter 3, Functions, teaches you why functions are the basic building blocks of Julia, and how to effectively use them.

Chapter 4, Control Flow, shows Julia's elegant control constructs, how to perform error handling, and how to use coroutines (called Tasks in Julia) to structure the execution of your code.

Chapter 5, Collection Types, explores the different types that group individual values, such as arrays and matrices, tuples, dictionaries, and sets.

Chapter 6, More on Types, Methods, and Modules, digs deeper into the type concept and how it is used in multiple dispatch to get C-like performance. Modules, a higher code organizing concept, are discussed as well.

Chapter 7, Metaprogramming in Julia, touches on deeper layers of Julia, such as expressions and reflection capabilities, and demonstrates the power of macros.

Chapter 8, I/O, Networking, and Parallel Computing, shows how to work with data in files and databases by using DataFrames. It also looks at networking capabilities, and how to set up a parallel computing environment with Julia.

Chapter 9, Running External Programs, looks at how Julia interacts with the command-line and with other languages and also discusses performance tips.

Chapter 10, The Standard Library and Packages, digs deeper into the standard library, and demonstrates important packages for the visualization of data.

Chapter 11, Creating Our First Julia App, will show you how to perform data analysis against the Iris dataset with Julia. We take a look at RDatasets, a package that provides access to 700 learning datasets distributed with the R language. We'll load the Iris dataset and we'll manipulate it using standard data analysis functions. We also look more closely at the data by employing common visualization techniques using Gadfly. In the process, we cover strings and regular expressions, numbers, tuples, ranges, and arrays. Finally, we'll see how to persist and (re)load our data with CSV, Feather, and MongoDB.

Chapter 12, Setting Up the Wiki Game, introduces our first fully featured Julia project, a Wikipedia web crawler disguised as a popular game. In the first iteration, we will build a program that gets a random web page from Wikipedia. Then we'll learn about parsing the HTML response using CSS selectors. We'll use this to introduce key concepts such as functions, pairs, dictionaries, exceptions, and conditional evaluation.

Chapter 13, Building the Wiki Game Web Crawler, will build upon the foundations set in the previous chapter, and we'll build a Wikipedia web scraper that implements the requirements of the wiki game.

Chapter 14, Adding a Web UI for the Wiki Game, will see us finish the Wiki Game by adding a web UI. We'll build a simple web app that will allow the player to start a new game, render the Wikipedia articles picked by the game engine, and navigate between linked Wikipedia articles. The UI will also keep track of and display current game progress and determine a session as a win or a loss.

Chapter 15, Implementing Recommender Systems with Julia, will have you take on a more challenging example project and build a few basic recommender systems. We'll set up a supervised machine learning system powered by Julia and we will develop some simple movie recommenders.

Chapter 16, Machine Learning for Recommender Systems, will show you how to implement a more powerful recommender system using the Recommender.jl package. We will use a sample dataset to train our system and generate book recommendations as we'll learn about model-based recommenders.

To get the most out of this book

To run the code examples in the book, you will need the Julia 1.0 platform for your computer, which can be downloaded from http://julialang.org/downloads/. To work more comfortably with Julia scripts, a development environment such as IJulia, Sublime Text, or Visual Studio Code is advisable. The first chapter contains detailed instructions on how to set up your Julia environment.

Download the example code files

You can download the example code files for this book from your account at `www.packt.com`. If you purchased this book elsewhere, you can visit `www.packt.com/support` and register to have the files emailed directly to you.

You can download the code files by following these steps:

1. Log in or register at `www.packt.com`.
2. Select the **SUPPORT** tab.
3. Click on **Code Downloads & Errata**.
4. Enter the name of the book in the **Search** box and follow the onscreen instructions.

Once the file is downloaded, please make sure that you unzip or extract the folder using the latest version of:

- WinRAR/7-Zip for Windows
- Zipeg/iZip/UnRarX for Mac
- 7-Zip/PeaZip for Linux

The code bundle for the book is also hosted on GitHub at `https://github.com/TrainingByPackt/Julia-1-Programming-Complete-Reference-Guide`.In case there's an update to the code, it will be updated on the existing GitHub repository.

We also have other code bundles from our rich catalog of books and videos available at `https://github.com/PacktPublishing/`. Check them out!

Download the color images

We also provide a PDF file that has color images of the screenshots/diagrams used in this book. You can download it here: `https://www.packtpub.com/sites/default/files/downloads/9781838822248_ColorImages.pdf`.

Conventions used

There are a number of text conventions used throughout this book.

`CodeInText`: Indicates code words in text, database table names, folder names, filenames, file extensions, pathnames, dummy URLs, user input, and Twitter handles. Here is an example:
"Add `/Applications/Julian.m.app/Contents/Resources/julia/bin/Julia` to make Julia available everywhere on your computer."

A block of code is set as follows:

```
for arg in ARGS
 println(arg)
end
```

Any command-line input or output is written as follows:

```
julia> include("hello.jl")
```

Bold: Indicates a new term, an important word, or words that you see onscreen. For example, words in menus or dialog boxes appear in the text like this. Here is an example:
"Start it up, go to **Settings**, and then **Install Panel**."

Warnings or important notes appear like this.

Tips and tricks appear like this.

Get in touch

Feedback from our readers is always welcome.

General feedback: If you have questions about any aspect of this book, mention the book title in the subject of your message and email us at customercare@packtpub.com.

Errata: Although we have taken every care to ensure the accuracy of our content, mistakes do happen. If you have found a mistake in this book, we would be grateful if you would report this to us. Please visit www.packt.com/submit-errata, selecting your book, clicking on the Errata Submission Form link, and entering the details.

Piracy: If you come across any illegal copies of our works in any form on the Internet, we would be grateful if you would provide us with the location address or website name. Please contact us at copyright@packt.com with a link to the material.

If you are interested in becoming an author: If there is a topic that you have expertise in and you are interested in either writing or contributing to a book, please visit authors.packtpub.com.

Reviews

Please leave a review. Once you have read and used this book, why not leave a review on the site that you purchased it from? Potential readers can then see and use your unbiased opinion to make purchase decisions, we at Packt can understand what you think about our products, and our authors can see your feedback on their book. Thank you!

For more information about Packt, please visit packt.com.

Installing the Julia Platform

1

This chapter guides you through the download and installation process of all the necessary components of Julia. The topics covered in this chapter are as follows:

- Installing Julia
- Working with Julia's REPL
- Startup options and Julia scripts
- Packages
- Installing and working with IJulia
- Installing Juno
- Installing julia-vscode
- Installing Sublime-IJulia
- Other editors and IDEs
- How Julia works

By the end of this chapter, you will have a running Julia platform. Moreover, you will be able to work with Julia's shell as well as with editors or integrated development environments with a lot of built-in features to make development more comfortable.

Installing Julia

The Julia platform, in binary (that is, executable) form, can be downloaded from `http://julialang.org/downloads/`. It exists for three major platforms (Windows, Linux, and OS X) in 32- and 64-bit format, and it is delivered as a package or in an archive version. FreeBSD 64-bit is also supported.

You should use the current official stable release when doing serious professional work with Julia. At the time of writing, Julia has reached its version 1.0 production release. The previous link contains detailed and platform-specific instructions for the installation. We will not repeat these instructions here completely, but we will summarize some important points.

Windows OS

Keep in mind that your Windows OS must be version 7 or higher. Now, follow the steps shown here:

1. Download the `julia-n.m.p-win64.exe` file into a temporary folder (`n.m.p` is the version number, such as `0.7.0` or `0.1.0`; `win32`/`win64` are the 32- and 64-bit versions, respectively; a release candidate file looks like `julia-1.0.0-rc1-nnnnnnn-win64` (where `nnnnnnn` is a checksum number such as `0480f1b`)).

2. Double-click on the file (or right-click and select **Run as Administrator** if you want Julia installed for all users on the machine). Click **OK** on the security dialog message. Then, choose the installation directory (for example, for `C:\julia`, the default installation folder is: `C:\Users\UserName\AppData\Local\Julia-n.m.p` (where `n.m.p` is the version number)) and the setup program will extract the archive into the chosen folder, producing the following directory structure, and taking some 800 MB of disk space:

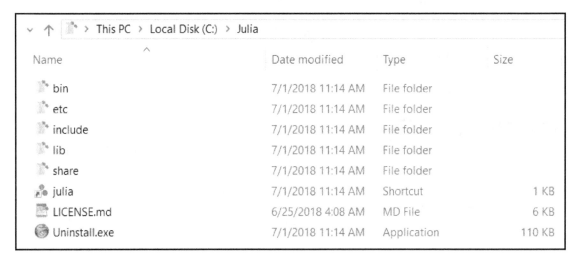

The Julia folder structure in Windows

3. A menu shortcut will be created which, when clicked, starts the Julia command-line version or **Read Evaluate Print Loop** (**REPL**), as shown in the following screenshot:

The Julia REPL

4. On Windows, if you have chosen `C:\Julia` as your installation directory, this is the `C:\Julia\bin\julia.exe` file. Add `C:\Julia\bin` to your `PATH` variable if you want the REPL to be available on any command window.
5. More information on Julia's installation for the Windows OS can be found at `https://github.com/JuliaLang/julia/blob/master/README.windows.md`.

OS X

Installation for OS X is straightforward, and can be done using the standard software installation tools for the platform. Add `/Applications/Julia-n.m.app/Contents/Resources/julia/bin/Julia` to make Julia available everywhere on your computer.

Linux OS

Generic Linux binaries for x86 can be downloaded. This will get you a compressed `tar.gz` archive that will have a name similar to `julia-1.0-linux-x86_64.tar.gz`, for example, in your `~/Downloads` directory in Ubuntu. Open up a Terminal window and navigate to the `Downloads` directory using `cd Downloads`. Move the `tar.gz` file to a directory of your choice, and then extract the `tar.gz` file using the `tar -zxvf julia-1.0-linux-x86_64.tar.gz` command. A directory with the extracted contents will be generated in the same parent directory as the compressed archive with a name similar to `julia-n.m.p`, where `n.m.p` is Julia's version number.

This is the directory from which Julia will be run; no further installation is needed. To run it, simply navigate to the `julia-n.m.p\bin` directory in your Terminal and type: `./julia`.

If you want to be at the bleeding edge of development, you can download the nightly builds instead of the stable releases from `https://julialang.org/downloads/nightlies.html`. The nightly builds are generally less stable, but will contain the most recent features. They are available for Windows, Linux, and OS X.

The path to the Julia executable is contained in the environment variable, `JULIA_BINDIR` (for example, in our installation procedure, this was `C:\Julia\bin` on Windows).

If you want code to be run whenever you start a Julia session, put it in `/home/.juliarc.jl` on Ubuntu, `~/.juliarc.jl` on OS X, or `C:\Users\username\.juliarc.jl` on Windows.

Building from source

Download the source code, rather than the binaries, if you intend to contribute to the development of Julia itself, or if no Julia binaries are provided for your operating system or particular computer architecture. The Julia source code can be found on GitHub at `https://github.com/JuliaLang/julia.git`. Compiling the source code will get you the latest Julia version, not the stable version (if you want the latter, download the binaries, and refer to the previous section).

Because of the diversity of platforms and the possible issues involved, we refer you to `https://github.com/JuliaLang/julia`, and in that, the *Source Download and Compilation* section.

JuliaPro

Another alternative is JuliaPro, which is available from `https://juliacomputing.com/products/juliapro.html`. This is an Anaconda-style Julia repository, which, at present, is only up to version 0.6.4. It does come with about 200+ verified ready-to-go packages, and is a very good way for beginners to start. JuliaPro version 1.0 will probably become available after some time.

There are two ways of using Julia. As described in the previous section, we can use the Julia shell for interactive work. Alternatively, we can write programs in a text file, save them with a .jl extension, and let Julia execute the program by starting it by running julia program.jl.

Working with Julia's REPL

We started with Julia's REPL in the previous section to verify the correctness of the installation by issuing the julia command in a Terminal session. The REPL is Julia's working environment, where you can interact with the **just in time** (**JIT**) compiler to test out pieces of code. When satisfied, you can copy and paste this code into a file with a .jl extension, such as program.jl. Alternatively, you can continue to work on this code from within a text editor or an IDE, such as the ones we will point out later in this chapter. After the banner with Julia's logo has appeared, you will get a julia> prompt for the input. To end this session and get to the OS Command Prompt, type *Ctrl + D*, and hit *Enter*. To evaluate an expression, type it and press *Enter* to show the result, as shown in the following screenshot:

```
julia> 6 * 7
42

julia> ans
42

julia> 8 * 5;

julia> ans
40

julia> ans + 10
50

julia>
```

Working with the REPL (1)

If, for some reason, you don't need to see the result, end the expression with a ; (semicolon) such as 8 * 5; In both the cases, the resulting value is stored, for convenience, in a variable named `ans` that can be used in expressions, but only inside the REPL. You can bind a value to a variable by entering an assignment as a = 3. Julia is dynamic, and we don't need to enter a type for a, but we do need to enter a value for the variable so that Julia can infer its type. Using a variable b that is not bound to the a value results in the ERROR: UndefVarError: b not defined message. Strings are delineated by double quotes (" "), as in b = "Julia". The following screenshot illustrates this in the REPL:

```
julia> a = 3
3

julia> b
ERROR: UndefVarError: b not defined

julia> b = "Julia"
"Julia"

julia> b
"Julia"

julia>
```

Working with the REPL (2)

Previous expressions can be retrieved in the same session by working with the up and down arrow keys. The following key bindings are also handy:

- To clear or interrupt a current command, press *Ctrl + C*
- To clear the screen, press *Ctrl + L* (variables are kept in memory)

Commands from the previous sessions can still be retrieved, because they are stored (with a timestamp) in a `repl_history.jl` file (in `/home/$USER/.julia/logs` on Ubuntu, `C:\Users\username\.julia\logs` on Windows, or `~/.julia/logs/repl_history` on OS X). *Ctrl + R* (produces a `reverse-i-search` prompt) searches through these commands.

Typing ? starts up the help mode (help?>) to give you quick access to Julia's documentation. Information on function names, types, macros, and so on, is given when typing in their names. Alternatively, to get more information on a variable, for example, a, type ?a, and to get more information on a function such as sort, type ?sort. To find all the places where a function such as println is defined or used, type apropos("println"), which gives the following output:

```
Base.Pair
Base.any
Base.@isdefined
Base.eachindex
Base.all
Base.Generator
Base.Timer
...
Printf.@sprintf
REPL.TerminalMenus.request
```

Thus, we can see that it is defined in the Base module, and that it is used in several other functions.

Different complete expressions on the same line have to be separated by a ; (semicolon), and only the last result is shown. You can enter multiline expressions, as shown in the following screenshot. If the shell detects that the statement is syntactically incomplete, it will not attempt to evaluate it. Rather, it will wait for the user to enter additional lines until the multiline statement can be evaluated:

```
julia> a = 1; b = 2; c = 3
3

julia> if 10 > 0
            println("10 is bigger than 0")
        end
10 is bigger than 0

julia>
```

Working with the REPL (3)

A handy autocomplete feature also exists. Type one or more letters, press the *Tab* key twice, and then a list of functions starting with these letters appears. For example, type `so`, press the *Tab* key twice, and then you will get the list as `sort sort! sortcols sortperm sortperm! sortrows`.

If you start a line with `;`, the rest of the line is interpreted as a system shell command (try, for example, `ls`, `cd`, `mkdir`, `whoami` on Linux). The *Backspace* key returns to the Julia prompt.

A Julia script can be executed in the REPL by calling it with `include`. For example, for `hello.jl`, which contains the `println("Hello, Julia World!")` statement, the command is as follows:

```
julia> include("hello.jl")
```

The preceding command prints the output as follows:

```
Hello, Julia World!
```

Experiment a bit with different expressions to get a feeling for this environment.

Startup options and Julia scripts

Without any options, the `julia` command starts up the REPL environment. A useful option to check your environment is `julia -v`. This shows Julia's version, for example, `julia version 1.0.0`. (The `versioninfo()` function in REPL is more detailed, and the `VERSION` constant only gives you the version number: `v"1.0.0"`). An option that lets you evaluate expressions on the command line itself is `-e`, for example:

```
julia -e 'a = 6 `* 7;
println(a)'
```

The preceding commands print out `42` (this also works in a PowerShell window on Windows, but in an ordinary Windows Command Prompt, use " instead of the ' character).

Some other options that are useful for parallel processing will be discussed in `Chapter 9`, *Running External Programs*. Type `julia -h` for a list of all options.

A `script.jl` file with Julia source code can be started from the command line with the following command:

```
julia script.jl arg1 arg2 arg3
```

Here, `arg1`, `arg2`, and `arg3` are optional arguments to be used in the script's code. They are available from the global constant `ARGS`. Take a look at the `args.jl` file, which contains the following:

```
for arg in ARGS
    println(arg)
end
```

The `julia args.jl 1 Red C` command prints out `1`, `Red`, and `C` on consecutive lines.

A script file can also execute other source files by including them in the REPL; for example, `main.jl` contains `include("hello.jl")`, which will execute the code from `hello.jl` when called with `julia main.jl`.

Sometimes, it can be useful to know when code is executed interactively in the REPL, or when started up with the Julia VM with the `julia` command. This can be tested with the `isinteractive()` function. The `isinteractive.jl` script contains the following code:

```
println("Is this interactive? $(isinteractive())")
```

If you start this up in the REPL with `include("isinteractive.jl")`, the output will be `Is this interactive? true`.

When started up in a Terminal window as `julia isinteractive.jl`, the output is `Is this interactive? false`.

You can download the example code files from your account at `http://www.packtpub.com` for all the Packt Publishing books you have purchased. If you purchased this book elsewhere, you can visit `https://github.com/TrainingByPackt/Julia-1-Programming-Complete-Reference-Guide`.

Packages

Most of the standard library in Julia (which can be found in `/share/julia/base` and `/share/julia/stdlib`, relative to where Julia was installed) is written in Julia itself. The rest of Julia's code ecosystem is contained in packages that are simply GitHub repositories. They are most often authored by external contributors, and already provide functionality for such diverse disciplines such as bioinformatics, chemistry, cosmology, finance, linguistics, machine learning, mathematics, statistics, and high-performance computing. A package listing can be found at `http://pkg.julialang.org`.

Julia's installation contains a built-in package manager, `Pkg`, for installing additional packages that are written in Julia. Version and dependency management is handled automatically by `Pkg`.

`Pkg` has a REPL mode, which can be started from within the Julia REPL by entering the `]` key, which is often called the REPL's package mode. The `Pkg` mode is shown as a blue prompt, like this: `(v1.0) pkg>`.

From this mode, we can start all functions of `Pkg`. To return to the normal REPL mode, press *Backspace* or *Ctrl + C*.

To initialize your environment, enter the `init` command, which creates an empty `Project.toml` file in your Julia installation folder.

Adding a new package

Before adding a new package, it is always a good idea to update your package database for the already installed packages with the `up` command. Then, add a new package by issuing the `add PackageName` command, and execute it by using `PackageName` in the code or in the REPL.

For example, to add 2D plotting capabilities, install the `Plots` package with `add Plots` in the `Package` mode by first typing `]`. This installs the `Plots` package and all of its dependencies, building them when needed.

To make a graph of 100 random numbers between 0 and 1, execute the following commands:

```
using Plots
plot(rand(100))
```

The `rand(100)` function is an array with 100 random numbers. This produces the following output:

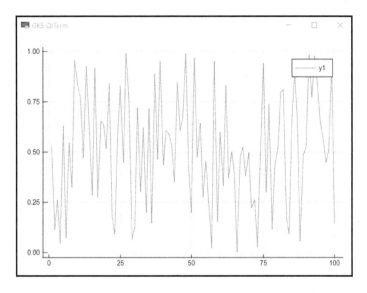

A plot of white noise with Plots

After installing a new Julia version, update all the installed packages by running `up` in the `Pkg` REPL-mode.

Installing and working with IJulia

IJulia (`https://github.com/JuliaLang/IJulia.jl`) is a combination of the Jupyter Notebook interactive environment (`http://jupyter.org/`) with a Julia language backend. It allows you to work with a powerful graphical notebook (which combines code, formatted text, math, and multimedia in a single document) with a regular REPL. Detailed instructions for installation can be found at the GitHub page for IJulia (`https://github.com/JuliaLang/IJulia.jl`) and in the Julia at MIT notes (`https://github.com/stevengj/julia-mit/blob/master/README.md`). Add the IJulia package in the REPL package mode with `add IJulia`.

Then, whenever you want to use it, start up a Julia REPL and type the following commands:

```
using IJulia
notebook()
```

If you want to run it from the command line, type:

```
jupyter notebook
```

The IJulia dashboard should look as follows:

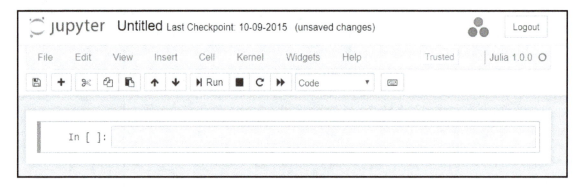

The IJulia dashboard

You should see the Jupyter logo in the upper-left corner of the browser window. Julia code is entered in the input cells (the input can be multiline) and then executed with *Shift + Enter*.

Here is a small example (`ijulia-example.jl`):

The output should be something as follows:

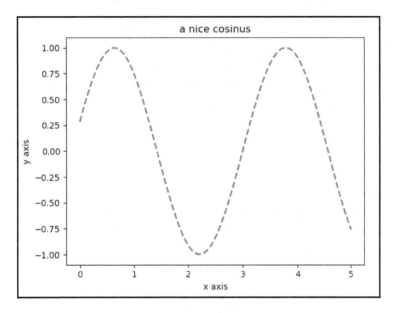

An IJulia session example

In the first input cell, the value of b is calculated from a:

```
a = 5
b = 2a^2 + 30a + 9
```

In the second input cell, we use PyPlot. Install this package with add PyPlot in the REPL package mode, and by issuing using PyPlot in the REPL.

The range(0,stop=5,length=101) command defines an array of 100 equally spaced values between 0 and 5; y is defined as a function of x and is then shown graphically with the plot command, as follows:

```
using PyPlot
x = range(0,stop=5,length=101)
y = cos.(2x .+ 5)
plot(x, y, linewidth=2.0, linestyle="--")
title("a nice cosinus")
xlabel("x axis")
ylabel("y axis")
```

Save a notebook in file format (with the .ipynb extension) by downloading it from the menu.

Installing Juno

Juno (`http://junolab.org/`) is a full-fledged IDE for Julia by Mike Innes, which is based on the Atom environment. The setup page at `https://github.com/JunoLab/uber-juno/blob/master/setup.md` provides detailed instructions for installing and configuring Juno. Here is a summary of the steps:

1. Download and install Atom (`https://atom.io/`)
2. Start it up, go to **Settings**, and then click **Install Panel**
3. Enter `uber-juno` into the search box

Atom works extensively with a command palette that you can open by typing *Ctrl +* spacebar, entering a command, and then selecting it. Juno provides an integrated console, and you can evaluate single expressions in the code editor directly by typing *Ctrl + Enter* at the end of the line. A complete script is evaluated by typing *Ctrl + Shift + Enter*. More on basic usage can be found here: `http://docs.junolab.org/latest/man/basic_usage.html`.

Installing julia-vscode

Another IDE called `julia-vscode` is based on the Visual Studio Code editor (`https://code.visualstudio.com/`). Install it by following the instructions given here: `https://github.com/JuliaEditorSupport/julia-vscode`. This IDE provides syntax highlighting, code snippets, Julia-specific commands (execute code by pressing *F5*), an integrated Julia REPL, code completion, hover help, a linter, code navigation, and tasks for running tests, builds, benchmarks, and build documentation.

Installing Sublime-IJulia

The Sublime Text editor (`http://www.sublimetext.com/3`) has a plugin called `Julia-sublime`: `https://github.com/JuliaEditorSupport/Julia-sublime`. It gives you syntax highlighting, autocompletion, auto-indentation, and code snippets. To install it, select `Julia` from the `Package Control: Install Package` drop-down list in the **Command Palette**.

Other editors and IDEs

For Terminal users, the available editors are as follows:

- Vim, together with `julia-vim`, works great
  (`https://github.com/JuliaLang/julia-vim`)
- Emacs, with `julia-mode.el`, from the
  `https://github.com/JuliaLang/julia/tree/master/contrib` directory

On Linux, gedit is very good. The Julia plugin works well and provides autocompletion. Notepad++ also has Julia support from the `contrib` directory mentioned earlier.

The CoCalc project (`https://cocalc.com/`) runs Julia in the cloud within a Terminal and lets you work with Jupyter notebooks. You can also work and teach with Julia in the cloud by using the JuliaBox platform (`https://juliabox.org/`).

How Julia works

(You can safely skip this section on a first reading.) Julia works with an LLVM JIT compiler framework that is used for JIT generation of machine code. The first time you run a Julia function, it is parsed, and the types are inferred. Then, LLVM code is generated by the JIT compiler, which is then optimized and compiled down to native code. The second time you run a Julia function, the native code that's already generated is called. This is the reason why, the second time you call a function with arguments of a specific type, it takes much less time to run than the first time (keep this in mind when doing benchmarks of Julia code).

This generated code can be inspected. Suppose, for example, that we have defined a `f(x) = 2x + 5` function in a REPL session. Julia responds with the message f (generic function with one method); the code is dynamic because we didn't have to specify the type of x or f. Functions are, by default, generic in Julia because they are ready to work with different data types for their variables.

The `code_llvm` function can be used to see the JIT bytecode. This is the bytecode generated by LLVM, and it will be different for each target platform. For example, for the Intel x64 platform, if the x argument is of type `Int64`, it will be as follows:

```
julia> code_llvm(f, (Int64,))

; Function f
; Location: REPL[7]:1
```

```
; Function Attrs: uwtable
define i64 @julia_f_33833(i64) #0 {
top:
; Function *; {
; Location: int.jl:54
  %1 = shl i64 %0, 1
;}
; Function +; {
; Location: int.jl:53
  %2 = add i64 %1, 5
;}
  ret i64 %2
}
```

The `code_native` function can be used to see the assembly code that was generated for the same type of x:

```
julia> code_native(f, (Int64,))

        .text
; Function f {
; Location: REPL[7]:1
        pushq   %rbp
        movq    %rsp, %rbp
; Function +; {
; Location: int.jl:53
        leaq    5(%rcx,%rcx), %rax
;}
        popq    %rbp
        retq
        nopl    (%rax,%rax)
;}
```

Compare this with the code generated when x is of type `Float64`:

```
julia> code_native(f, (Float64,))

        .text
; Function f {
; Location: REPL[7]:1
        pushq   %rbp
        movq    %rsp, %rbp
; Function *; {
; Location: promotion.jl:314
; Function *; {
; Location: float.jl:399
        vaddsd  %xmm0, %xmm0, %xmm0
        movabsq $424735072, %rax        # imm = 0x1950F160
```

```
;}}
; Function +; {
; Location: promotion.jl:313
; Function +; {
; Location: float.jl:395
        vaddsd   (%rax), %xmm0, %xmm0
;}}
        popq     %rbp
        retq
        nopl     (%rax,%rax)
;}
```

Julia code is fast because it generates specialized versions of functions for each data type. Julia also implements automatic memory management. The user doesn't have to worry about allocating and keeping track of the memory for specific objects. Automatic deletion of objects that are not needed anymore (and hence, reclamation of the memory associated with those objects) is done using a **garbage collector** (**GC**).

The GC runs at the same time as your program. Exactly when a specific object is garbage collected is unpredictable. The GC implements an incremental mark-and-sweep algorithm. You can start garbage collection yourself by calling GC.gc(), or if you don't need it, you can disable it by calling GC.enable(false).

The standard library is implemented in Julia itself. The I/O functions rely on the libuv library for an efficient, platform-independent I/O. The standard library is contained in a package called Base, which is automatically imported when starting Julia.

Summary

By now, you should have been able to install Julia in the working environment you prefer using. You should also have some experience with working in the REPL. We will put this to good use starting in the next chapter, where we will meet the basic data types in Julia by testing out everything in the REPL.

Variables, Types, and Operations

2

Julia is an optionally typed language, which means that the user can choose to specify the type of arguments passed to a function and the type of variables used inside a function. Julia's type system is the key for its performance; understanding it well is important, and it can pay off to use type annotations, not only for documentation or tooling, but also for execution speed. This chapter discusses the realm of elementary built-in types in Julia, the operations that can be performed on them, as well as the important concepts of types and scope.

The following topics are covered in this chapter:

- Variables, naming conventions, and comments
- Types
- Integers
- Floating point numbers
- Elementary mathematical functions and operations
- Rational and complex numbers
- Characters
- Strings
- Regular expressions
- Ranges and arrays
- Dates and times
- Scope and constants

You will need to follow along by typing in the examples in the REPL, or executing the code snippets in the code files of this chapter.

Variables, naming conventions, and comments

Data is stored in values such as 1, 3.14, and "Julia", and every other value has a type, for example, the type of 3.14 is Float64. Some other examples of elementary values and their data types are 42 of the Int64 type, true and false of the Bool type, and 'X' of the Char type.

Julia, unlike many modern programming languages, differentiates between single characters and strings. Strings can contain any number of characters, and are specified using double quotes—single quotes are only used for a character literal. Variables are the names that are bound to values by assignments, such as x = 42. They have the type of the value they contain (or reference); this type is given by the typeof function. For example, typeof(x) returns Int64.

The type of a variable can change, because putting x = "I am Julia" now results in typeof(x) returning String. In Julia, we don't have to declare a variable (that indicates its type) such as in C or Java, for instance, but a variable must be initialized (that is, bound to a value) so that Julia can deduce its type:

```
julia> y = 7
7
typeof(y)    # Int64
julia> y + z
ERROR: UndefVarError: z not defined
```

In the preceding example, z was not assigned a value before we used it, so we got an error. By combining variables through operators and functions such as the + operator (as in the preceding example), we get expressions. An expression always results in a new value after computation. Contrary to many other languages, everything in Julia is an expression, so it returns a value. That's why working in a REPL is so great: because you can see the values at each step.

The type of variables determines what you can do with them, that is, the operators with which they can be combined. In this sense, Julia is a strongly typed language. In the following example, x is still a `String` value, so it can't be summed with y, which is of type `Int64`, but if we give x a float value, the sum can be calculated, as shown in the following example:

```
julia> x + y
ERROR: MethodError: no method matching +(::String, ::Int64)
julia> x = 3.5; x + y
10.5
```

Here, the semicolon (;) ends the first expression and suppresses its output. Names of the variables are case-sensitive. By convention, lowercase is used with multiple words separated by an underscore. They start with a letter and, after that, you can use letters, digits, underscores, and exclamation points. You can also use Unicode characters. Use clear, short, and to-the-point names. Here are some valid variable names: `mass`, `moon_velocity`, `current_time`, `pos3`, and ω1. However, the last two are not very descriptive, and they should better be replaced with, for example, `particle_position` and `particle_ang_velocity`.

A line of code preceded by a hash sign (#) is a comment, as we can see in the following example:

```
# Calculate the gravitational acceleration grav_acc:
gc = 6.67e-11 # gravitational constant in m3/kg s2
mass_earth = 5.98e24   # in kg
radius_earth = 6378100 # in m
grav_acc = gc * mass_earth / radius_earth^2 # 9.8049 m/s2
```

Multiline comments are helpful for writing comments that span across multiple lines or commenting out code. In Julia, all lines between #= and =# are treated as a comment. For printing out values, use the `print` or `println` functions, as follows:

```
julia> print(x)
3.5
```

If you want your printed output to be in color, use `printstyled("I love Julia!", color=:red)`, which returns the argument string in the color indicated by the second argument.

The term object (or instance) is frequently used when dealing with variables of more complex types. However, we will see that, when doing actions on objects, Julia uses functional semantics. We write `action(object)` instead of `object.action()`, as we do in more object-oriented languages such as Java or C#.

In a REPL, the value of the last expression is automatically displayed each time a statement is evaluated (unless it ends with a `;` sign). In a standalone script, Julia will not display anything unless the script specifically instructs it to. This is achieved with a `print` or `println` statement. To display any object in the way the REPL does in code, use `display(object)` or `show(object)` (`show` is a basic function that prints a text representation of an object, which is often more specific than `print`).

Types

Julia's type system is unique. Julia behaves as a dynamically typed language (such as Python, for instance) most of the time. This means that a variable bound to an integer at one point might later be bound to a string. For example, consider the following:

```
julia> x = 10
10
julia> x = "hello"
"hello"
```

However, one can, optionally, add type information to a variable. This causes the variable to only accept values that match that specific type. This is done through a type of annotation. For instance, declaring `x::String` implies that only strings can be bound to `x`; in general, it looks like `var::TypeName`. These are used the most often to qualify the arguments a function can take. The extra type information is useful for documenting the code, and often allows the JIT compiler to generate better-optimized native code. It also allows the development environments to give more support, and code tools such as a linter that can check your code for possible wrong type use.

Here is an example: a function with the `calc_position` name defined as the function `calc_position(time::Float64)` indicates that this function takes one argument named `time` of type `Float64`.

Julia uses the same syntax for type assertions, which are used to check whether a variable or an expression has a specific type. Writing `(expr)::TypeName` raises an error if `expr` is not of the required type. For instance, consider the following:

```
julia> (2+3)::String
ERROR: TypeError: in typeassert, expected String, got Int64
```

Notice that the type comes after the variable name, unlike in most other languages. In general, the type of a variable can change in Julia, but this is detrimental to performance. For utmost performance, you need to write *type-stable code*. Code is type-stable if the type of every variable does not vary over time. Carefully thinking in terms of the types of variables is useful in avoiding performance bottlenecks. Adding type annotations to variables that are updated in the inner loop of a critical region of code can lead to drastic improvements in the performance by helping the JIT compiler remove some type checking. To see an excellent example where this is important, read the article available at
`http://www.johnmyleswhite.com/notebook/2013/12/06/writing-type-stable-code-in-j`
`ulia/`.

A lot of types exist; in fact, a whole type hierarchy is built-in in Julia. If you don't specify the type of a function argument, it has the `Any` type, which is effectively the root or parent of all types. Every object is at least of the universal type `Any`. At the other end of the spectrum, there is type `Nothing`, which has no values. No object can have this type, but it is a subtype of every other type. While running the code, Julia will infer the type of the parameters passed in a function, and with this information, it will generate optimal machine code.

You can define your own custom types as well, for instance, a `Person` type. We'll come back to this in `Chapter 6`, *More on Types, Methods, and Modules*. By convention, the names of types begin with a capital letter, and if necessary, the word separation is shown with `CamelCase`, such as `BigFloat` or `AbstractArray`.

If x is a variable, then `typeof(x)` gives its type, and `isa(x, T)` tests whether x is of type T. For example, `isa("ABC", String)` returns `true`, and `isa(1, Bool)` returns `false`.

Everything in Julia has a type, including types themselves, which are of type `DataType`: `typeof(Int64)` returns `DataType`. Conversion of a variable var to a type `Type1` can be done using the type name as a function, such as `Type1(var)`. For example, `Int64(3.0)` returns `3`.

However, this raises an error if type conversion is impossible, as follows:

```
julia> Int64("hello")
ERROR: MethodError: Cannot `convert` an object of type String to an object
of type Int64
```

Integers

Julia offers support for integer numbers ranging from types `Int8` to `Int128`, with 8 to 128 representing the number of bits used, and with unsigned variants with a `U` prefix, such as `UInt8`. The default type (which can also be used as `Int`) is `Int32` or `Int64`, depending on the target machine architecture. The bit width is given by the `Sys.WORD_SIZE` variable. The number of bits used by the integer affects the maximum and minimum value this integer can have. The minimum and maximum values are given by the `typemin()` and `typemax()` functions, respectively; for example, `typemax(Int16)` returns `32767`.

If you try to store a number larger than that allowed by `typemax`, overflow occurs. For example, note the following:

```
julia> typemax(Int)
9223372036854775807 # might be different on 32 bit platform
julia> ans + 1
-9223372036854775808
```

Overflow checking is not automatic, so an explicit check (for example, the result has the wrong sign) is needed when this can occur. Integers can also be written in binary (`0b`), octal (`0o`), and hexadecimal (`0x`) format.

For computations needing arbitrary-precision integers, Julia has a `BigInt` type. These values can be constructed as `BigInt(number)` or `big(number)`, and support the same operators as normal integers. Conversions between numeric types are automatic, but not between the primitive types and the big types. The normal operations of addition (+), subtraction (–), and multiplication (*) apply for integers. A division (/) always gives a floating point number. If you only want integer divisor and remainder, use `div` and `rem`. The symbol ^ is used to obtain the power of a number.

The logical values, `true` and `false`, of type `Bool` are also integers with 8 bits. `0` amounts to `false`, and `1` to `true`. Negation can be done with the `!` operator; for example, `!true` is `false`. Comparing numbers with == (equal), != or < and > returns a `Bool` value, and comparisons can be chained after one another (as in `0 < x < 3`).

Floating point numbers

Floating point numbers follow the IEEE 754 standard and represent numbers with a decimal point, such as `3.14`, or an exponent notation, such as `4e-14`, and come in the types `Float16` up to `Float64`, the last one being used for double precision.

Single precision is achieved through the use of the `Float32` type. Single precision float literals must be written in scientific notation, such as `3.14f0`, but with `f`, where one normally uses e. That is, `2.5f2` indicates `2.5*10^2` with single precision, while `2.5e2` indicates `2.5*10^2` in double precision. Julia also has a `BigFloat` type for arbitrary-precision floating numbers computations.

A built-in type promotion system takes care of all the numeric types that can work together seamlessly, so that there is no explicit conversion needed. Special values exist: `Inf` and `-Inf` are used for infinity, and `NaN` is used for "not a number" values such as the result of `0/0` or `Inf - Inf`.

Floating point arithmetic in all programming languages is often a source of subtle bugs and counter-intuitive behavior. For instance, note the following:

```
julia> 0.1 + 0.2
0.30000000000000004
```

This happens because of the way the floating point numbers are stored internally. Most numbers cannot be stored internally with a finite number of bits, such as 1/3 having no finite representation in base 10. The computer will choose the closest number it can represent, introducing a small **round-off error**. These errors might accumulate over the course of long computations, creating subtle problems.

Maybe the most important consequence of this is the need to avoid using equality when comparing floating point numbers:

```
julia> 0.1 + 0.2 == 0.3
false
```

A better solution is to use >= or <= comparisons in logical tests that involve floating point numbers, wherever possible.

Elementary mathematical functions and operations

You can view the binary representation of any number (integer or float) with the `bitstring` function, for example, `bitstring(3)` returns `"0000000000000000000000000000000000000000000000000000000000000011"`.

To round a number, use the `round()` function which returns a floating point number. All standard mathematical functions are provided, such as `sqrt()`, `cbrt()`, `exp()`, `log()`, `sin()`, `cos()`, `tan()`, `erf()` (the error function), and many more (refer to the URL mentioned at the end of this section). To generate a random number, use `rand()`.

Use parentheses `( )` around expressions to enforce precedence. Chained assignments, such as a = b = c = d = 1, are allowed. The assignments are evaluated right-to-left. Assignments for different variables can be combined, as shown in the following example:

```
a = 1; b = 2; c = 3; d = 4
a, b = c, d
```

Now, a has a value of 3 and b has a value of 4. In particular, this makes an easy swap possible:

```
a, b = b, a    # now a is 4 and b is 3
```

Like in many other languages, the Boolean operators working on the `true` and `false` values for *and, or,* and *not* have &&, ||, and ! as symbols, respectively. Julia applies a short-circuit optimization here. That means the following:

- In a && b, b is not evaluated when a is false (since && is already false)
- In a || b, b is not evaluated when a is true (since || is already true)

The operators & and | are also used for non-short-circuit Boolean evaluations.

Julia also supports bitwise operations on integers. Note that n++ or n-- with n as an integer does not exist in Julia, as it does in C++ or Java. Use n += 1 or n -= 1 instead.

For more detailed information on operations, such as the bitwise operators, special precedence, and so on, refer to http://docs.julialang.org/en/latest/manual/mathematical-operations/.

Rational and complex numbers

Julia supports these types out of the box. The global constant `im` represents the square root of −1, so that 3.2 + 7.1im is a complex number with floating point coefficients, so it is of the type `Complex{Float64}`.

This is the first example of a **parametric type** in Julia. For this example, we can write this as `Complex{T}`, where type `T` can take a number of different type values, such as `Int32`, `Int64`, or `Float64`.

All operations and elementary functions, such as `exp()`, `sqrt()`, `sinh()`, `real()`, `imag()`, `abs()`, and so on, are also defined on complex numbers; for example, `abs(3.2 + 7.1im)` = `7.787810988975015`.

If `a` and `b` are two variables that contain a number, use `complex(a,b)` to form a complex number with them. Rational numbers are useful when you want to work with exact ratios of integers, for example, `3//4`, which is of type `Rational{Int64}`.

Again, comparisons and standard operations are defined: `float()` converts to a floating point number, and `num()` and `den()` gives the numerator and denominator. Both types work together seamlessly with all the other numeric types.

Characters

Like C or Java, but unlike Python, Julia implements a type for a single character, the `Char` type. A character literal is written as `'A'`, where `typeof('A')` returns `Char`. A `Char` value is a Unicode code point, and it ranges from `'\0'` to `'\Uffffffff'`. Convert this to its code point with `Int()`: `Int('A')` returns `65`, and `Int('α')` returns `945`, so this takes two bytes.

The reverse also works: `Char(65)` returns `'A'`, `Char(945)` returns `'\u3b1'`, which is the code point for α (`3b1` is hexadecimal for `945`).

Unicode characters can be entered by a `\u` in single quotes, followed by four hexadecimal digits (ranging from 0-9 or A-F), or `\U` followed by eight hexadecimal digits. The `isvalid(Char, value)` function can test whether a number returns an existing Unicode character: `isvalid(Char,0x3b1)` returns `true`. The normal escape characters, such as `\t` (tab), `\n` (newline), `\'`, and so on, also exist in Julia.

Strings

Literal strings are always of type `String`:

```
julia> typeof("hello")
String
```

This is also true if they contain UTF-8 characters that cannot be represented in ASCII, as in this example:

```
julia> typeof("Güdrun")
String
```

UTF-16 and UTF-32 are also supported. Strings are contained in double quotes (" ") or triple quotes (""" """). They are immutable, which means that they cannot be altered once they have been defined:

```
julia> s = "Hello, Julia"
julia> s[2] = 'z'
ERROR: MethodError: no method matching setindex!(::String, ::Char, ::Int64)
```

`String` is a succession, or an array of characters (see the *Ranges and arrays* section) that can be extracted from the string by indexing it, starting from 1: with `str = "Julia"`, `str[1]` returns the character `'J'`, and `str[end]` returns the character `'a'`, the last character in the string. The index of the last byte is also given by `endof(str)`, and `length()` returns the number of characters. These two are different if the string contains multi-byte Unicode characters, for example, `endof("Güdrun")` gives 7, while `length("Güdrun")` gives 6.

Using an index less than one or greater than the index of the last byte gives a `BoundsError`. In general, strings can contain Unicode characters, which can take up to four bytes, so not every index is a valid character index. For example, for `str2 = "I am the α: the beginning"`, we have `str2[10]`, which returns `'\u3b1'` (the two-byte character representing α), `str2[11]` returns `ERROR: StringIndexError` (because this is the second byte of the α character), and `str2[12]` returns colon (`:`).

We can see 25 characters. `length(str2)` returns 25, but the last index given by `lastindex(str2)` returns 26. For this reason, looping over a string's characters can best be done as an iteration and not by using the index, as follows:

```
for c in str2
    println(c)
end
```

A substring can be obtained by taking a range of `indices: str[3:5]` or using `str[3:end]`, which returns `"lia"`. A string that contains a single character is different from that `Char` value: `'A' == "A"` returns `false`.

Julia has an elegant string interpolation mechanism for constructing strings: $var inside a string is replaced by the value of var, and $(expr), where expr is an expression, is replaced by its computed value. When a is 2 and b is 3, the following expression "$a * $b = $(a * b)" returns "2 * 3 = 6". If you need to write the $ sign in a string, escape it as \$.

You can also concatenate strings with the * operator or with the string() function: "ABC" * "DEF" returns "ABCDEF", and string("abc", "def", "ghi") returns "abcdefghi".

Strings prefixed with : are of type Symbol, such as :green; we already used it in the printstyled function. They are more efficient than strings and are used for IDs or keys. Symbols cannot be concatenated. They should only be used if they are expected to remain constant over the course of the execution of the program.

The String type is very rich, and it has 96 functions defined on it, given by methodswith(String). Some useful methods include the following:

- replace(string, str1, str2): This changes substrings str1 to str2 in string, for example, replace("Julia","u" => "o") returns "Jolia".
- split(string, char or [chars]): This splits a string on the specified character or characters, for example, split("34,Tom Jones,Pickwick Street 10,Aberdeen", ',') returns the four strings in an array: ["34","Tom Jones","Pickwick Street 10","Aberdeen"]. If char is not specified, the split is done on space characters (spaces, tabs, newlines, and so on).

Formatting numbers and strings

The @printf macro from the Printf package (we'll look deeper into macros in Chapter 7, *Metaprogramming in Julia*) takes a format string and one or more variables to substitute into this string while being formatted. It works in a manner similar to printf in C. You can write a format string that includes placeholders for variables, for example, as follows:

```
julia> name = "Pascal"
julia> using Printf
julia> @printf("Hello, %s \n", name) # returns Hello, Pascal
```

Because @printf now lives in another package, you have to do this using Printf first (prior to 1.0, it belonged to Base).

If you need a string as the return value, use the macro @sprintf.

The following `formatting.jl` script shows the most common formats:

```
using Printf
# d for integers:
@printf("%d\n", 1e5) #> 100000
x = 7.35679
# f = float format, rounded if needed:
@printf("x = %0.3f\n", x) #> 7.357
aa = 1.5231071779744345
bb = 33.976886930000695
@printf("%.2f %.2f\n", aa, bb) #> 1.52 33.98
# or to create another string:
str = @sprintf("%0.3f", x)
show(str) #> "7.357"
println()
# e = scientific format with e:
@printf("%0.6e\n", x) #> 7.356790e+00
# c = for characters:
@printf("output: %c\n", 'α') #> output: α
# s for strings:
@printf("%s\n", "I like Julia")
# right justify:
@printf("%50s\n", "text right justified!")
# p for pointers:
@printf("a pointer: %p\n", 1e10) #> a pointer: 0x00000002540be400
```

The following output is obtained upon running the preceding script:

```
100000
x = 7.357
1.52 33.98
"7.357"
7.356790e+00
output: α
I like Julia
                       text right justified!
a pointer: 0x00000002540be400
```

A special kind of string is `VersionNumber`, which the form `v"0.3.0"` (note the preceding v), with optional additional details. They can be compared, and are used for Julia's versions, but also in the package versions and dependency mechanism of `Pkg` (refer to the *Packages* section of `Chapter 1`, *Installing the Julia Platform*). If you have the code that works differently for different versions, use something as follows:

```
if v"0.5" <= VERSION < v"0.6-"
# do something specific to 0.5 release series
end
```

Regular expressions

To search for and match patterns in text and other data, regular expressions are an indispensable tool for the data scientist. Julia adheres to the Perl syntax of regular expressions. For a complete reference, refer to
http://www.regular-expressions.info/reference.html. Regular expressions are represented in Julia as a double (or triple) quoted string preceded by r, such as r"..." (optionally, followed by one or more of the i, s, m, or x flags), and they are of type Regex. The regexp.jl script shows some examples.

In the first example, we will match the email addresses (#> shows the result):

```
email_pattern = r".+@.+"
input = "john.doe@mit.edu"
println(occursin(email_pattern, input)) #> true
```

The regular expression pattern + matches any (non-empty) group of characters. Thus, this pattern matches any string that contains @ somewhere in the middle.

In the second example, we will try to determine whether a credit card number is valid or not:

```
visa = r"^(?:4[0-9]{12}(?:[0-9]{3})?)$"  # the pattern
input = "4457418557635128"
occursin(visa, input)  #> true
if occursin(visa, input)
    println("credit card found")
    m = match(visa, input)
    println(m.match) #> 4457418557635128
    println(m.offset) #> 1
    println(m.offsets) #> []
end
```

The occursin(regex, string) function returns true or false, depending on whether the given regex matches the string, so we can use it in an if expression. If you want the detailed information of the pattern matching, use match instead of occursin. This either returns nothing when there is no match, or an object of type RegexMatch when the pattern is found (nothing is, in fact, a value to indicate that nothing is returned or printed, and it has a type of Nothing).

The `RegexMatch` object has the following properties:

- `match` contains the entire substring that matches (in this example, it contains the complete number)
- `offset` states at what position the matching begins (here, it is 1)
- `offsets` gives the same information as the preceding line, but for each of the captured substrings
- `captures` contains the captured substrings as a tuple (refer to the following example)

Besides checking whether a string matches a particular pattern, regular expressions can also be used to capture parts of the string. We can do this by enclosing parts of the pattern in parentheses ( ). For instance, to capture the username and hostname in the email address pattern used earlier, we modify the pattern as follows:

```
email_pattern = r"(.+)@(.+)"
```

Notice how the characters before @ are enclosed in brackets. This tells the regular expression engine that we want to capture this specific set of characters. To see how this works, consider the following example:

```
email_pattern = r"(.+)@(.+)"
input = "john.doe@mit.edu"
m = match(email_pattern, input)
println(m.captures) #> Union{Nothing,
SubString{String}}["john.doe", "mit.edu"]
```

Here is another example:

```
m = match(r"(ju|l)(i)?(a)", "Julia")
println(m.match) #> "lia"
println(m.captures) #> l - i - a
println(m.offset) #> 3
println(m.offsets) #> 3 - 4 - 5
```

The `search` and `replace` functions also take regular expressions as arguments, for example, `replace("Julia", r"u[\w]*l" => "red")` returns `"Jredia"`. If you want to work with all the matches, `matchall` and `eachmatch` come in handy:

```
str = "The sky is blue"
reg = r"[\w]{3,}" # matches words of 3 chars or more
r = collect((m.match for m = eachmatch(reg, str)))
show(r) #> ["The","sky","blue"]
```

```
iter = eachmatch(reg, str)
for i in iter
    println("\"$(i.match)\" ")
end
```

The `collect` function returns an array with `RegexMatch` for each match. `eachmatch` returns an iterator, `iter`, over all the matches, which we can loop through with a simple `for` loop. The screen output is `"The"`, `"sky"`, and `"blue"`, printed on consecutive lines.

Ranges and arrays

Ranges come in handy when you have to work with an interval of numbers, for example, one up to thousand: `1:1000`. The type of this object, `typeof(1:1000)`, is `UnitRange{Int64}`. By default, the step is 1, but this can also be specified as the second number; `0:5:100` gives all multiples of 5 up to `100`. You can iterate over a range, as follows:

```
# code from file chapter2\arrays.jl
for i in 1:2:9
    println(i)
end
```

This prints out 1, 3, 5, 7, 9 on consecutive lines.

In the previous section on *Strings*, we already encountered the array type when discussing the `split` function:

```
a = split("A,B,C,D",",")
typeof(a) #> Array{SubString{String},1}
show(a) #> SubString{String}["A","B","C","D"]
```

Julia's arrays are very efficient, powerful, and flexible. The general type format for an array is `Array{Type, n}`, with n number of dimensions (we will discuss multidimensional arrays or matrices in Chapter 6, *More on Types, Methods, and Modules*). As with the complex type, we can see that the `Array` type is generic, and all the elements have to be of the same type. A one-dimensional array (also called a **vector** in Julia) can be initialized by separating its values by commas and enclosing them in square brackets, for example, `arr = [100, 25, 37]` is a 3-element `Array{Int64,1}`; the type is automatically inferred with this notation. If you want the type to be `Any`, then define it as follows: `arra = Any[100, 25, "ABC"]`.

The index starts from 1:

```
julia> arr[0]
ERROR: BoundsError: attempt to access 3-element Array{Int64,1} at index [0]
julia> arr[1]
100
```

Notice that we don't have to indicate the number of elements. Julia takes care of that and lets an array grow dynamically when needed.

Arrays can also be constructed by passing a type parameter and a number of elements:

```
arr2 = Array{Int64}(undef, 5) # is a 5-element Array{Int64,1}
show(arr2) #> [326438368, 326438432, 326438496, 326438560, 326438624]
```

undef makes sure that your array gets populated with random values of the given type.

You can define an array with 0 elements of type Float64 as follows:

```
arr3 = Float64[] #> 0-element Array{Float64,1}
```

To populate this array, use push!; for example, push!(arr3, 1.0) returns 1-element Array{Float64,1}.

Creating an empty array with arr3 = [] is not very useful because the element type is Any. Julia wants to be able to infer the type!

Arrays can also be initialized from a range with the collect function:

```
arr4 = collect(1:7) #> 7-element Array{Int64,1}
show(arr4) #> [1, 2, 3, 4, 5, 6, 7]
```

Of course, when dealing with large arrays, it is better to indicate the final number of elements from the start for the performance. Suppose you know beforehand that arr2 will need 10^5 elements, but not more. If you use sizehint!(arr2, 10^5), you'll be able to push! at least 10^5 elements without Julia having to reallocate and copy the data already added, leading to a substantial improvement in performance.

Arrays store a sequence of values of the same type (called elements), indexed by integers 1 through the number of elements (as in mathematics, but unlike most other high-level languages such as Python). Like with strings, we can access the individual elements with the bracket notation; for example, with arr being [100, 25, 37], arr[1] returns 100, and arr[end] is 37. Use an invalid index result in an exception, as follows:

```
arr[6] #> ERROR: BoundsError: attempt to access 3-element Array{Int64,1} at
index [6]
```

You can also set a specific element the other way around:

```
arr[2] = 5 #> [100, 5, 37]
```

The main characteristics of an array are given by the following functions:

- The element type is given by `eltype(arr)`; in our example, this is `Int64`
- The number of elements is given by `length(arr)`, and here this is 3
- The number of dimensions is given by `ndims(arr)`, and here this is 1
- The number of elements in dimension n is given by `size(arr, n)`, and here, `size(arr, 1)` returns 3

A `for...in` loop over an array is read-only, and you cannot change elements of the array inside it:

```
da = [1,2,3,4,5]
for n in da
    n *= 2
end
da #> 5-element Array{Int64,1}: 1 2 3 4 5
```

Instead, use an index `i`, like this:

```
for i in 1:length(da)
    da[i] *= 2
end
da #> 5-element Array{Int64,1}: 2 4 6 8 10
```

It is easy to join the array elements to a string separated by a comma character and a space, for example, with `arr4 = [1, 2, 3, 4, 5, 6, 7]`:

```
join(arr4, ", ") #> "1, 2, 3, 4, 5, 6, 7"
```

We can also use this range syntax (called a slice as in Python) to obtain subarrays:

```
arr4[1:3] #>#> 3-element array [1, 2, 3]
arr4[4:end] #> 3-element array [4, 5, 6, 7]
```

Slices can be assigned to, with one value or with another array:

```
arr = [1,2,3,4,5]
arr[2:4] = [8,9,10]
println(arr) #> 1 8 9 10 5
```

Other ways to create arrays

For convenience, `zeros(n)` returns an n element array with all the elements equal to `0.0`, and `ones(n)` does the same with elements equal to `1.0`.

`range(start, stop=value, length=value)` creates a vector of n equally spaced numbers from start to stop, for example, as follows:

```
eqa = range(0, step=10, length=5) #> 0:10:40
show(eqa) #> 0:10:40
```

You can use the following to create an array with undefined values `#undef`, as shown here:

```
println(Array{Any}(undef, 4)) #> Any[#undef,#undef,#undef,#undef]
```

To fill an array `arr` with the same value for all the elements, use `fill!(arr, 42)`, which returns `[42, 42, 42, 42, 42]`.

To create a five-element array with random `Int32` numbers, execute the following:

```
v1 = rand(Int32,5)
5-element Array{Int32,1}:
   905745764
   840462491
  -227765082
  -286641110
    16698998
```

Some common functions for arrays

If `b = [1:7]` and `c = [100,200,300]`, then you can concatenate b and c with the following command:

```
append!(b, c) #> Now b is [1, 2, 3, 4, 5, 6, 7, 100, 200, 300]
```

The array, b, is changed by applying this `append!` method—that's why it ends in an exclamation mark (`!`). This is a general convention.

A function whose name ends in a ! changes its first argument.

Likewise, push! and pop! append one element at the end, or take one away and return that, while the array is changed:

```
pop!(b) #> 300, b is now [1, 2, 3, 4, 5, 6, 7, 100, 200]
push!(b, 42) # b is now [1, 2, 3, 4, 5, 6, 7, 100, 200, 42]
```

If you want to do the same operations on the front of the array, use popfirst! and pushfirst! (formerly unshift! and shift!, respectively):

```
popfirst!(b) #> 1, b is now [2, 3, 4, 5, 6, 7, 100, 200, 42]
pushfirst!(b, 42) # b is now [42, 2, 3, 4, 5, 6, 7, 100, 200, 42]
```

To remove an element at a certain index, use the splice! function, as follows:

```
splice!(b,8) #> 100, b is now [42, 2, 3, 4, 5, 6, 7, 200, 42]
```

Checking whether an array contains an element is very easy with the in function:

```
in(42, b) #> true , in(43, b) #> false
```

To sort an array, use sort! if you want the array to be changed in place, or sort if the original array must stay the same:

```
sort(b) #> [2,3,4,5,6,7,42,42,200], but b is not changed:
println(b) #> [42,2,3,4,5,6,7,200,42]
sort!(b) #>                                    println(b)
#> b is now changed to [2,3,4,5,6,7,42,42,200]
```

To loop over an array, you can use a simple for loop:

```
for e in arr
    print("$e ") # or process e in another way
end
```

If a dot (.) precedes operators such as + or *, the operation is done element-wise, that is, on the corresponding elements of the arrays:

```
arr = [1, 2, 3]
arr .+ 2 #> [3, 4, 5]
arr * 2  #> [2, 10, 6]
```

As another example, if a1 = [1, 2, 3] and a2 = [4, 5, 6], then a1 .* a2 returns the array [4, 10, 18]. On the other hand, if you want the dot (or scalar) product of vectors, use the LinearAlgebra.dot(a1, a2) function, which returns 32, so this gives the same result as sum(a1 .* a2):

```
using LinearAlgebra
LinearAlgebra.dot(a1, a2) #> 32
sum(a1 .* a2)
```

Lots of other useful methods exist, such as repeat([1, 2, 3], inner = [2]), which produces [1,1,2,2,3,3].

The methodswith(Array) function returns 47 methods. You can use help in the REPL, or search the documentation for more information.

When you assign an array to another array, and then change the first array, both the arrays change. Consider the following example:

```
a = [1,2,4,6]
a1 = a
show(a1) #> [1,2,4,6]
a[4] = 0
show(a) #> [1,2,4,0]
show(a1) #> [1,2,4,0]
```

This happens because they point to the same object in memory. If you don't want this, you have to make a copy of the array. Just use b = copy(a) or b = deepcopy(a) if some elements of a are arrays that have to be copied recursively.

As we have seen, arrays are mutable (in contrast to strings), and as arguments to a function, they are passed by reference. As a consequence, the function can change them, as in this example:

```
a = [1,2,3]

function change_array(arr)
   arr[2] = 25
end

change_array(a)
println(a) #>[ 1, 25, 3]
```

Suppose you have an array `arr = ['a', 'b', 'c']`. Which function on `arr` do we need to return all characters in one string?

The function `join` will do the trick: `join(arr)` returns the string `"abc"`.

`string(arr)` does not: this returns `['a', 'b', 'c']`, but `string(arr...)` does return `"abc"`. This is because `...` is the **splice operator** (also known as splat). It causes the contents of `arr` to be passed as individual arguments, rather than passing `arr` as an array.

Dates and times

To get the basic time information, you can use the `time()` function that returns, for example, `1.408719961424e9`, which is the number of seconds since a predefined date called the **epoch** (normally, the 1st of January 1970 on a Unix system). This is useful for measuring the time interval between two events, for example, to benchmark how long a long calculation takes:

```
start_time = time()
# long computation
time_elapsed = time() - start_time
println("Time elapsed: $time_elapsed")
```

Use the `Dates` module that is built in into the standard library, with `Date` for days and `DateTime` for times down to milliseconds, to implement this. Additional time zone functionality can be added through the `Timezones.jl` package.

The `Date` and `DateTime` functions can be constructed as follows, or with simpler versions with less information:

- `d = Date(2014,9,1)` returns `2014-09-01`
- `dt = DateTime(2014,9,1,12,30,59,1)` returns `2014-09-01T12:30:59.001`

These objects can be compared and subtracted to get the duration. The `Date` function parts or fields can be retrieved through accessor functions, such as `year(d)`, `month(d)`, `week(d)`, and `day(d)`. Other useful functions exist, such as `dayofweek`, `dayname`, `daysinmonth`, `dayofyear`, `isleapyear`, and so on.

Scope and constants

The region in the program where a variable is known is called the **scope** of that variable. Until now, we have only seen how to create top-level or global variables that are accessible from anywhere in the program. By contrast, variables defined in a local scope can only be used within that scope. A common example of a local scope is the code inside a function. Using global scope variables is not advisable for several reasons, notably the performance. If the value and type can change at any moment in the program, the compiler cannot optimize the code.

So, restricting the scope of a variable to local scope is better. This can be done by defining them within a function or a control construct, as we will see in the following chapters. This way, we can use the same variable name more than once without name conflicts.

Let's take a look at the following code fragment:

```
# code in chapter 2\scope.jl
x = 1.0 # x is Float64
x = 1 # now x is Int
y::Float64 = 1.0
# ERROR: syntax: type declarations on global variables are not yet
supported

function scopetest()
    println(x) # 1, x is known here, because it's in global scope
    y::Float64 = 1.0
# y must be Float64, this is not possible in global scope
end

scopetest()
#> 1
#> 1.0

println(y) #> ERROR: UndefVarError: y not defined
```

Variable x changes its type, which is allowed, but because it makes the code type unstable, it could be the source of a performance hit. From the definition of y in the third line, we can see that type annotations can only be used in local scope (here, in the `scopetest()` function).

Some code constructs introduce scope blocks. They support local variables. We have already mentioned functions, but `for`, `while`, `try`, `let`, and `type` blocks can all support a local scope. Any variable defined in a `for`, `while`, `try`, or `let` block will be local unless it is used by an enclosing scope before the block.

The following structure, called a **compound expression**, does not introduce a new scope. Several (preferably short) sub-expressions can be combined in one compound expression if you start it with begin, as in this example:

```
x = begin
    a = 5
    2 * a
end # now x is 10
println(a) #> a is 5
```

After end, x has the value 10 and a is 5. This can also be written with ( ) as follows:

```
x = (a = 5; 2 * a)   #> 10
```

The value of a compound expression is the value of the last sub-expression. Variables introduced in it are still known after the expression ends.

Values that don't change during program execution are constants, which are declared with const. In other words, they are immutable, and their type is inferred. It is a good practice to write their name in uppercase letters, like this:

```
const GC = 6.67e-11 # gravitational constant in m3/kg s2
```

Julia defines a number of constants, such as ARGS (an array that contains the command-line arguments), VERSION (the version of Julia that is running), and OS_NAME (the name of the operating system such as Linux, Windows, or Darwin), mathematical constants (such as pi and e), and Datetime constants (such as Friday, Fri, August, and Aug).

If you try to give a global constant a new value, you get a warning, but if you change its type, you get an error, as follows:

```
julia> GC = 3.14
    Warning: redefining constant GC
julia> GC = 10
    ERROR: invalid redefinition of constant GC
```

 Constants can only be assigned a value once, and their type cannot change, so they can be optimized. Use them whenever possible in the global scope.

So, global constants are more about type than value, which makes sense, because Julia gets its speed from knowing the correct types. If, however, the constant variable is of a mutable type (for example, `Array`, `Dict` (refer to Chapter 8, *I/O, Networking, and Parallel Computing*)), then you can't change it to a different array, but you can always change the contents of that variable:

```
julia> const ARR = [4,7,1]
julia> ARR[1] = 9
julia> show(ARR) #> [9,7,1]
julia> ARR = [1, 2, 3]
   Warning: redefining constant ARR
```

To review what we have learned in this chapter, we will play with characters, strings, and arrays in the following program (`strings_arrays.jl`):

```
using Statistics
# a newspaper headline:
str = "The Gold and Blue Loses a Bit of Its Luster"
println(str)
nchars = length(str)
println("The headline counts $nchars characters") # 43
str2 = replace(str, "Blue" => "Red")

# strings are immutable
println(str) # The Gold and Blue Loses a Bit of Its Luster
println(str2)
println("Here are the characters at position 25 to 30:")
subs = str[25:30]
print("-$(lowercase(subs))-") # "-a bit -"
println("Here are all the characters:")
for c in str
    println(c)
end
arr = split(str,' ')
show(arr)
#["The","Gold","and","Blue","Loses","a","Bit","of","Its","Luster"]
nwords = length(arr)
println("The headline counts $nwords words") # 10
println("Here are all the words:")
for word in arr
    println(word)
end
arr[4] = "Red"
show(arr) # arrays are mutable
println("Convert back to a sentence:")
nstr = join(arr, ' ')
println(nstr) # The Gold and Red Loses a Bit of Its Luster
```

```
# working with arrays:
println("arrays: calculate sum, mean and standard deviation ")
arr = collect(1:100)
typeof(arr)  #> Array{Int64,1}
println(sum(arr))  #> 5050
println(mean(arr))  #> 50.5
```

Summary

In this chapter, we reviewed some basic elements of Julia, such as constants, variables, and types. We also learned how to work with the basic types such as numbers, characters, strings, and ranges, and encountered the very versatile array type. In the next chapter, we will look in-depth at functions and realize that Julia deserves to be called a functional language.

3
Functions

Julia is first and foremost a functional language because computations and data transformations are done through functions; they are first-class citizens in Julia. Programs are structured around defining functions and to overload them for different combinations of argument types. This chapter discusses this keystone concept, covering the following topics:

- Defining functions
- Optional and keyword arguments
- Anonymous functions
- First-class functions and closures
- Recursive functions
- Broadcasting
- Map, filter, and list comprehensions
- Generic functions and multiple dispatch

Defining functions

A function is an object that gets a number of arguments (the argument list, `arglist`) as the input, then does something with these values in the function body, and returns none, one, or more value(s). Multiple arguments are separated by commas (,) in an `arglist` (in fact, they form a tuple, as do the return values; refer to the *Tuples* section of Chapter 5, *Collection Types*). The arguments are also optionally typed, and the type(s) can be user-defined. The general syntax is as follows:

```
function fname(arglist)
    # function body...
    return value(s)
end
```

A function's argument list can also be empty; in this case, it is written as `fname()`.

The following is a simple example:

```
# code in functions101.jl
function mult(x, y)
        println("x is $x and y is $y")
        return x * y
end
```

Function names such as `mult` are, by convention, in lower-case. They can contain Unicode characters, which are useful in mathematical notations. The `return` keyword in the last line is optional; we could have written the line as `x * y`. In general, the value of the last expression in the function is returned, but writing `return` is mostly a good idea in multiline functions to increase readability.

The function called with `n = mult(3, 4)` returns `12`, and assigns the return value to a new variable, `n`. You can also execute a function just by calling `fname(arglist)` if you only need its side-effects (that is, how the function affects the program state; for instance, by changing the global variables). The `return` keyword can also be used within a condition in other parts of the function body to exit the function earlier, as in this example:

```
function mult(x, y)
    println("x is $x and y is $y")
    if x == 1
      return y
    end
    x * y
end
```

In this case, `return` can also be used without a value so that the function returns `nothing`.

Functions are not limited to returning a single value. Here is an example with multiple return values:

```
function multi(n, m)
    n*m, div(n,m), n%m
end
```

This returns the tuple `(16,4,0)` when called with `multi(8, 2)`. The return values can be extracted to other variables such as `x, y, z = multi(8, 2)`; then x becomes `16`, y becomes `4`, and z becomes `0`. In fact, you can say that Julia always returns a single value, but this value can be a tuple that can be used to pass multiple variables back to the program.

We can also have a variable with a number of arguments using the ellipsis operator
(. . .). An example of this operator is as follows:

```
function varargs(n, m, args...)
    println("arguments : $n $m $args")
  end
```

Here, n and m are just positional arguments (there can be more or none at all). The args...
argument takes in all the remaining parameters in a tuple. If we call the function with
varargs(1, 2, 3, 4), then n is 1, m is 2, and args has the value (3, 4). When there are
still more parameters, the tuple can grow; or if there are none, it can be empty (). The same
splat operator can also be used to unpack a tuple or an array into individual arguments. For
example, we can define a second variable argument function as follows:

```
function varargs2(args...)
    println("arguments2: $args")
  end
```

With x = (3, 4), we can call varargs2 as varargs2(1, 2, x...). Now, args
becomes the tuple (1, 2, 3, 4); the tuple x was spliced. This also works for arrays. If x
= [10, 11, 12], then args becomes (1, 2, 10, 11, 12). The receiving function does
not need to be a variable argument function, but then the number of spliced parameters
must exactly match the number of arguments.

It is important to realize that, in Julia, all arguments to functions (with the exception of
plain data such as numbers and chars) are passed by reference. Their values are not copied
when they are passed, which means they can be changed from inside the function, and the
changes will be visible to the calling code.

For example, consider the following code:

```
function insert_elem(arr)
   push!(arr, -10)
end

arr = [2, 3, 4]
insert_elem(arr)
# arr is now [ 2, 3, 4, -10 ]
```

As this example shows, arr itself has been modified by the function.

Due to the way Julia compiles, a function must be defined by the time it is actually called
(but it can be used before that in other function definitions).

It can also be useful to indicate the argument types, to restrict the kind of parameters passed when calling. Our `function` header for floating point numbers would then look like: `function mult(x::Float64, y::Float64)`. When this is the only `mult` function, and we call this function with `mult(5, 6)`, we receive an error, `ERROR: MethodError: no method matching mult(::Int64, ::Int64)`, proving that Julia is indeed a strongly typed language. It does not accept integer parameters for floating point arguments.

If we define a function without types, it is generic; the Julia JIT compiler is ready to generate versions called `methods` for different argument types when needed. Define the previous function `mult` in the REPL, and you will see the output as `mult (generic function with 1 method)`.

There is also a more compact, one-line function syntax (the assignment form) for short functions, for example, `mult(x, y) = x * y`. Use this, preferably, for simple one-line functions, as it will lend the code greater clarity. Because of this, mathematical functions can also be written in an intuitive form:

```
f(x, y) = x^3 - y + x * y; f(3, 2) #=> 31
```

A function defines its own scope. The set of variables that are declared inside a function are only known inside the function, and this is also true for the arguments. Functions can be defined as top-level (global) or nested (a function can be defined within another function). Usually, functions with related functionality are grouped in their own Julia file, which is included in a main file. Or, if the function is big enough, it can have its own file, preferably with the same name as the function.

Optional and keyword arguments

When defining functions, one or more arguments can be given a default value such as `f(arg = val)`. If no parameter is supplied for `arg`, then `val` is taken as the value of `arg`. The position of these arguments in the function's input is important, just as it is for normal arguments; that's why they are called **optional positional arguments**. Here is an example of an `f` function with an optional argument `b`:

```
# code in arguments.jl:
f(a, b = 5) = a + b
```

For example, if it's f(1), then it returns 6; f(2, 5) returns 7; and f(3) returns 8. However, calling it with f() or f(1,2,3) returns an error, because there is no matching function f with zero or three arguments. These arguments are still only defined by position: calling f(2, b = 5) raises an error as ERROR: function f does not accept keyword arguments.

Until now, arguments were only defined by position. For code clarity, it can be useful to explicitly call them by name, so they are called **optional keyword arguments**. Because the arguments are given explicit names, their order is irrelevant, but they must come last and be separated from the positional arguments by a semi-colon (;) in the argument list, as shown in this example:

```
k(x; a1 = 1, a2 = 2) = x * (a1 + a2)
```

Now, k(3, a2 = 3) returns 12, k(3, a2 = 3, a1 = 0) returns 9 (so their position doesn't matter), but k(3) returns 9 (demonstrating that the keyword arguments are optional). Normal, optional positional, and keyword arguments can be combined as follows:

```
function allargs(normal_arg, optional_positional_arg=2; keyword_arg="ABC")
    print("normal arg: $normal_arg" - )
    print("optional arg: $optional_positional_arg" - )
    print("keyword arg: $keyword_arg")
end
```

If we call allargs(1, 3, keyword_arg=4), it prints normal arg: 1 - optional arg: 3 - keyword arg: 4.

A useful case is when the keyword arguments are splatted as follows:

```
function varargs2(;args...)
    args
end
```

Calling this with varargs2(k1="name1", k2="name2", k3=7) returns pairs(::NamedTuple) with three entries: (:k1,"name1") (:k2,"name2") (:k3,7). Now, args is a collection of (key, value) tuples, where each key comes from the name of the keyword argument, and it is also a symbol (refer to the *Strings* section of Chapter 2, *Variables, Types, and Operations*) because of the colon (:) as prefix.

Anonymous functions

The function f(x, y) at the end of the *Defining functions* section can also be written with no name, as an anonymous function: (x, y) -> x^3 - y + x * y. We can, however, bind it to a name, such as f = (x, y) -> x^3 - y + x * y, and then call it, for example, as f(3, 2). Anonymous functions are also often written using the following syntax (note the space before (x)):

```
function (x)
    x + 2
end
(anonymous function)
julia> ans(3)
5
```

Often, they are also written with a lambda expression as (x) -> x + 2. Before the stab character (->) are the arguments, and after the stab character we have the return value. This can be shortened to x -> x + 2. A function without arguments would be written as () -> println("hello, Julia").

Here is an anonymous function taking three arguments: (x, y, z) -> 3x + 2y - z. When the performance is important, try to use named functions instead, because calling anonymous functions involves a huge overhead. Anonymous functions are mostly used when passing a function as an argument to another function, which is precisely what we will discuss in the next section.

First-class functions and closures

In this section, we will demonstrate the power and flexibility of functions (example code can be found in Chapter 3\first_class.jl). Firstly, functions have their own type: Function. Functions can also be assigned to a variable by their name:

```
julia> m = mult
julia> m(6, 6) #> 36
```

This is useful when working with anonymous functions, such as `c = x -> x + 2`, or as follows:

```
julia> plustwo = function (x)
                    x + 2
              end
(anonymous function)
julia> plustwo(3)
5
```

Operators are just functions written with their arguments in an infix form; for example, `x + y` is equivalent to `+(x, y)`. In fact, the first form is parsed to the second form when it is evaluated. We can confirm it in the REPL: `+(3,4)` returns 7 and `typeof(+)` returns `Function`.

A function can take *a function* (or multiple functions) as its argument, which calculates the numerical derivative of a function `f`; as defined in the following function:

```
function numerical_derivative(f, x, dx=0.01)
    derivative = (f(x+dx) - f(x-dx))/(2*dx)
    return derivative
end
```

The function can be called as `numerical_derivative(f, 1, 0.001)`, passing an anonymous function `f` as an argument:

```
f = x -> 2x^2 + 30x + 9
println(numerical_derivative(f, 1, 0.001)) #> 33.99999999999537
```

A function can also return another function (or multiple functions) as its value. This is demonstrated in the following code, which calculates the derivative of a function (this is also a function):

```
function derivative(f)
    return function(x)
    # pick a small value for h
        h = x == 0 ? sqrt(eps(Float64)) : sqrt(eps(Float64)) * x
        xph = x + h
        dx = xph - x
        f1 = f(xph) # evaluate f at x + h
        f0 = f(x) # evaluate f at x
        return (f1 - f0) / dx   # divide by h
    end
end
```

As we can see, both are excellent use cases for anonymous functions.

Here is an example of a `counter` function that returns (a tuple of) two anonymous functions:

```
function counter()
    n = 0
    () -> n += 1, () -> n = 0
end
```

We can assign the returned functions to variables:

```
(addOne, reset) = counter()
```

Notice that n is not defined outside the function:

```
julia> n
ERROR: n not defined
```

Then, when we call `addOne` repeatedly, we get the following output:

```
addOne() #=> 1
addOne() #=> 2
addOne() #=> 3
reset()  #=> 0
```

What we see is that, in the `counter` function, the variable n is captured in the anonymous functions. It can only be manipulated by the functions, `addOne` and `reset`. The two functions are said to be **closed** over the variable n and both have references to n. That's why they are called **closures**.

Currying (also called a partial application) is the technique of translating the evaluation of a function that takes multiple arguments (or a tuple of arguments) into evaluating a sequence of functions, each with a single argument. Here is an example of function currying:

```
function add(x)
    return function f(y)
        return x + y
    end
end
```

The output returned is `add (generic function with 1 method)`.

Calling this function with add(1)(2) returns 3. This example can be written more succinctly as add(x) = f(y) = x + y or, with an anonymous function, as add(x) = y -> x + y. Currying is especially useful when passing functions around, as we will see in the *Map, filter, and list comprehensions* section.

functions

Functions can be nested, as demonstrated in the following example:

```
function a(x)
    z = x * 2
    function b(z)
        z += 1
    end
    b(z)
end

d = 5
a(d)  #=> 11
```

A function can also be recursive, that is, it can call itself. To show some examples, we need to be able to test a condition in code. The simplest way to do this in Julia is to use the ternary operator ? of the form expr ? b : c (ternary because it takes three arguments). Julia also has a normal if construct. (Refer to the *Conditional evaluation* section of Chapter 4, *Control Flow*.) expr is a condition and, if it is true, then b is evaluated and the value is returned, else c is evaluated. This is used in the following recursive definition to calculate the sum of all the integers up to and including a certain number:

```
sum(n) = n > 1 ? sum(n-1) + n : n
```

The recursion ends because there is a base case: when n is 1, this value is returned. Here is the famous function to calculate the nth Fibonacci number that is defined as the sum of the two previous Fibonacci numbers:

```
fib(n) = n < 2 ? n : fib(n-1) + fib(n-2)
```

When using recursion, care should be taken to define a base case to stop the calculation. Also, although Julia can nest very deeply, watch out for stack overflows, because, until now, Julia has not done tail call optimization automatically.

Broadcasting

A function f can be broadcast over all elements of an array (or matrix) by using the dot notation f.(matrix); for example:

```
arr = [1.0, 2.0, 3.0]
sin.(arr) #>
3-element Array{Float64,1}:
#   0.8414709848078965
#   0.9092974268256817
#   0.1411200080598672
```

Here is another example:

```
f(x,y) = x + 7y
f.(pi, arr)
#> 3-element Array{Float64,1}:
# 10.141592653589793
# 17.141592653589793
# 24.141592653589793
```

Broadcasting is very useful in Julia to write compact expressions with arrays and matrices.

Map, filter, and list comprehensions

Maps and filters are typical for functional languages. A map is a function of the form map(func, coll), where func is a (often anonymous) function that is successively applied to every element of the coll collection, so map returns a new collection. Some examples are as follows:

- map(x -> x * 10, [1, 2, 3]) returns [10, 20, 30]
- cubes = map(x-> Base.power_by_squaring(x, 3), collect(1:5)) returns [1, 8, 27, 64, 125]

 power_by_squaring is an internal function in Base, which means it is not exported, so it has to be qualified with Base.

The map function can also be used with functions that take more than one argument. In this case, it requires a collection for each argument; for example, map(*, [1, 2, 3], [4, 5, 6]) works per element and returns [4, 10, 18].

When the function passed to `map` requires several lines, it can be a bit unwieldy to write as an anonymous function. For instance, consider using the following function:

```
map( x-> begin
            if x == 0 return 0
            elseif iseven(x) return 2
            elseif isodd(x) return 1
            end
        end, collect(-3:3))
```

This function returns `[1,2,1,0,1,2,1]`. This can be simplified with a `do` block as follows:

```
map(collect(-3:3)) do x
    if x == 0 return 0
    elseif iseven(x) return 2
    elseif isodd(x) return 1
    end
end
```

The `do x` statement creates an anonymous function with the argument `x` and passes it as the first argument to `map`.

A `filter` is a function of the form `filter(func, coll)`, where `func` is a (often anonymous) Boolean function that is checked on each element of the collection `coll`. Filter returns a new collection with only the elements on which `func` is evaluated to be true. For example, the following code filters the even numbers and returns `[2, 4, 6, 8, 10]`:

```
filter( n -> iseven(n), collect(1:10))
```

An incredibly powerful and simple way to create an array is to use a list comprehension. This is a kind of implicit loop which creates the result array and fills it with values. Some examples are as follows:

- `arr = Float64[x^2 for x in 1:4]` creates 4-element `Array{Float64,1}` with elements `1.0`, `4.0`, `9.0`, and `16.0`.
- `cubes = [x^3 for x in collect(1:5)]` returns `[1, 8, 27, 64, 125]`.
- `mat1 = [x + y for x in 1:2, y in 1:3]` creates a 2 x 3 array (`Array{Int64,2}`):

  ```
  2  3  4
  3  4  5
  ```

- `table10 = [x * y for x=1:10, y=1:10]` creates a 10 x 10 array (`Array{Int64,2}`), and returns the multiplication table of 10.

- `arrany = Any[i * 2 for i in 1:5]` **creates** `5-element Array{Any,1}` with elements `2`, `4`, `6`, `8`, and `10`.

For more examples, you can refer to the *Dictionaries* section in `Chapter 5`, *Collection Types*.

Constraining the type, as with `arr`, is often helpful for performance. Using typed comprehensions everywhere for explicitness and safety in production code is certainly the best practice.

Generic functions and multiple dispatch

We have already seen that functions are inherently defined as generic, that is, they can be used for different types of their arguments. The compiler will generate a separate version of the function each time it is called with arguments of a new type. In Julia, a concrete version of a function for a specific combination of argument types is called a **method**. To define a new method for a function (also called **overloading**), just use the same function name but a different signature, that is, with different argument types. A list of all the methods is stored in a virtual method table (`vtable`) on the function itself; methods do not belong to a particular type. When a function is called, Julia will lookup in `vtable` at runtime to find which concrete method it should call, based on the types of all its arguments; this is Julia's multiple dispatch mechanism, which Python, C++, or Fortran do not implement this. It allows open extensions where normal object-oriented code would have forced you to change a class or subclass to an existing class and thus change your library. Note that only positional arguments are taken into account for multiple dispatch, and not keyword arguments.

For each of these different methods, specialized low-level code is generated, targeted to the processor's instruction set. In contrast to **object-oriented** (**OO**) languages, `vtable` is stored in the function, and not in the type (or class). In OO languages, a method is called on a single object, `object.method()`, which is generally called **single dispatch**. In Julia, one can say that a function belongs to multiple types, or that a function is specialized or overloaded for different types. Julia's ability to compile code that reads like a high-level dynamic language into machine code that performs almost entirely like C is derived from its ability to do multiple dispatch.

To make this idea more concrete, a function such as `square(x) = x * x` actually defines a potentially infinite family of methods, one for each of the possible types of the argument x. For example, `square(2)` will call a specialized method that uses the CPU's native integer multiplication instruction, whereas `square(2.0)` will use the CPU's native floating point multiplication instruction.

Let's see multiple dispatch in action. We will define a function f that takes two arguments n and m returning a string, but, in some methods, the type of n or m, or both, is annotated. (Number is a supertype of Integer, refer to the *The type hierarchy – subtypes and supertypes* section in Chapter 6, *More on Types, Methods, and Modules*.) This can be seen in the following example:

```
f(n, m) = "base case"
f(n::Number, m::Number) = "n and m are both numbers"
f(n::Number, m) = "n is a number"
f(n, m::Number) = "m is a number"
f(n::Integer, m::Integer) = "n and m are both integers"
```

This returns f (generic function with 5 methods).

When n and m have no type, as in "base case", then their type is Any, the supertype of all types. Let's take a look at how the most appropriate method is chosen in each of the following function calls:

- f(1.5, 2) returns n and m are both numbers
- f(1, "bar") returns n is a number
- f(1, 2) returns n and m are both integers
- f("foo", [1,2]) returns base case

Calling f(n, m) will never result in an error, because if no other method matches, the base case will be invoked when we add a new method:

```
f(n::Float64, m::Integer) = "n is a float and m is an integer"
```

So, the call to f(1.5,2) now returns n is a float and m is an integer.

To get a quick overview of all the versions of a function, type methods(fname) into the REPL. For example, methods(+) shows a listing of 174 methods for a generic function +:

```
+(x::Bool) at bool.jl:36
+(x::Bool,y::Bool) at bool.jl:39
...
+(a,b,c) at operators.jl:82
+(a,b,c,xs...) at operators.jl:83
```

You can even take a look in the source code at how they are defined, as in base/bool.jl in the local Julia installation or at https://github.com/JuliaLang/julia/blob/master/base/bool.jl, where we can see the addition of Bool variables equal to the addition of integers: +(x::Bool, y::Bool) = int(x) + int(y), where int(false) is 0 and int(true) is 1.

As a second example, `methods(sort)` shows `# 6 methods for the generic function "sort"`.

The macro `@which` gives you the exact method that is used and where in the source code that method is defined, for example, `@which 2 * 2` returns `*(x::Int64, y::Int64)` at `int.jl:47`. This also works the other way around. If you want to know which methods are defined for a certain type, or use that type, ask `methodswith(Type)` from the `InteractiveUtils` module. For example, here is a part of the output of `InteractiveUtils .methodswith(String)`:

```
[18] getindex(s::String, r::UnitRange{Int64}) in Base at
strings/string.jl:240
[19] getindex(s::String, i::Int64) in Base at strings/string.jl:205
[20] getindex(s::String, r::UnitRange{#s56} where #s56<:Integer) in Base at
strings/string.jl:237 ...
```

As already noted, type stability is crucial for optimal performance. A function is type-stable if the return type(s) of all the output variables can be deduced from the types of the inputs. So try to design your functions with type stability in mind.

Some crude performance measurements (execution time and memory used) on the execution of functions can be obtained from the macro `@time`, for example:

```
@time fib(35)
elapsed time: 0.115188593 seconds (6756 bytes allocated) 9227465
```

`@elapsed` only returns the execution time. `@elapsed fib(35)` returns `0.115188593`.

In Julia, the first call of a method invokes the LLVM JIT compiler backend (refer to the *How Julia works* section in `Chapter 1`, *Installing the Julia Platform*), to emit machine code for it, so this warm-up call will take a bit longer. Start timing or benchmarking from the second call onward, after doing a dry run.

When writing a program with Julia, first write an easy version that works. Then, if necessary, improve the performance of that version by profiling it and then fixing performance bottlenecks. We'll come back to performance measurements in the *Performance tips* section of `Chapter 9`, *Running External Programs*.

Summary

In this chapter, we saw that functions are the basic building blocks of Julia. We explored the power of functions, their arguments and return values, closures, maps, filters, and comprehensions. However, to make the code in a function more interesting, we need to see how Julia does basic control flow, iterations, and loops. This is the topic of the next chapter.

4
Control Flow

Julia offers many control statements that are familiar to the other languages, while also simplifying the syntax for many of them. However, tasks are probably new; they are based on the coroutine concept to make computations more flexible.

We will cover the following topics in this chapter:

- Conditional evaluation
- Repeated evaluation
- Exception handling
- Scope revisited
- Tasks

Conditional evaluation

Conditional evaluation means that pieces of code are evaluated, depending on whether a Boolean expression is either true or false. The familiar if...elseif...else...end syntax is used here, which is as follows:

```
# code in Chapter 4\conditional.jl
var = 7
if var > 10
    println("var has value $var and is bigger than 10.")
elseif var < 10
    println("var has value $var and is smaller than 10.")
else
    println("var has value $var and is 10.")
end
# => prints "var has value 7 and is smaller than 10."
```

The `elseif` (of which there can be more than one) or `else` branches are optional. The condition in the first branch is evaluated, only the code in that branch is executed when the condition is true, and so on; so only one branch ever gets evaluated. No parentheses around condition(s) are needed, but they can be used for clarity. Each expression tested must effectively result in a true or false value, and no other values (such as 0 or 1) are allowed.

Because every expression in Julia returns a value, so also does the `if` expression. We can use this expression to do an assignment depending on a condition. In the preceding case, the return value is nothing since that is what `println` returns.

However, in the following snippet, the value 15 is assigned to z:

```
a = 10
b = 15
z = if a > b   a
    else       b
    end
```

These kinds of expression can be simplified using the ternary operator ? (which we introduced in the *Recursive functions* section in Chapter 3, *Functions*) as follows:

```
z = a > b ? a : b
```

Here, only a or b is evaluated and parentheses ( ) can be added around each clause, as they are necessary for clarity. The ternary operator can be chained, but then it often becomes harder to read. Our first example can be rewritten as follows:

```
var = 7
varout = "var has value $var"
cond = var > 10 ? "and is bigger than 10." : var < 10 ? "and is
    smaller than 10" : "and is 10."
println("$varout $cond") # var has value 7 and is smaller than 10
```

Using short-circuit evaluation (refer to the *Elementary mathematical functions* section in Chapter 2, *Variables, Types, and Operations*), the statements with `if...only` are often written as follows:

```
if <cond> <statement> end is written as <cond> && <statement
if !<cond> <statement> end is written as <cond> || <statement>
```

To make this clearer, the first can be read as `<cond>` *and then* `<statement>`, and the second as `<cond>` *or else* `<statement>`.

This feature can come in handy when guarding the parameter values passed into the arguments, which calculates the square root, like in the following function:

```
function sqroot(n::Int)
    n >= 0 || error("n must be non-negative")
    n == 0 && return 0
    sqrt(n)
end
sqroot(4)  #=> 2.0
sqroot(0)  #=> 0.0
sqroot(-6) #=> ERROR: LoadError: n must be non-negative
```

The `error` statement effectively throws an exception with the given message and stops the code execution (refer to the *Exception handling* section in this chapter).

Julia has no switch/case statement, and the language provides no built-in pattern matching (although one can argue that multiple dispatch is a kind of pattern matching that is based not on value, but on type).

Repeated evaluation

Julia has a `for` loop for iterating over a collection or repeating some code a certain number of times. You can use a `while` loop when the repetition depends on a condition, and you can influence the execution of both loops through `break` and `continue`.

for loops

We already encountered the `for` loop when iterating over the element e of a collection `coll` (refer to the *Strings, Ranges and Arrays* sections in `Chapter 2`, *Variables, Types, and Operations*). This takes the following general form:

```
# code in Chapter 4\repetitions.jl
for e in coll
    # body: process(e) executed for every element e in coll
end
```

Here, `coll` can be a range, a string, an array, or any other iterable collection (for other uses, also refer to Chapter 5, *Collection Types*). The variable e is not known outside the `for` loop. When iterating over a numeric range, often = (equal to) is used instead of `in`:

```
for n = 1:10
    print(n^3)
end
```

(This code can be a one-liner, but is spread over three lines for clarity.) The `for` loop is generally used when the number of repetitions is known.

> Use `for i in 1:n` rather than `for i in [1:n]` since the latter allocates an array while the former uses a simpler range object.

You can also use ϵ instead of `in` or =.

If you need to know the index when iterating over the elements of an array, run the following code:

```
arr = [x^2 for x in 1:10]
for i = 1:length(arr)
    println("the $i-th element is $(arr[i])")
end
```

A more elegant way to accomplish this uses the `enumerate` function, as follows:

```
for (ix, val) in enumerate(arr)
    println("the $ix-th element is $val")
end
```

Nested `for` loops are possible, as in this code snippet, for a multiplication table:

```
for n = 1:5
    for m = 1:5
        println("$n * $m = $(n * m)")
    end
end
```

However, nested `for` loops can often be combined into a single outer loop, as follows:

```
for n = 1:5, m = 1:5
    println("$n * $m = $(n * m)")
end
```

while loops

When you want to use looping as long as a condition stays true, use the `while` loop, which is as follows:

```
a = 10; b = 15
while a < b
    # body: process(a)
    println(a)
    global a += 1
end
# prints on consecutive lines: 10 11 12 13 14
```

In the body of the loop, something has to change the value of `a` so that the initial condition becomes false and the loop ends. If the initial condition is false at the start, the body of the `while` loop is never executed. The `global` keyword makes `a` in the current scope refer to the global variable of that name.

If you need to loop over an array while adding or removing elements from the array, use a `while` loop, as follows:

```
arr = [1,2,3,4]
while !isempty(arr)
    print(pop!(arr), ", ")
end
```

The preceding code returns the output as `4, 3, 2, 1`.

The break statement

Sometimes, it is convenient to stop the loop repetition inside the loop when a certain condition is reached. This can be done with the `break` statement, which is as follows:

```
a = 10; b = 150
while a < b
    # process(a)
    println(a)
    global a += 1
    if a >= 50
        break
    end
end
```

This prints out the numbers 10 to 49, and then exits the loop when `break` is encountered. The following is an idiom that is often used; how to search for a given element in an array, and stop when we have found it:

```
arr = rand(1:10, 10)
println(arr)
# get the index of search in an array arr:
searched = 4
for (ix, curr) in enumerate(arr)
  if curr == searched
    println("The searched element $searched occurs on index $ix")
    break
  end
end
```

A possible output might be as follows:

```
[8, 4, 3, 6, 3, 5, 4, 4, 6, 6]
The searched element 4 occurs on index 2
```

The `break` statement can be used in `for` loops as well as in `while` loops. It is, of course, mandatory in a `while true...end` loop.

The continue statement

What should you do when you want to skip one (or more) loop repetitions then, nevertheless, continue with the next loop iteration? For this, you need `continue`, as in this example:

```
for n in 1:10
  if 3 <= n <= 6
    continue # skip current iteration
  end
  println(n)
end
```

This prints out, 1 2 7 8 9 10, skipping the numbers three to six, using a chained comparison.

There is no `repeat...until` or `do...while` construct in Julia. A `do...while` loop can be simulated as follows:

```
while true
# code
  condition || break
end
```

Exception handling

When executing a program, abnormal conditions can occur that force the Julia runtime to throw an exception or error, show the exception message and the line where it occurred, and then exit. For example (follow along with the code in `Chapter 4\errors.jl`):

- Using the wrong index for an array, for example, `arr = [1,2,3]` and then asking for `arr[0]` causes a program to stop with `ERROR: BoundsError()`
- Calling `sqrt()` on a negative value, for example, `sqrt(-3)` causes `ERROR: DomainError: sqrt will only return a complex result if called with a complex argument, try sqrt(complex(x));` the `sqrt(complex(-3))` function gives the correct result `0.0 + 1.7320508075688772im`
- A syntax error in Julia code will usually result in `LoadError`

Similar to these, there are 18 predefined exceptions that Julia can generate (refer to `http://docs.julialang.org/en/latest/manual/control-flow/#man-exception-handling`). They are all derived from a base type, `Exception`.

How can you signal an error condition yourself? You can *call* one of the built-in exceptions by *throwing* such an exception; that is, calling the `throw` function with the exception as an argument. Suppose an input field, `code`, can only accept the codes listed in `codes = ["AO", "ZD", "SG", "EZ"]`. If `code` has the value, `AR`, the following test produces `DomainError`:

```
if code in codes
    println("This is an acceptable code")
else
    throw(DomainError())
end
```

A `rethrow()` statement can be useful to hand the current exception to a higher calling code level.

Note that you can't give your own message as an argument to `DomainError()`. This is possible with the `error(message)` function (refer to the *Conditional evaluation* section) with a `String` message. This results in a program stopping with an `ErrorException` function and an `ERROR: message` message.

Creating user-defined exceptions can be done by deriving from the base type, `Exception`, such as `mutable struct CustomException <: Exception end` (for an explanation of `<`, refer to the *The type hierarchy - subtypes and supertypes* section in `Chapter 6`, *More on Types, Methods, and Modules*). These can also be used as arguments to be thrown.

In order to catch and handle possible exceptions yourself so that the program can continue to run, Julia uses the familiar `try...catch...finally` construct, which includes the following:

- The dangerous code that comes in the `try` block
- The `catch` block that stops the exception and allows you to react to the code that threw the exception

Here is an example:

```
a = []
try
    pop!(a)
catch ex
    println(typeof(ex))
    showerror(STDOUT, ex)
end
```

This example prints the output, as follows:

```
ArgumentError
    array must be non-empty
```

Popping an empty array generates an exception. The variable, ex, contains the exception object, but a plain catch without a variable can also be used. The `showerror` function is a handy function; its first argument can be any I/O stream, so it could be a file.

To differentiate between the different types of exception in the `catch` block, you can use the following code:

```
try
   # try this code
catch ex
   if isa(ex, DomainError)
      # do this
   elseif isa(ex, BoundsError)
      # do this
   end
end
```

Similar to `if` and `while`, `try` is an expression, so you can assign its return value to a variable. So, run the following code:

```
ret = try
            global a = 4 * 2
        catch ex
        end
```

After running the preceding code, `ret` contains the value 8.

Sometimes, it is useful to have a set of statements to be executed no matter what, for example, to clean up resources. Typical use cases are when reading from a file or a database. We want the file or the database connection to be closed after the execution, regardless of whether an error occurred while the file or database was being processed. This is achieved with the `finally` clause of a `try...catch...finally` construct, as in the following code snippet:

```
try
    global f = open("file1.txt") # returns an IOStream(<file file1.txt>)
   # operate on file f
catch ex
finally
    close(f)
end
```

`f` must be defined as `global` in `try`, otherwise it is not known in the `finally` branch.

Here is a more concrete example:

```
try
   open("file1.txt", "r") do f
            k = 0
            while(!eof(f))
                a=readline(f)
```

```
                    println(a)
                    k += 1
             end
          println("\nNumber of lines in file: $k")
       end
   catch ex
   finally
       close(f)
   end
```

The `try...catch...finally` full construct guarantees that the `finally` block is always executed, even when there is a return in `try`. In general, all three combinations of `try...catch`, `try...finally`, and `try...catch...finally` are possible.

It is important to realize that `try...catch` should not be used in performance bottlenecks, because the mechanism impedes performance. Whenever feasible, test a possible exception with normal conditional evaluation.

The preceding code can be written more idiomatically as follows:

```
open("file1.txt", "w") do f
    # operate on file f
end
```

`close(f)` is no longer needed: it is done implicitly with the `end`.

Scope revisited

A variable that is defined at the top level is said to have **global scope**.

The `for`, `while`, and `try` blocks (but not the `if` blocks) all introduce a new scope. Variables defined in these blocks are only known to that scope. This is called the **local scope**, and nested blocks can introduce several levels of local scope. However, global variables are not accessible in `for` and `while` loops.

Variables with the same name in different scopes can safely be used simultaneously. If a variable exists both in global and local scope, you can decide which one you want to use by prefixing them with the `global` or `local` keyword:

- `global`: This indicates that you want to use the variable from the outer, global scope. This applies to the whole of the current scope block.
- `local`: This means that you want to define a new variable in the current scope.

The following example will clarify this, as follows:

```
# code in Chapter 4\scope.jl
x = 9
function funscope(n)
  x = 0 # x is in the local scope of the function
  for i = 1:n
    local x # x is local to the for loop
    x = i + 1
    if (x == 7)
        println("This is the local x in for: $x") #=> 7
    end
  end
  x
  println("This is the local x in funscope: $x") #=> 0
  global x = 15
end

funscope(10)
println("This is the global x: $x") #=> 15
```

This prints out the following result:

```
This is the local x in for: 7
This is the local x in funscope: 0
This is the global x: 15
```

If the local keyword was omitted from the for loop, the second print statement would print out 11 instead of 7, as follows:

```
This is the local x in for: 7
This is the local x in funscope: 11
This is the global x: 15
```

What is the output when the global x = 15 statement is left out? In this situation, the program prints out this result:

```
This is the local x in for: 7
This is the local x in funscope: 11
This is the global x: 9
```

However, needless to say, such name conflicts obscure the code and are a source of bugs, so try to avoid them if possible.

If you need to create a new local binding for a variable, use the `let` block. Execute the following code snippet:

```
anon = Array{Any}(undef, 2)
for i = 1:2
  anon[i] = ()-> println(i)
  i += 1
end
```

Here, both `anon[1]` and `anon[2]` are anonymous functions. When they are called with `anon[1]()` and `anon[2]()`, they print 2 and 3 (the values of `i` when they were created plus one). What if you wanted them to stick with the value of `i` at the moment of their creation? Then, you have to use `let` and change the code to the following:

```
anon = Array{Any}(undef, 2)
for i = 1:2
  let i = i
      anon[i] = ()-> println(i)
  end
  i += 1
end
```

Now, `anon[1]()` and `anon[2]()` print 1 and 2, respectively. Because of `let`, they kept the value of `i` the same as when they were created.

The `let` statement also introduces a new scope. You can, for example, combine it with `begin`, like this:

```
begin
    local x = 1
    let
       local x = 2
       println(x)  #> 2
    end
    x
    println(x)  #> 1
end
```

`for` loops and comprehensions differ in the way they scope an iteration variable. When i is initialized to 0 before a `for` loop, after executing `for i = 1:10 end`, the variable i is now 10:

```
i = 0
for i = 1:10
end
println(i)   #> 10
```

After executing a comprehension such as `[i for i = 1:10]`, the variable i is still 0:

```
i = 0
[i for i = 1:10 ]
println(i)   #> 0
```

Tasks

Julia has a built-in system for running tasks, which are, in general, known as **coroutines**. With this, a computation that generates values into a `Channel` (with a `put!` function) can be suspended as a task, while a consumer task can pick up the values (with a `take!` function). This is similar to the `yield` keyword in Python.

As a concrete example, let's take a look at a `fib_producer` function that calculates the first 10 Fibonacci numbers (refer to the *Recursive functions* section in `Chapter 3`, *Functions*), but it doesn't return the numbers, it produces them:

```
# code in Chapter 4\tasks.jl
  function fib_producer(c::Channel)
        a, b = (0, 1)
        for i = 1:10
            put!(c, b)
            a, b = (b, a + b)
        end
    end
```

Construct a `Channel` by providing this function as an argument:

```
chnl = Channel(fib_producer)
```

The task's state is now runnable. To get the Fibonacci numbers, start consuming them with `take!` until `Channel` is closed, and the task is finished (state is `:done`):

```
take!(chnl) #> 1
take!(chnl) #> 1
take!(chnl) #> 2
take!(chnl) #> 3
take!(chnl) #> 5
take!(chnl) #> 8
take!(chnl) #> 13
take!(chnl) #> 21
take!(chnl) #> 34
take!(chnl) #> 55
take!(chnl) #> ERROR: InvalidStateException("Channel is closed.", :closed)
```

It is as if the `fib_producer` function was able to return multiple times, once for each `take!` call. Between calls to `fib_producer`, its execution is suspended, and the consumer has control.

The same values can be more easily consumed in a `for` loop, where the loop variable becomes one by one the produced values:

```
for n in chnl
    println(n)
end
```

This produces: `1  1  2  3  5  8  13  21  34  55`.

There is a macro `@task` that does the same thing:

```
chnl = @task fib_producer(c::Channel)
```

Coroutines are not executed in different threads, so they cannot run on separate CPUs. Only one coroutine is running at once, but the language runtime switches between them. An internal scheduler controls a queue of runnable tasks and switches between them based on events, such as waiting for data, or data coming in.

Here is another example, which uses @async to start a task asynchronously, binds a channel to the task, and then prints out the contents of the channel:

```
fac(i::Integer) = (i > 1) ? i*fac(i - 1) : 1
c = Channel(0)
task = @async foreach(i->put!(c,fac(i)), 1:5)
bind(c,task)
for i in c
    @show i
end
```

This prints out the following:

```
i = 1
i = 2
i = 6
i = 24
i = 120
```

Tasks should be seen as a form of cooperative multitasking in a single thread. Switching between tasks does not consume stack space, unlike normal function calls. In general, tasks have very low overhead; so you can use lots of them if needed. Exception handling in Julia is implemented using Tasks as well as servers that accept many incoming connections (refer to the *Working with TCP sockets and servers* section in Chapter 8, *IO, Networking, and Parallel Computing*).

True parallelism in Julia is discussed in the *Parallel operations and computing* section of Chapter 8, *IO, Networking, and Parallel Computing*.

Summary

In this chapter, we explored different control constructs, such as if and while. We also saw how to catch exceptions with try or catch, and how to throw our own exceptions. Some subtleties of scope were discussed, and finally, we got an overview of how to use coroutines in Julia with tasks. Now we are well-equipped to explore more complex types that consist of many elements. This is the topic of the next chapter, *Collection Types*.

5
Collection Types

Collections of values appear everywhere in programs, and Julia has the most important built-in collection types. In Chapter 2, *Variables, Types, and Operations*, we introduced two important types of collection: **arrays** and **tuples**. In this chapter, we will look more deeply into multidimensional arrays (or matrices), and into the tuple type as well. A dictionary type, where you can look up a value through a key, is indispensable in a modern language, and Julia has this too. Finally, we will explore the set type. Like arrays, all these types are parameterized; the type of their elements can be specified at the time of object construction.

Collections are also iterable types, the types over which we can loop with `for` or an iterator producing each element of the collection successively. The iterable types include string, range, array, tuple, dictionary, and set.

So, the following are the topics for this chapter:

- Matrices
- Tuples
- Dictionaries
- Sets
- An example project—word frequency

Matrices

We know that the notation [1, 2, 3] is used to create an array. In fact, this notation denotes a special type of array, called a (column) **vector** in Julia, as shown in the following screenshot:

```
julia> [1, 2, 3]
3-element Array{Int64,1}:
 1
 2
 3
```

To create this as a row vector (1 2 3), use the notation `[1 2 3]` with spaces instead of commas. This array is of type `1 x 3 Array{Int64,2}`, so it has two dimensions. (The spaces used in `[1, 2, 3]` are for readability only, we could have written this as `[1,2,3]`).

A matrix is a two- or multidimensional array (in fact, a matrix is an alias for the two-dimensional case). We can write this as follows:

```
Array{Int64, 1} == Vector{Int64} #> true
Array{Int64, 2} == Matrix{Int64} #> true
```

As matrices are so prevalent in data science and numerical programming, Julia has an amazing range of functionalities for them.

To create a matrix, use space-separated values for the columns and semicolon-separated for the rows:

```
// code in Chapter 5\matrices.jl:
matrix = [1 2; 3 4]
    2x2 Array{Int64,2}:
    1   2
    3   4
```

So, the column vector from the beginning can also be written as `[1; 2; 3]`. However, you cannot use commas and semicolons together.

To get the value from a specific element in the matrix, you need to index it by row and then by column, for example, `matrix[2, 1]` returns the value 3 (second row, first column).

Using the same notation, one can calculate products of matrices such as `[1 2] * [3 ; 4]`; this is calculated as `[1 2] * [3 4]`, which returns the value 11 (which is equal to `1*3 + 2*4`). In contrast to this, conventional matrix multiplication is defined with the operator `.*`:

```
[1 2] .* [3 ; 4]
# 2 Array{Int64,2}:
#   3   6
#   4   8
```

To create a matrix from random numbers between 0 and 1, with three rows and five columns, use `ma1 = rand(3, 5)`, which shows the following results:

```
3x5 Array{Float64,2}:
 0.0626778   0.616528   0.60699    0.709196   0.900165
 0.511043    0.830033   0.671381   0.425688   0.0437949
 0.0863619   0.621321   0.78343    0.908102   0.940307
```

The `ndims` function can be used to obtain the number of dimensions of a matrix. Consider the following example:

```julia
julia> ndims(ma1) #> 2
julia> size(ma1) #> a tuple with the dimensions (3, 5)
```

To get the number of rows (3), run the following command:

```julia
julia>    size(ma1,1) #> 3
```

The number of columns (5) is given by:

```julia
julia> size(ma1,2) #> 5
julia> length(ma1) #> 15, the number of elements
```

That's why you will often see this: `nrows, ncols = size(ma)`, where `ma` is a matrix, `nrows` is the number of rows, and `ncols` is the number of columns.

If you need an identity matrix, where all the elements are zero, except for the elements on the diagonal that are `1.0`, use the `I` function (from the `LinearAlgebra` package) with the argument 3 for a 3 x 3 matrix:

```julia
using LinearAlgebra
  idm = Matrix(1.0*I, 3, 3)
#> 3x3 Array{Float64,2}:
  1.0  0.0  0.0
  0.0  1.0  0.0
  0.0  0.0  1.0
```

You can easily work with parts of a matrix, known as **slices**; these are similar to those used in Python and NumPy as follows:

- `idm[1:end, 2]` or shorter `idm[:, 2]` returns the entire second column
- `idm[2, :]` returns the entire second row
- `idmc = idm[2:end, 2:end]` returns the output as follows:

  ```julia
  2x2 Array{Float64,2}
      1.0  0.0
      0.0  1.0
  ```

- `idm[2, :] .= 0` sets the entire second row to 0
- `idm[2:end, 2:end] = [ 5 7 ; 9 11 ]` will change the matrix as follows:

  ```julia
      1.0  0.0  0.0
      0.0  5.0  7.0
      0.0  9.0  11.0
  ```

Slicing operations create views into the original array rather than copying the data, so a change in the slice changes the original array or matrix.

Any multidimensional matrix can also be seen as a one-dimensional vector in column order, as follows:

```
a = [1 2;3 4]
2 Array{Int64,2}:
  1  2
  3  4

a[:]
4-element Array{Int64,1}:
  1
  3
  2
  4
```

To make an array of arrays (a **jagged** array), use an `Array` initialization, and then `push!` each array in its place, for example:

```
jarr = (Array{Int64, 1})[]
push!(jarr, [1,2])
push!(jarr, [1,2,3,4])
push!(jarr, [1,2,3])
#=>
3-element Array{Array{Int64,1},1}:
  [1,2]
  [1,2,3,4]
  [1,2,3]
```

If `ma` is a matrix, say `[1 2; 3 4]`, then `ma'` is the transpose matrix, that is `[1 3; 2 4]`:

```
ma:    1  2            ma'  1  3
       3  4                 2  4
```

 `ma'` is an operator notation for the `transpose(ma)` function.

Multiplication is defined between matrices, as in mathematics, so `ma * ma'` returns the 2 x 2 matrix or type `Array{Int64,2}` as follows:

```
  5    11
  11   25
```

If you need element-wise multiplication, use `ma .* ma'`, which returns 2 x 2 `Array{Int64,2}`:

```
1    6
6   16
```

The inverse of a matrix `ma` (if it exists) is given by the `inv(ma)` function. The `inv(ma)` function returns 2 x 2 `Array{Float64,2}`:

```
-2.0    1.0
 1.5   -0.5
```

The inverse means that `ma * inv(ma)` produces the identity matrix:

```
1.0    0.0
0.0    1.0
```

 Trying to take the inverse of a singular matrix (a matrix that does not have a well-defined inverse) will result in `LAPACKException` or `SingularException`, depending on the matrix type. Suppose you want to solve the `ma1 * X = ma2` equation, where `ma1`, `X`, and `ma2` are matrices. The obvious solution is `X = inv(ma1) * ma2`. However, this is actually not that good. It is better to use the built-in solver, where `X = ma1 \ ma2`. If you have to solve the `X * ma1 = ma2` equation, use the solution `X = ma2 / ma1`. Solutions that use `/` and `\` are much more numerically stable, and also much faster.

If `v = [1.,2.,3.]` and `w = [2.,4.,6.]`, and you want to form a 3 x 2 matrix with these two column vectors, then use `hcat(v, w)` (for horizontal concatenation) to produce the following output:

```
1.0    2.0
2.0    4.0
3.0    6.0
```

`vcat(v,w)` (for vertical concatenation) results in a one-dimensional array with all the six elements with the same result as `append!(v, w)`.

Thus, `hcat` concatenates vectors or matrices along the second dimension (columns), while `vcat` concatenates along the first dimension (rows). The more general `cat` can be used to concatenate multidimensional arrays along arbitrary dimensions.

There is an even simpler literal notation: to concatenate two matrices a and b with the same number of rows to a matrix c, just execute c = [a b]. now b is appended to the right of a. To put b beneath c, use c = [a; b]. The following is a concrete example, a = [1 2; 3 4] and b = [5 6; 7 8]:

a	b	c = [a b]	c = [a; b]
1 2 3 4	5 6 7 8	1 2 5 6 3 4 7 8	1 2 3 4 5 6 7 8

The reshape function changes the dimensions of a matrix to new values if this is possible, for example:

```
reshape(1:12, 3, 4) #> returns a 3x4 array with the values 1 to 12
3x4 Array{Int64,2}:
 1   4   7   10
 2   5   8   11
 3   6   9   12
a = rand(3, 3)   #> produces a 3x3 Array{Float64,2}
3x3 Array{Float64,2}:
 0.332401    0.499608   0.355623
 0.0933291   0.132798   0.967591
 0.722452    0.932347   0.809577
reshape(a, (9,1)) #> produces a 9x1 Array{Float64,2}:
9x1 Array{Float64,2}:
 0.332401
 0.0933291
 0.722452
 0.499608
 0.132798
 0.932347
 0.355623
 0.967591
 0.809577
reshape(a, (2,2)) #> does not succeed:
ERROR: DimensionMismatch("new dimensions (2,2) must be consistent
   with array size 9")
```

When working with arrays that contain arrays, it is important to realize that such an array contains references to the contained arrays, not their values. If you want to make a copy of an array, you can use the copy() function, but this produces only a *shallow copy* with references to the contained arrays. In order to make a complete copy of the values, we need to use the deepcopy() function.

The following example makes this clear:

```
x = Array{Any}(undef, 2) #> 2-element Array{Any,1}: #undef #undef
x[1] = ones(2) #> 2-element Array{Float64} 1.0 1.0
x[2] = trues(3) #> 3-element BitArray{1}: true true true
x #> 2-element Array{Any,1}: [1.0,1.0] Bool[true,true,true]
a = x
b = copy(x)
c = deepcopy(x)
# Now if we change x:
x[1] = "Julia"
x[2][1] = false
x #> 2-element Array{Any,1}: "Julia" Bool[false,true,true]
a #> 2-element Array{Any,1}: "Julia" Bool[false,true,true]
isequal(a, x) #> true, a is identical to x
b #> 2-element Array{Any,1}: [1.0,1.0] Bool[false,true,true]
isequal(b, x) #> false, b is a shallow copy of x
c #> 2-element Array{Any,1}: [1.0,1.0] Bool[true,true,true]
isequal(c, x) #> false
```

The value of a remains identical to x when this changes, because it points to the same object in the memory. The deep copy c function remains identical to the original x. The b value retains the changes in a contained array of x, but not if one of the contained arrays becomes another array.

To further increase performance, consider using the statically-sized and immutable vectors and matrices from the `ImmutableArrays` package, which is a lot faster, certainly for small matrices, and particularly for vectors.

Tuples

A **tuple** is a fixed-sized group of values, separated by commas and optionally surrounded by parentheses ( ). The type of these values can be the same, but it doesn't have to be; a tuple can contain values of different types, unlike arrays. A tuple is a heterogeneous container, whereas an array is a homogeneous container. The type of a tuple is just a tuple of the types of the values it contains. So, in this sense, a tuple is very much the counterpart of an array in Julia. Also, changing a value in a tuple is not allowed; tuples are immutable.

In Chapter 2, *Variables, Types, and Operations*, we saw fast assignment, which is made possible by tuples:

```
// code in Chapter 5\tuples.jl:
a, b, c, d = 1, 22.0, "World", 'x'
```

This expression assigns a value 1, b becomes 22.0, c takes up the value World, and d becomes x.

The expression returns a tuple (1, 22.0, "World", 'x'), as the REPL shows as follows:

```
julia> a, b, c, d = 1, 22.0, "World", 'x'
(1,22.0,"World",'x')
```

If we assign this tuple to a variable t1 and ask for its type, we get the following result:

```
typeof(t1) #> Tuple{Int64,Float64,String,Char}
```

The argument list of a function (refer to the *Defining functions* section in Chapter 3, Functions) is, in fact, also a tuple. Similarly, Julia simulates the possibility of returning multiple values by packaging them into a single tuple, and a tuple also appears when using functions with variable argument lists. ( ) represents the empty tuple, and (1,) is a one-element tuple. The type of a tuple can be specified explicitly through a type annotation (refer to the *Types* section in Chapter 2, *Variables, Types, and Operations*), such as ('z', 3.14)::Tuple{Char, Float64}.

The following snippet shows that we can index tuples in the same way as arrays by using brackets, indexing starting from 1, slicing, and index control:

```
t3 = (5, 6, 7, 8)
t3[1] #> 5
t3[end] #> 8
t3[2:3] #> (6, 7)
t3[5] #> BoundsError: attempt to access (5, 6, 7, 8) at index [5]
t3[3] = 9 #> Error: 'setindex' has no matching ...
author = ("Ivo", "Balbaert", 62)
author[2] #> "Balbaert"
```

To iterate over the elements of a tuple, use a for loop:

```
for i in t3
    println(i)
end # #> 5  6  7  8
```

A tuple can be *unpacked* or deconstructed like this: a, b = t3; now a is 5 and b is 6. Notice that we don't get an error despite the left-hand side not being able to take all the values of t3. To do this, we would have to write a, b, c, d = t3.

In the preceding example, the elements of the author tuple are unpacked into separate variables: first_name, last_name, and age = author.

So, tuples are nice and simple types that make a lot of things possible. We'll find them again in the next section as elements of a dictionary.

Dictionaries

When you want to store and look up values based on a unique key, then the dictionary type `Dict` (also called hash, associative collection, or map in other languages) is what you need. It is basically a collection of two-element tuples of the form `(key, value)`. To define a dictionary `d1` as a literal value, the following syntax is used:

```
// code in Chapter 5\dicts.jl:
d1 = Dict(1 => 4.2, 2 => 5.3)
```

It returns `Dict{Int64,Float64}` with two entries: `2 => 5.3` and `1 => 4.2`, so there are two key-value tuples here, `(1, 4.2)` and `(2, 5.3)`; the key appears before the `=>` symbol and the value appears after it, and the tuples are separated by commas.

To explicitly specify the types, use:

```
d1 = Dict{Int64,Float64}(1 => 4.2, 2 => 5.3)
```

If you use the former `[]` notation to try to define a dictionary, you now get `Array{Pairs{}}` instead:
```
d1 = [1 => 4.2, 2 => 5.3]
# 2-element Array{Pair{Int64,Float64},1}:
# 1 => 4.2
# 2 => 5.3
```

Here are some other examples:

```
d2 = Dict{Any,Any}("a"=>1, (2,3)=>true)
d3 = Dict(:A => 100, :B => 200)
```

The `Any` type is inferred when a common type among the keys or values cannot be detected.

So a `Dict` can have keys of different types, and the same goes for the values: their type is then indicated as `Any`. In general, dictionaries that have type `{Any, Any}` tend to lead to lower performance since the JIT compiler does not know the exact type of the elements. Dictionaries used in performance-critical parts of the code should therefore be explicitly typed. Notice that the `(key, value)` pairs are not returned (or stored) in the key order.

If the keys are of the `Char` or `String` type, you can also use `Symbol` as the key type, which could be more appropriate since `Symbols` are immutable, for example:

```
d3 = Dict{Symbol,Int64}(:A => 100, :B => 200)
```

Use the bracket notation, with a key as an index, to get the corresponding value: `d3[:B]` returns 200. However, the key must exist, otherwise we will get an error, `d3[:Z]`, that returns `ERROR: KeyError: key not found: :Z`. To get around this, use the `get` method and provide a default value that is returned instead of the error, `get(d3, :Z, 999)` returns 999.

Here is a dictionary that resembles an object, storing the field names as symbols in the keys:

```
dmus = [ :first_name => "Louis", :surname => "Armstrong",
    :occupation => "musician", :date_of_birth => "4/8/1901" ]
```

To test if a key is present in `Dict`, you can use the function `haskey` as follows:

- `haskey(d3, :Z)` returns `false`
- `haskey(d3, :B)` returns `true`

Dictionaries are mutable. If we tell Julia to execute `d3[:A] = 150`, then the value for key `:A` in d3 has changed to 150. If we do this with a new key, then that tuple is added to the dictionary:

```
d3[:C] = 300
```

d3 is now `Dict(:A=>150,:B=>200,:C=>300)`, and it has three elements: `length(d3)` returns 3.

`d4 = Dict()` is an empty dictionary of type `Any`, and you can start populating it in the same way as in the example with d3.

`d5 = Dict{Float64, Int64}()` is an empty dictionary with key type `Float64` and value type `Int64`. As to be expected, adding keys or values of another type to a typed dictionary is an error. `d5["c"] = 6` returns `ERROR: MethodError 'convert' has no method matching convert(::Type{Float64}, ::ASCIIString)` and `d3["CVO"] = 500` returns `ERROR: ArgumentError: CVO is not a valid key for type Symbol`.

Deleting a key mapping from a collection is also straightforward. `delete!(d3, :B)` removes `(:B, 200)` from the dictionary, and returns the collection that contains only `:A => 100`.

Keys and values – looping

To isolate the keys of a dictionary, use the `keys` function `ki = keys(d3)`, with `ki` being a `KeyIterator` object, which we can use in a `for` loop as follows:

```
for k in keys(d3)
    println(k)
end
```

Assuming d3 is again `d3 = Dict(:A => 100, :B => 200)`, this prints out A and B. This also gives us an alternative way to test if a key exists with `in`. For example, `:A in keys(d3)` returns `true` and `:Z in keys(d3)` returns `false`.

If you want to work with an array of keys, use `collect(keys(d3))`, which returns a two-element `Array{Symbol,1}` that contains `:A` and `:B`. To obtain the values, use the `values` function: `vi = values(d3)`, with `vi` being a `ValueIterator` object, which we can also loop through with `for`:

```
for v in values(d3)
    println(v)
end
```

This returns `100` and `200`, but the order in which the values or keys are returned is undefined.

Creating a dictionary from arrays with `keys` and `values` is trivial because we have a `Dict` constructor that can use these; as in the following example:

```
keys1 = ["J.S. Bach", "Woody Allen", "Barack Obama"] and
values1 =  [ 1685, 1935, 1961]
```

Then, `d5 = Dict(zip(keys1, values1))` results in a `Dict{String,Int64}` with three entries as follows:

```
"J.S. Bach"    => 1685
"Woody Allen"  => 1935
"Barack Obama" => 1961
```

Working with both the `key` and `value` pairs in a loop is also easy. For instance, the `for` loop over d5 is as follows:

```
for (k, v) in d5
        println("$k was born in $v")
    end
```

This will print the following output:

```
J.S. Bach was born in 1685
Barack Obama was born in 1961
Woody Allen was born in 1935
```

Alternatively, we can use an index in the tuple:

```
for p in d5
  println("$(p[1]) was born in $(p[2])")
end
```

Here are some more neat tricks, where `dict` is a dictionary:

- Copying the keys of a dictionary to an array with a list comprehension:

  ```
  arrkey = [key for (key, value) in dict]
  ```

  This is the same as `collect(keys(dict))`.

- Copying the values of a dictionary to an array with a list comprehension:

  ```
  arrval = [value for (key, value) in dict]
  ```

  This is the same as `collect(values(dict))`

Sets

Array elements are ordered, but can contain duplicates, that is, the same value can occur at different indices. In a dictionary, keys have to be unique, but the values do not, and the keys are not ordered. If you want a collection where order does not matter, but where the elements have to be unique, then use a **Set**. Creating a set is as easy as this:

```
// code in Chapter 5\sets.jl:
s = Set([11, 14, 13, 7, 14, 11])
```

The `Set()` function creates an empty set `Set(Any[])`. The preceding line returns `Set([7, 14, 13, 11])`, where the duplicates have been eliminated.

Operations from the set theory are also defined for s1 = Set([11, 25]) and s2 = Set([25, 3.14]) as follows:

- union(s1, s2) produces Set([3.14,25,11])
- intersect(s1, s2) produces Set([25])
- setdiff(s1, s2) produces Set{Any}([11]), whereas setdiff(s2, s1) produces Set([3.14])
- issubset(s1, s2) produces false, but issubset(s1, Set([11, 25, 36])) produces true

To add an element to a set is easy: push!(s1, 32) adds 32 to set s1. Adding an existing element will not change the set. To test whether a set contains an element, use in. For example, in(32, s1) returns true and in(100, s1) returns false.

Set([1,2,3]) produces a set of integers Set([2,3,1]) of the Set{Int64} type. To get a set of arrays, use Set([[1,2,3]]), which returns Set(Array{Int64,1}[[1, 2, 3]]).

Sets are commonly used when we need to keep track of objects in no particular order. For instance, we might be searching through a graph. We can then use a set to remember which nodes of the graph we have already visited in order to avoid visiting them again. Checking whether an element is present in a set is independent of the size of the set. This is extremely useful for very large sets of data, for example:

```
x = Set(collect(1:100))
@time 2 in x
#> 0.003186 seconds (33 allocations: 2.078 KiB)
x2 = Set(collect(1:1000000))
@time 2 in x2
# 0.000003 seconds (4 allocations: 160 bytes)
```

The second statement executes much faster using much less memory, despite the fact that x2 is four orders of magnitude larger than x.

Take a look at the Collections module if you need more specialized containers. It contains a priority queue as well as some lower-level heap functions.

An example project – word frequency

A lot of the concepts and techniques that we have seen so far in this book come together in this little project. Its aim is to read a text file, remove all characters that are not used in words, and count the frequency of the words in the remaining text. This can be useful, for example, when counting the word density on a web page, the frequency of DNA sequences, or the number of hits on a website that came from various IP addresses. This can be done in some ten lines of code. For example, when `words1.txt` contains the sentence `to be, or not to be, that is the question!`, then this is the output of the program:

```
Word : frequency
be : 2
is : 1
not : 1
or : 1
question : 1
that : 1
the : 1
to : 2
```

Here is the code with comments:

```julia
# code in chapter 5\word_frequency.jl:
# 1- read in text file:
str = read("words1.txt", String)
# 2- replace non alphabet characters from text with a space:
nonalpha = r"(\W\s?)" # define a regular expression
str = replace(str, nonalpha => ' ')
digits = r"(\d+)"
str = replace(str, digits => ' ')
# 3- split text in words:
word_list = split(str, ' ')
# 4- make a dictionary with the words and count their frequencies:
word_freq = Dict{String, Int64}()
for word in word_list
    word = strip(word)
    if isempty(word) continue end
    haskey(word_freq, word) ?
      word_freq[word] += 1 :
      word_freq[word] = 1
end
# 5- sort the words (the keys) and print out the frequencies:
println("Word : frequency \n")
words = sort!(collect(keys(word_freq)))
for word in words
    println("$word : $(word_freq[word])")
end
```

The `strip()` function removes white space from a string at the front/back.

The `isempty` function is quite general and can be used on any collection.

Try the code out with the example text files `words1.txt` or `words2.txt`. See the output in `results_words1.txt` and `results_words2.txt`.

Summary

In this chapter, we looked at the built-in collection types Julia has to offer. We saw the power of matrices, the elegance of dictionaries, and the usefulness of tuples and sets. However, to dig deeper into the fabric of Julia, we need to learn how to define new types, which is another concept necessary that we need to organize code. We must know how types can be constructed, and how they are used in multiple dispatch. This is the main topic of the next chapter, where we will also see modules, which serve to organize code, but at an even higher level than types.

6
More on Types, Methods, and Modules

Julia has a rich built-in type system, and most data types can be parameterized, such as `Array{Float64, 2}` or `Dict{Symbol, Float64}`. Typing a variable (or more exactly the value it is bound to) is optional. However, indicating the type of some variables, although they are not statically checked, can provide some of the advantages of static-type systems as in C++, Java, or C#. A Julia program can run without any indication of types, which can be useful in a prototyping stage, and it will still run fast. However, some type indications can increase the performance by allowing more specialized multiple dispatch. Type assertions also help the LLVM compiler to create more compact, better optimized code. Moreover, typing function parameters makes the code easier to read and understand. The robustness of the program is also enhanced by throwing exceptions, in cases where certain type operations are not allowed. These failures will manifest themselves during testing, or the code can provide an exception handling mechanism.

All functions in Julia are inherently generic or polymorphic, that is, they can operate on different types of their arguments. The most appropriate method (an implementation of the function where argument types are indicated) will be chosen at runtime to be executed, depending on the type of arguments passed to the function. As we will see in this chapter, you can also define your own types, and Julia provides a limited form of abstract types and subtyping.

A lot of these topics have already been discussed in previous chapters; for example, refer to the *Generic functions and multiple dispatch* section in Chapter 3, *Functions*. In this chapter, we broaden the previous discussions by covering the following topics:

- Type annotations
- The type hierarchy—subtypes and supertypes
- Concrete and abstract types
- User-defined and composite types

- Types and collections—inner constructors
- Type unions
- Parametric types and methods
- Standard modules and paths

Type annotations

As we saw in Chapter 2, *Variables, Types, and Operations*, type-annotating a variable is done with the :: operator, such as in the function definition `function write(io::IO, s::String) #... end`, where the parameter `io` has to be of type `IO`, and `s` of type `String`. To put it differently, `io` has to be an instance of type `IO`, and `s` an instance of type `String`. The :: operator is, in fact, an assertion that affirms that the value on the left is of the type on the right. If this is not true, a `typeassert` error is thrown. Try this out in the REPL:

```
# see the code in Chapter 6\conversions.jl:
(31+42)::Float64
```

We get an `ERROR: TypeError: in typeassert, expected Float64, got Int64` error message.

This is, in addition to the method specialization for multiple dispatch, an important reason why type annotations are used in function signatures.

The operator :: can also be used in the sense of a type declaration, but only in local scope, such as in functions, as follows:

```
n::Int16 or local n::Int16 or n::Int16 = 5
```

Every value assigned to `n` will be implicitly converted to the indicated type with the `convert` function.

Type conversions and promotions

The `convert` function can also be used explicitly in the code as `convert(Int64, 7.0)`, which returns 7.

In general, `convert(Type, x)` will attempt to put the `x` value in an instance of `Type`. In most cases, `type(x)` will also do the trick, as in `Int64(7.0)`, returning 7.

The conversion, however, doesn't always work:

- When precision is lost—Int64(7.01) returns an ERROR: InexactError() error message
- When the target type is incompatible with the source value—convert(Int64, "CV") returns an ERROR: MethodError: Cannot `convert` an object of type String to an object of type Int64 error message

This last error message really shows us how multiple dispatch works; the types of the input arguments are matched against the methods available for that function.

We can define our own conversions by providing new methods for the convert function. For example, for information on how to do this, refer to http://docs.julialang.org/en/latest/manual/conversion-and-promotion/#conversion.

Julia has a built-in system called **automatic type promotion** to promote arguments of mathematical operators and assignments to a common type: in 4 + 3.14, the integer 4 is promoted to a Float64 value, so that the addition can take place and results in 7.140000000000001. In general, promotion refers to the conversion of values of different types to one common type. This can be done with the promote function, which takes a number of arguments, and returns a tuple of the same values, converting them to a common type. An exception is thrown if promotion is not possible. Some examples are as follows:

- promote(1, 2.5, 3//4) returns (1.0, 2.5, 0.75)
- promote(1.5, im) returns (1.5 + 0.0im, 0.0 + 1.0im)
- promote(true, 1.0) returns (1.0, 1.0)

Thanks to the automatic type promotion system for numbers, Julia doesn't have to define, for example, the + operator for any combinations of numeric types. Instead, it is defined as +(x::Number, y::Number) = +(promote(x,y)...).

It basically says: first, promote the arguments to a common type, and then perform the addition. Number is a common supertype for all values of numeric types. To determine the common promotion type of the two types, use promote_type(Int8, UInt16) to find whether it returns UInt16.

This is because, somewhere in the standard library, the following promote_rule function was defined as promote_rule(::Type{Int8}, ::Type{Uint16}) = UInt16.

You can take a look at how promoting is defined in the source code Julia in `base/promotion.jl`. These kinds of promotion rules can be defined for your own types too if needed.

The type hierarchy – subtypes and supertypes

In Julia, every value has a type, for example, `typeof(2)` is `Int64` (or `Int32` on 32-bit systems). Julia has a lot of built-in types, in fact, a whole hierarchy starting from the type `Any` at the top. Every type in this structure also has a type, namely, `DataType`, so it is very consistent. `typeof(Any)`, `typeof(Int64)`, `typeof(Complex{Int64})`, and `typeof(DataType)` all return `DataType`. So, types in Julia are also objects; all concrete types, except tuple types, which are a tuple of the types of its arguments, are of type `DataType`.

 Follow along with the code in `type_hierarchy.jl`.

This type hierarchy is like a tree; each type has one parent given by the `supertype` function:

- `supertype(Int64)` returns `Signed`
- `supertype(Signed)` returns `Integer`
- `supertype(Integer)` returns `Real`
- `supertype(Real)` returns `Number`
- `supertype(Number)` returns `Any`
- `supertype(Any)` returns `Any`

A type can have a lot of children or `subtypes` (a function from the `InteractiveUtils` package) as follows:

- `subtypes(Integer)` form 3-element `Array{Any,1}`, which contains `Bool`, `Signed`, and `Unsigned`
- `subtypes(Signed)` form 6-element `Array{Any,1}`, which contains `BigInt`, `Int128`, `Int16`, `Int32`, `Int64`, and `Int8`
- `subtypes(Int64)` is 0-element `Array{Any,1}`, which has no subtypes

To indicate the subtype relationship, the operator < is used: `Bool <: Integer` and `Bool <: Any` returns true, while `Bool <: Char` is false. The following is a visualization of part of this type tree:

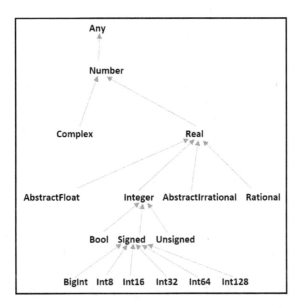

Concrete and abstract types

In this hierarchy, some types, such as `Number`, `Integer`, and `Signed`, are abstract, which means that they have no concrete objects or values of their own. Instead, objects or values are of concrete types given by the result of applying `typeof(value)`, such as `Int8`, `Float64`, and `String`. For example, the concrete type of the value 5 is `Int64` given by `typeof(5)` (on a 64-bit machine). However, a value also has the type of all of its supertypes; for example, `isa(5, Number)` returns true (we introduced the `isa` function in the *Types* section of `Chapter 2`, *Variables, Types, and Operations*).

Concrete types have no subtypes and might only have abstract types as their supertypes. Schematically, we can differentiate them as follows:

Type	Instantiate	Subtypes
concrete	Y	N
abstract	N	Y

An abstract type (such as `Number` and `Real`) is only a name that groups multiple subtypes together, but it can be used as a type annotation or used as a type in array literals. These types are the nodes in the type hierarchy that mainly serve to support the type tree. Also, note that an abstract type cannot have any fields.

The abstract type `Any` is the supertype of all types, and all the objects are also instances of `Any`.

At the other end is `Union{}`: this type has no values and no subtypes. All types are supertypes of `Union{}`, and no object is an instance of `Union{}`. It is unlikely that you will ever have to use this type. The `Nothing` type has one value called `nothing`.

When a function is only used for its side-effects, convention dictates that it returns `nothing`. We have seen this with the `println` function, where the printing is the side-effect, for instance:

```
x = println("hello") #> hello
x == nothing #> true
```

User-defined and composite types

In Julia, as a developer you can define your own types to structure data used in applications. For example, if you need to represent points in a three-dimensional space, you can define a type `Point`, as follows:

```
# see the code in Chapter 6\user_defined.jl:
mutable struct Point
    x::Float64
    y::Float64
    z::Float64
end
```

`mutable` here means that `Point` values can be modified. If your type values cannot be changed, simply use `struct`.

The type `Point` is a concrete type. Objects of this type can be created as `p1 = Point(2, 4, 1.3)`, and it has no subtypes: `typeof(p1)` returns `Point` (constructor with 2 methods), `subtypes(Point)` returns `0-element Array{Any,1}`.

Such a user-defined type is composed of a set of named fields with an optional type annotation; that's why it is a composite type, and its type is also `DataType`. If the type of a named field is not given, then it is `Any`. A composite type is similar to `struct` in C, or a class without methods in Java.

Unlike in other object-oriented languages such as Python or Java, where you call a function on an object such as `object.func(args)`, Julia uses the `func(object, args)` syntax.

Julia has no classes (as types with functions belong to that type); this keeps the data and functions separate. Functions and methods for a type will be defined outside that type. Methods cannot be tied to a single type, because multiple dispatch connects them with different types. This provides more flexibility, because when adding a new method for a type, you don't have to change the code of the type itself, as you would have to do with the code of the class in object-oriented languages.

The names of the fields that belong to a composite type can be obtained with the `names` function of the type or object: `fieldnames(Point)` or `fieldnames(typeof(p1))` returns `(:x, :y, :z)`.

A user-defined type has two default implicit *constructors* that have the same name as the type and take an argument for each field. You can see this by asking for the methods of `Point`: `methods(Point)`; it returns two methods for generic function `Point`: `Point(x::Float64, y::Float64, z::Float64)` and `Point(x ,y ,z)`. Here, the field values can be of type `Any`.

You can now make objects simply like this:

```
orig = Point(0, 0, 0)
p1 = Point(2, 4, 1.3).
```

Fields that together contain the state of the object can be accessed by name, as in: `p1.y`, which returns `4.0`.

Objects of such a type are mutable, for example, I can change the z field to a new value with `p1.z = 3.14`, resulting in `p1` now having the value `Point(2.0, 4.0, 3.14)`. Of course, types are checked: `p1.z = "A"` results in an error.

Objects as arguments to functions are *passed by reference*, so that they can be changed inside the function (for example, refer to the function `insert_elem(arr)` in the *Defining types* section of `Chapter 3`, *Functions*).

If you don't want your objects to be changeable, replace `type` with the keyword `struct`, for example:

```
struct Vector3D
    x::Float64
    y::Float64
    z::Float64
end
```

Calling `p = Vector3D(1, 2, 3)` returns `Vector3D(1.0, 2.0, 3.0)` and `p.y = 5` returns `ERROR: type Vector3D is immutable`.

Immutable types enhance performance, because Julia can optimize the code for them. Another big advantage of immutable types is thread safety: an immutable object can be shared between threads without needing synchronization. If, however, such an immutable type contains a mutable field such as an array, the contents of that field can be changed. So, define your immutable types without mutable fields.

A type once defined cannot be changed. If we try to define a new type `Point` with fields of type `Int64`, or with added fields, we get an `ERROR: invalid redefinition of constant TypeName` error message.

A new type that is exactly the same as an existing type can be defined as an *alias* through a simple assignment, for instance, `Point3D = Point`. Now, objects of type `Point3D` can also be created: `p31 = Point3D(1, 2, 3)` returns `Point(1.0, 2.0, 3.0)`. Julia also uses this internally; the alias `Int` is used for either `Int64` or `Int32`, depending on the architecture of the system that is being used.

When are two values or objects equal or identical?

Whether two values are equal or not can be decided by the `==` operator, for example, `5 == 5` and `5 == 5.0` are both `true`. Equivalent to this operator is the `isequal()` function:

```
isequal(5, 5)   #> true
isequal(5, 5.0) #> true
```

Both the preceding statements return `true`, because objects such as numbers are immutable and they are compared at the bits level.

To see whether the two objects x and y are identical, they must be compared with the ===
operator. The result is a `Bool` value, `true` or `false`: x === y -> Bool, for example:

```
5 === 5 #> true
5 === 5.0 #> false
```

For objects that are more complex, such as strings, arrays, or objects that are constructed
from composite types, the addresses in the memory are compared to check whether they
point to the same memory location. For immutable object such as `struct`, this gets
optimized so that instances with the same value point to the same object:

```
struct Vector3D
    x::Float64
    y::Float64
    z::Float64
end

q = Vector3D(4.0, 3.14, 2.71)
r = Vector3D(4.0, 3.14, 2.71)
isequal(q, r) #> true
q === r #> true
```

However, if objects are mutable, they are different objects even if they have the same value,
as follows:

```
mutable struct MVector3D
    x::Float64
    y::Float64
    z::Float64
end

q = MVector3D(4.0, 3.14, 2.71)
r = MVector3D(4.0, 3.14, 2.71)
isequal(q, r) #> false
q === r #> false
```

A multiple-dispatch example

Let's now explore an example about people working in a company to show multiple
dispatch in action. Let's define an abstract type `Employee` and a type `Developer` that is a
subtype:

```
abstract type Employee
end
```

```
mutable struct Developer <: Employee
    name::String
    iq
    favorite_lang::String
end
```

We cannot make objects from an abstract type: calling `Employee()` only returns an `ERROR:` `MethodError: no constructors have been defined for Employee` error message.

The type `Developer` has two implicit constructors, but we can define another outer constructor, which uses a default constructor as follows:

```
Developer(name, iq) = Developer(name, iq, "Java")
```

Outer constructors provide additional convenient methods to construct objects. Now, we can make the following two developer objects:

- `devel1 = Developer("Bob", 110)`, which returns `Developer("Bob",110,"Java")`

- `devel2 = Developer("William", 145, "Julia")`, which returns `Developer("William",145,"Julia")`

Similarly, we can define a type `Manager` and an instance of it as follows:

```
mutable struct Manager
    name::String
    iq
    department::String
end
man1 = Manager("Julia", 120, "ICT")
```

Concrete types, such as `Developer` or `Manager`, cannot be subtyped:

```
mutable struct MobileDeveloper <: Developer
  platform
end
```

This returns `ERROR: invalid subtyping in definition of MobileDeveloper`.

If we now define a function `cleverness` as `cleverness(emp::Employee) = emp.iq`, then `cleverness(devel1)` returns `110`, but `cleverness(man1)` returns an `ERROR:` `MethodError: `cleverness` has no method matching cleverness(::Manager)` error message; the function has no method for a manager.

The following function makes us think that managers are always cleverer, which is, of course, not true:

```
function cleverer(m::Manager, e::Employee)
    println("The manager $(m.name) is cleverer!")
end

cleverer(man1, devel1) #> The manager Julia is cleverer!
cleverer(man1, devel2) #> The manager Julia is cleverer!
```

Suppose we introduce a function `cleverer` with the following argument types:

```
function cleverer(d::Developer, e::Employee)
    println("The developer $(d.name) is cleverer I think!")
end
```

The `cleverer(devel1, devel2)` call will now print `"The developer Bob is cleverer I think!"`. (Clearly, the function isn't yet coded right.) It matches a method because `devel2` is also an employee.

However, `cleverer(devel1, man1)` will give an `ERROR: MethodError: `cleverer` has no method matching cleverer(::Developer,::Manager)` error message, as a manager is not an employee, and a method with this signature was not defined.

We should now define another method for `cleverer` as follows:

```
function cleverer(e::Employee, d::Developer)
    if e.iq <= d.iq
        println("The developer $(d.name) is cleverer!")
    else
        println("The employee $(e.name) is cleverer!")
    end
end
```

If we now call `cleverer(devel1, devel2)` an ambiguity arises; Julia detects a problem in the definitions and gives us the following error:

```
#> ERROR: MethodError: cleverer(::Developer, ::Developer) is ambiguous.
Candidates:
 cleverer(e::Employee, d::Developer) in Main at REPL[32]:2
 cleverer(d::Developer, e::Employee) in Main at REPL[29]:2
Possible fix, define
 cleverer(::Developer, ::Developer)
```

The ambiguity is that, if cleverer is called with e being a Developer, which of the two defined methods should be chosen? To remove this ambiguity, we will now define the more specific (and correct) method, as follows:

```
function cleverer(d1::Developer, d2::Developer)
    if d1.iq <= d2.iq
        println("The developer $(d2.name) is cleverer!")
    else
        println("The developer $(d1.name) is cleverer!")
    end
end
```

Now, cleverer(devel1, devel2) prints "The developer William is cleverer!" as well as cleverer(devel2, devel1). This illustrates multiple dispatching. When defined, the more specific method definition (here, the second method cleverer) is chosen; more specific means the method with more specialized type annotations for its arguments. More specialized doesn't only mean subtypes, it can also mean using type aliases.

Always avoid method ambiguities by specifying an appropriate method for the intersection case.

Types and collections – inner constructors

Here is another type with only default constructors:

```
# see the code in Chapter 6\inner_constructors.jl
mutable struct Person
    firstname::String
    lastname::String
    sex::Char
    age::Float64
    children::Array{String, 1}
end

p1 = Person("Alan", "Bates", 'M', 45.5, ["Jeff", "Stephan"])
```

This example demonstrates that an object can contain collections, such as arrays or dictionaries. Custom types can also be stored in a collection, just like built-in types, for example:

```
people = Person[]
```

This returns 0-element `Array{Person,1}`:

```
push!(people, p1)
push!(people, Person("Julia", "Smith", 'F', 27, ["Viral"]))
```

The `show(people)` function now returns the following output:

```
Person[Person("Alan", "Bates", 'M', 45.5, ["Jeff", "Stephan"]),
       Person("Julia", "Smith", 'F', 27.0, ["Viral"])]
```

Now we can define a function `fullname` on type `Person`. You will notice that the definition stays outside the type's code:

```
fullname(p::Person) = "$(p.firstname) $(p.lastname)"
```

Or, slightly more performant:

```
fullname(p::Person) = string(p.firstname, " ", p.lastname)
```

Now `print(fullname(p1))` returns `Alan Bates`.

If you need to include error checking or transformations as part of the type construction process, you can use inner constructors (so-called because they are defined inside the type itself), as shown in the following example:

```
mutable struct Family
    name::String
    members::Array{String, 1}
    big::Bool
  Family(name::String) = new(name, String[], false)
  Family(name::String, members) = new(name, members,
    length(members) > 4)
end
```

We can make a `Family` object as follows:

```
fam = Family("Bates-Smith", ["Alan", "Julia", "Jeff", "Stephan",
  "Viral"])
```

Then the output is as follows:

```
Family("Bates-Smith",String["Alan","Julia","Jeff","Stephan","Viral"],true)
```

The keyword `new` can only be used in an inner constructor to create an object of the enclosing type. The first constructor takes one argument and generates a default for the other two values. The second constructor takes two arguments and infers the value of `big`. Inner constructors give you more control over how the values of the type can be created. Here, they are written with the short function notation, but if they are multiline, they will use the normal function syntax.

Note that when you use inner constructors, there are no default constructors any more. Outer constructors, calling a limited set of inner constructors, are often the best practice.

Type unions

In geometry, a two-dimensional point and a vector are not the same, even if they both have an x and y component. In Julia, we can also define them as different types, as follows:

```
# see the code in Chapter 6\unions.jl
mutable struct Point
    x::Float64
    y::Float64
end

mutable struct Vector2D
    x::Float64
    y::Float64
end
```

Here are the two objects:

- `p = Point(2, 5)` that returns `Point(2.0, 5.0)`

- `v = Vector2D(3, 2)` that returns `Vector2D(3.0, 2.0)`

Suppose we want to define the sum for these types as a point which has coordinates as the sum of the corresponding coordinates:

```
+(p, v)
```

This results in an `ERROR: MethodError: `+` has no method matching +(::Point, ::Vector2D)` error message.

To define a + method here, first do an `import Base.+`

Even after defining the following, + (p, v) still returns the same error because of multiple dispatch. Julia has no way of knowing that + (p, v) should be the same as + (v, p):

```
+(p::Point, q::Point) = Point(p.x + q.x, p.y + q.y)
+(u::Vector2D, v::Vector2D) = Point(u.x + v.x, u.y + v.y)
+(u::Vector2D, p::Point) = Point(u.x + p.x, u.y + p.y)
```

Only when we define the type matching method as + (p::Point, v::Vector2D) = Point(p.x + v.x, p.y + v.y), do we get a result + (p, v), which returns Point(5.0,7.0).

Now you can ask the question: Don't multiple dispatch and many types give rise to code duplication, as is the case here?

The answer is no, because, in such a case, we can define a union type, VecOrPoint:

```
VecOrPoint = Union{Vector2D, Point}
```

If p is a point, it is also of type VecOrPoint, and the same is true for v which is Vector2D. isa(p, VecOrPoint) and isa(v, VecOrPoint); both return true.

Now we can define one + method that works for any of the preceding four cases:

```
+(u::VecOrPoint, v:: VecOrPoint) = VecOrPoint(u.x + v.x, u.y +
  v.y)
```

So, now we only need one method instead of four.

Parametric types and methods

An array can take elements of different types. Therefore, we can have, for example, arrays of the following types: Array{Int64,1}, Array{Int8,1}, Array{Float64,1}, or Array{String, 1}, and so on. That is why an Array is a parametric type; its elements can be of any arbitrary type T, written as Array{T, 1}.

In general, types can take type parameters, so that type declarations actually introduce a whole family of new types. Returning to the Point example of the previous section, we can generalize it to the following:

```
# see the code in Chapter 6\parametric.jl
mutable struct Point{T}
  x::T
  y::T
end
```

This is conceptually similar to the generic types in Java or templates in C++.

This abstract type creates a whole family of new possible concrete types (but they are only compiled as needed at runtime), such as `Point{Int64}`, `Point{Float64}`, and `Point{String}`.

These are all subtypes of `Point`: `Point{String} <: Point` returns `true`. However, this is not the case when comparing different `Point` types, whose parameter types are subtypes of one another: `Point{Float64} <: Point{Real}` returns `false`.

To construct objects, you can indicate the type `T` in the constructor, as in `p = Point{Int64}(2, 5)`, but this can be shortened to `p = Point(2, 5)`. Or let's consider another example: `p = Point("London", "Great-Britain")`.

If you want to restrict the parameter type `T` to only the subtypes of `Real`, this can be written as follows:

```
mutable struct Point{T <: Real}
  x::T
  y::T
end
```

Now, the statement `p = Point("London", "Great-Britain")` results in an `ERROR: MethodError: `Point{T<:Real}` has no method matching Point{T<:Real}(::String, :String)` error message, because `String` is not a subtype of `Real`.

In much the same way, methods can also optionally have type parameters immediately after their name and before the tuple of arguments. For example, to constrain two arguments to be of the same type `T`, run the following command:

```
add(x::T, y::T) where T = x + y
```

Now, `add(2, 3)` returns `5` and `add(2, 3.0)` returns an `ERROR: MethodError: `add` has no method matching add(::Int64, ::Float64)` error message.

Here, we restrict `T` to be a subtype of `Number` in `add` as follows:

```
add(x::T, y::T) where T <: Number = x + y
```

As another example, here is how to check whether a `vecfloat` function only takes a vector of floating point numbers as the input. Simply define it with a type parameter `T` as follows:

```
function vecfloat(x::Vector{T}) where T <: AbstractFloat
    # code
end
```

Inner constructors can also take type parameters in their definition.

Standard modules and paths

The code for Julia packages (also called **libraries**) is contained in a module whose name starts with an uppercase letter by convention, like this:

```
# see the code in Chapter 6\modules.jl
module Package1

export Type1, perc

include("file1.jl")
include("file2.jl")

# code
mutable struct Type1
    total
end

perc(a::Type1) = a.total * 0.01

end
```

This serves to separate all its definitions from those in other modules so that no name conflicts occur. Name conflicts are solved by qualifying the function by the module name. For example, the packages `Winston` and `Gadfly` both contain a function plot. If we needed these two versions in the same script, we would write it as follows:

```
import Winston
import Gadfly
Winston.plot(rand(4))
Gadfly.plot(x=[1:10], y=rand(10))
```

All variables defined in the `global` scope are automatically added to the `Main` module. Thus, when you write x = 2 in the REPL, you are adding the variable x to the `Main` module.

Julia starts with `Main` as the current top-level module. The module `Core` is a set of non-Julia sources (in the `src` directory of the GitHub source); for example, C/C++ and Femtolisp, which are used to create `libjulia`, are used by the Julia source to interface to the OS through the API. The standard library is also available. The code for the standard library (the contents of `/base`) is contained in the following modules:

- `Base64`
- `FileWatching`
- `LinearAlgebra`
- `Printf`
- `Serialization`
- `SuiteSparse`
- `CRC32c`
- `Future`
- `Logging`
- `Profile`
- `SharedArrays`
- `Test`
- `Dates`
- `InteractiveUtils`
- `Markdown`
- `REPL`
- `Sockets`
- `UUIDs`
- `DelimitedFiles`
- `LibGit2`
- `Mmap`
- `Random`
- `SparseArrays`
- `Unicode`
- `Distributed`
- `Libdl`
- `Pkg`
- `SHA`
- `Statistics`

The type of a module is `Module: typeof(Base)`, which returns `Module`. If we call `names(Main)`, we get, for example, `5-element Array{Symbol,1}: :ans, :Main, :Core, :Base`, and `:InteractiveUtils`. If you have defined other variables or functions in the REPL, these would also show up.

All the top-level defined variables and functions, together with the default modules, are stored as symbols. The `varinfo()` function lists these objects with their types:

```
name                    size        summary

Base                                 Module
Core                                 Module
InteractiveUtils 157.063 KiB Module
Main                                 Module
```

This can also be used for another module. For example, `varinfo(Winston)` lists all the exported names from the module `Winston`.

A module can make some of its internal definitions (such as constants, variables, types, functions, and so on) visible to other modules (as if making them public) by declaring them with `export`. This can be seen in the following example:

```
export Type1, perc
```

For the preceding example, using `Package1` will make the type `Type1` and function `perc` available in other modules that import them through this statement. All the other definitions remain invisible (or private).

As we saw in `Chapter 1`, *Installing the Julia Platform*, a module can also include other source files in their entirety with `include("file1.jl")`. However, this means that the included files are not modules. Using `include("file1.jl")` is, to the compiler, no different from copying `file1.jl` and pasting it directly in the current file or the REPL.

In general, use `import` to import definitions from another module in the current module:

- After `import .LibA`, you can use all definitions from `LibA` inside the current module by qualifying them with `LibA.`, such as `LibA.a`

- The `import LibB.varB` or `import LibD.funcD` statement only imports one name; the function `funcD` must be used as `LibD.funcD`.

- Use `importall LibE` to import all the exported names from `LibE` in the current module.

Here is a more concrete example. Suppose we define a `TemperatureConverter` module as follows:

```
#code in Chapter 6\temperature_converter.jl
module TemperatureConverter

  function as_celsius(temperature, unit)
    if unit == :Celsius
      return temperature
    elseif unit == :Kelvin
      return kelvin_to_celsius(temperature)
    end
  end

  function kelvin_to_celsius(temperature)
    # 'private' function
    return temperature + 273
  end

end
```

We can now use this module in another program as follows:

```
#code in Chapter 6\using_module.jl
include("temperature_converter.jl")

println("$(TemperatureConverter.as_celsius(100, :Celsius))")
#> 100
println("$(TemperatureConverter.as_celsius(100, :Kelvin))")
#> 373
println("$(TemperatureConverter.kelvin_to_celsius(0))") #> 273
```

Imported variables are read-only, and the current module cannot create variables with the same names as the imported ones. A source file can contain many modules, or one module can be defined in several source files. If a module contains a function __init__(), this will be executed when the module is first loaded.

The variable `LOAD_PATH` contains a list of directories where Julia looks for (module) files when running the `using`, `import`, or `include` statements. Put this statement in the file `~/.julia/config/startup.jl` to extend `LOAD_PATH` on every Julia startup:

```
push!(LOAD_PATH, "new/path/to/search")
```

Summary

In this chapter, we delved into types and type hierarchies in Julia. We got a much better understanding of types and how functions work on them through multiple dispatch. The next chapter will reveal another power tool in Julia: metaprogramming and macros.

7
Metaprogramming in Julia

Everything in Julia is an expression that returns a value when executed. Every piece of the program code is internally represented as an ordinary Julia data structure, also called an **expression**. In this chapter, we will see how, by working on expressions, a Julia program can transform and even generate new code. This is a very powerful characteristic, also called **homoiconicity**. It inherits this property from **Lisp**, where code and data are just lists, and where it is commonly referred to with the phrase: *Code is data and data is code.*

In homoiconic languages, code can be expressed in terms of the language syntax. This is the case for the Lisp-like family of languages: Lisp, Scheme and, more recently, Clojure, which use s-expressions. Julia is homoiconic, as are others such as Prolog, IO, Rebol, and Red. As such, these are able to generate code during runtime, which can be subsequently executed.

We will explore this metaprogramming power by covering the following topics:

- Expressions and symbols
- Evaluation and interpolation
- Defining macros
- Built-in macros
- Reflection capabilities

Expressions and symbols

An **abstract syntax tree** (**AST**) is a tree representation of the abstract syntactic structure of source code written in a programming language. When Julia code is parsed by its LLVM JIT compiler, it is internally represented as an abstract syntax tree. The nodes of this tree are simple data structures of the type expression `Expr`. For more information on abstract syntax trees, refer to `http://en.wikipedia.org/wiki/Abstract_syntax_tree`.

An expression is simply an object that represents Julia code. For example, 2 + 3 is a piece of code, which is an expression of type Int64 (follow along with the code in Chapter 7\expressions.jl). Its syntax tree can be visualized as follows:

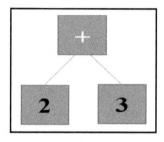

To make Julia see this as an expression and block its evaluation, we have to quote it, that is, precede it by a colon (:) as in : (2 + 3). When you evaluate : (2 + 3) in the REPL, it just returns : (2 + 3), which is of type Expr: typeof(: (2 + 3)) returns Expr. In fact, the : operator (also called the **quote** operator) sets out to treat its argument as data, not as code.

If this code is more than one line, enclose the lines between the quote and end keywords to turn the code into an expression. For example, this expression just returns itself:

```
quote
    a = 42
    b = a^2
    a - b
end
```

In fact, this is the same as : (a = 42; b = a^2; a - b). quote...end is just another way to convert blocks of code into expressions.

We can give an expression such as this a name, such as e1 = : (2 + 3). We can ask for the following information:

- e1.head returns :call, indicating the kind of expression, which here is a function call
- e1.args returns 3-element Array{Any,1}: :+ 2 3

Indeed the expression 2 + 3 is, in fact, a call of the + function with the argument 2, and 3: 2 + 3 == + (2, 3) returns true. The args argument consists of a symbol :+, and two literal values, 2 and 3. Expressions are made up of symbols and literals. More complicated expressions will consist of literal values, symbols, and sub- or nested expressions, which can, in turn, be reduced to symbols and literals.

For example, consider the expression e2 = : (2 + a * b - c), which can be visualized by the following syntax tree:

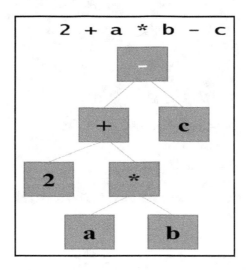

e2 consists of e2.args, which is a 3-element Array{Any,1} that contains :- and :c, which are symbols, and : (2 + a * b), which is also an expression. This last expression, in turn, is itself an expression with args :+, 2, and : (a * b); : (a * b) is an expression with arguments and symbols: : *, :a, and :b. We can see that this works recursively; we can simplify every subexpression in the same way until we end up with elementary symbols and literals.

In the context of an expression, *symbols are used to indicate access to variables*; they represent the variable in the tree structure for the code. In fact, the **prevent evaluation** character of the quote operator (:) is already at work with symbols: after x = 5, x returns 5, but :x returns :x.

The `dump` function presents the abstract syntax tree for its argument in a nice way. For example, `dump(:(2 + a * b - c))` returns the output, as shown in the following screenshot:

```
julia> dump(:(2 + a * b - c))
Expr
  head: Symbol call
  args: Array{Any}((3,))
    1: Symbol -
    2: Expr
      head: Symbol call
      args: Array{Any}((3,))
        1: Symbol +
        2: Int64 2
        3: Expr
          head: Symbol call
          args: Array{Any}((3,))
            1: Symbol *
            2: Symbol a
            3: Symbol b
    3: Symbol c
```

Evaluation and interpolation

With the definition of type `Expr` from the preceding section, we can also build expressions directly from the constructor for `Expr`. For example: `e1 = Expr(:call, *, 3, 4)` returns `:((*)(3, 4))` (follow along with the code in `Chapter 7\eval.jl`).

The result of an expression can be computed with the `eval` function, `eval(e1)`, which returns `12` in this case. At the time an expression is constructed, not all the symbols have to be defined, but they have to be defined at the time of evaluation, otherwise an error occurs.

For example, `e2 = Expr(:call, *, 3, :a)` returns `:((*)(3, a))`, and `eval(e2)` then gives `ERROR: UndefVarError: a not defined`. Only after we say, for example, `a = 4` does `eval(e2)` return `12`.

Expressions can also change the state of the execution environment, for example, the expression `e3 = :(b = 1)` assigns a value to `b` when evaluated, and even defines `b`, if it doesn't exist already.

To make writing expressions a bit simpler, we can use the $ operator to do **interpolation** in expressions, as with $ in strings, and this will evaluate immediately when the expression is made. The expressions a = 4 and b = 1, e4 = :(a + b) return :(a + b), and e5 = :($a + b) returns :(4 + b); both expressions evaluate to 5. So, there are two kinds of evaluation here:

- Expression interpolation (with $) evaluates when the expression is constructed (at parse time)
- Quotation (with : or quote) evaluates only when the expression is passed to eval at runtime

We now have the capability to build code programmatically. Inside a Julia program, we can construct arbitrary code while it is running, and then evaluate this with eval. So, Julia can generate the code from inside itself during the normal program execution.

This happens all the time in Julia and it is used, for example, to do things such as generating bindings for external libraries, to reducing the repetitive boilerplate code needed to bind big libraries, or generating lots of similar routines in other situations. Also, in the field of robotics, the ability to generate another program and then run it is very useful. For example: a chirurgical robot learns how to move by perceiving a human surgeon demonstrating a procedure. Then, the robot generates the program code from that perception, so that it is able to perform the procedure by itself.

One of the most powerful Julia tools emerging from what we discussed before is **macros**, which exist in all the languages of the Lisp family.

Julia version 1.0 also introduces the concept of **generated functions**: such functions are prefixed by the @generated macro and, instead of normal values, they return expressions. We won't discuss this advanced concept here in this book.

Defining macros

In previous chapters, we have already used macros, such as @printf, in Chapter 2, *Variables, Types, and Operations*, and @time in Chapter 3, *Functions*. Macros are like functions, but instead of values they take expressions (which can also be symbols or literals) as input arguments. When a macro is evaluated, the input expression is expanded, that is, the macro returns a modified expression. This expansion occurs at parse time when the syntax tree is being built, not when the code is actually executed.

The following descriptions highlight the difference between macros and functions when they are called or invoked:

- **Function**: It takes the input values and returns the computed values at runtime
- **Macro**: It takes the input expressions and returns the modified expressions at parse time

In other words, a macro is a custom program transformation. Macros are defined with the keyword as follows:

```
macro mname
# code returning expression
end
```

It is invoked as `@mname exp1 exp2` or `@mname(exp1, exp2)` (the @ sign distinguishes it from a normal function call). The macro block defines a new scope. Macros allow us to control when the code is executed.

Here are some examples:

- A first simple example is `macint` macro, which does the interpolation of its argument expression `ex`:

    ```
    # see the code in Chapter 7\macros.jl)
    macro macint(ex)
        quote
            println("start")
            $ex
            println("after")
        end
    end
    ```

    `@macint println("Where am I?")` will result in:

    start
    Where am I?
    after

- The second example is an `assert` macro that takes an expression `ex` and tests whether it is true or not; in the last case, an error is thrown:

```
macro assert(ex)
:($ex ? nothing : error("Assertion failed: ",
       $(string(ex))))
end
```

For example: `@assert 1 == 1.0` returns `nothing`. `@assert 1 == 42` returns `ERROR: Assertion failed: 1 == 42`.

The macro replaces the expression with a ternary operator expression, which is evaluated at runtime. To examine the resulting expression, use the `macroexpand` function as follows:

```
macroexpand(Main, :(@assert 1 == 42))
```

This returns the following expression:

```
:(if 1 == 42
        nothing
    else
        (Base.throw)((Base.AssertionError)("1 == 42"))
    end)
```

This `assert` function is just a macro example, using the built-in assert function in the production code. (Refer to the *Testing* subsection of the *Built-in macros* section.)

- The third example mimics an `unless` construct, where `branch` is executed if the condition `test_cond` is not true:

```
macro unless(test_cond, branch)
    quote
        if !$test_cond
            $branch
        end
    end
end
```

Suppose `arr = [3.14, 42, 'b']`, then `@unless 42 in arr println("arr does not contain 42")` returns `nothing`, but `@unless 41 in arr println("arr does not contain 41")` prints out the following command:

```
arr does not contain 41
```

Here, `macroexpand(Main, :(@unless 41 in arr println("arr does not contain 41")))` returns the following output:

```
quote
    #= REPL[49]:3 =#
    if !(41 in Main.arr)
        #= REPL[49]:4 =#
        (Main.println)("arr does not contain 41")
    end
end
```

Unlike functions, macros inject the code directly into the namespace in which they are called, possibly this is also in a different module than the one in which they were defined. It is therefore important to ensure that this generated code does not clash with the code in the module in which the macro is called. When a macro behaves appropriately like this, it is called a **hygienic macro**. The following rules are used when writing hygienic macros:

- Declare the variables used in the macro as `local`, so as not to conflict with the outer variables
- Use the escape function `esc` to make sure that an interpolated expression is not expanded, but instead is used literally
- Don't call `eval` inside a macro (because it is likely that the variables you are evaluating don't even exist at that point)

These principles are applied in the following `timeit` macro, which times the execution of an expression `ex` (like the built-in macro `@time`):

```
macro timeit(ex)
    quote
        local t0 = time()
        local val = $(esc(ex))
        local t1 = time()
        print("elapsed time in seconds: ")
        @printf "%.3f" t1 - t0
        val
    end
end
```

The expression is executed through `$`, and `t0` and `t1` are respectively the start and end times.

`@timeit factorial(10)` returns elapsed time in seconds: 0.0003628800.

`@timeit a^3` returns elapsed time in seconds: 0.0013796416.

Hygiene with macros is all about differentiating between the macro context and the calling context.

Macros are valuable tools which save you a lot of tedious work, and, with the quoting and interpolation mechanism, they are fairly easy to create. You will see them being used everywhere in Julia for lots of different tasks. Ultimately, they allow you to create **domain-specific languages (DSLs)**. To get a better idea of this concept, we suggest you experiment with the other examples in the accompanying code file.

Built-in macros

Needless to say, the Julia team has put macros to good use. To get help information about a macro, enter a ? in the REPL, and type @macroname after the help> prompt. Apart from the built-in macros we encountered in the examples in the previous chapters, here are some other very useful ones (refer to the code in Chapter 7\built_in_macros.jl).

Testing

The @assert macro actually exists in the standard library. The standard version also allows you to give your own error message, which is printed after ERROR: assertion failed.

The Test library contains some useful macros to compare the numbers:

```
using Test
@test 1 == 3
```

This returns the following:

```
Test Failed at REPL[5]:1
  Expression: 1 == 3
    Evaluated: 1 == 3
ERROR: There was an error during testing.
```

@test with the ≈ operator tests whether the two numbers are approximately equal. @test 1 ≈ 1.1 returns Test Failed because they are not equal within the machine tolerance. However, you can give the interval as the last argument within which they should be equal: @test 1 ≈ 1.1 atol=0.2, which returns Test Passed, so 1 and 1.1 are within 0.2 from each other.

Debugging

If you want to look up in the source code where and how a particular method is defined, use @which. For example: if arr = [1, 2] then @which sort(arr) returns sort(v::AbstractArray{T,1}) where T) in Base.Sort at sort.jl:683 at sort.jl:334.

@show shows the expression and its result, which is handy for checking the embedded results: 456 * 789 + (@show 2 + 3) gives 2 + 3 => 5   359789.

Benchmarking

For benchmarking purposes, we already know @time and @elapsed; @timed gives you the @time results as a tuple:

@time [x^2 for x in 1:1000] prints elapsed time: 3.911e-6 seconds (8064 bytes allocated) and returns 1000-element Array{Int64,1}: ....

@timed [x^2 for x in 1:1000] returns the following:

    ([1, 4, 9, 16, 25, 36, 49, 64, 81, 100 ... 982081, 984064, 986049, 988036, 990025, 992016, 994009, 996004, 998001, 1000000], 3.911e-6, 8064, 0.0)

@elapsed [x^2 for x in 1:1000] returns 3.422e-6.

If you are specifically interested in the allocated memory, use @allocated [x^2 for x in 1:1000], which returns 8064.

If you are looking for a package, consult BenchmarkingTools. This has some macros and also a good method for benchmarking.

Starting a task

Tasks (refer to the *Tasks* section in Chapter 4, *Control Flow*) are independent units of code execution. Often, we want to start executing them, and then continue executing the main code without waiting for the task result. In other words, we want to start the task *asynchronously*. This can be done with the @async macro:

    a = @async 1 + 2 # Task (done) @0x000000002d70faf0

Reflection capabilities

We saw in this chapter that code in Julia is represented by expressions that are data structures of the `Expr` type. The structure of a program and its types can therefore be explored programmatically just like any other data. This means that a running program can dynamically discover its own properties, which is called **reflection**. We have already encountered some of these macros or functions before:

- Use the `@isdefined` macro to check whether a variable is already declared, for example if a is not declared, you get:

    ```
    @isdefined a #> false
    ```

- Use the `typeof` and `InteractiveUtils.subtypes` to query the type hierarchy (refer to Chapter 6, *More on Types, Methods, and Modules*)
- Use the `methods(f)` to see all the methods of a function f (refer to Chapter 3, *Functions*)
- `names` and `types`: given a type `Person`:

    ```
    mutable struct Person
        name:: String
        height::Float64
    end
    ```

    Then, `fieldnames(Person)` returns the field names as a tuple of symbols: (`:name, :height`)

    `Person.types` returns a tuple with the field types (`String, Float64`).

- To inspect how a function is represented internally, you can use `code_lowered`:

    ```
    code_lowered(+, (Int, Int))
    ```

    This returns the following output:

    ```
    1-element Array{Core.CodeInfo,1}:
      CodeInfo(
    53 1 ─ %1 = Base.add_int(%%x, %%y)::Any
       │
       └──             return %1
       │
       )
    ```

Or you can use `code_typed` to see the type-inferred form:

```
code_typed(+, (Int, Int))
```

This returns the following:

```
1-element Array{Any,1}:
 1-element Array{Any,1}:
  CodeInfo(
 53 1 ─ %1 = Base.add_int(%%x, %%y)::Int64
    │
    └──           return %1
    │
 ) => Int64
```

Using `code_typed` can show you whether your code is type-optimized for performance: if the `Any` type is used instead of an appropriate specific type that you would expect, then the type annotation in your code can certainly be improved, leading most likely to speeding up the program's execution.

- To inspect the code generated by the LLVM engine, use `code_llvm`, and, to see the assembly code generated, use `code_native` (refer to the *How Julia works* section in `Chapter 1`, *Installing the Julia Platform*).

While reflection is not necessary for many of the programs that you will write, it is very useful for IDEs to be able to inspect the internals of an object, as well as for tools generating automatic documentation, and for profiling tools. In other words, reflection is indispensable for tools that need to inspect the internals of code objects programmatically.

You should also look at the `MacroTools` package (from Mike Innes) which has some good examples of macros.

Summary

In this chapter, we explored the expression format in which Julia is parsed. Because this format is a data structure, we can manipulate this in the code, and this is precisely what macros can do. We explored a number of them, and also some built-in ones that can be useful.

In the next chapter, we will extend our vision to the network environment in which Julia runs, and we will explore its powerful capabilities for parallel execution.

8
I/O, Networking, and Parallel Computing

In this chapter, we will explore how Julia interacts with the outside world, reading from standard input and writing to standard output, files, networks, and databases. Julia provides asynchronous networking I/O using the `libuv` library. We will see how to handle data in Julia. We will also explore Julia's parallel processing model.

In this chapter, the following topics are covered:

- Basic input and output
- Working with files (including CSV files)
- Using DataFrames
- Working with TCP sockets and servers
- Interacting with databases
- Parallel operations and computing

Basic input and output

Julia's vision on **input/output (I/O)** is **stream-oriented**, that is, reading or writing streams of bytes. We will introduce different types of stream, file streams, in this chapter. **Standard input (stdin)** and **standard output (stdout)** are constants of the `TTY` type (an abbreviation for the old term, `Teletype`) that can be read from and written to in Julia code (refer to the code in `Chapter 8\io.jl`):

- `read(stdin, Char)`: This command waits for a character to be entered, and then returns that character; for example, when you type in J, this returns `'J'`

- `write(stdout, "Julia")`: This command types out `Julia5` (the added 5 is the number of bytes in the output stream; it is not added if the command ends in a semicolon `;`)

`stdin` and `stdout` are simply streams and can be replaced by any stream object in read/write commands. `readbytes` is used to read a number of bytes from a stream into a vector:

- `read(stdin, 3)`: This command waits for an input, for example, `abe` reads three bytes from it, and then returns `3-element Array{Uint8,1}: 0x61 0x62 0x65`.
- `readline(stdin)`: This command reads all the input until a newline character, \n, is entered. For example, type `Julia` and press *Enter*; this returns `"Julia\r\n"` on Windows and `"Julia\n"` on Linux.

If you need to read all the lines from an input stream, use the `eachline` method in a `for` loop, for example:

```
stream = stdin
for line in eachline(stream)
    println("Found $line")
    # process the line
end
```

Include the following REPL dialog as an example:

```
First line of input
Found First line of input
2nd line of input
Found 2nd line of input
3rd line...
Found 3rd line...
```

To test whether you have reached the end of an input stream, use `eof(stream)` in combination with a `while` loop, as follows:

```
while !eof(stream)
    x = read(stream, Char)
    println("Found: $x")
# process the character
end
```

We can experiment with the preceding code by replacing `stream` with `stdin` in these examples.

Working with files

To work with files, we need the `IOStream` type. `IOStream` is a type with the `IO` supertype and has the following characteristics:

- The fields are given by `fieldnames(IOStream)`:

    `(:handle, :ios, :name, :mark)`

- The types are given by `IOStream.types`:

    `(Ptr{Nothing}, Array{UInt8,1}, AbstractString, Int64)`

The file handle is a pointer of the `Ptr` type, which is a reference to the file object.

Opening and reading a line-oriented file with the `example.dat` name is very easy:

```
// code in Chapter 8\io.jl
fname = "example.dat"
f1 = open(fname)
```

`fname` is a string that contains the path to the file, using the escaping of special characters with \ when necessary. For example, in Windows, when the file is in the `test` folder on the `D:` drive, this would become `d:\\test\\example.dat`. The `f1` variable is now an `IOStream(<file example.dat>)` object.

To read all lines one after another in an array, use `data = readlines(f1)`, which returns 3-element `Array{String,1}`:

```
"this is line 1."
"42; 3.14"
"this is line 3."
```

For processing line by line, now only a simple loop is needed:

```
for line in data
  println(line) # or process line
end
close(f1)
```

Always close the `IOStream` object to clean and save resources. If you want to read the file into one string, use `readall` (for example, see the `word_frequency` program in Chapter 5, *Collection Types*). Use this only for relatively small files because of the memory consumption; this can also be a potential problem when using `readlines`.

There is a convenient shorthand with the do syntax for opening a file, applying a function process, and closing it automatically. This goes as follows (file is the IOStream object in this code):

```
open(fname) do file
    process(file)
end
```

As you can recall, in the *Map, filter, and list comprehensions* section in Chapter 3, *Functions*, do creates an anonymous function, and passes it to open. Thus, the previous code example would have been equivalent to open(process, fname). Use the same syntax for processing a fname file line by line without the memory overhead of the previous methods, for example:

```
open(fname) do file
    for line in eachline(file)
        print(line) # or process line
    end
end
```

Writing a file requires first opening it with a "w" flag, writing strings to it with write, print, or println, and then closing the file handle that flushes the IOStream object to the disk:

```
fname =    "example2.dat"
f2 = open(fname, "w")
write(f2, "I write myself to a file\n")
# returns 24 (bytes written)
println(f2, "even with println!")
close(f2)
```

Opening a file with the "w" option will clear the file if it exists. To append to an existing file, use "a".

To process all the files in the current folder (or a given folder as an argument to readdir()), use this for loop:

```
for file in readdir()
  # process file
end
```

For example, try out this code, which goes up to the parent directory, prints them out, and then comes back:

```
mydir = pwd()
cd("..")

for fn in readdir()
    println(fn)
end
cd(mydir)
```

Reading and writing CSV files

A **CSV** file is a **comma-separated file**. The data fields in each line are separated by commas, `,`, or another delimiter, such as semicolons, `;`. These files are the de-facto standard for exchanging small and medium amounts of tabular data. Such files are structured so that one line contains data about one data object, so we need a way to read and process the file line by line. As an example, we will use the `Chapter 8\winequality.csv` datafile, which contains 1,599 sample measurements, 12 data columns, such as `pH` and `alcohol`, per sample, separated by a semicolon. In the following screenshot, you can see the top 20 rows:

	fixed acidi	volatile ac	citric acid	residual su	chlorides	free sulfur	total sulfu	density	pH	sulphates	alcohol	quality
1												
2	7.4	0.7	0	1.9	0.076	11	34	0.9978	3.51	0.56	9.4	5
3	7.8	0.88	0	2.6	0.098	25	67	0.9968	3.2	0.68	9.8	5
4	7.8	0.76	0.04	2.3	0.092	15	54	0.997	3.26	0.65	9.8	5
5	11.2	0.28	0.56	1.9	0.075	17	60	0.998	3.16	0.58	9.8	6
6	7.4	0.7	0	1.9	0.076	11	34	0.9978	3.51	0.56	9.4	5
7	7.4	0.66	0	1.8	0.075	13	40	0.9978	3.51	0.56	9.4	5
8	7.9	0.6	0.06	1.6	0.069	15	59	0.9964	3.3	0.46	9.4	5
9	7.3	0.65	0	1.2	0.065	15	21	0.9946	3.39	0.47	10	7
10	7.8	0.58	0.02	2	0.073	9	18	0.9968	3.36	0.57	9.5	7
11	7.5	0.5	0.36	6.1	0.071	17	102	0.9978	3.35	0.8	10.5	5
12	6.7	0.58	0.08	1.8	0.097	15	65	0.9959	3.28	0.54	9.2	5
13	7.5	0.5	0.36	6.1	0.071	17	102	0.9978	3.35	0.8	10.5	5
14	5.6	0.615	0	1.6	0.089	16	59	0.9943	3.58	0.52	9.9	5
15	7.8	0.61	0.29	1.6	0.114	9	29	0.9974	3.26	1.56	9.1	5
16	8.9	0.62	0.18	3.8	0.176	52	145	0.9986	3.16	0.88	9.2	5
17	8.9	0.62	0.19	3.9	0.17	51	148	0.9986	3.17	0.93	9.2	5
18	8.5	0.28	0.56	1.8	0.092	35	103	0.9969	3.3	0.75	10.5	7
19	8.1	0.56	0.28	1.7	0.368	16	56	0.9968	3.11	1.28	9.3	5
20	7.4	0.59	0.08	4.4	0.086	6	29	0.9974	3.38	0.5	9	4

In general, the `readdlm` function from the `DelimitedFiles` package is used to read in the data from the CSV files:

```
# code in Chapter 8\csv_files.jl:
fname = "winequality.csv"
using DelimitedFiles
data = DelimitedFiles.readdlm(fname, ';')
```

The second argument is the delimiter character (here, it is `;`). The resulting data is a `1600x12 Array{Any,2}` array of the `Any` type because no common type could be found:

"fixed acidity"	"volatile acidity"	"alcohol"	"quality"
7.4	0.7	9.4	5.0
7.8	0.88	9.8	5.0
7.8	0.76	9.8	5.0
...			

The problem with what we have done so far is that the header (the column titles) was read as part of the data. Fortunately, we can pass the `header=true` argument to let Julia put the first line in a separate array. It then naturally gets the correct datatype, `Float64`, for the data array. We can also specify the type explicitly, such as this:

```
data3 = DelimitedFiles.readdlm(fname, ';', Float64, '\n', header=true)
```

The third argument here is the type of data, which is a numeric type, `String` or `Any`. The next argument is the line-separator character, and the fifth indicates whether or not there is a header line with the field (column) names. If so, then `data3` is a tuple with the data as the first element and the header as the second, in our case, `([7.4 0.7 ... 9.4 5.0; 7.8 0.88 ... 9.8 5.0; ... ; 5.9 0.645 ... 10.2 5.0; 6.0 0.31 ... 11.0 6.0], AbstractString["fixed acidity" "volatile acidity" ... "alcohol" "quality"])` (there are other optional arguments to define `readdlm`; use ? `DelimitedFiles.readdlm`). In this case, the actual data is given by `data3[1]` and the header by `data3[2]`.

Let's continue working with variable data. The data forms a matrix, and we can get the rows and columns of data using the normal array-matrix syntax (refer to the *Matrices* section in Chapter 5, *Collection Types*). For example, the third row is given by `row3 = data[3, :]` with data: `7.8 0.88 0.0 2.6 0.098 25.0 67.0 0.9968 3.2 0.68 9.8 5.0`, representing the measurements for all the characteristics of a certain wine.

The measurements of a certain characteristic for all wines are given by a `data` column; for example, `col3 = data[ :, 3]` represents the measurements of citric acid and returns a `1600-element Array{Any,1}`: `"citric acid" 0.0 0.0 0.04 0.56 0.0 0.0 ... 0.08 0.08 0.1 0.13 0.12 0.47` column vector.

If we need columns two to four (`volatile acidity` to `residual sugar`) for all wines, extract the data with `x = data[:, 2:4]`. If we need these measurements only for the wines on rows 70-75, get these with `y = data[70:75, 2:4]`, returning a 6 x 3 `Array{Any, 2}` output, as follows:

```
0.32    0.57   2.0
0.705   0.05   1.9
. . .
0.675   0.26   2.1
```

To get a matrix with the data from columns 3, 6, and 11, execute the following command:

```
z = [data[:,3] data[:,6] data[:,11]]
```

This includes the headers; if you don't want these, use the following:

```
z = [data[2:end,3] data[2:end,6] data[2:end,11]]
```

It would be useful to create a `Wine` type in the code.

For example, if the data is to be passed around functions, it will improve the code quality to encapsulate all the data in a single data type, like this:

```
struct Wine
    fixed_acidity::Array{Float64}
    volatile_acidity::Array{Float64}
    citric_acid::Array{Float64}
    # other fields
    quality::Array{Float64}
end
```

Then, we can create objects of this type to work with them, like in any other object-oriented language, for example, `wine1 = Wine(data[1, :]...)`, where the elements of the row are splatted with the `...` operator into the `Wine` constructor.

To write to a CSV file, the simplest way is to use the `writecsv` function for a comma separator, or the `writedlm` function if you want to specify another separator. For example, to write an array data to a `partial.dat` file, you need to execute the following command:

```
writedlm("partial.dat", data, ';')
```

If more control is necessary, you can easily combine the more basic functions from the previous section. For example, the following code snippet writes 10 tuples of three numbers each to a file:

```
// code in Chapter 8\tuple_csv.jl
fname = "savetuple.csv"
```

```
csvfile = open(fname,"w")
# writing headers:
write(csvfile, "ColName A, ColName B, ColName C\n")
for i = 1:10
  tup(i) = tuple(rand(Float64,3)...)
  write(csvfile, join(tup(i),","), "\n")
end
close(csvfile)
```

Using DataFrames

If you measure n variables (each of a different type) of a single object, then you get a table with n columns for each object row. If there are m observations, then we have m rows of data. For example, given the student grades as data, you might want to know compute the average grade for each socioeconomic group, where grade and socioeconomic group are both columns in the table, and there is one row per student.

DataFrame is the most natural representation to work with such a (*m x n*) table of data. They are similar to Pandas DataFrames in Python or data.frame in R. DataFrame is a more specialized tool than a normal array for working with tabular and statistical data, and it is defined in the DataFrames package, a popular Julia library for statistical work. Install it in your environment by typing in add DataFrames in the REPL. Then, import it into your current workspace with using DataFrames. Do the same for the DataArrays and RDatasets packages (which contain a collection of example datasets mostly used in the R literature).

A common case in statistical data is that data values can be missing (the information is not known). The Missings package provides us with a unique value, missing, which represents a non-existing value, and has the Missing type. The result of the computations that contain the missing values mostly cannot be determined, for example, 42 + missing returns missing.

DataFrame is a kind of in-memory database, versatile in the various ways you can work with data. It consists of columns with names such as Col1, Col2, and Col3. All of these columns are DataArrays that have their own type, and the data they contain can be referred to by the column names as well, so we have substantially more forms of indexing. Unlike two-dimensional arrays, columns in DataFrame can be of different types. One column might, for instance, contain the names of students and should therefore be a string. Another column could contain their age and should be an integer.

We construct `DataFrame` from the program data as follows:

```
// code in Chapter 8\dataframes.jl
using DataFrames, Missings
# constructing a DataFrame:
df = DataFrame()
df[:Col1] = 1:4
df[:Col2] = [exp(1), pi, sqrt(2), 42]
df[:Col3] = [true, false, true, false]
show(df)
```

Notice that the column headers are used as symbols. This returns the following 4 x 3 `DataFrame` object:

```
show(df)
4x3 DataFrame
| Row | Col1 | Col2    | Col3  |
|-----|------|---------|-------|
| 1   | 1    | 2.71828 | true  |
| 2   | 2    | 3.14159 | false |
| 3   | 3    | 1.41421 | true  |
| 4   | 4    | 42.0    | false |
```

`show(df)` produces a nicely formatted output (whereas `show(:Col2)` does not). This is because there is a `show()` routine defined in the package for the entire contents of `DataFrame`.

We could also have used the full constructor, as follows:

```
df = DataFrame(Col1 = 1:4, Col2 = [e, pi, sqrt(2), 42],
      Col3 = [true, false, true, false])
```

You can refer to columns either by an index (the column number) or by a name; both of the following expressions return the same output:

```
show(df[2])
show(df[:Col2])
```

This gives the following output:

```
[2.718281828459045, 3.141592653589793, 1.4142135623730951,42.0]
```

To show the rows or subsets of rows and columns, use the familiar splice (`:`) syntax, for example:

- To get the first row, execute `df[1, :]`. This returns `1x3 DataFrame`:

```
| Row | Col1 | Col2    | Col3 |
|-----|------|---------|------|
| 1   | 1    | 2.71828 | true |
```

- To get the second and third row, execute `df [2:3, :]`.
- To get only the second column from the previous result, execute `df[2:3, :Col2]`. This returns `[3.141592653589793, 1.4142135623730951]`.
- To get the second and third columns from the second and third row, execute `df[2:3, [:Col2, :Col3]]`, which returns the following output:

```
2x2 DataFrame
| Row | Col2    | Col3  |
|---- |-----   -|-------|
| 1   | 3.14159 | false |
| 2   | 1.41421 | true  |
```

The following functions are very useful when working with `DataFrames`:

- The `head(df)` and `tail(df)` functions show you the first six and the last six lines of data, respectively. You can see this in the following example:

```
df0 = DataFrame(i = 1:10, x = rand(10),
                y = rand(["a", "b",  "c"], 10))
head(df0
```

- The `names` function gives the names of the `names(df)` columns. It returns `3-element Array{Symbol,1}: :Col1 :Col2 :Col3`.
- The `eltypes` function gives the data types of the `eltypes(df)` columns. It gives the output as `3-element Array{Type{T<:Top},1}: Int64 Float64 Bool`.
- The `describe` function tries to give some useful summary information about the data in the columns, depending on the type. For example, `describe(df)` gives for column 2 (which is numeric) the minimum, maximum, median, mean, number of unique, and the number of missing:

```
3R8 DataFrame
 Row | variable | mean    | min     | median  | max  | nunique | nmissing | eltype
  1  | Col1     | 2.5     | 1       | 2.5     | 4    |         |          | Int64
  2  | Col2     | 12.3185 | 1.41421 | 2.92994 | 42.0 |         |          | Float64
  3  | Col3     | 0.5     | false   | 0.5     | true |         |          | Bool
```

To load in data from a local CSV file, use the `read` method from the CSV package (the following are the docs for that package: https://juliadata.github.io/CSV.jl/stable/). The returned object is of the `DataFrame` type:

```
// code in Chapter 8\dataframes.jl
using DataFrames, CSV
fname = "winequality.csv"
data = CSV.read(fname, delim = ';')
typeof(data) # DataFrame
size(data) # (1599,12)
```

Here is a fraction of the output:

```
1599x12 DataFrame
| Row  | fixed_acidity | volatile_acidity | citric_acid | residual_sugar |
|------|---------------|------------------|-------------|----------------|
| 1    | 7.4           | 0.7              | 0.0         | 1.9            |
| 2    | 7.8           | 0.88             | 0.0         | 2.6            |
| 3    | 7.8           | 0.76             | 0.04        | 2.3            |
:
| 1596 | 5.9           | 0.55             | 0.1         | 2.2            |
| 1597 | 6.3           | 0.51             | 0.13        | 2.3            |
| 1598 | 5.9           | 0.645            | 0.12        | 2.0            |
| 1599 | 6.0           | 0.31             | 0.47        | 3.6            |
```

The `readtable` method also supports reading in the `gzip` CSV files.

Writing `DataFrame` to a file can be done with the `CSV.write` function, which takes the filename and `DataFrame` as arguments, for example, `CSV.write ("dataframe1.csv", df, delim = ';')`. By default, `write` will use the delimiter specified by the filename extension and write the column names as headers.

Both `read` and `write` support numerous options for special cases. Refer to the docs for more information.

To demonstrate some of the power of `DataFrames`, here are some queries you can do:

- Make a vector with only quality information, `data[:quality]`.
- Give wines whose alcohol percentage is equal to `9.5`, for example, `data[data[:alcohol] .== 9.5, :]`.

  Here, we use the `.==` operator, which does an element-wise comparison. `data[:alcohol] .== 9.5` returns an array of Boolean values (true for datapoints, where `:alcohol` is `9.5`, and false otherwise). `data[boolean_array, :]` selects those rows where `boolean_array` is true.

- Count the number of wines grouped by quality with `by(data, :quality, data -> size(data, 1))`, which returns the following:

```
6x2 DataFrame
| Row | quality | x1  |
|-----|---------|-----|
| 1   | 3       | 10  |
| 2   | 4       | 53  |
| 3   | 5       | 681 |
| 4   | 6       | 638 |
| 5   | 7       | 199 |
| 6   | 8       | 18  |
```

- The `DataFrames` package contains the `by` function, which takes in three arguments:
    - `DataFrame`, here it takes `data`
    - A column to split `DataFrame` on, here it takes `quality`
    - A function or an expression to apply to each subset of `DataFrame`, here `data -> size(data, 1)`, which gives us the number of wines for each quality value

Another easy way to get the distribution among quality is to execute the histogram `hist` function, `hist(data[:quality])`, which gives the counts over the range of quality (`2.0:1.0:8.0, [10,53,681,638,199,18]`). More precisely, this is a tuple with the first element corresponding to the edges of the histogram bins, and the second denoting the number of items in each bin. So there are, for example, 10 wines with quality between 2 and 3.

To extract the counts as a `count` variable of the `Vector` type, we can execute `_, count = hist(data[:quality]);` `_;` this means that we neglect the first element of the tuple. To obtain the quality classes as a `DataArray` class, we execute the following:

```
class = sort(unique(data[:quality]))
```

We can now construct `df_quality`, a `DataFrame` type with `class` and `count` columns as `df_quality = DataFrame(qual=class, no=count)`. This gives the following output:

```
6x2 DataFrame
| Row | qual | no  |
|-----|------|-----|
| 1   | 3    | 10  |
| 2   | 4    | 53  |
| 3   | 5    | 681 |
| 4   | 6    | 638 |
| 5   | 7    | 199 |
| 6   | 8    | 18  |
```

To deepen your understanding and learn about the other features of Julia's `DataFrames` (such as joining, reshaping, and sorting), refer to the documentation available at `http://juliadata.github.io/DataFrames.jl/latest/index.html`.

Other file formats

Julia can work with other human-readable file formats through specialized packages:

- For JSON, use the `JSON` package. The `parse` method converts JSON strings into dictionaries, and the `json` method turns any Julia object into a JSON string.
- For XML, use the `LightXML` package.
- For YAML, use the `YAML` package.
- For HDF5 (a common format for scientific data), use the `HDF5` package.
- For working with Windows `INI` files, use the `IniFile` package.

Working with TCP sockets and servers

To send data over a network, the data has to conform to a certain format or protocol. The **Transmission Control Protocol / Internet Protocol (TCP/IP)** is one of the core protocols to be used on the internet.

The following screenshot shows how to communicate over TCP/IP between a Julia TCP server and a client (see the code in `Chapter 8\tcpserver.jl`):

```
                 _                Documentation: https://docs.julialang.org
     _       _ _(_)_     |
    (_)     | (_) (_)    |        Type "?" for help, "]?" for Pkg help.
     _ _   _| |_  __ _   |
    | | | | | | |/ _` |  |        Version 1.0.0 (2018-08-08)
    | | |_| | | | (_| |  |        Official https://julialang.org/ release
   _/ |\__'_|_|_|\__'_|  |
  |__/                   |

julia> using Sockets

julia> server = Sockets.listen(8080)
Sockets.TCPServer(Base.Libc.WindowsRawSocket(0x0000000000000358) active)

julia> conn = accept(server)
TCPSocket(Base.Libc.WindowsRawSocket(0x0000000000000364) open, 0 bytes waiting)

julia>

julia> line = readline(conn)
"hello Julia server!"

julia> write(conn, "Hello back from server to client, what can I do for you?")
56

julia> close(conn)                Selecteren Opdrachtprompt

julia>                            e:\Downloads>nc localhost 8080
                                  hello Julia server!
                                  Hello back from server to client, what can I do for you?
                                  e:\Downloads>
```

The server (in the upper-left corner) is started in a Julia session with `server = Sockets.listen(8080)`, which returns a `TcpServer` object listening on port `8080`. The `conn = accept(server)` line waits for an incoming client to make a connection. In a second terminal (in the lower-right corner), we start the **netcat (nc)** tool at the prompt to make a connection with the Julia server on port `8080`, for example, `nc localhost 8080`. Then, the `accept` function creates a `TcpSocket` object on which the server can read or write.

Then, the server issues the `line = readline(conn)` command, blocking the server until it gets a full line (ending with a newline character) from the client. The client types `"hello Julia server!"` followed by *Enter*, which appears at the server console. The server can also write text to the client over the TCP connection with the `write(conn, "message ")` function, which then appears at the client side. The server can, when finished, close the `TcpSocket` connection to close the TCP connection with `close(conn)`; this also closes the `netcat` session.

Of course, a normal server must be able to handle multiple clients. Here, you can see the code for a server that echoes back to the clients everything they send to the server:

```
// code in Chapter8\echoserver.jl
using Sockets
server = Sockets.listen(8080)
while true
  conn = accept(server)   @async begin
    try
      while true
        line = readline(conn)
        println(line)   # output in server console
        write(conn,line)
      end
    catch ex
      print("connection ended with error $ex")
    end
  end # end coroutine block
end
```

To achieve this, we place the `accept()` function within an infinite `while` loop, so that each incoming connection is accepted. The same is true for reading and writing to a specific client; the server only stops listening to that client when the client disconnects. Because the network communication with the clients is a possible source of errors, we have to surround it within a `try/catch` expression. When an error occurs, it is bound to the `ex` object. For example, when a client terminal exits, you get the `connection ended with error ErrorException("stream is closed or unusable")` message.

However, we also see an `@async` macro here; what is its function? The `@async` macro starts a new coroutine (refer to the *Tasks* section in `Chapter 4`, *Control Flow*) in the local process to handle the execution of the `begin...end` block that starts right after it. So, the `@async` macro handles the connection with each particular client in a separate coroutine. Thus, the `@async` block returns immediately, enabling the server to continue accepting new connections through the outer `while` loop. Because coroutines have a very low overhead, making a new one for each connection is perfectly acceptable. If it weren't for the `async` block, the program would block it until it was done with its current client before accepting a new connection.

On the other hand, the `@sync` macro is used to enclose a number of `@async` (or `@spawn` or `@parallel` calls, refer to the *Parallel operations and computing* section), and the code execution waits at the end of the `@sync` block until all the enclosed calls are finished.

Start this server example by typing the following command:

```
julia echoserver.jl
```

We can experiment with a number of netcat sessions in separate terminals. Client sessions can also be made by typing in a Julia console:

```
using Sockets
conn = Sockets.connect(8080)
#> TCPSocket(Base.Libc.WindowsRawSocket(0x0000000000000340) open, 0 bytes
waiting)
write(conn, "Do you hear me?\n")
```

The `listen` function has some variants, for example, `listen(IPv6(0),2001)` creates a TCP server that listens on port `2001` on all IPv6 interfaces. Similarly, instead of `readline`, there are also simpler `read` methods:

- `read(conn, UInt8)`: This method blocks until there is a byte to read from `conn`, and then returns it. Use `convert(Char, n)` to convert a `UInt8` value into `Char`. This will let you see the ASCII letter for `UInt8` you read in.
- `read(conn, Char)`: This method blocks until there is a byte to read from `conn`, and then returns it.

The important aspect about the communication API is that the code looks like synchronous code executing line by line, even though the I/O is actually happening asynchronously through the use of tasks. We don't have to worry about writing callbacks as in some other languages. For more details about possible methods, refer to the *I/O and Network* section at `https://docs.julialang.org/en/latest/base/io-network/`.

Interacting with databases

Open Database Connectivity (**ODBC**) is a low-level protocol for establishing connections with the majority of databases and datasources (for more details, refer to `http://en.wikipedia.org/wiki/Open_Database_Connectivity`).

Julia has an `ODBC` package that enables Julia scripts to talk to ODBC data sources. Install the package through `Pkg.add("ODBC")`, and at the start of the code, run it `using ODBC`.

The package can work with a system **Data Source Name** (**DSN**) that contains all the concrete connection information, such as server name, database, credentials, and so on. Every operating system has its own utility to make DSNs. In Windows, the ODBC administrator can be reached by navigating to **Control Panel** | **Administrative Tools** | **ODBC Data Sources**; on other systems, you have IODBC or Unix ODBC.

For example, suppose we have a database called pubs running in a SQL Server or a MySQL Server, and the connection is described with a DSN pubsODBC. (Included in the code download is a script, instpubs.sql, to install the pubs database with only the titles table in a SQL Server; the script can be easily adapted for MySQL.)

Now, I can connect to this database as follows:

```
// code in Chapter 8\odbc.jl
using ODBC
ODBC.DSN("pubsODBC",<user>,<password>)
```

This returns an output as follows:

```
Connection Data Source: pubsODBC
pubsODBC Connection Number: 1
    Contains resultset? No
```

You can also store this DSN object in a dsn variable, as follows:

```
dsn = ODBC.DSN("pubsODBC",<user>,<password>)
```

This way, you are able to close the connection when necessary through ODBC.disconnect!(dsn) to save database resources, or handle multiple connections.

To launch a query on the titles table, you only need to use the query function, as follows:

```
results = ODBC.query(dsn, "select * from titles")
```

The result is of the DataFrame type and the dimensions are 18 x 10, because the table contains 18 rows and 10 columns, for example; here are some of the columns:

Row	title
1	"The Busy Executive's Database Guide"
2	"Cooking with Computers: Surreptitious Balance Sheets"
3	"You Can Combat Computer Stress!"
4	"Straight Talk About Computers"
5	"Silicon Valley Gastronomic Treats"
6	"The Gourmet Microwave"

Row	_type	pub_id	price	advance	royalty	ytd_sales
1	"business "	"1389"	19.99	5000.0	10	4095
2	"business "	"1389"	11.95	5000.0	10	3876
3	"business "	"0736"	2.99	10125.0	24	18722
4	"business "	"1389"	19.99	5000.0	10	4095
5	"mod_cook "	"0877"	19.99	0.0	12	2032
6	"mod_cook "	"0877"	2.99	15000.0	24	22246

If you haven't stored the query results in a variable, you can always retrieve them from `conn.resultset`, where `conn` is an existing connection. Now we have all the functionalities of `DataFrames` at our disposal to work with this data. Launching data-manipulation queries works in the same way:

```
updsql = "update titles set type = 'psychology' where
    title_id='BU1032'"
stmt = ODBC.prepare(dsn, updsql)
ODBC.execute!(stmt)
```

In order to see which ODBC drivers are installed on the system, ask for `ODBC.listdrivers()`. The already available DSNs are listed with `ODBC.listdsns()`.

Julia already has database drivers for Memcache, FoundationDB, MongoDB, Redis, MySQL, SQLite, and PostgreSQL (for more information, refer to `https://github.com/JuliaDatabases`).

Parallel operations and computing

In our multicore CPU and clustered computing world, it is imperative for a new language to have excellent parallel computing capabilities. This is one of the main strengths of Julia: providing an environment based on message-passing between multiple processes that can execute on the same machine or on remote machines.

In that sense, it implements the actor model (as Erlang, Elixir, and Pony do), but we'll see that the actual coding happens on a higher level than receiving and sending messages between processes, or workers (processors) as Julia calls them. The developer only needs to explicitly manage the main process from which all other workers are started. The message send and receive operations are simulated by higher-level operations that look like function calls.

Creating processes

To start with processes, add and make available the `Distributed` package with `add Distributed`, and `using Distributed`.

Julia can be started as a REPL or as a separate application with a number of workers, n, available. The following command starts n processes on the local machine (this command includes the `Distributed` package automatically):

```
// code in Chapter 8\parallel.jl
julia -p n   # starts REPL with n workers
```

These workers are different processes, not threads, so they do not share memory.

To get the most out of a machine, set n equal to the number of processor cores. For example, when n is 8, you have, in fact, nine workers: one for the REPL shell itself, and eight others that are ready to do parallel tasks. Every worker has its own integer identifier, which we can see by calling the `workers` function, `workers()`. This returns the following:

```
8-element Array{Int64,1} containing:   2  3  4  5  6  7  8  9
```

Process 1 is the REPL worker. We can now iterate over the workers with the following command:

```
for pid in workers()
  # do something with each process (pid = process id)
end
```

Each worker can get its own process ID with the `myid()` function. If you need more workers, adding new ones is easy:

```
addprocs(5)
```

This returns `5-element Array{Any,1}`, which contains their process identifiers, 10 11 12 13 14. The default method adds workers on the local machine, but the `addprocs` method accepts arguments to start processes on remote machines via SSH. This is the secure shell protocol that enables you to execute commands on a remote computer via a shell in a totally encrypted manner.

The number of available workers is given by `nprocs()`; in our case, this is 14. A worker can be removed by calling `rmprocs()` with its identifier; for example, `rmprocs(3)` stops the worker with the ID 3.

All these workers communicate via TCP ports and run on the same machine, which is why it is called a local cluster. To activate workers on a cluster of computers, start Julia as follows:

```
julia --machine-file machines driver.jl
```

Here, `machines` is a file that contains the names of the computers you want to engage, as follows:

```
node01
node01
node02
node02
node03
```

Here `node01`, `node02`, and `node03` are the three names of computers in the cluster, and we want to start two workers each on `node01` and `node02`, and one worker on `node03`.

The `driver.jl` file is the script that runs the calculations and has a process identifier of `1`. This command uses a password-less SSH login to start the worker processes on the specified machines. The following screenshot shows all the eight processors on an eight-core machine when engaged in a parallel operation:

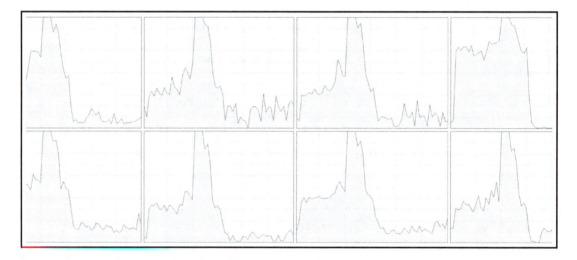

The horizontal axis is time, and the vertical is the CPU usage. On each core, a worker process is engaged in a long-running Fibonacci calculation.

Processors can be dynamically added or removed to a master Julia process, locally on symmetric multiprocessor systems, remotely on a computer cluster, as well as in the cloud. If more versatility is needed, you can work with the `ClusterManager` type (see http://docs.julialang.org/en/latest/manual/parallel-computing/).

Using low-level communications

Julia's native parallel computing model is based on two primitives: **remote calls** and **remote references**. At this level, we can give a certain worker a function with arguments to execute with `remotecall`, and get the result back with fetch. As a trivial example in the following code, we call upon worker 2 to execute a square function on the number 1000:

```
r1 = remotecall(x -> x^2, 2, 1000)
```

This returns Future(2, 1, 15, nothing).

The arguments are: the worker ID, the function, and the function's arguments. Such a remote call returns immediately, thus not blocking the main worker (the REPL in this case). The main process continues executing while the remote worker does the assigned job. The `remotecall` function returns a variable, r1, of the Future type, which is a reference to the computed result, which we can get using fetch:

```
fetch(r1)
```

This returns 1000000.

The call to fetch will block the main process until worker 2 has finished the calculation. The main processor can also run wait(r1), which also blocks until the result of the remote call becomes available. If you need the remote result immediately in the local operation, use the following command:

```
remotecall_fetch(sin, 5, 2pi)
```

Which returns −2.4492935982947064e-16.

This is more efficient than fetch(remotecall(..)).

You can also use the @spawnat macro, which evaluates the expression in the second argument on the worker specified by the first argument:

```
r2 = @spawnat 4 sqrt(2) # lets worker 4 calculate sqrt(2)
   fetch(r2)  # returns 1.4142135623730951
```

This is made even easier with @spawn, which only needs an expression to evaluate, because it decides for itself where it will be executed: r3 = @spawn sqrt(5) returns RemoteRef(5,1,26) and fetch(r3) returns 2.23606797749979.

To execute a certain function on all the workers, we can use a comprehension:

```
r = [@spawnat w sqrt(5) for w in workers()]
fetch(r[3]) # returns 2.23606797749979
```

To execute the same statement on all the workers, we can also use the @everywhere macro:

```
@everywhere println(myid()) 1
            From worker 2: 2
            From worker 3: 3
            From worker 4: 4
            From worker 7: 7
            From worker 5: 5
            From worker 6: 6
            From worker 8: 8
            From worker 9: 9
```

All the workers correspond to different processes; they therefore do not share variables, for example:

```
x = 5 #> 5
@everywhere println(x) #> 5
  # exception on worker 2: ERROR: UndefVarError: x not defined ...
        ...and 11 more exception(s)
```

The x variable is only known in the main process, all the other workers return the ERROR: x not defined error message.

@everywhere can also be used to make the data, such as the w variable, available to all processors, for example, @everywhere w = 8.

The following example makes a defs.jl source file available to all the workers:

```
@everywhere include("defs.jl")
```

Or, more explicitly, a fib(n) function, as follows:

```
@everywhere function fib(n)
  if (n < 2) then
    return n
  else return fib(n-1) + fib(n-2)
  end
end
```

In order to be able to perform its task, a remote worker needs access to the function it executes. You can make sure that all workers know about the functions they need by loading the `functions.jl` source code with `include`, making it available to all workers:

```
include("functions.jl")
```

In a cluster, the contents of this file (and any files loaded recursively) will be sent over the network.

A best practice is to separate your code into two files: one file (`functions.jl`) that contains the functions and parameters that need to be run in parallel, and the other file (`driver.jl`) that manages the processing and collects the results. Use the `include("functions.jl")` command in `driver.jl` to import the functions and parameters to all processors.

An alternative is to specify that the files load on the command line. If you need the `file1.jl` and `file2.jl` source files on all the n processors at startup time, use the `julia -p n -L file1.jl -L file2.jl driver.jl` syntax, where `driver.jl` is the script that organizes the computations.

Data-movement between workers (such as when calling `fetch`) needs to be reduced as much as possible in order to get performance and scalability.

If every worker needs to know the d variable, this can be broadcast to all processes with the following code:

```
for pid in workers()
    remotecall(pid, x -> (global d; d = x; nothing), d)
end
```

Each worker then has its local copy of data. Scheduling the workers is done with tasks (refer to the *Tasks* section of Chapter 4, *Control Flow*), so that no locking is required; for example, when a communication operation such as `fetch` or `wait` is executed, the current task is suspended, and the scheduler picks another task to run. When the wait event completes (for example, the data shows up), the current task is restarted.

In many cases, however, you do not have to specify or create processes to do parallel programming in Julia, as we will see in the next section.

Parallel loops and maps

A `for` loop with a large number of iterations is a good candidate for parallel execution, and Julia has a special construct to do this: the `@parallel` macro, which can be used for the `for` loops and comprehensions.

Let's calculate an approximation for Π using the famous Buffon's needle problem. If we drop a needle onto a floor with equal parallel strips of wood, what is the probability that the needle will cross a line between two strips? Let's take a look at the following screenshot:

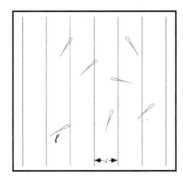

Without getting into the mathematical intricacies of this problem (if you are interested, see `http://en.wikipedia.org/wiki/Buffon's_needle`), a `buffon(n)` function can be deduced from the model assumptions that returns an approximation for Π when throwing the needle n times (assuming the length of the needle, `l`, and the width, `d`, between the strips both equal 1):

```
// code in Chapter 8\parallel_loops_maps.jl
function buffon(n)
  hit = 0
  for i = 1:n
    mp = rand()
    phi = (rand() * pi) - pi / 2 # angle at which needle falls
    xright = mp + cos(phi)/2 # x location of needle
    xleft = mp - cos(phi)/2
    # does needle cross either x == 0 or x == 1?
    p = (xright >= 1 || xleft <= 0) ? 1 : 0
    hit += p
  end
  miss = n - hit
  piapprox = n / hit * 2
end
```

With ever-increasing n, the calculation time increases, because the number of the `for` iterations that have to be executed in one thread on one processor increases, but we also get a better estimate for Π:

```
@time buffon(100000)
    0.208500 seconds (504.79 k allocations: 25.730 MiB, 7.10% gc time)
  3.1441597233139444

@time buffon(100000000)
    4.112683 seconds (5 allocations: 176 bytes)
    3.141258861373451
```

However, what if we could spread the calculations over the available processors? For this, we have to rearrange our code a bit. In the sequential version, the variable hit is increased on every iteration inside the `for` loop with the p amount (which is 0 or 1). In the parallel version, we rewrite the code, so that this p is exactly the result of the `for` loop (one calculation) done on one of the involved processors.

Julia also provides a `@distributed` macro that acts on a `for` loop, splitting the range and distributing it to each process. It optionally takes a "reducer" as its first argument. If a reducer is specified, the results from each remote procedure will be aggregated using the reducer. In the following example, we use the `(+)` function as a reducer, which means that the last values of the parallel blocks on each worker will be summed to calculate the final value of `hit`:

```
function buffon_par(n)
  hit = @distributed (+) for i = 1:n
      mp = rand()
      phi = (rand() * pi) - pi / 2
      xright = mp + cos(phi)/2
      xleft = mp - cos(phi)/2
        (xright >= 1 || xleft <= 0) ? 1 : 0
    end
  miss = n - hit
  piapprox = n / hit * 2
end
```

On my machine with eight processors, this gives the following results:

```
@time buffon_par(100000)
  1.058487 seconds (951.35 k allocations: 48.192 MiB, 2.04% gc time)
  3.15059861373661

@time buffon_par(100000000)
  0.735853 seconds (1.84 k allocations: 133.156 KiB)
  3.1418106012575633
```

We see much better performance for the higher number of iterations (a factor of 5.6 in this case). By changing a normal `for` loop into a parallel-reducing version, we were able to get substantial improvements in the calculation time, at the cost of higher memory consumption. In general, always test whether the parallel version really is an improvement over the sequential version in your specific case!

The first argument of `@distributed` is the reducing operator (here, `(+)`), the second is the `for` loop, which must start on the same line. The calculations in the loop must be independent of one another, because the order in which they run is arbitrary, given that they are scheduled over the different workers. The actual reduction (summing up in this case) is done on the calling process.

Any variables used inside the parallel loop will be copied (broadcasted) to each process. Because of this, the code, such as the following, will fail to initialize the `arr` array, because each process has a copy of it:

```
arr = zeros(100000)
@distributed for i=1:100000
  arr[i] = i
end
```

Afterward the loop, `arr` still contains all the zeros, because it is the copy on the master worker.

If the computational task is to apply a function to all elements in some collection, you can use a **parallel map** operation through the `pmap` function. The `pmap` function takes the following form: `pmap(f, coll)`, applies an `f` function on each element of the `coll` collection in parallel, but preserves the order of the collection in the result. Suppose we have to calculate the rank of a number of large matrices. We can do this sequentially, as follows:

```
using LinearAlgebra
function rank_marray()
  marr = [rand(1000,1000) for i=1:10]
  for arr in marr
      println(LinearAlgebra.rank(arr))
  end
end

@time rank_marray() # prints out ten times 1000
7.310404 seconds (91.33 k allocations: 162.878 MiB, 1.15% gc time)
```

In the following, parallelizing also gives benefits (a factor of `1.6`):

```
function prank_marray()
  marr = [rand(1000,1000) for i=1:10]
  println(pmap(LinearAlgebra.rank, marr))
end

@time prank_marray()
5.966216 seconds (4.15 M allocations: 285.610 MiB, 2.15% gc time)
```

The `@distributed` macro and `pmap` are both powerful tools to tackle **map-reduce** problems.

Julia's model for building a large parallel application works by means of a global distributed address space. This means that you can hold a reference to an object that lives on another machine participating in a computation. These references are easily manipulated and passed around between machines, making it simple to keep track of what's being computed where. Also, machines can be added in mid-computation when needed.

Summary

In this chapter, we explored a lot of material. We learned how the I/O system in Julia is constructed, how to work with files and `DataFrames`, and how to connect with databases using ODBC. The basics of network programming in Julia were also discussed, and then we got an overview of the parallel computing functionality, from primitive operations to map-reduce functions and distributed arrays.

In the next chapter, we will take a look at how Julia interacts with the command line and with other languages, and discuss a number of performance tips.

Running External Programs

9

Sometimes, your code needs to interact with programs in the outside world, be it the operating system in which it runs or other languages such as C or Fortran. This chapter shows how straightforward it is to run external programs from Julia and covers the following topics:

- Running shell commands—interpolation and pipelining
- Calling C and Fortran
- Calling Python
- Performance tips

Running shell commands

To interact with the operating system from within the Julia REPL, there are a few helper functions available, as follows:

- `pwd()`: this function prints the current directory, for example, `"d:\\test"`
- `cd("d:\\test\\week1")`: this function helps to navigate to subdirectories
- `;`: in the interactive shell, you can also use shell mode using the `;` modifier, for example: `; cd folder`: navigates to `folder`

However, what if you want to run a shell command by using the operating system (the OS)? Julia offers efficient shell integration through the `run` function, which takes an object of type `Cmd`, defined by enclosing a command string in backticks (`` ` ` ``).

The following are some examples for Linux or macOS X (at the time of writing: September 2018):

```
# Code in Chapter 9\shell.jl:
cmd = `echo Julia is smart`
    typeof(cmd) #> Cmd
    run(cmd) # returns Julia is smart
    run(`date`) #> Sat Jul 14 09:44:50 GMT 2018
    cmd = `cat file1.txt`
    run(cmd) # prints the contents of file1.txt
```

The preceding code does not work on Windows, although it worked until version 0.6. This is a bug in version 1.0 and is expected to be resolved in the near future.

Be careful to enclose the command text in backticks (`` ` ``), not single quotes (').

If the execution of `cmd` by the OS goes wrong, `run` throws a `failed process` error. You might want to test the command first before running it; `success(cmd)` will return `true` if it executes successfully, otherwise it returns `false`.

Julia forks commands as **child processes** from the Julia process. Instead of immediately running the command in the shell, backticks create a `Cmd` object to represent the command. This can then be run, connected to other commands via pipes, and read or written to.

Interpolation

String interpolation with the `$` operator is allowed in a command object, like this:

```
file = "file1.txt"
cmd = `cat $file` # equivalent to `cat file1.txt`
run(cmd) #> prints the contents of file1.txt
```

This is very similar to the string interpolation with `$` in strings (refer to the *Strings* section in Chapter 2, *Variables, Types, and Operations*).

Pipelining

Julia defines a `pipeline` function to redirect the output of a command as the input to the following command:

```
run(pipeline(`cat $file`,"test.txt"))
```

This writes the contents of the file referred to by `$file` into `test.txt`, which is shown as follows:

```
run(pipeline("test.txt",`cat`))
```

This `pipeline` function can even take several successive commands, as follows:

```
run(pipeline(`echo $("\nhi\nJulia")`,`cat`,`grep -n J`)) #>
    3:Julia
```

If the file `tosort.txt` contains B, A, and C on consecutive lines, then the following command will sort the lines:

```
run(pipeline(`cat "tosort.txt"`,`sort`))   # returns A B C
```

Another example is to search for the word `is` in all the text files in the current folder. Use the following command:

```
run(`grep is $(readdir())`)
```

To capture the result of a command in Julia, use `read` or `readline`:

```
a = read(pipeline(`cat "tosort.txt"`,`sort`))
```

Now a has the value A\r\nB\r\nC\n.

Multiple commands can be run in parallel with the `&` operator:

```
run(`cat "file1.txt"` & `cat "tosort.txt"`)
```

This will print the lines of the two files intermingled, because the printing happens concurrently.

Using this functionality requires careful testing, and, probably, the code will differ according to the operating system on which your Julia program runs. You can obtain the OS from the variable `Sys.KERNEL`, or use the functions `iswindows`, `isunix`, `islinux`, and `isosx` from the `Sys` package, which was specifically designed to handle platform variations. For example, let's say we want to execute the function `fun1()` (unless we are on Windows, in which case the function is `fun2()`). We can write this as follows:

```
Sys.iswindows() ? fun1 : fun2
```

Or we can write it with the more usual `if...else` keyword:

```
if Sys.iswindows()
    fun1
else
    fun2
end
```

Calling C and Fortran

While Julia can rightfully claim to obviate the need to write some C or Fortran code, it is possible that you will need to interact with the existing C or Fortran shared libraries. Functions in such a library can be called directly by Julia, with no glue code, boilerplate code, or compilation needed. Because Julia's LLVM compiler generates native code, calling a C function from Julia has exactly the same overhead as calling the same function from C code itself. However, first, we need to know a few more things:

- For calling out to C, we need to work with pointer types; a native pointer `Ptr{T}` is nothing more than the memory address for a variable of type `T`. You can use `Cstring` if the value is null-terminated.
- At this lower level, the term `primitive` is also used. `primitive` is a concrete type whose data consists of bits, such as `Int8`, `UInt8`, `Int32`, `Float64`, `Bool`, and `Char`.
- To pass a string to C, it is converted to a contiguous byte array representation with the function `unsafe_string()`; given `Ptr` to a C string, it returns a Julia string.

Here is how to call a C function in a shared library (calling Fortran is done similarly). Suppose we want to know the value of an environment variable in our system, say, the language; we can obtain this by calling the C function `getenv` from the shared library `libc`:

```
# code in Chapter 9\callc.jl:
lang = ccall( (:getenv, "libc"), Cstring, (Cstring,), "LANG")
```

This returns a `Cstring`. To see its string contents, execute `unsafe_string(lang)`, which returns en_US.

In general, `ccall` takes the following arguments:

- A (`:function`, `"library"`) tuple, where the name of the C function (here, `getenv`) is used as a symbol, and the library name (here, `libc`) as a string
- The return type (here, `Cstring`), which can also be any `primitive`, or `Ptr`
- A `Cstring` as input arguments: note the tuple notation (`Cstring,`)
- The actual arguments, if there are any (here, `"LANG"`)

It is generally advisable to test for the existence of a library before doing the call. This can be tested like this: `find_library(["libc"])`, which returns `"libc"` when the library is found, or `" "` when it cannot find the library.

When calling a Fortran function, all inputs must be passed by reference. Arguments to C functions are, in general, automatically converted, and the returned values in C types are also converted to Julia types. Arrays of Booleans are handled differently in C and Julia and cannot be passed directly, so they must be manually converted. The same applies for some system-dependent types.

The `ccall` function will also automatically ensure that all of its arguments will be preserved from garbage collection until the call returns. C types are mapped to Julia types. For example, `short` is mapped to `Int16`, and `double` to `Float64`.

A complete table of these mappings, as well as a lot more intricate details, can be found in the Julia docs at `http://docs.julialang.org/en/latest/manual/calling-c-and-fortran-code/`. The other way around is also possible, by calling Julia functions from C code (or embedding Julia in C); refer to `http://docs.julialang.org/en/latest/manual/embedding/`. Julia and C can also share array data without copying.

If you have the existing C code, you must compile it as a shared library to call it from Julia. With GCC, you can do this using the `-shared -fPIC` command-line arguments. Support for C++ is more limited and is provided by the `Cpp` and `Clang` packages.

Calling Python

The `PyCall` package provides us with the ability to call Python from Julia code. As always, add this package to your Julia environment with `add PyCall`. Then, you can start using it in the REPL, or in a script as follows:

```
using PyCall
py"10*10"                    #> 100
@pyimport math
math.sin(math.pi / 2) #> 1.0
```

As we can see with the `@pyimport` macro, we can easily import any Python library; functions inside such a library are called with the familiar dot notation.

For more details, refer to `https://github.com/stevengj/PyCall.jl`.

Performance tips

Throughout this book, we have paid attention to performance. Here, we summarize some highlighted performance topics and give some additional tips. These tips need not always be used, and you should always benchmark or profile the code and the effect of a tip. However, applying some of them can often yield a remarkable performance improvement. Using type annotations everywhere is certainly *not* the way to go; Julia's type inferring engine does that work for you:

- **Refrain from using global variables**. If unavoidable, make them constant with `const`, or at least annotate the types. It is better to use local variables instead; they are often only kept on the stack (or even in registers), especially if they are immutable.
- Use a `main()` function to structure your code.
- Use functions that do their work on local variables via function arguments, rather than mutating global objects.

- Type stability is very important:
  - Avoid changing the types of variables over time
  - The return type of a function should only depend on the type of the arguments

Even if you do not know the types that will be used in a function, but you do know it will always be of the same type T, then functions should be defined keeping that in mind, as in the following code snippet:

```
function myFunc(a::T, c::Int) where T
    # code
end
```

- If large arrays or dictionaries are needed, indicate their final size with `sizehint!` from the start (refer to the *Ranges and arrays* section of Chapter 2, *Variables, Types, and Operations*). The following is an example of its use:

```
d1 = Dict();
sizehint!(d1, 10000);
for i in [1:10000] d1[string(i)] = 2*i; end;
```

- If `arr` is a very large array that you no longer need, you can free the memory it occupies by setting `arr = nothing`. The occupied memory will be released the next time the garbage collector runs. You can force this to happen by invoking `GC.gc()`.
- In certain cases (such as real-time applications), disabling garbage collection (temporarily) with `GC.enable(false)` can be useful.
- Use named functions instead of anonymous functions.
- In general, use small functions.
- Don't test for the types of arguments inside a function, use an argument type annotation instead.
- If necessary, code different versions of a function (several methods) according to the types, so that multiple dispatch applies. Normally, this won't be necessary, because the JIT compiler is optimized to deal with types as they come.
- Use types for keyword arguments; avoid using the splat operator (. . .) for dynamic lists of keyword arguments.
- Using mutating APIs (functions with ! at the end) is helpful, for example, to avoid copying large arrays.
- Prefer array operations to comprehensions, for example, `x.^2` is considerably faster than `[val^2 for val in x]`.
- Don't use `try`/`catch` in the inner loop of a calculation.

- Use immutable types (`cfr.` package `ImmutableArrays`).
- Avoid using type `Any`, especially in collection types.
- Avoid using abstract types in a collection.
- Type annotate fields in composite types.
- Avoid using a large number of variables, large temporary arrays, and collections, because this provokes a great deal of garbage collection. Also, don't make copies of variables if you don't have to.
- Avoid using string interpolation (`$`) when writing to a file, just write the values.
- Devectorize your code, that is, use explicit `for` loops on array elements instead of simply working with the arrays and matrices. (This is the exact opposite of advice commonly given to R, MATLAB, or Python users.)
- If appropriate, use a parallel reducing form with `@distributed` instead of a normal `for` loop (refer to `Chapter 8`, *IO, Networking, and Parallel Computing*).
- Reduce data movement between workers in a parallel execution as much as possible (refer to `Chapter 8`, *IO, Networking, and Parallel Computing*).
- Fix deprecation warnings.
- Use the macro `@inbounds` so that no array bounds checking occurs in expressions (if you are absolutely certain that no `BoundsError` occurs!).
- Avoid using `eval` at runtime.

In general, split your code into functions. Data types will be determined at function calls, and when a function returns. Types that are not supplied will be inferred, but the `Any` type does not translate to efficient code. If types are stable (that is, variables stick to the same type) and can be inferred, then your code will run quickly.

Tools to use

Execute a function with certain parameter values, and then use `@time` (refer to the *Generic functions and multiple dispatch* section in `Chapter 3`, *Functions*) to measure the elapsed time and memory allocation. If too much memory is allocated, investigate the code for type problems.

Experiment with different tips and techniques in the script `array_product_benchmark.jl`. Use `code_typed` (refer to the *Reflection capabilities* section in `Chapter 7`, *Metaprogramming in Julia*) to see if type `Any` is inferred.

A **profiler** tool is available in the standard library to measure the performance of your running code and identify possible bottleneck lines. This works through calling your code with the `@profile` macro (refer to `https://docs.julialang.org/en/latest/manual/profile/`).

The `ProfileView` package provides a nice graphical browser to investigate profile results (follow the tutorial at `https://github.com/timholy/ProfileView.jl`).

`BenchmarkingTools` is an excellent package with macros and tools for benchmarking your code.

For more tips, examples, and argumentation about performance, look up `http://docs.julialang.org/en/latest/manual/performance-tips/`.

Summary

In this chapter, we saw how easy it is to run commands at the operating system level. Interfacing with C is not that much more difficult, although it is somewhat specialized. Finally, we reviewed the best practices at our disposal to make Julia perform at its best. In the previous chapter, we got to know some of the more important packages when using Julia in real projects.

In the next chapter, we will be digging deeper into the standard library and on how to use the package manager to explore different packages in Julia.

10
The Standard Library and Packages

In this chapter, we will look anew at the standard library and explore the ever-growing ecosystem of packages for Julia. We will discuss the following topics:

- Digging deeper into the standard library
- Julia's package manager
- Graphics in Julia
- Using Plots on data

Digging deeper into the standard library

The standard library is written in Julia and is comprised of a very broad range of functionalities: from regular expressions, working with dates and times, a package manager, internationalization and Unicode, linear algebra, complex numbers, specialized mathematical functions, statistics, I/O and networking, **Fast Fourier Transformations (FFT)**, and parallel computing, to macros, and reflection. Julia provides a firm and broad foundation for numerical computing and data science (for example, much of what NumPy has to offer is provided). Despite being targeted at numerical computing and data science, Julia aims to be a general-purpose programming language.

The source code of the standard library can be found in the `share\julia\base` and `share\julia\stdlib` subfolders of Julia's root installation folder. Coding in Julia leads almost naturally to this source code, for example, when viewing all the methods of a particular function with `methods()`, or when using the `@which` macro to find out more about a certain method (refer to the *Generic functions and multiple dispatch* section in Chapter 3, *Functions*).

Here, we see the output of the command `methods(+)`, which lists 167+ methods available in Julia version 1.0, together with their source locations:

```
julia> methods(+)
# 167 methods for generic function "+":
[1] +(x::Bool, z::Complex{Bool}) in Base at complex.jl:277
[2] +(x::Bool, y::Bool) in Base at bool.jl:104
[3] +(x::Bool) in Base at bool.jl:101
[4] +(x::Bool, y::T) where T<:AbstractFloat in Base at bool.jl:112
[5] +(x::Bool, z::Complex) in Base at complex.jl:284
[6] +(a::Float16, b::Float16) in Base at float.jl:392
[7] +(x::Float32, y::Float32) in Base at float.jl:394
[8] +(x::Float64, y::Float64) in Base at float.jl:395
[9] +(z::Complex{Bool}, x::Bool) in Base at complex.jl:278
[10] +(z::Complex{Bool}, x::Real) in Base at complex.jl:292
[11] +(::Missing, ::Missing) in Base at missing.jl:92
[12] +(::Missing) in Base at missing.jl:79
[13] +(::Missing, ::Number) in Base at missing.jl:93
[14] +(level::Base.CoreLogging.LogLevel, inc::Integer) in Base.CoreLogging at logging.jl:106
```

The same command in a Jupyter notebook even provides hyperlinks to the source code.

We covered some of the most important types and functions in the previous chapters, and you can refer to the manual for a more exhaustive overview at `https://docs.julialang.org/en/latest/base/base/`.

It is certainly important to know that Julia contains a wealth of functional constructs to work with collections, such as the `reduce`, `fold`, `min`, `max`, `sum`, `any`, `all`, `map`, and `filter` functions. Some examples are as follows:

- `filter(f, coll)` applies the function `f` to all the elements of the collection `coll`:

    ```
    # code in Chapter 10\stdlib.jl:
    filter(x -> iseven(x), 1:10)
    ```

This returns `5-element Array{Int64,1}`, which consists of 2, 4, 6, 8, and 10.

- `mapreduce(f, op, coll)` applies the function `f` to all the elements of `coll` and then reduces this to one resulting value by applying the operation `op`:

```
mapreduce(x -> sqrt(x), +, 1:10) #> 22.4682781862041
# which is equivalent to:
sum(map(x -> sqrt(x), 1:10))
```

When working in the REPL, it can be handy to store a variable in the operating system's clipboard if you want to clean the REPL's variables memory with `workspace()`. Consider the ensuing example:

```
a = 42
using InteractiveUtils
clipboard(a)
# quit and restart REPL:
a # returns ERROR: a not defined
a = clipboard() # returns "42"
```

This also works while copying information from another application, for example, a string from a website or from a text editor.

Julia's package manager

The *Packages* section in `Chapter 1`, *Installing the Julia Platform*, introduced us to Julia's package system (some 1,906 packages in September 2018 and counting) and its manager program `Pkg`. Most Julia libraries are written exclusively in Julia; this makes them not only more portable, but also an excellent source for learning and experimenting with Julia in your own modified versions. The packages that are useful for data scientists are `Stats`, `Distributions`, `GLM`, and `Optim`. You can search for applicable packages in the `https://pkg.julialang.org/` repository.

Installing and updating packages

Use the `status` command in the package REPL mode to see which packages have already been installed:

```
(v1.0) pkg> status
    Status `C:\Users\CVO\.julia\environments\v1.0\Project.toml`
  [336ed68f] CSV v0.3.1
  [0fe7c1db] DataArrays v0.7.0
  [a93c6f00] DataFrames v0.13.1
  [aaf54ef3] DistributedArrays v0.5.1
  [f67ccb44] HDF5 v0.10.0
  [7073ff75] IJulia v1.10.0
  [83e8ac13] IniFile v0.5.0
  [682c06a0] JSON v0.19.0
  [9c8b4983] LightXML v0.8.0
  [d4b2101a] Lint v0.5.2
  [e1d29d7a] Missings v0.3.0
  [91a5bcdd] Plots v0.20.1
  [438e738f] PyCall v1.18.3
  [d330b81b] PyPlot v2.6.2
  [ce6b1742] RDatasets v0.5.0
  [ddb6d928] YAML v0.3.2
```

It is advisable to regularly (and certainly before installing a new package) execute the `up` command to ensure that your local package repository is up-to-date and synchronized, as shown in the following screenshot:

```
(v1.0) pkg> up
  Updating registry at `C:\Users\CVO\.julia\registries\General`
  Updating git-repo `https://github.com/JuliaRegistries/General.git`
Resolving package versions...
  Updating `C:\Users\CVO\.julia\environments\v1.0\Project.toml`
[no changes]
  Updating `C:\Users\CVO\.julia\environments\v1.0\Manifest.toml`
[no changes]

(v1.0) pkg>
```

If you only want to update one package, specify the package name after the `up` command.

The `rm` command is used for deleting a package, but it removes only the reference to it. To completely remove the sources, use the `gc` command.

As we saw in `Chapter 1`, *Installing the Julia Platform*, packages are installed via `add PackageName` and brought into scope using `PackageName`. You can also clone a package from a `git` repository as follows:

```
Pkg.clone("git@github.com:ericchiang/ANN.jl.git")
```

If you need to force a certain package to a certain version (perhaps an older version), use `pin`. For example, use `pin HDF5, v"0.4.3"` to force the use of version 0.4.3 of package `HDF5`, even when you already have version 0.4.4 installed.

Graphics in Julia

Several packages exist to plot data and visualize data relations; `Plots` and `PyPlot` are some of the most commonly used:

- `PyPlot`: (refer to the *Installing and working with Jupyter* section in `Chapter 1`, *Installing the Julia Platform*) This package works with no overhead through the `PyCall` package. The following is a summary of the main commands:
  - `plot(y)`, `plot(x,y)` plots y versus 0,1,2,3 or versus x: `loglog(x,y)`
  - `semilogx(x,y)`, `semilogy(x,y)` for log scale plots
  - `title("A title")`, `xlabel("x-axis")`, and `ylabel("foo")` to set labels
  - `legend(["curve 1", "curve 2"], "northwest")` to write a legend at the upper-left
  - `grid()`, `axis( "equal")` adds grid lines, and uses equal x and y scaling
  - `title(L"the curve $e^\sqrt{x}$")` sets the title with a LaTeX equation
  - `savefig( "fig.png")`, `savefig( "fig.eps")` saves as the PNG or EPS image

- `Plots`: (refer to the *Adding a new package* section in `Chapter 1`, *Installing the Julia Platform*) This is the favorite package in the Julia Computing community. It is a visualization interface and toolset that works with several backends, in particular GR (the default backend), `PyPlot`, and `PlotyJS`. To start using a certain backend, type `gr()` or `pyplot()` after you have given the command `using PyPlots`.

Plot styles can be adapted by so-called **attributes** (documented at `http://docs.juliaplots.org/latest/attributes/`). Some of the most used attributes are:

- `* xaxis`, `yaxis`, and `zaxis`
- `line`—to adapt line visualizations
- `fill`—to fill surfaces with color and transparency
- The `subplot` category to modify visualization of an entire plot
- The `plot` category to modify visualization of an entire plot

Lots of other plots can be drawn in `Plots`, such as scatter plots, 2D histograms, and box plots. You can even draw in the REPL if you want to.

Comprehensive documentation and a tutorial can be found here: `http://docs.juliaplots.org/latest/`

We apply `Plots` to visualize data in the next section.

Using Plots on data

Let's apply `Plots` to show a graph on the famous Iris flower data set, which can be found in the `Rdatasets` package (don't forget to first add this package). We also need the `StatPlots` package when visualizing `DataFrames`. It contains an `@df` macro, which makes this much easier. Here is the code to draw a scatter plot:

```
# code in Chapter 10\plots_iris.jl
using PyPlots, StatPlots, RDatasets
iris = dataset("datasets", "iris")
@df iris scatter(:SepalLength, :SepalWidth, group=:Species,m=(0.5,
[:+ :h :star7], 4), bg=RGB(1.0,1.0,1.0))
```

We plot the `sepalwidth` property against the `sepallength` of the flowers. In the preceding code, `iris` is the name of our `DataFrame`, which is passed as the first argument to the `@df` macro. We then call the scatter function to obtain the following plot:

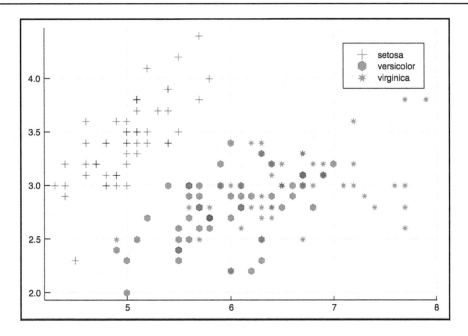

Summary

In this chapter, we looked at the built-in functionality Julia has to offer in its standard library. We also took a peek at some of the more useful packages to apply in the data sciences.

We hope that you now have a clear overview of Julia's capabilities and it's time to put them to some good use as in the next chapter you will be creating your first Julia app.

11
Creating Our First Julia App

Now that you have a working Julia installation and your IDE of choice is ready to run, it's time to put them to some good use. In this chapter, you'll learn how to apply Julia for data analysis—a domain that is central to the language, so expect to be impressed!

We will learn to perform exploratory data analysis with Julia. In the process, we'll take a look at `RDatasets`, a package that provides access to over 700 learning datasets. We'll load one of them, the Iris flowers dataset, and we'll manipulate it using standard data analysis functions. Then we'll look more closely at the data by employing common visualization techniques. And finally, we'll see how to persist and (re)load our data.

But, in order to do that, first we need to revisit and take a look at some of the language's most important building blocks.

We will cover the following topics in this chapter:

- Declaring variables (and constants)
- Working with `Strings` of characters and `regular expressions`
- Numbers and numeric types
- Our first Julia data structures—`Tuple`, `Range`, and `Array`
- * Exploratory data analysis using the Iris flower dataset—`RDatasets` and core `Statistics`
- Quick data visualization with `Gadfly`
- * Saving and loading tabular data with `CSV` and `Feather`
- Interacting with MongoDB databases

Technical requirements

The Julia package ecosystem is under continuous development and new package versions are released on a daily basis. Most of the times this is great news, as new releases bring new features and bug fixes. However, since many of the packages are still in beta (version 0.x), any new release can introduce breaking changes. As a result, the code presented in the book can stop working. In order to ensure that your code will produce the same results as described in the book, it is recommended to use the same package versions. Here are the external packages used in this chapter and their specific versions:

```
CSV@v0.4.3
DataFrames@v0.15.2
Feather@v0.5.1
Gadfly@v1.0.1
IJulia@v1.14.1
JSON@v0.20.0
RDatasets@v0.6.1
```

In order to install a specific version of a package you need to run:

```
pkg> add PackageName@vX.Y.Z
```

For example:

```
pkg> add IJulia@v1.14.1
```

Alternatively you can install all the used packages by downloading the `Project.toml` file provided with the chapter and using `pkg>` instantiate as follows:

```
julia>
download("https://github.com/TrainingByPackt/Julia-1-Programming-Complete-R
eference-Guide/tree/master/Chapter11/Project.toml", "Project.toml")
pkg> activate .
pkg> instantiate
```

Defining variables

We have seen in the previous chapter how to use the REPL in order to execute computations and have the result displayed back to us. Julia even lends a helping hand by setting up the `ans` variable, which automatically holds the last computed value.

But, if we want to write anything but the most trivial programs, we need to learn how to define variables ourselves. In Julia, a variable is simply a name associated to a value. There are very few restrictions for naming variables, and the names themselves have no semantic meaning (the language will not treat variables differently based on their names, unlike say Ruby, where a name that is all caps is treated as a constant).

Let's see some examples:

```julia
julia> book = "Julia v1.0 By Example"
julia> pi = 3.14
julia> ANSWER = 42
julia> my_first_name = "Adrian"
```

 You can follow along through the examples in the chapter by loading the accompanying Jupyter/IJulia notebook provided with this chapter's support files.

The variables, names are case-sensitive, meaning that ANSWER and answer (and Answer and aNsWeR) are completely different things:

```julia
julia> answer
ERROR: UndefVarError: answer not defined
```

Unicode names (UTF-8-encoded) are also accepted as variables names:

```julia
julia> δ = 130
```

Remember that you can type many Unicode math symbols by typing backslash (\) then the name of the symbol and then the *Tab* key. For example, \pi[*Tab*] will output π.

Emojis also work, if your terminal supports them:

```julia
julia> 🚀 = "apollo 11"
```

The only explicitly disallowed names for variables are the names of built-in Julia statements (do, end, try, catch, if, and else, plus a few more):

```julia
julia> do = 3
ERROR: syntax: invalid "do" syntax
julia> end = "Paris"
ERROR: syntax: unexpected end
```

Attempting to access a variable that hasn't been defined will result in an error:

```
julia> MysteryVar
ERROR: UndefVarError: MysteryVar not defined
```

It's true that the language does not impose many restrictions, but a set of code style conventions is always useful—and even more so for an open source language. The Julia community has distilled a set of best practices for writing code. In regard to naming variables, the names should be lowercase and in just one word; word separation can be done with underscores (_), but only if the name would be difficult to read without them. For example, `myvar` versus `total_length_horizontal`.

Given that the degree of difficulty in reading a name is a subjective thing, I'm a bit split about this naming style. I normally prefer the crystal-clear clarity of separating at word boundaries. But nevertheless, it is better to follow the recommendation, given that function names in the Julia API adhere to it. By adhering to the same conventions, your code will be consistent throughout.

Constants

Constants are variables that, once declared, can't be changed. They are declared by prefixing them with the `const` keyword:

```
julia> const firstmonth = "January"
```

Very importantly in Julia, constants are not concerned with their value, but rather with their *type*. It is a bit too early to discuss types in Julia, so for now it suffices to say that a type represents what kind of a value we're dealing with. For instance, `"abc"` (within double quotes) is of type `String`, `'a'` (within single quotes) is of type `Char`, and `1000` is of type `Int` (because it's an integer). Thus, in Julia, unlike most other languages, we can change the value assigned to a constant as long as the `type` remains the same. For instance, we can at first decide that eggs and milk are acceptable meal choices and go `vegetarian`:

```
julia> const mealoption = "vegetarian"
```

And we can change our mind later on, if we decide to go `vegan`. Julia will let it slide with just a warning:

```
julia> mealoption = "vegan"
WARNING: redefining constant mealoption
"vegan"
```

However, attempting to say that `mealoption` = 2 will result in an error:

```
julia> mealoption = 2
ERROR: invalid redefinition of constant mealoption
```

This makes sense, right? Who's ever heard of that kind of diet?

However, the nuances can be more subtle than that, most notably when working with numbers:

```
julia> const amount = 10.25
10.25
julia> amount = 10
ERROR: invalid redefinition of constant amount
```

Julia doesn't allow it because internally `10` and `10.00`, despite having the same arithmetical value, are values of different types (`10` is an integer, while `10.00` is a `float`). We'll take a closer look at numeric types in just a moment, so it will all become clearer:

```
julia> amount = 10.00
WARNING: redefining constant amount
10.0
```

Thus, we need to pass the new value as `10.00`—a `float`, in order to obey the same type requirement.

Why are constants important?

It's mostly about performance. Constants can be especially useful as global values. Because global variables are long-lived and can be modified at any time and from any location in your code, the compiler is having a hard time optimizing them. If we tell the compiler that the value is constant and thus that the type of the value won't change, the performance problem can be optimized away.

 Of course, just because constants alleviate some critical performance problems brought about by global variables, it doesn't mean that we are encouraged to use them. Global values in Julia, like in other languages, must be avoided whenever possible. Besides performance issues, they can create subtle bugs that are hard to catch and understand. Also, keep in mind that, since Julia allows changing the value of a constant, accidental modification becomes possible.

Comments

Common programming wisdom says the following:

"Code is read much more often than it is written, so plan accordingly."

Code comments are a powerful tool that make the programs easier to understand later on. In Julia, comments are marked with the # sign. Single-line comments are denoted by a # and everything that follows this, until the end of the line, is ignored by the compiler. Multiline comments are enclosed between #= ... =#. Everything within the opening and the closing comment tags is also ignored by the compiler. Here is an example:

```
julia> #=
          Our company charges a fixed
          $10 fee per transaction.
       =#
const flatfee = 10 # flat fee, per transaction
```

In the previous snippet, we can see both multiline and single-line comments in action. A single-line comment can also be placed at the beginning of the line.

Strings

A string represents a sequence of characters. We can create a string by enclosing the corresponding sequence of characters between double quotes, as shown in the following:

```
julia> "Measuring programming progress by lines of code is like measuring
aircraft building progress by weight."
```

If the string also includes quotes, we can escape these by prefixing them with a backslash \:

```
julia> "Beta is Latin for \"still doesn't work\"."
```

Triple-quoted strings

However, escaping can get messy, so there's a much better way of dealing with this—by using triple quotes """...""".

```
julia> """Beta is Latin for "still doesn't work"."""
```

Within triple quotes, it is no longer necessary to escape the single quotes. However, make sure that the single quotes and the triple quotes are separated—or else the compiler will get confused:

```
julia> """Beta is Latin for "still doesn't work""""
syntax: cannot juxtapose string literal
```

The triple quotes come with some extra special powers when used with multiline text. First, if the opening """ is followed by a newline, this newline is stripped from the string. Also, whitespace is preserved but the string is dedented to the level of the least-indented line:

```
julia> """
                    Hello
            Look
        Here"""


julia> print(ans)
Hello
Look
Here
```

The previous snippet illustrates how the first line is stripped and the whitespace is preserved—but the indentation starts with the least indented line (the space in front of Here was removed).

Here is how it looks in Jupyter/IJulia:

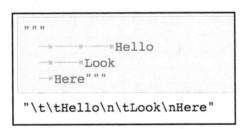

The longer arrow stands for a *Tab* (represented by a \t in the output), while the shorter arrow is a space. Note that each line had a space as the first character—but it was removed. The least indented line, the last one, was shifted to the left, removing all its whitespace and beginning with **Here**, while the remaining whitespace on the other lines was preserved (now beginning with a *Tab*).

Concatenating strings

Two or more strings can be joined together (concatenated) to form a single string by using the star * operator:

```
julia> "Hello " * "world!" "Hello world!"
```

Alternatively, we can invoke the string function, passing in all the words we want to concatenate:

```
julia> string("Itsy", " ", "Bitsy", " ", "Spider")
"Itsy Bitsy Spider"
```

Concatenation works great with variables too:

```
julia> username = "Adrian"
julia> greeting = "Good morning"
julia> greeting * ", " * username
"Good morning, Adrian"
```

However, again, we need to be careful when dealing with types (types are central to Julia, so this will be a recurring topic). Concatenation only works for strings:

```
julia> username = 9543794
julia> greeting = "Good morning"
julia> greeting * ", " * username
MethodError: no method matching *(::String, ::Int64)
```

Performing the concatenation by invoking the string function does work even if not all the arguments are strings:

```
julia> string(greeting, ", ", username)
 "Good morning, 9543794"
```

Thus, string has the added advantage that it automatically converts its parameters to strings. The following example works too:

```
julia> string(2, " and ", 3)
"2 and 3"
```

But this does not:

```
julia> 2 * " and " * 3
ERROR: MethodError: no method matching *(::Int64, ::String)
```

 > There is also a `String` method (with capital S). Remember that in Julia names are case-sensitive, so `string` and `String` are two different things. For most purposes we'll need the lowercase function, `string`. You can use Julia's help system to access the documentation for `String`, if you want to learn about it.

Interpolating strings

When creating longer, more complex strings, concatenation can be noisy and error-prone. For such cases, we're better off using the `$` symbol to perform variable interpolation into strings:

```
julia> username = "Adrian"
julia> greeting = "Good morning"
julia> "$greeting, $username"
"Good morning, Adrian"
```

More complex expressions can be interpolated by wrapping them into `$(...)`:

```
julia> "$(uppercase(greeting)), $(reverse(username))"
"GOOD MORNING, nairdA"
```

Here we invoke the `uppercase` function which changes all the letters of the string into their uppercase counterparts—and the `reverse` function which reverses the order of the letters in the word. Their output is then interpolated in a string. Between the `$(...)` boundaries, we can use any Julia code we want.

Just like the `string` function, interpolation takes care of converting the values to strings:

```
julia> "The sum of 1 and 2 is $(1 + 2)"
"The sum of 1 and 2 is 3"
```

Manipulating strings

Strings can be treated as a list of characters, so we can index into them—that is, access the character at a certain position in the word:

```julia
julia> str = "Nice to see you"
julia> str[1]
'N': ASCII/Unicode U+004e (category Lu: Letter, uppercase)
```

The first character of the string Nice to see you is N.

Indexing in Julia is 1-based, which means that the first element of a list is found at index 1. This can be surprising if you've programmed before, given that most programming languages use 0-based indexing. However, I assure you that 1-based indexing makes for a very pleasant and straightforward coding experience.

 Julia has support for arrays with arbitrary indices, allowing, for example, to start numbering at 0. However, arbitrary indexing is a more advanced feature that we won't cover here. If you are curious, you can check the official documentation at https://docs.julialang.org/en/v1/devdocs/offset-arrays/.

We can also extract a part of the string (a substring) by indexing with a range, providing the starting and the ending positions:

```julia
julia> str[9:11]
"see"
```

It is important to notice that indexing via a singular value returns a Char , while indexing via a range returns a String (remember, for Julia these are two completely different things):

```julia
julia> str[1:1]
"N"
```

N is a String of just one letter, as indicated by its double quotes:

```julia
julia> str[1]
'N': ASCII/Unicode U+004e (category Lu: Letter, uppercase)
```

N is a `Char`, as shown by the single quotes:

```
julia> str[1:1] == str[1]
false
```

They are not equal.

Unicode and UTF-8

In Julia, string literals are encoded using UTF-8. UTF-8 is a variable-width encoding, meaning that not all characters are represented using the same number of bytes. For example, ASCII characters are encoded using a single byte—but other characters can use up to four bytes. This means that not every byte index into a UTF-8 string is necessarily a valid index for a corresponding character. If you index into a string at such an invalid byte index, an error will be thrown. Here is what I mean:

```
julia> str = "Søren Kierkegaard was a Danish Philosopher"
julia> str[1]
'S': ASCII/Unicode U+0053 (category Lu: Letter, uppercase)
```

We can correctly retrieve the character at index 1:

```
julia> str[2]
'ø': Unicode U+00f8 (category Ll: Letter, lowercase)
```

And at index 2, we successfully get the ø character:

```
julia> str[3]
StringIndexError("Søren Kierkegaard was a Danish Philosopher", 3)
```

However, ø has two bytes, so index 3 is used by ø as well and we cannot access the string at this position:

```
julia> str[4]
'r': ASCII/Unicode U+0072 (category Ll: Letter, lowercase)
```

The third letter, r, is found at position 4.

Thus ø is a two-byte character that occupies the locations 2 and 3—so the index 3 is invalid, matching the second byte of ø. The next valid index can be computed using `nextind(str, 2)`—but the recommended way is to use iteration over the characters (we'll discuss `for` loops a bit later in this chapter):

```
julia> for s in str
            println(s)
        end
S
ø
r
e
n

K
... output truncated...
```

Because of variable-length encodings, the number of characters in a string is not necessarily the same as the last index (as you have seen, the third letter, r, was at index 4):

```
julia> length(str) 42
julia> str[42] 'e': ASCII/Unicode U+0065 (category Ll: Letter, lowercase)
```

For such cases, Julia provides the `end` keyword, which can be used as a shorthand for the last index. You can perform arithmetic and other operations with `end`, just like a normal value:

```
julia> str[end]
'r': ASCII/Unicode U+0072 (category Ll: Letter, lowercase)
julia> str[end-10:end]
"Philosopher"
```

The `end` value can be computed programmatically using the `endof(str)` function. Attempting to index outside the bounds of a string will result in a `BoundsError`:

```
julia> str[end+1]
ERROR: BoundsError: attempt to access "Søren Kierkegaard was a Danish
Philosopher"
  at index [44]
```

Regular expressions

Regular expressions are used for powerful pattern-matching of substrings within strings. They can be used to search for a substring in a string, based on patterns—and then to extract or replace the matches. Julia provides support for Perl-compatible regular expressions.

The most common way to input regular expressions is by using the so-called **nonstandard string literals**. These look like regular double-quoted strings, but carry a special prefix. In the case of regular expressions, this prefix is "r". The prefix provides for a different behavior, compared to a normal string literal.

For example, in order to define a regular string that matches all the letters, we can use `r"[a-zA-Z]*"`.

Julia provides quite a few nonstandard string literals—and we can even define our own if we want to. The most widely used are for regular expressions (`r"..."`), byte array literals (`b"..."`), version number literals (`v"..."`), and package management commands (`pkg"..."`).

Here is how we build a regular expression in Julia—it matches numbers between 0 and 9:

```
julia> reg = r"[0-9]+"
r"[0-9]+"
julia> match(reg, "It was 1970")
RegexMatch("1970")
```

Our regular expression matches the substring `1970`.

We can confirm that the nonstandard string literal `reg` is in fact a `Regex` and not a regular `String` by checking its `type` with the `typeof` function:

```
julia> typeof(reg)
Regex
```

This gives away the fact that there's also a `Regex` constructor available:

```
julia> Regex("[0-9]+")
r"[0-9]+"
```

The two constructs are similar:

```
julia> Regex("[0-9]+") == reg
true
```

Using the constructor can come in handy when we need to create regular expressions using more complex strings that might include interpolation or concatenation. But in general, the `r"..."` format is more used.

The behavior of the regular expression can be affected by using some combination of the flags `i`, `m`, `s`, and `x`. These modifiers must be placed right after the closing double quote mark:

```
julia> match(r"it was", "It was 1970") # case-sensitive no match
julia> match(r"it was"i, "It was 1970") # case-insensitive match
RegexMatch("It was")
```

As you might expect, `i` performs a case-insensitive pattern match. Without the `i` modifier, `match` returns `nothing`—a special value that does not print anything at the interactive prompt—to indicate that the regex does not match the given string.

These are the available modifiers:

- `i`—case-insensitive pattern matching.
- `m`—treats string as multiple lines.
- `s`—treats string as single line.
- `x`—tells the regular expression parser to ignore most whitespace that is neither backslashed nor within a character class. You can use this to break up your regular expression into (slightly) more readable parts. The `#` character is also treated as a metacharacter introducing a comment, just as in ordinary code.

The `occursin` function is more concise if all we need is to check if a regex or a substring is contained in a string—if we don't want to extract or replace the matches:

```
julia> occursin(r"hello", "It was 1970")
false
julia> occursin(r"19", "It was 1970")
true
```

When a regular expression does match, it returns a `RegexMatch` object. These objects encapsulate how the expression matches, including the substring that the pattern matches and any captured substrings:

```
julia> alice_in_wonderland = "Why, sometimes I've believed as many as six
impossible things before breakfast."

julia> m = match(r"(\w+)+", alice_in_wonderland)
RegexMatch("Why", 1="Why")
```

The \w regex will match a *word*, so in this snippet we captured the first word, Why.

We also have the option to specify the index at which to start the search:

```
m = match(r"(\w+)+", alice_in_wonderland, 6)
RegexMatch("sometimes", 1="sometimes")
```

Let's try something a bit more complex:

```
julia> m = match(r"((\w+)(\s+|\W+))", alice_in_wonderland)
RegexMatch("Why, ", 1="Why, ", 2="Why", 3=", ")
```

The resultant RegexMatch object m exposes the following properties (or fields, in Julia's lingo):

- m.match (Why,) contains the entire substring that matched.
- m.captures (an array of strings containing Why, Why, and ,) represents the captured substrings.
- m.offset, the offset at which the whole match begins (in our case 1).
- m.offsets, the offsets of the captured substrings as an array of integers (for our example being [1, 1, 4]).

Julia does not provide a g modifier, for a *greedy* or *global* match. If you need all the matches, you can iterate over them using eachmatch(), with a construct like the following:

```
julia> for m in eachmatch(r"((\w+)(\s+|\W+))", alice_in_wonderland)
           println(m)
       end
```

Or, alternatively, we can put all the matches in a list using collect():

```
julia> collect(eachmatch(r"((\w+)(\s+|\W+))", alice_in_wonderland))
13-element Array{RegexMatch,1}:
RegexMatch("Why, ", 1="Why, ", 2="Why", 3=", ")
RegexMatch("sometimes ", 1="sometimes ", 2="sometimes", 3=" ")
RegexMatch("I'", 1="I'", 2="I", 3="'")
RegexMatch("ve ", 1="ve ", 2="ve", 3=" ")
RegexMatch("believed ", 1="believed ", 2="believed", 3=" ")
RegexMatch("as ", 1="as ", 2="as", 3=" ")
RegexMatch("many ", 1="many ", 2="many", 3=" ")
RegexMatch("as ", 1="as ", 2="as", 3=" ")
RegexMatch("six ", 1="six ", 2="six", 3=" ")
RegexMatch("impossible ", 1="impossible ", 2="impossible", 3=" ")
RegexMatch("things ", 1="things ", 2="things", 3=" ")
RegexMatch("before ", 1="before ", 2="before", 3=" ")
RegexMatch("breakfast.", 1="breakfast.", 2="breakfast", 3=".")
```

For more info about regular expressions, check the official documentation at `https://docs.julialang.org/en/stable/manual/strings/#Regular-Expressions-1`.

Raw string literals

If you need to define a string that does not perform interpolation or escaping, for example to represent code from another language that might contain $ and \ which can interfere with the Julia parser, you can use raw strings. They are constructed with `raw"..."` and create ordinary `String` objects that contain the enclosed characters exactly as entered, with no interpolation or escaping:

```
julia> "This $will error out"
ERROR: UndefVarError: will not defined
```

Putting a $ inside the string will cause Julia to perform interpolation and look for a variable called `will`:

```
julia> raw"This $will work"
"This \$will work"
```

But by using a raw string, the $ symbol will be ignored (or rather, automatically escaped, as you can see in the output).

Numbers

Julia provides a broad range of primitive numeric types, together with the full range of arithmetic and bitwise operators and standard mathematical functions. We have at our disposal a rich hierarchy of numeric types, with the most generic being `Number`—which defines two subtypes, `Complex` and `Real`. Conversely, `Real` has four subtypes—`AbstractFloat`, `Integer`, `Irrational`, and `Rational`. Finally, `Integer` branches into four other subtypes—`BigInt`, `Bool`, `Signed`, and `Unsigned`.

Let's take a look at the most important categories of numbers.

Integers

Literal integers are represented simply as follows:

```
julia> 42
```

The default Integer type, called `Int`, depends on the architecture of the system upon which the code is executed. It can be either `Int32` or `Int64`. On my 64-bit system, I get it as follows:

```
julia> typeof(42)
Int64
```

The `Int` type will reflect that, as it's just an alias to either `Int32` or `Int64`:

```
julia> @show Int
Int = Int64
```

Overflow behavior

The minimum and maximum values are given by the `typemin()` and `typemax()` functions:

```
julia> typemin(Int), typemax(Int)
(-9223372036854775808, 9223372036854775807)
```

Attempting to use values that go beyond the boundaries defined by the minimum and the maximum values will not throw an error (or even a warning), resulting instead in a wraparound behavior (meaning that it will jump over at the other end):

```
julia> typemin(Int) - 1
9223372036854775807
julia> typemin(Int) - 1 == typemax(Int)
true
```

Substracting 1 from the minimum value will return the maximum value instead:

```
julia> typemax(Int) + 1 == typemin(Int)
true
```

The reverse is also `true`—adding 1 to the maximum value will return the minimum value.

For working with values outside these ranges, we'll use the `BigInt` type:

```
julia> BigInt(typemax(Int)) + 1
9223372036854775808
```

No wraparound here; the result is what we expected.

Floating-point numbers

Floating-point numbers are represented by numerical values separated by a dot:

```
julia> 3.14
3.14
julia> -1.0
-1.0
julia> 0.25
0.25
julia> .5
0.5
```

By default they are `Float64` values, but they can be converted to `Float32`:

```
julia> typeof(1.)
Float64
julia> f32 = Float32(1.)
1.0f0
julia> typeof(f32)
Float32
```

To improve readability, the underscore (_) separator can be used with both integers and floats:

```
julia> 1_000_000, 0.000_000_005
(1000000, 5.0e-9)
```

Rational numbers

Julia also provides a Rational number type. This allows us to work with exact ratios, instead of having to deal with the precision loss inherent in floats. Rational numbers are represented as their numerator and denominator values, separated by two forward slashes //:

```julia
julia> 3//2
3//2
```

Rational numbers can be converted to other types, if there is no data loss:

```julia
julia> 1//2 + 2//4
1//1

julia> Int(1//1)
1

julia> float(1//3)
0.3333333333333333

julia> Int(1//3)
ERROR: InexactError: Int64(Int64, 1//3)

julia> float(1//3) == 1/3
true
```

Julia also includes support for Complex numbers. We won't discuss, them but you can read about the topic in the official documentation at https://docs.julialang.org/en/v1/manual/complex-and-rational-numbers/#Complex-Numbers-1.

Numerical operators

Julia supports the full range of arithmetic operators for its numeric types:

- +—(unary and binary plus)
- −—(unary and binary minus)
- *—(times)

- /—(divide)
- \—(inverse divide)
- ^—(power)
- %—(remainder)

The language also supports handy update operators for each of these (+=,−=,*=,/=,\=,÷=,%=,and ^=). Here they are in the wild:

```julia
julia> a = 2
2
julia> a *= 3 # equivalent of a = a * 3
6
julia> a ^= 2 # equivalent of a = a ^ 2
36
julia> a += 4 # equivalent of a = a + 4
40
```

Numerical comparisons can be performed with the following set of operators:

- ==—(equality)
- != or ≠—(inequality)
- <—(less than)
- <= or ≤—(less than or equal to)
- >—(greater than)
- >= or ≥—(greater than or equal to)

In Julia, the comparisons can also be chained:

```julia
julia> 10 > 5 < 6 == 6 >= 3 != 2
true
```

Vectorized dot operators

Julia defines corresponding *dot* operations for every binary operator. These are designed to work element-wise with collections of values (called **vectorized**). That is, the operator that is *dotted* is applied for each element of the collection.

In the following example, we'll square each element of the `first_five_fib` collection:

```
julia> first_five_fib = [1, 1, 2, 3, 5]
5-element Array{Int64,1}:
 1
 1
 2
 3
 5
julia> first_five_fib .^ 2
5-element Array{Int64,1}:
 1
 1
 4
 9
 25
```

In the previous example, `first_five_fib` was not touched and the resultant collection was returned, but *dotted* updating operators are also available, updating the values in place. They match the previously discussed update operators (with the added *dot*). For example, to update `first_five_fib` in place, we'd use the following:

```
julia> first_five_fib .^= 2
```

 Vectorized code is an important part of the language due to its readability and conciseness, but also because it provides important performance optimizations. For more details, check `https://docs.julialang.org/en/stable/manual/functions/#man-vectorized-1`.

There's more to it

This section barely scratches the surface. For a deeper dive into Julia's numeric types, read the official documentation at `https://docs.julialang.org/en/stable/manual/mathematical-operations/`.

Tuples

Tuples are one of the simplest data types and data structures in Julia. They can have any length and can contain any kind of value—but they are immutable. Once created, a tuple cannot be modified. A tuple can be created using the literal tuple notation, by wrapping the comma-separated values within brackets (. . .):

```
(1, 2, 3)
```

```
julia> ("a", 4, 12.5)
("a", 4, 12.5)
```

In order to define a one-element tuple, we must not forget the trailing comma:

```
julia> (1,)
(1,)
```

But it's OK to leave off the parenthesis:

```
julia> 'e', 2
('e', 2)
```

```
julia> 1,
(1,)
```

We can index into tuples to access their elements:

```
julia> lang = ("Julia", v"1.0")
("Julia", v"1.0.0")
```

```
julia> lang[2]
v"1.0.0"
```

Vectorized *dot* operations also work with tuples:

```
julia> (3,4) .+ (1,1) (4, 5)
```

Named tuples

A named tuple represents a tuple with labeled items. We can access the individual components by label or by index:

```julia
julia> skills = (language = "Julia", version = v"1.0")
(language = "Julia", version = v"1.0.0")

julia> skills.language
"Julia"


julia> skills[1]
"Julia"
```

Named tuples can be very powerful as they are similar to full-blown objects, but with the limitation that they are immutable.

Ranges

We've seen ranges a bit earlier, when learning to index into `strings`. They can be as simple as the following:

```julia
julia> r = 1:20
1:20
```

As with previous collections, we can index into ranges:

```julia
julia> abc = 'a':'z'
'a':1:'z'

julia> abc[10]
'j': ASCII/Unicode U+006a (category Ll: Letter, lowercase)

julia> abc[end]
'z': ASCII/Unicode U+007a (category Ll: Letter, lowercase)
```

A range can be expanded into its corresponding values by using the splat operator, "`...`". For example, we can splat it into a tuple:

```julia
julia> (1:20...,)
(1, 2, 3, 4, 5, 6, 7, 8, 9, 10, 11, 12, 13, 14, 15, 16, 17, 18, 19, 20)
```

We can also splat it into a list:

```
julia> [1:20...]
20-element Array{Int64,1}
```

The same is true for Tuples, which can also be splatted into lists, among other things: `[(1,2,3)...]`.

We can see that the range steps in increments of one, by default. We can change that by passing it an optional step parameter. Here is an example of a range between 0 and 20 with a step of five:

```
julia> (0:5:20...,)
(0, 5, 10, 15, 20)
```

Now our values go from 5 to 5.

This opens the possibility to also go in descending order, by using a negative step:

```
julia> (20:-5:-20...,)
(20, 15, 10, 5, 0, -5, -10, -15, -20)
```

Ranges are not limited to integers—you've seen earlier a range of `chars`; and these are ranges of `floats`:

```
julia> (0.5:10)
0.5:1.0:9.5
julia> (0.5:10...,)
(0.5, 1.5, 2.5, 3.5, 4.5, 5.5, 6.5, 7.5, 8.5, 9.5)
```

We can also use the `collect` function to expand the range into a list (an array):

```
julia> collect(0.5:0.5:10)
20-element Array{Float64,1}
```

Arrays

An array is a data structure (and the corresponding *type*) that represents an ordered collection of elements. More specifically, in Julia, an array is a collection of objects stored in a multi-dimensional grid.

Arrays can have any number of dimensions and are defined by their type and number of dimensions—Array{Type, Dimensions}.

A one-dimensional array, also called a **vector**, can be easily defined using the array literal notation, the square brackets [. . .]:

```
julia> [1, 2, 3]
3-element Array{Int64,1}:
 1
 2
 3
```

You can also constrain the type of the elements:

```
julia> Float32[1, 2, 3, 4]
4-element Array{Float32,1}:
 1.0
 2.0
 3.0
 4.0
```

A two D array (also called a **matrix**) can be initialized using the same array literal notation, but this time without the commas:

```
julia> [1 2 3 4]
1×4 Array{Int64,2}:
 1  2  3  4
```

We can add more rows using semicolons:

```
julia> [1 2 3; 4 5 6; 7 8 9]
3×3 Array{Int64,2}:
 1  2  3
 4  5  6
 7  8  9
```

Julia comes with a multitude of functions that can construct and initialize arrays with different values, such as zeroes, ones, trues, falses, similar, rand, fill, and more. Here are a few of these in action:

```
julia> zeros(Int, 2)
2-element Array{Int64,1}:
 0
 0
```

```
julia> zeros(Float64, 3)
3-element Array{Float64,1}:
```

```
 0.0
 0.0
 0.0

julia> ones(2)
2-element Array{Float64,1}:
 1.0
 1.0

julia> ones(Int, 2)
2-element Array{Int64,1}:
 1
 1

julia> ones(Int, 3, 4)
3×4 Array{Int64,2}:
 1  1  1  1
 1  1  1  1
 1  1  1  1

julia> trues(2)
2-element BitArray{1}:
 true
 true

julia> rand(Int, 4, 2)
4×2 Array{Int64,2}:
  9141724849782088627   6682031028895615978
 -3827856130755187476  -1731760524632072533
 -3369983903467340663  -7550830795386270701
 -3159829068325670125   1153092130078644307

julia> rand(Char, 3, 2)
3×2 Array{Char,2}:
 '\U63e7a'  '\Ub8723'
 '\Uda56f'  '林'
 '\U7b7fd'  '\U5f749'

julia> fill(42, 2, 3)
2×3 Array{Int64,2}:
 42  42  42
 42  42  42
```

`Array` elements can be accessed by their index, passing in a value for each dimension:

```
julia> arr1d = rand(5) 5-element Array{Float64,1}: 0.845359 0.0758361
0.379544 0.382333 0.240184
julia> arr1d[5]
 0.240184
julia> arr2d = rand(5,2)
5×2 Array{Float64,2}:
 0.838952   0.312295
 0.800917   0.253152
 0.480604   0.49218
 0.716717   0.889667
 0.703998   0.773618

julia> arr2d[4, 1]
0.7167165812985592
```

We can also pass a colon (:) to select all indices within the entire dimension—or a range to define subselections:

```
julia> arr2d = rand(5,5)
5×5 Array{Float64,2}:
 0.618041   0.887638    0.633995   0.868588   0.19461
 0.400213   0.699705    0.719709   0.328922   0.326825
 0.322572   0.807488    0.866489   0.960801   0.476889
 0.716221   0.504356    0.206264   0.600758   0.843445
 0.705491   0.0334613   0.240025   0.235351   0.740302
```

This is how we select rows 1 to 3 and columns 3 to 5:

```
julia> arr2d[1:3, 3:5]
3×3 Array{Float64,2}:
 0.633995   0.868588   0.19461
 0.719709   0.328922   0.326825
 0.866489   0.960801   0.476889
```

The solitary colon : stands for all—so here we pick all the rows and columns 3 to 5:

```
julia> arr2d[:, 3:5]
5×3 Array{Float64,2}:
 0.633995   0.868588   0.19461
 0.719709   0.328922   0.326825
 0.866489   0.960801   0.476889
 0.206264   0.600758   0.843445
 0.240025   0.235351   0.740302
```

Another option is an `Array` of Booleans to select elements at its `true` indices. Here we select the rows corresponding to the `true` values and the columns 3 to 5:

```julia
julia> arr2d[[true, false, true, true, false], 3:5]
3×3 Array{Float64,2}:
 0.633995  0.868588  0.19461
 0.866489  0.960801  0.476889
 0.206264  0.600758  0.843445
```

In a similar way to indexing into an array, we can also assign values to the selected items:

```julia
julia> arr2d[1, 1] = 0.0
```

```julia
julia> arr2d[[true, false, true, true, false], 3:5] = ones(3, 3)
julia> arr2d
5×5 Array{Float64,2}:
 0.0       0.641646  1.0       1.0        1.0
 0.750895  0.842909  0.818378  0.484694   0.661247
 0.938833  0.193142  1.0       1.0        1.0
 0.195541  0.338319  1.0       1.0        1.0
 0.546298  0.920886  0.720724  0.0529883  0.238986
```

Iteration

The simplest way to iterate over an array is with the `for` construct:

```julia
for element in yourarray
    # do something with element
end
```

Here's an example:

```julia
julia> for person in ["Alison", "James", "Cohen"]
           println("Hello $person")
       end

Hello Alison
Hello James
Hello Cohen
```

If you also need the index while iterating, Julia exposes the `eachindex(yourarray)` iterator:

```julia
julia> people = ["Alison", "James", "Cohen"]
3-element Array{String,1}:
 "Alison"
```

```
  "James"
  "Cohen"

julia> for i in eachindex(people)
           println("$i. $(people[i])")
       end


1. Alison
2. James
3. Cohen
```

Mutating arrays

We can add more elements to the end of a collection by using the push! function:

```
julia> arr = [1, 2, 3]
3-element Array{Int64,1}:
 1
 2
 3


julia> push!(arr, 4)
4-element Array{Int64,1}:
 1
 2
 3
 4

julia> push!(arr, 5, 6, 7)
7-element Array{Int64,1}:
  1
  2
  3
  4
  5
  6
  7
```

Note the ending exclamation mark ! for the push! function. This is a perfectly legal function name in Julia. It is a convention to warn that the function is *mutating*—that is, it will modify the data passed as argument to it, instead of returning a new value.

We can remove elements from the end of an `array` using `pop!`:

```
julia> pop!(arr)
7

julia> arr
6-element Array{Int64,1}:
  1
  2
  3
  4
  5
  6
```

The call to the `pop!` function has removed the last element of `arr` and returned it.

If we want to remove an element other than the last, we can use the `deleteat!` function, indicating the index that we want to be removed:

```
julia> deleteat!(arr, 3)
5-element Array{Int64,1}:
  1
  2
  4
  5
  6
```

Finally, a word of warning when mutating arrays. In Julia, the arrays are passed to functions by reference. This means that the original array is being sent as the argument to the various mutating functions, and not its copy. Beware not to accidentally make unwanted modifications. Similarly, when assigning an array to a variable, a new reference is created, but the data is not copied. So for instance:

```
julia> arr = [1,2,3]
3-element Array{Int64,1}:
  1
  2
  3

julia> arr2 = arr
3-element Array{Int64,1}:
  1
  2
  3
```

Now we pop an element off arr2:

```
julia> pop!(arr2)
3
```

So, arr2 looks like this:

```
julia> arr2
2-element Array{Int64,1}:
 1
 2
```

But our original array was modified, too:

```
julia> arr
2-element Array{Int64,1}:
 1
 2
```

Assigning arr to arr2 does not copy the values of arr into arr2 , it only creates a new binding (a new name) that points to the original arr array. To create a separate array with the same values, we need to use the copy function:

```
julia> arr
2-element Array{Int64,1}:
 1
 2

julia> arr2 = copy(arr)
2-element Array{Int64,1}:
 1
 2
```

Now, if we pop an element off the copied array:

```
julia> pop!(arr2)
2
```

Our original array is untouched:

```
julia> arr
2-element Array{Int64,1}:
 1
 2
```

Only the copy was modified:

```
julia> arr2
1-element Array{Int64,1}:
 1
```

Comprehensions

Array comprehensions provide a very powerful way to construct arrays. It is similar to the previously discussed array literal notation, but instead of passing in the actual values, we use a computation over an iterable object.

An example will make it clear:

```
julia> [x += 1 for x = 1:5]
10-element Array{Int64,1}:
 2
 3
 4
 5
 6
```

This can be read as—*for each element* x *within the range* 1 *to* 5, *compute* x+1 *and put the resultant value in the array.*

Just like with the *plain* array literals, we can constrain the type:

```
julia> Float64[x+=1 for x = 1:5]
5-element Array{Float64,1}:
 2.0
 3.0
 4.0
 5.0
 6.0
```

Similarly, we can create multi-dimensional arrays:

```
julia> [x += y for x = 1:5, y = 11:15]
5x5 Array{Int64,2}:
 12  13  14  15  16
 13  14  15  16  17
 14  15  16  17  18
 15  16  17  18  19
 16  17  18  19  20
```

Comprehensions can be filtered using the `if` keyword:

```
julia> [x += 1 for x = 1:10 if x/2 > 3]
4-element Array{Int64,1}:
  8
  9
 10
 11
```

In this case, we only kept the values where x/2 was greater than 3.

Generators

But the superpower of the comprehensions is activated when they are used for creating generators. Generators can be iterated to produce values on demand, instead of allocating an array and storing all the values in advance. You'll see what that means in a second.

Generators are defined just like array comprehensions, but without the square brackets:

```
julia> (x+=1 for x = 1:10)
Base.Generator{UnitRange{Int64},##41#42}(#41, 1:10)
```

They allow us to work with potentially infinite collections. Check the following example, where we want to print the numbers from one to one million with a cube less than or equal to `1_000`:

```
julia> for i in [x^3 for x=1:1_000_000]
           i >= 1_000 && break
           println(i)
       end
1
8
27
64
125
216
343
512
729
```

This computation uses significant resources because the comprehension creates the full array of 1 million items, despite the fact that we only iterate over its first nine elements.

We can see that by benchmarking the code using the handy `@time` construct:

```
@time for i in [x^3 for x=1:1_000_000]
    i >= 1_000 && break
    println(i)
end
```

```
0.035739 seconds (58.46 k allocations: 10.493 MiB)
```

Over 10 MB of memory and almost 60,000 allocations. Compare this with using a generator:

```
@time for i in (x^3 for x=1:1_000_000)
    i >= 1_000 && break
    println(i)
end
```

```
0.019681 seconds (16.63 k allocations: 898.414 KiB)
```

Less than 1 MB and a quarter of the number of allocations. The difference will be even more dramatic if we increase from 1 million to 1 billion:

```
julia> @time for i in [x^3 for x=1:1_000_000_000]
           i >= 1_000 && break
           println(i)
       end
1
8
27
64
125
216
343
512
729
```

```
10.405833 seconds (58.48 k allocations: 7.453 GiB, 3.41% gc time)
```

Over 10 seconds and 7 GB of memory used!

On the other hand, the generator runs practically in constant time:

```
julia> @time for i in (x^3 for x=1:1_000_000_000)
           i >= 1_000 && break
           println(i)
       end
1
```

```
8
27
64
125
216
343
512
729
```

```
0.020068 seconds (16.63 k allocations: 897.945 KiB
```

Exploratory data analysis with Julia

Now that you have a good understanding of Julia's basics, we can apply this knowledge to our first project. We'll start by applying **exploratory data analysis** (**EDA**) to the Iris flower dataset.

If you already have experience with data analysis, you might've used the Iris dataset before. If so, that's great! You'll be familiar with the data and the way things are done in your (previous) language of choice, and can now focus on the Julia way.

On the contrary, if this is the first time you've heard about the Iris flower dataset, no need to worry. This dataset is considered the `Hello World` of data science—and we'll take a good look at it using Julia's powerful toolbox. Enjoy!

The Iris flower dataset

Also called **Fisher's Iris dataset**, it was first introduced in 1936 by British statistician and biologist Ronald Fisher. The dataset consists of 50 samples from each of three species of Iris flower (Iris setosa, Iris virginica, and Iris versicolor). It is sometimes called **Anderson's Iris dataset** because Edgar Anderson collected the data. Four features were measured—the length and the width of the sepals and petals (in centimeters).

Using the RDatasets package

Finding good-quality data for learning, teaching, and statistical software development can be challenging. That's why the industry practically standardized the use of over 10,00 high-quality datasets. These were originally distributed with the statistical software environment R. Hence, they've been aptly named the `RDatasets`.

The Iris flower dataset is part of this collection. There are many ways to download it, but the most convenient is through the `RDatasets` package. This package provides an easy way for Julia users to experiment with most of the standard datasets available in R or included with R's most popular packages. Sounds great; let's add it.

First, switch to package management mode:

```
julia> ]
pkg> add RDatasets
```

Once the package is added, let's tell Julia that we want to use it:

```
julia> using RDatasets
```

We can peek at the included datasets by calling `RDatasets.datasets()`. It returns a list of all the 700+ datasets available with `RDatasets`. It includes details about the data package, the name of the dataset, its title (or info), number of rows, and number of columns. These are the first 20 rows:

```
julia> RDatasets.datasets()
```

The output is as follows:

Row	Package	Dataset	Title	Rows	Columns
1	COUNT	affairs	affairs	601	18
2	COUNT	azdrg112	azdrg112	1798	4
3	COUNT	azpro	azpro	3589	6
4	COUNT	badhealth	badhealth	1127	3
5	COUNT	fasttrakg	fasttrakg	15	9
6	COUNT	lbw	lbw	189	10
7	COUNT	lbwgrp	lbwgrp	6	7
8	COUNT	loomis	loomis	410	11
9	COUNT	mdvis	mdvis	2227	13
10	COUNT	medpar	medpar	1495	10
11	COUNT	rwm	rwm	27326	4
12	COUNT	rwm5yr	rwm5yr	19609	17
13	COUNT	ships	ships	40	7
14	COUNT	titanic	titanic	1316	4
15	COUNT	titanicgrp	titanicgrp	12	5
16	Ecdat	Accident	Ship Accidents	40	5
17	Ecdat	Airline	Cost for U.S. Airlines	90	6
18	Ecdat	Airq	Air Quality for Californian Metropolitan Areas	30	6
19	Ecdat	Benefits	Unemployement of Blue Collar Workers	4877	18
20	Ecdat	Bids	Bids Received By U.S. Firms	126	12

You can see that the datasets are part of a `Package`—we can use that to filter by it. The Iris flower dataset is part of the *datasets* package.

All we have to do now is load the data:

```julia
julia> iris = dataset("datasets", "iris")
```

The output is as follows:

```
150×5 DataFrame
 Row │ SepalLength   SepalWidth   PetalLength   PetalWidth   Species

   1    5.1           3.5          1.4           0.2          setosa
   2    4.9           3.0          1.4           0.2          setosa
   3    4.7           3.2          1.3           0.2          setosa
   4    4.6           3.1          1.5           0.2          setosa
   5    5.0           3.6          1.4           0.2          setosa
   6    5.4           3.9          1.7           0.4          setosa
   7    4.6           3.4          1.4           0.3          setosa
   8    5.0           3.4          1.5           0.2          setosa
   9    4.4           2.9          1.4           0.2          setosa
  10    4.9           3.1          1.5           0.1          setosa
```

The returned value is a DataFrame object with 150 rows and five columns—SepalLength, SepalWidth, PetalLength, PetalWidth, and Species, plus an automatically added id column called Row.

Dataframes are the *de facto* standard for working with tabular data in Julia. They are a key part of Julia's data analysis toolset and we'll discuss them in detail in the next chapters. For now, it suffices to say that, as you can see in the previous examples, it represents a data structure that looks very much like a table or a spreadsheet.

You can programmatically retrieve the names of the columns using the following:

```julia
julia> names(iris)
5-element Array{Symbol,1}:
 :SepalLength
 :SepalWidth
 :PetalLength
 :PetalWidth
 :Species
```

To check the size, use the following:

```julia
julia> size(iris)
(150, 5)
```

The result is a tuple that matches the number of rows and columns—(rows, cols). Yep, as already established, 150 rows over 5 columns.

Let's take a look at the data:

```julia
julia> head(iris)
```

The output is as follows:

```
6×5 DataFrame
 Row │ SepalLength │ SepalWidth │ PetalLength │ PetalWidth │ Species

  1  │ 5.1        │ 3.5        │ 1.4         │ 0.2        │ setosa
  2  │ 4.9        │ 3.0        │ 1.4         │ 0.2        │ setosa
  3  │ 4.7        │ 3.2        │ 1.3         │ 0.2        │ setosa
  4  │ 4.6        │ 3.1        │ 1.5         │ 0.2        │ setosa
  5  │ 5.0        │ 3.6        │ 1.4         │ 0.2        │ setosa
  6  │ 5.4        │ 3.9        │ 1.7         │ 0.4        │ setosa
```

The head function shows the top six rows. Optionally, it takes a second parameter to indicate the number of rows: head(iris, 10). There's also its twin, tail(), which will display the bottom rows of the DataFrame:

```julia
julia> tail(iris, 10)
```

The output is as follows:

```
10×5 DataFrame
 Row │ SepalLength │ SepalWidth │ PetalLength │ PetalWidth │ Species

  1  │ 6.7        │ 3.1        │ 5.6         │ 2.4        │ virginica
  2  │ 6.9        │ 3.1        │ 5.1         │ 2.3        │ virginica
  3  │ 5.8        │ 2.7        │ 5.1         │ 1.9        │ virginica
  4  │ 6.8        │ 3.2        │ 5.9         │ 2.3        │ virginica
  5  │ 6.7        │ 3.3        │ 5.7         │ 2.5        │ virginica
  6  │ 6.7        │ 3.0        │ 5.2         │ 2.3        │ virginica
  7  │ 6.3        │ 2.5        │ 5.0         │ 1.9        │ virginica
  8  │ 6.5        │ 3.0        │ 5.2         │ 2.0        │ virginica
  9  │ 6.2        │ 3.4        │ 5.4         │ 2.3        │ virginica
 10  │ 5.9        │ 3.0        │ 5.1         │ 1.8        │ virginica
```

In regard to the species present in the dataset, we see *setosa* in the head rows and *virginica* at the bottom. We should have three species, though, according to the description of the data. Let's ask for a row count grouped by Species:

```julia
julia> by(iris, :Species, nrow)
```

The output is as follows:

```
3×2 DataFrame
 Row │ Species    │ x1
─────┼────────────┼────
  1  │ setosa     │ 50
  2  │ versicolor │ 50
  3  │ virginica  │ 50
```

The `by` function takes three parameters—the dataset, the name of the column, and a grouping function—in this case, `nrow`, which computes the number of rows. We can see that the third species is *versicolor*, and for each of the species we have 50 records.

> I'm sure you're wondering why, in the preceding example, the name of the column is prefixed by a colon ":". It is a `Symbol`. We'll discuss more about symbols when we learn about metaprogramming. For now, you can just think of symbols as identifiers or labels.

Using simple statistics to better understand our data

Now that it's clear how the data is structured and what is contained in the collection, we can get a better understanding by looking at some basic stats.

To get us started, let's invoke the `describe` function:

```
julia> describe(iris)
```

The output is as follows:

```
5×8 DataFrame
 Row │ variable     │ mean    │ min    │ median │ max       │ nunique │ nmissing │ eltype
─────┼─────────────┼─────────┼────────┼────────┼───────────┼─────────┼──────────┼──────────────────────
  1  │ SepalLength │ 5.84333 │ 4.3    │ 5.8    │ 7.9       │         │          │ Float64
  2  │ SepalWidth  │ 3.05733 │ 2.0    │ 3.0    │ 4.4       │         │          │ Float64
  3  │ PetalLength │ 3.758   │ 1.0    │ 4.35   │ 6.9       │         │          │ Float64
  4  │ PetalWidth  │ 1.19933 │ 0.1    │ 1.3    │ 2.5       │         │          │ Float64
  5  │ Species     │         │ setosa │        │ virginica │ 3       │          │ CategoricalString{UInt8}
```

This function summarizes the columns of the `iris` DataFrame. If the columns contain numerical data (such as `SepalLength`), it will compute the minimum, median, mean, and maximum. The number of missing and unique values is also included. The last column reports the type of data stored in the row.

A few other stats are available, including the 25th and the 75th percentile, and the first and the last values. We can ask for them by passing an extra `stats` argument, in the form of an array of symbols:

```julia
julia> describe(iris, stats=[:q25, :q75, :first, :last])
```

The output is as follows:

```
5×5 DataFrame
 Row │ variable     q25   q75   first    last
─────┼──────────────────────────────────────────────
 1   │ SepalLength  5.1   6.4   5.1      5.9
 2   │ SepalWidth   2.8   3.3   3.5      3.0
 3   │ PetalLength  1.6   5.1   1.4      5.1
 4   │ PetalWidth   0.3   1.8   0.2      1.8
 5   │ Species                  setosa   virginica
```

Any combination of stats labels is accepted. These are all the options—`:mean`, `:std`, `:min`, `:q25`, `:median`, `:q75`, `:max`, `:eltype`, `:nunique`, `:first`, `:last`, and `:nmissing`.

In order to get all the stats, the special `:all` value is accepted:

```julia
julia> describe(iris, stats=:all)
```

The output is as follows:

Row	variable	mean	std	min	q25	median	q75	max	nunique	nmissing	first	last	eltype
1	SepalLength	5.84333	0.828066	4.3	5.1	5.8	6.4	7.9			5.1	5.9	Float64
2	SepalWidth	3.05733	0.435866	2.0	2.8	3.0	3.3	4.4			3.5	3.0	Float64
3	PetalLength	3.758	1.7653	1.0	1.6	4.35	5.1	6.9			1.4	5.1	Float64
4	PetalWidth	1.19933	0.762238	0.1	0.3	1.3	1.8	2.5			0.2	1.8	Float64
5	Species			setosa				virginica	3		setosa	virginica	CategoricalString{UInt8}

We can also compute these individually by using Julia's `Statistics` package. For example, to calculate the mean of the `SepalLength` column, we'll execute the following:

```julia
julia> using Statistics
julia> mean(iris[:SepalLength])
5.843333333333334
```

In this example, we use `iris[:SepalLength]` to select the whole column. The result, not at all surprisingly, is the same as that returned by the corresponding `describe()` value.

In a similar way we can compute the `median()`:

```
julia> median(iris[:SepalLength])
5.8
```

And there's (a lot) more, such as, for instance, the standard deviation `std()`:

```
julia> std(iris[:SepalLength])
0.828066127977863
```

Or, we can use another function from the `Statistics` package, `cor()`, in a simple script to help us understand how the values are correlated:

```
julia> for x in names(iris)[1:end-1]
          for y in names(iris)[1:end-1]
            println("$x \t $y \t $(cor(iris[x], iris[y]))")
          end
          println("-----------------------------------------")
       end
```

Executing this snippet will produce the following output:

```
SepalLength     SepalLength     1.0
SepalLength     SepalWidth      -0.11756978413300191
SepalLength     PetalLength     0.8717537758865831
SepalLength     PetalWidth      0.8179411262715759
-----------------------------------------------------
SepalWidth      SepalLength     -0.11756978413300191
SepalWidth      SepalWidth      1.0
SepalWidth      PetalLength     -0.42844010433053953
SepalWidth      PetalWidth      -0.3661259325364388
-----------------------------------------------------
PetalLength     SepalLength     0.8717537758865831
PetalLength     SepalWidth      -0.42844010433053953
PetalLength     PetalLength     1.0
PetalLength     PetalWidth      0.9628654314027963
-----------------------------------------------------
PetalWidth      SepalLength     0.8179411262715759
PetalWidth      SepalWidth      -0.3661259325364388
PetalWidth      PetalLength     0.9628654314027963
PetalWidth      PetalWidth      1.0
-----------------------------------------------------
```

The script iterates over each column of the dataset with the exception of Species (the last column, which is not numeric), and generates a basic correlation table. The table shows strong positive correlations between SepalLength and PetalLength (87.17%), SepalLength and PetalWidth (81.79%), and PetalLength and PetalWidth (96.28%). There is no strong correlation between SepalLength and SepalWidth.

We can use the same script, but this time employ the cov() function to compute the covariance of the values in the dataset:

```
julia> for x in names(iris)[1:end-1]
         for y in names(iris)[1:end-1]
           println("$x \t $y \t $(cov(iris[x], iris[y]))")
         end
         println("----------------------------------------------")
       end
```

This code will generate the following output:

```
SepalLength     SepalLength     0.6856935123042507
SepalLength     SepalWidth      -0.04243400447427293
SepalLength     PetalLength     1.2743154362416105
SepalLength     PetalWidth      0.5162706935123043
---------------------------------------------------
SepalWidth      SepalLength     -0.04243400447427293
SepalWidth      SepalWidth      0.189979418344519
SepalWidth      PetalLength     -0.3296563758389262
SepalWidth      PetalWidth      -0.12163937360178968
---------------------------------------------------
PetalLength     SepalLength     1.2743154362416105
PetalLength     SepalWidth      -0.3296563758389262
PetalLength     PetalLength     3.1162778523489933
PetalLength     PetalWidth      1.2956093959731543
---------------------------------------------------
PetalWidth      SepalLength     0.5162706935123043
PetalWidth      SepalWidth      -0.12163937360178968
PetalWidth      PetalLength     1.2956093959731543
PetalWidth      PetalWidth      0.5810062639821031
---------------------------------------------------
```

The output illustrates that SepalLength is positively related to PetalLength and PetalWidth, while being negatively related to SepalWidth. SepalWidth is negatively related to all the other values.

Moving on, if we want a random data sample, we can ask for it like this:

```
julia> rand(iris[:SepalLength])
7.4
```

Optionally, we can pass in the number of values to be sampled:

```
julia> rand(iris[:SepalLength], 5)
5-element Array{Float64,1}:
 6.9
 5.8
 6.7
 5.0
 5.6
```

We can convert one of the columns to an array using the following:

```
julia> sepallength = Array(iris[:SepalLength])
150-element Array{Float64,1}:
 5.1
 4.9
 4.7
 4.6
 5.0
# ... output truncated ...
```

Or we can convert the whole `DataFrame` to a matrix:

```
julia> irisarr = convert(Array, iris[:,:])
150×5 Array{Any,2}:
 5.1  3.5  1.4  0.2  CategoricalString{UInt8} "setosa"
 4.9  3.0  1.4  0.2  CategoricalString{UInt8} "setosa"
 4.7  3.2  1.3  0.2  CategoricalString{UInt8} "setosa"
 4.6  3.1  1.5  0.2  CategoricalString{UInt8} "setosa"
 5.0  3.6  1.4  0.2  CategoricalString{UInt8} "setosa"
# ... output truncated ...
```

Visualizing the Iris flowers data

Visualization is a powerful tool in exploratory data analysis, helping us to identify patterns that would otherwise be hard to spot just by looking at the numbers. Julia provides access to some excellent plotting packages that are very easy to set up and use.

We'll illustrate with some plots created with Gadfly.

We'll start by adding Gadfly with `pkg> add "Gadfly"`and we'll continue with `julia> using Gadfly`. This will bring into scope Gadfly's `plot()` method. Now, let's find some interesting data to visualize.

In the previous section, we have identified that there is a strong covariant relation between `SepalLength` and `PetalLength`. Let's plot the data:

```julia
julia> plot(iris, x=:SepalLength, y=:PetalLength, color=:Species)
```

 At the time of writing, Gadfly support for Julia v1 was still incomplete. If that is still the case, the unstable yet working version of Gadfly can be installed using—`pkg> add Compose#master, Gadfly#master, Hexagon`.

Executing the `plot()` function will generate the following graph:

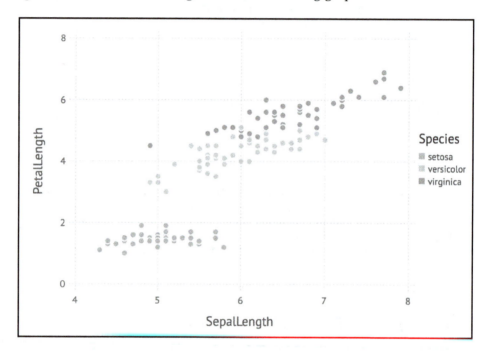

Sure enough, the plot will indicate that `SepalLength` and `PetalLength` vary together for both Iris versicolor and Iris virginica. For Iris setosa, it's not that obvious, with `PetalLength` staying pretty much unchanged while the sepal length grows.

A box plot will confirm the same; the sepal length of Iris setosa has little variation:

```julia
julia> plot(iris, x=:Species, y=:PetalLength, Geom.boxplot)
```

Plotting our values looks like this:

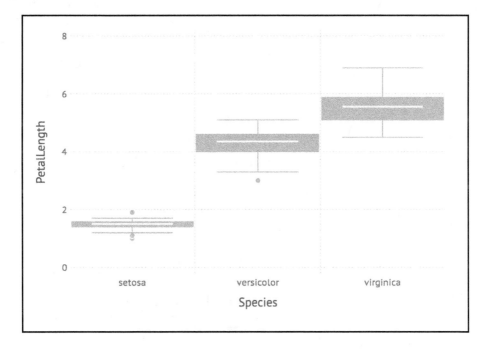

I have a feeling that a histogram would be even better for illustrating the distribution of the `PetalLength`:

```julia
julia> plot(iris, x=:PetalLength, color=:Species, Geom.histogram)
```

Generating a histogram using the `PetalLength` produces the following:

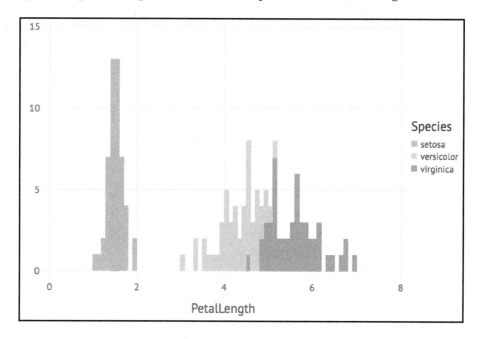

If we visualize the `PetalWidth` values as a histogram, we'll notice a similar pattern:

```julia
julia> plot(iris, x=:PetalWidth, color=:Species, Geom.histogram)
```

The output is as follows:

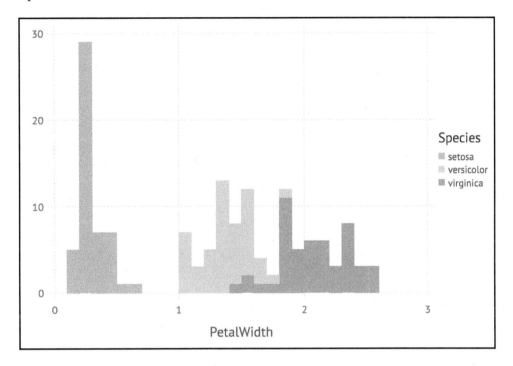

Plotting the petal width and height for the three species should now provide a strong indication that, for example, we can successfully classify Iris setosa based on the two values:

```julia
julia> plot(iris, x=:PetalWidth, y=:PetalLength, color=:Species)
```

The output is as follows:

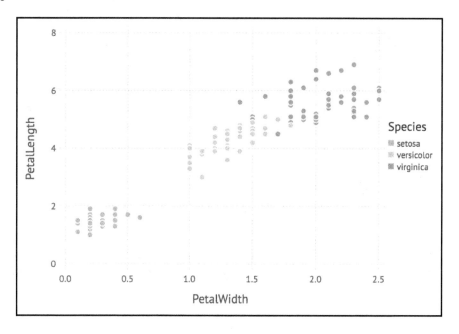

Loading and saving our data

Julia comes with excellent facilities for reading and storing data out of the box. Given its focus on data science and scientific computing, support for tabular-file formats (CSV, TSV) is first class.

Let's extract some data from our initial dataset and use it to practice persistence and retrieval from various backends.

We can reference a section of a `DataFrame` by defining its bounds through the corresponding columns and rows. For example, we can define a new `DataFrame` composed only of the `PetalLength` and `PetalWidth` columns and the first three rows:

```
julia> iris[1:3, [:PetalLength, :PetalWidth]]
3×2 DataFrames.DataFrame
| Row | PetalLength | PetalWidth |
|-----|-------------|------------|
| 1   | 1.4         | 0.2        |
| 2   | 1.4         | 0.2        |
| 3   | 1.3         | 0.2        |
```

The generic indexing notation is `dataframe[rows, cols]`, where `rows` can be a number, a range, or an `Array` of `boolean` values where `true` indicates that the row should be included:

```julia
julia> iris[trues(150), [:PetalLength, :PetalWidth]]
```

This snippet will select all the `150` rows since `trues(150)` constructs an `array` of 150 elements that are all initialized as `true`. The same logic applies to `cols`, with the added benefit that they can also be accessed by name.

Armed with this knowledge, let's take a sample from our original dataset. It will include some 10% of the initial data and only the `PetalLength`, `PetalWidth`, and `Species` columns:

```julia
julia> test_data = iris[rand(150) .<= 0.1, [:PetalLength, :PetalWidth,
:Species]]
10×3 DataFrames.DataFrame
```

Row	PetalLength	PetalWidth	Species
1	1.1	0.1	"setosa"
2	1.9	0.4	"setosa"
3	4.6	1.3	"versicolor"
4	5.0	1.7	"versicolor"
5	3.7	1.0	"versicolor"
6	4.7	1.5	"versicolor"
7	4.6	1.4	"versicolor"
8	6.1	2.5	"virginica"
9	6.9	2.3	"virginica"
10	6.7	2.0	"virginica"

What just happened here? The secret in this piece of code is `rand(150) .<= 0.1`. It does a lot—first, it generates an array of random `Float` values between 0 and 1; then, it compares the array, element-wise, against 0.1 (which represents 10% of 1); and finally, the resultant `Boolean` array is used to filter out the corresponding rows from the dataset. It's really impressive how powerful and succinct Julia can be!

In my case, the result is a `DataFrame` with the preceding 10 rows, but your data will be different since we're picking random rows (and it's quite possible you won't have exactly 10 rows either).

Saving and loading using tabular file formats

We can easily save this data to a file in a tabular file format (one of CSV, TSV, and others) using the CSV package. We'll have to add it first and then call the write method:

```
pkg> add CSV
julia> using CSV
julia> CSV.write("test_data.csv", test_data)
```

And, just as easily, we can read back the data from tabular file formats, with the corresponding CSV.read function:

```
julia> td = CSV.read("test_data.csv")
10×3 DataFrames.DataFrame
 │ Row │ PetalLength │ PetalWidth │ Species       │
 ├─────┼─────────────┼────────────┼───────────────┼──────
 │
 │  1  │ 1.1         │ 0.1        │ "setosa"      │
 │  2  │ 1.9         │ 0.4        │ "setosa"      │
 │  3  │ 4.6         │ 1.3        │ "versicolor"  │
 │  4  │ 5.0         │ 1.7        │ "versicolor"  │
 │  5  │ 3.7         │ 1.0        │ "versicolor"  │
 │  6  │ 4.7         │ 1.5        │ "versicolor"  │
 │  7  │ 4.6         │ 1.4        │ "versicolor"  │
 │  8  │ 6.1         │ 2.5        │ "virginica"   │
 │  9  │ 6.9         │ 2.3        │ "virginica"   │
 │ 10  │ 6.7         │ 2.0        │ "virginica"   │
```

Just specifying the file extension is enough for Julia to understand how to handle the document (CSV, TSV), both when writing and reading.

Working with Feather files

Feather is a binary file format that was specially designed for storing data frames. It is fast, lightweight, and language-agnostic. The project was initially started in order to make it possible to exchange data frames between R and Python. Soon, other languages added support for it, including Julia.

Support for Feather files does not come out of the box, but is made available through the homonymous package. Let's go ahead and add it and then bring it into scope:

```
pkg> add Feather
julia> using Feather
```

Now, saving our `DataFrame` is just a matter of calling `Feather.write`:

```
julia> Feather.write("test_data.feather", test_data)
```

Next, let's try the reverse operation and load back our Feather file. We'll use the counterpart `read` function:

```
julia> Feather.read("test_data.feather")
10×3 DataFrames.DataFrame
```

Row	PetalLength	PetalWidth	Species
1	1.1	0.1	"setosa"
2	1.9	0.4	"setosa"
3	4.6	1.3	"versicolor"
4	5.0	1.7	"versicolor"
5	3.7	1.0	"versicolor"
6	4.7	1.5	"versicolor"
7	4.6	1.4	"versicolor"
8	6.1	2.5	"virginica"
9	6.9	2.3	"virginica"
10	6.7	2.0	"virginica"

Yeah, that's our sample data all right!

 In order to provide compatibility with other languages, the Feather format imposes some restrictions on the data types of the columns. You can read more about Feather in the package's official documentation at `https://juliadata.github.io/Feather.jl/latest/index.html`.

Saving and loading with MongoDB

Before closing this chapter, let's take a look at using a NoSQL backend for persisting and retrieving our data. Don't worry, we'll extensively cover interaction with relational databases in the upcoming chapters too.

In order to follow through this chapter, you'll need a working MongoDB installation. You can download and install the correct version for your operating system from the official website, at `https://www.mongodb.com/download-center?jmp=nav#community`. I will use a Docker image which I installed and started up through Docker's Kitematic (available for download at `https://github.com/docker/kitematic/releases`).

Next, we need to make sure to add the `Mongo` package. The package also has a dependency on `LibBSON`, which is automatically added. `LibBSON` is used for handling `BSON`, which stands for *Binary JSON*, a binary-encoded serialization of JSON-like documents. While we're at it, let's add the `JSON` package as well; we will need it. I'm sure you know how to do that by now—if not, here is a reminder:

```
pkg> add Mongo, JSON
```

At the time of writing, Mongo.jl support for Julia v1 was still a work in progress. This code was tested using Julia v0.6.

Easy! Let's let Julia know that we'll be using all these packages:

```
julia> using Mongo, LibBSON, JSON
```

We're now ready to connect to MongoDB:

```
julia> client = MongoClient()
```

Once successfully connected, we can reference a `dataframes` collection in the `db` database:

```
julia> storage = MongoCollection(client, "db", "dataframes")
```

Julia's MongoDB interface uses dictionaries (a data structure called `Dict` in Julia) to communicate with the server. We'll look at `dict`s in more detail in the next chapter. For now, all we need to do is to convert our `DataFrame` to such a `Dict`. The simplest way to do it is to sequentially serialize and then deserialize the `DataFrame` by using the `JSON` package. It generates a nice structure that we can later use to rebuild our `DataFrame`:

```
julia> datadict = JSON.parse(JSON.json(test_data))
```

Thinking ahead, to make any future data retrieval simpler, let's add an identifier to our dictionary:

```
julia> datadict["id"] = "iris_test_data"
```

Now we can insert it into Mongo:

```
julia> insert(storage, datadict)
```

In order to retrieve it, all we have to do is query the Mongo database using the "id" field we've previously configured:

```
Julia> data_from_mongo = first(find(storage, query("id" =>
"iris_test_data")))
```

We get a `BSONObject`, which we need to convert back to a `DataFrame`. Don't worry, it's straightforward. First, we create an empty `DataFrame`:

```
julia> df_from_mongo = DataFrame()
0×0 DataFrames.DataFrame
```

Then we populate it using the data we retrieved from Mongo:

```
for i in 1:length(data_from_mongo["columns"])
  df_from_mongo[Symbol(data_from_mongo["colindex"]["names"][i])] =
Array(data_from_mongo["columns"][i])
end
julia> df_from_mongo
10×3 DataFrames.DataFrame
```

Row	PetalLength	PetalWidth	Species
1	1.1	0.1	"setosa"
2	1.9	0.4	"setosa"
3	4.6	1.3	"versicolor"
4	5.0	1.7	"versicolor"
5	3.7	1.0	"versicolor"
6	4.7	1.5	"versicolor"
7	4.6	1.4	"versicolor"
8	6.1	2.5	"virginica"
9	6.9	2.3	"virginica"
10	6.7	2.0	"virginica"

And that's it! Our data has been loaded back into a `DataFrame`.

Summary

Julia's intuitive syntax makes for a lean learning curve. The optional typing and the wealth of shorthand constructors result in readable, noise-free code, while the large collection of third-party packages makes accessing, manipulating, visualizing, plotting, and saving data a breeze.

Just by learning Julia's basic data structures and a few related functions, coupled with its powerful data manipulation toolset, we were able to implement an efficient data analysis workflow and extract valuable insight from the Iris flowers dataset. That was all we needed in order to perform efficient exploratory data analysis with Julia.

In the next chapter, we'll continue our journey by learning how to build a web crawler. Web mining, the process of extracting information from the web, is an important part of data mining and a key component of data acquisition in general. Julia is a great choice when building web mining software, given not only its built-in performance and its rapid prototyping features, but also the availability of powerful libraries that cover everything, from HTTP clients, to DOM parsing, to text analysis.

Setting Up the Wiki Game
12

I hope you're excited about Julia by now. The friendly, expressive, and intuitive syntax, the powerful **read-eval-print loop** (**REPL**), the great performance, and the richness of both built-in and third-party libraries are a game-changing combination for data science in particular—and programming in general.

The foundation we've laid in the previous chapters are now strong enough to allow us to develop pretty much any kind of program using Julia. Hard to believe? Well, here's the proof—in the next three chapters, we'll develop a web-based game with Julia!

It will follow the narrative of the internet-famous *Six Degrees of Wikipedia*. If you've never heard of it, the idea is that any two articles on Wikipedia can be connected, using only the links on the pages, in six clicks or fewer. It is also called **six degrees of separation**.

In case you're wondering what this has to do with Julia, it is a playful excuse to learn about data mining and web scraping and to learn more about the language and apply our newly acquired knowledge to build a web app.

In this chapter, we will lay the foundations of the web scraper. We'll take a look at how requests are made over the web in a client-server architecture and how to use the HTTP package to fetch web pages. We'll learn about HTML documents, HTML and CSS selectors, and Gumbo, a HTML parser for Julia. In the process, we'll experiment with more code in the REPL and we'll learn about other key features of the language, such as dictionaries, error handling, functions, and conditional statements. We'll also get to set up our first Julia project.

The topics we will cover in this chapter include the following:

- What web scraping is and how it is used for data harvesting
- How to use Julia to make requests and fetch web pages
- Understanding the `Pair` type
- Learning about the dictionary, one of Julia's more versatile data structures
- Exception handling, to help us capture errors in our code
- Functions, the basic building blocks and one of the most important code units in Julia—we'll learn how to define and use them to create reusable, modular code
- A handful of useful Julia tricks, such as the pipe operator and short-circuit evaluation
- Setting up a Julia project using `Pkg`

Technical requirements

The Julia package ecosystem is under continuous development and new package versions are released on a daily basis. Most of the times this is great news, as new releases bring new features and bug fixes. However, since many of the packages are still in beta (version 0.x), any new release can introduce breaking changes. As a result, the code presented in the book can stop working. In order to ensure that your code will produce the same results as described in the book, it is recommended to use the same package versions. Here are the external packages used in this chapter and their specific versions:

```
Gumbo@v0.5.1
HTTP@v0.7.1
IJulia@v1.14.1
OrderedCollections@v1.0.2
```

In order to install a specific version of a package you need to run:

```
pkg> add PackageName@vX.Y.Z
```

For example:

```
pkg> add IJulia@v1.14.1
```

Alternatively you can install all the used packages by downloading the `Project.toml` file provided with the chapter and using `pkg>` instantiate as follows:

```
julia>
download("https://github.com/TrainingByPackt/Julia-1-Programming-Complete-R
eference-Guide/tree/master/Chapter12/Project.toml", "Project.toml")
pkg> activate .
pkg> instantiate
```

Data harvesting through web scraping

The technique for extracting data from web pages using software is called **web scraping**. It is an important component of data harvesting, typically implemented through programs called **web crawlers**. Data harvesting or data mining is a useful technique, often used in data science workflows to collect information from the internet, usually from websites (as opposed to APIs), and then to process that data for different purposes using various algorithms.

At a very high level, the process involves making a request for a web page, fetching its content, parsing its structure, and then extracting the desired information. This can be images, paragraphs of text, or tabular data containing stock information and prices, for example—pretty much anything that is present on a web page. If the content is spread across multiple web pages, the crawler will also extract the links and will automatically follow them to pull the rest of the pages, repeatedly applying the same crawling process.

The most common use of web scrapers is for web indexing, as done by search engines such as Google or Bing. Online price monitoring and price comparison, personal data mining (or contact scraping), and online reputation systems, as well as product review platforms, represent other common use cases for web scrapers.

How the web works – a crash course

The internet has become an integral part of our lives over the last decade. Most of us use it extensively to access a wealth of information, day in and day out. Googling things like rambunctious (noisy and lacking in restraint or discipline), catching up with friends on social networks, checking out the latest gourmet restaurants on Instagram, watching a blockbuster on Netflix, or reading the Wikipedia entry about Attitogon (a place in Togo where they practice voodoo)—they're all just a click away. All these, although different in nature, function in pretty much the same way.

An internet-connected device, be it a computer using Wi-Fi or a smartphone connected to a mobile data network, together with an app for accessing the web (generally a web browser such as Chrome or Firefox, but also a dedicated one such as Facebook or Netflix's mobile apps), represent *the client*. At the other end we have *the server*—a computer that stores the information, be it in the form of web pages, videos, or entire web apps.

When a client wants to access the information available on the server, it initiates a *request*. If the server determines that the client has the permission to access the resource, a copy of the information is downloaded from the server onto the client, to be displayed.

Making HTTP requests

The **Hypertext Transfer Protocol** (**HTTP**) is a communication protocol for transmitting documents over a network. It was designed for communication between web browsers and web servers. HTTP implements the standard client-server model, where a client opens a connection and makes a request, then waits for a response.

Learning about HTTP methods

HTTP defines a set of request methods to indicate the action to be performed for a given resource. The most common method is GET, which is meant to retrieve data from the server. It is used when navigating the internet using links. The POST method requests the server to accept an enclosed data payload, most commonly the result of submitting a web form. There are a few more methods, including HEAD, PUT, DELETE, PATCH, and others—but they are less used and less supported by clients and web servers. As we won't need them for our web crawler, they won't be covered.

If you're interested, you can read about them at
https://developer.mozilla.org/en-US/docs/Web/HTTP/Methods.

Understanding HTTPS

HTTP Secure (**HTTPS**) is basically HTTP over an encrypted connection. It started as an alternative protocol used primarily for processing payments over the web and transferring sensitive corporate information. But in recent years, it has begun to see widespread usage, with a push from major companies to replace plain HTTP connections on the internet. For the purpose of our discussion, HTTP and HTTPS can be used interchangeably.

Understanding HTML documents

In order to extract data from the fetched web pages, we need to isolate and manipulate the structural elements that contain the desired information. That's why a basic understanding of the generic structure of the web pages is helpful when performing web scraping. If you've done web scraping before, maybe using a different programming language, or if you just know enough about HTML documents, feel free to skip this section. On the other hand, if you're new to this or just need a quick refresher, please read on.

Hypertext Markup Language (**HTML**) is the gold standard for creating web pages and web applications. HTML goes hand in hand with HTTP, the protocol for transmitting HTML documents over the internet.

The building blocks of HTML pages are the *HTML elements*. They provide both the content and the structure of a web page. They can be nested to define complex relationships with each other (such as parents, children, siblings, ancestors, and so on). HTML elements are denoted by *tags*, written between angle brackets (`<tag>...</tag>`). The official W3C specification defines a wealth of such tags, representing everything from headings and paragraphs, to lists, forms, links, images, quotes, and much more.

To give you an idea, here's how the main heading is represented in HTML on Julia's Wikipedia page at `https://en.wikipedia.org/wiki/Julia_(programming_language)`:

```
<h1>Julia (programming language)</h1>
```

This HTML code renders in a modern browser, like this:

Julia (programming language)

A more elaborate example can present a nested structure such as the following:

```
<div>
    <h2>Language features</h2>
    <p>According to the official website, the main features of the language
are:</p>
    <ul>
        <li>Multiple dispatch</li>
        <li>Dynamic type sytem</li>
        <li>Good performance</li>
    </ul>
</div>
```

The snippet renders a secondary heading (`<h2>`), a paragraph of text (`<p>`), and an unordered list (`<ul>`), with three list items (`<li>`), all within a page section (`<div>`):

Language features

According to the official website, the main features of the language are:

- Multiple dispatch
- Dynamic type
- Good performance

HTML selectors

HTML's purpose is to provide content and structure. That's all we need in order to convey any kind of information, no matter how complex. However, as computers and web browsers became more powerful and the use of web pages more widespread, users and developers wanted more. They asked for ways to extend HTML to also include beautiful formatting (design) and rich behavior (interactivity).

That is why **Cascading Style Sheets** (**CSS**) was created—a style language that defines the design of HTML documents. Additionally, JavaScript emerged as the programming language of choice for the client side, adding interactivity to web pages.

The style rules and the interactive features provided by CSS and JavaScript are associated with well-defined HTML elements. That is, styling and interactivity have to explicitly target elements from the associated HTML document. For example, a CSS rule can target the main heading of the page—or a JavaScript validation rule can target text input in the login form. If you think of a web page as a structured collection of HTML elements, this targeting is achieved by *selecting* (sub-collections of) elements.

Selecting elements can be done, in its simplest form, by identifying the HTML tags by type and structure (hierarchy). In the previous example, where we looked at representing a list of Julia's features, we can select all the list items (the `<li>` elements) by indicating a hierarchy like `div > ul > li`, representing all the `li` items, nested within a `ul` element, nested within a `div`. These are called **HTML selectors**.

However, this approach has limitations. On the one hand, when dealing with large, complex, and deeply nested HTML documents, we have to handle equally complex hierarchies, a tedious and error-prone task. On the other hand, such an approach might not provide enough specificity to allow us to select the element we want to target. For example, on the same Julia Wikipedia page, how would we differentiate the list of features from the list of external links? They both have similar structures.

The list of **External links** on Julia's Wikipedia page looks like this:

> ## External links [edit]
>
> - Official website 🔗
> - The Julia manual 🔗
> - Julia Package Listing 🔗 – a searchable listing of all (currently over 1500 with combined over 30,000🔗 GitHub stars) *registered* packages

The **Language features** section has a similar structure:

> ## Language features [edit]
>
> According to the official website, the main features of the language are:
>
> - Multiple dispatch: providing ability to define function behavior across many combinations of argument types
> - Dynamic type system: types for documentation, optimization, and dispatch
> - Good performance, approaching that of statically-typed languages like C

The fact that the two HTML elements are structurally identical makes it difficult to select the list items for the language features alone.

Learning about the HTML attributes

This is where HTML attributes come into play. These are key-value pairs that enhance HTML tags, providing extra information. For example, in order to define a link, we're going to use the `<a>` tag—`<a>This is a link</a>`.

But clearly, this is not enough. If this is a link, what does it link to? As developers, we need to provide extra information about the linked location. This is done by adding the `href` attribute with its corresponding value:

```
<a href="https://julialang.org/">This is a link to Julia's home page</a>
```

Ah yes, now we're talking! A super handy link to Julia's home page.

In general, all the attributes can be used when selecting HTML elements. But not all of them are equally useful. The most important one is arguably the `id` attribute. It allows us to assign a unique identifier to an element and then reference it in a very efficient way. Another important attribute is the `class`, extensively used for CSS styling rules.

This is what our previous example would look like with extra attributes:

```
<a href="https://julialang.org/" id="julia_link" class="external_link">This
is a link to Julia's home page</a>
```

Learning about CSS and JavaScript selectors

Historically, JavaScript started off using selectors based on the `id` attribute and the names of the HTML elements (the tags). Later on, the CSS specification came with a more powerful set of selectors, employing not only the `class`, the `id`, and the tags, but also the presence of attributes and their values, states of the elements (such as `focused` or `disabled`), and more specific element hierarchies that take into account relationships.

Here are a few examples of CSS selectors that can be used to target the previously discussed `<a>` tag:

- `#julia_link` is the selector for the `id` attribute (the `#`)
- `.external_link` is the selector for the `class` attribute (the `.`)
- `a` is the selector for the `<a>` tag
- `a[href*="julialang.org"]` will select all the `<a>` tags with a `href` attribute that contains `"julialang.org"`

 You can read more about CSS selectors at `https://developer.mozilla.org/en-US/docs/Web/CSS/CSS_Selectors`. It's worth keeping this resource close as web scraping relies heavily on CSS selectors, as we'll see in the next chapter.

Understanding the structure of a link

Links, in technical lingo called **Uniform Resource Locators** (**URLs**), are strings of characters that uniquely identify a resource on the internet. They are informally known as **web addresses**. Sometimes you might see them called **Uniform Resource Identifiers** (**URIs**).

In our previous example, Julia's Wikipedia web page was accessible at the URL `https://en.wikipedia.org/wiki/Julia_(programming_language)`. This URL refers to the resource `/wiki/Julia_(programming_language)` whose representation, as a HTML document, can be requested via the HTTPS protocol (`https:`) from a network host whose domain name is `wikipedia.org`. (Wow, that's a mouthful, but now you can understand how complex the process of requesting a web page on the internet is).

Thus, a common URL can be broken down into the following parts—`scheme://host/path?query#fragment`.

For example, if we take a look at `https://en.wikipedia.org/wiki/Julia_(programming_language)?uselang=en#Interaction`, we have `https` as the `scheme`, `en.wikipedia.org` as the `host`, `/wiki/Julia_(programming_language)` as the `path`, `?uselang=en` as the `query`, and, finally, `#Interaction` as the `fragment`.

Accessing the internet from Julia

Now that you have a good understanding of how web pages are accessed on the internet through client-server interactions, let's see how we can do this with Julia.

The most common web clients are the web browsers—apps such as Chrome or Firefox. However, these are meant to be used by human users, rendering web pages with fancy styled UIs and sophisticated interactions. Web scraping can be done manually through a web browser, it's true, but the most efficient and scalable way is through a fully automated, software-driven process. Although web browsers can be automated (with something like Selenium from `https://www.seleniumhq.org`), it's a more difficult, error-prone, and resource-intensive task. For most use cases, the preferred approach is to use a dedicated HTTP client.

Making requests with the HTTP package

`Pkg`, Julia's built-in package manager, provides access to the excellent `HTTP` package. It exposes a powerful functionality for building web clients and servers—and we'll use it extensively.

As you're already accustomed to, extra functionality is only two commands away—`pkg> add HTTP` and `julia> using HTTP`.

Recall our discussion about HTTP methods from the previous section; the most important ones were `GET`, used to ask for a resource from the server, and `POST`, which sends a data payload to the server and accepts the response. The `HTTP` package exposes a matching set of functions—we get access to `HTTP.get`, `HTTP.post`, `HTTP.delete`, `HTTP.put`, and so on.

Let's say we want to request Julia's Wikipedia page. All we need is the page's URL and the `HTTP.get` method:

```julia
julia>
HTTP.get("https://en.wikipedia.org/wiki/Julia_(programming_language)")
```

The result will be a `Response` object that represents Julia's Wikipedia page in all its glory. The REPL displays the headers and the first lines of the response body, truncating the rest:

```
julia> HTTP.get("https://en.wikipedia.org/wiki/Julia_(programming_language)")
HTTP.Messages.Response:
"""
HTTP/1.1 200 OK
Date: Mon, 17 Sep 2018 10:35:38 GMT
Content-Type: text/html; charset=UTF-8
Content-Length: 193324
Connection: keep-alive
Server: mw2174.codfw.wmnet
Vary: Accept-Encoding,Cookie,Authorization
X-Content-Type-Options: nosniff
P3P: CP="This is not a P3P policy! See https://en.wikipedia.org/wiki/Special:CentralAutoLogin/P3P for more info."
X-Powered-By: HHVM/3.18.6-dev
Content-language: en
Last-Modified: Sun, 16 Sep 2018 06:23:32 GMT
Backend-Timing: D=94531 t=1537079074050651
X-Varnish: 343909603 326005351, 885580661 879616280, 1013404048 653558799
Via: 1.1 varnish (Varnish/5.1), 1.1 varnish (Varnish/5.1), 1.1 varnish (Varnish/5.1)
Age: 18448
X-Cache: cp2016 hit/5, cp3030 hit/2, cp3042 hit/26
X-Cache-Status: hit-front
Strict-Transport-Security: max-age=106384710; includeSubDomains; preload
Set-Cookie: WMF-Last-Access=17-Sep-2018;Path=/;HttpOnly;secure;Expires=Fri, 19 Oct 2018 00:00:00 GMT
Set-Cookie: WMF-Last-Access-Global=17-Sep-2018;Path=/;Domain=.wikipedia.org;HttpOnly;secure;Expires=Fri, 19 Oct 2018 0
0:00:00 GMT
X-Analytics: ns=0;page_id=38455554;https=1;nocookies=1
X-Client-IP: 83.51.206.212
Cache-Control: private, s-maxage=0, max-age=0, must-revalidate
Set-Cookie: GeoIP=ES:CT:Sitges:41.24:1.81:v4; Path=/; secure; Domain=.wikipedia.org
Accept-Ranges: bytes

<!DOCTYPE html>
<html class="client-nojs" lang="en" dir="ltr">
<head>
<meta charset="UTF-8"/>
<title>Julia (programming language) - Wikipedia</title>
<script>document.documentElement.className = document.documentElement.className.replace( /(^|\s)client-nojs(\s|$)/, "$
1client-js$2" );</script>
<script>(window.RLQ=window.RLQ||[]).push(function(){mw.config.set({"wgCanonicalNamespace":"","wgCanonicalSpecialPageNa
me":false,"wgNamespaceNumber":0,"wgPageName":"Julia_(programming_language)","wgTitle":"Julia (programming language)","
wgCurRevisionId":859773913,"wgRevisionId":859773913,"wgArticleId":38455554,"wgIsArticle":true,"wgIsRedirect":false,"wg
Action":"view","wgUserName":null,"wgUserGroups":["*"],"wgCategories":["CS1 maint: Multiple names: authors list","Use d
my dates from October 2015","Official website different in Wikidata and Wikipedia","2012 software","Array programming
languages","Computational notebook","Data mining and machine learning software","Data-centric programming languages"
⋮
193324-byte body
"""
```

The screenshot shows the details of the `HTTP.Messages.Response` object we received—the list of HTTP headers and the first part of the response body. Let's make sure we keep it in a variable so we can reference it later. Remember that Julia provisionally stores the result of the last computation in the `ans` REPL variable, so let's pick it up from there:

```
julia> resp = ans
```

Handling HTTP responses

After receiving and processing a request, the server sends back a HTTP response message. These messages have a standardized structure. They contain a wealth of information, with the most important pieces being the status code, the headers, and the body.

HTTP status codes

The status code is a three-digit integer where the first digit represents the category, while the next two digits are used to define the subcategory. They are as follows:

- **1XX - Informational**: Request was received. This indicates a provisional response.
- **2XX - Success**: This is the most important response status, acknowledging that the request was successfully received, understood, and accepted. It's what we're looking for in our web-mining scripts.
- **3XX - Redirection**: This class of status codes indicates that the client must take additional action. It usually means that additional requests must be made in order to get to the resource, so our scripts will have to handle this scenario. We also need to actively prevent cyclical redirects. We won't deal with such complex scenarios in our project, but in real-life applications, 3XX status codes will require specialized handling based on the subcategory.

 Wikipedia provides a good description of the various 3XX status codes and instructions for what to do in each case: https://en.wikipedia.org/wiki/List_of_HTTP_status_codes#3xx_Redirection.

- **4XX - Client Error**: This means that we've probably made a mistake when sending our request. Maybe the URL is wrong and the resource cannot be found (`404`) or maybe we're not allowed to access the page (`401` and `403` status codes). There's a long list of 4XX response codes and, similar to 3XX ones, our program should handle the various scenarios to ensure that the requests are eventually successful.
- **5XX - Server Error**: Congratulations, you found or caused a problem on the server! Depending on the actual status code, this may or may not be actionable. `503` (service unavailable) or `504` (gateway timeout) are relevant as they indicate that we should try again later.

Learning about HTTP headers

HTTP headers allow the client and the server to pass additional information. We won't go into the details of header transmission since Julia's `HTTP` library saves us from having to deal with raw headers. However, a few are worth mentioning, as they are important for web scraping:

- `Age`, `Cache-Control`, and `Expires` represent the validity of the page and can be used to set data refresh times
- `Last-Modified`, `Etag`, and `If-Modified-Since` can be used for content versioning, to check if the page has changed since it was last retrieved
- `Cookie` and `Set-Cookie` have to be used in order to read and write cookies that are required for correct communication with the server
- The `Content-*` family of headers, such as `Content-Disposition`, `Content-Length`, `Content-Type`, `Content-Encoding`, and so on, help when handling and validating the response message

Check `https://developer.mozilla.org/en-US/docs/Web/HTTP/Headers` and `https://en.wikipedia.org/wiki/List_of_HTTP_header_fields` for a complete discussion on the HTTP header fields.

The HTTP message body

The message body, the most important part and the reason for web scraping (the content of the web page itself), is actually an optional part of the response. The presence of the body, its properties, and its size are specified by the `Content-*` family of headers.

Understanding HTTP responses

The result of the HTTP.get invocation is an object that closely mirrors a raw HTTP response. The package makes our lives easier by extracting the raw HTTP data and neatly setting it up in a data structure, which makes manipulating it a breeze.

Let's take a look at its properties (or *fields* in Julia's lingo):

```julia
julia> fieldnames(typeof(resp))
(:version, :status, :headers, :body, :request)
```

The fieldnames function accepts a type as its argument and returns a tuple containing the names of the fields (or properties) of the argument. In order to get the type of a value, we can use the typeof function, like in the previous example.

Right! The status, headers, and body fields should by now sound familiar. The version field represents the version of the HTTP protocol (the HTTP/1.1 part in the first line of the response). Most web servers on the internet today use version 1.1 of the protocol, but a new major version, 2.0, is almost ready for wide deployment. Finally, the request field holds a reference to the HTTP.Messages.Request object that triggered the current response.

The status code

Let's take a closer look at the status code:

```julia
julia> resp.status 200
```

Sure enough, we got back a valid response, hereby confirmed by the 200 status code.

The headers

What about the headers? As already mentioned, they contain critical information indicating whether a message body is present. Let's check them out:

```julia
julia> resp.headers
```

The output is as follows:

```
25-element Array{Pair{SubString{String},SubString{String}},1}:
                    "Date" ⟹ "Mon, 17 Sep 2018 11:02:39 GMT"
            "Content-Type" ⟹ "text/html; charset=UTF-8"
          "Content-Length" ⟹ "193324"
              "Connection" ⟹ "keep-alive"
                  "Server" ⟹ "mw2174.codfw.wmnet"
                    "Vary" ⟹ "Accept-Encoding,Cookie,Authorization"
    "X-Content-Type-Options" ⟹ "nosniff"
                     "P3P" ⟹ "CP=\"This is not a P3P policy! See https://en.wikipedia.org/wiki/Special:Central/
            "X-Powered-By" ⟹ "HHVM/3.18.6-dev"
        "Content-language" ⟹ "en"
           "Last-Modified" ⟹ "Sun, 16 Sep 2018 06:23:32 GMT"
         "Backend-Timing" ⟹ "D=94531 t=1537079074050651"
               "X-Varnish" ⟹ "343909603 326005351, 885580661 879616280, 2790139 653558799"
                     "Via" ⟹ "1.1 varnish (Varnish/5.1), 1.1 varnish (Varnish/5.1), 1.1 varnish (Varnish/5.1)"
                     "Age" ⟹ "20069"
                 "X-Cache" ⟹ "cp2016 hit/5, cp3030 hit/2, cp3042 hit/29"
          "X-Cache-Status" ⟹ "hit-front"
  "Strict-Transport-Security" ⟹ "max-age=106384710; includeSubDomains; preload"
              "Set-Cookie" ⟹ "WMF-Last-Access=17-Sep-2018;Path=/;HttpOnly;secure;Expires=Fri, 19 Oct 2018 00:0(
              "Set-Cookie" ⟹ "WMF-Last-Access-Global=17-Sep-2018;Path=/;Domain=.wikipedia.org;HttpOnly;secure;|
             "X-Analytics" ⟹ "ns=0;page_id=38455554;https=1;nocookies=1"
             "X-Client-IP" ⟹ "83.51.206.212"
           "Cache-Control" ⟹ "private, s-maxage=0, max-age=0, must-revalidate"
              "Set-Cookie" ⟹ "GeoIP=ES:CT:Sitges:41.24:1.81:v4; Path=/; secure; Domain=.wikipedia.org"
           "Accept-Ranges" ⟹ "bytes"
```

Your output will be different in regard to some of the values, but it should be easy to spot the key HTTP headers we mentioned before. `Content-Length` confirms the presence of a response body. The `Content-Type` provides information about how to interpret the encoding of the message body (it's a HTML document using UTF-8 character encoding). And we can use the `Last-Modified` value to optimize the caching and the update frequency of our web crawler.

The message body

Since we just confirmed that we have a response body, let's see it:

```
julia> resp.body
193324-element Array{UInt8,1}:
 0x3c
 0x21
 0x44
# ... output truncated ...
```

Oops, that doesn't look like the web page we were expecting. No worries though, these are the bytes of the raw response—which we can easily convert to a human-readable HTML string. Remember that I mentioned the `String` method when learning about strings? Well, this is where it comes in handy:

```
julia> resp_body = String(resp.body)
```

Your REPL should now be outputting a long HTML string that represents Julia's Wikipedia page.

If we take a look at the first `500` characters, we'll start to see familiar patterns:

```
julia> resp_body[1:500]
```

The output is as follows:

```
"<!DOCTYPE html>\n<html class=\"client-nojs\" lang=\"en\" dir=\"ltr\">\n<head>\n<meta charset=\"UTF-8\"/>\n<
title>Julia (programming language) - Wikipedia</title>\n<script>document.documentElement.className = documen
t.documentElement.className.replace( /(^|\\s)client-nojs(\\s|\$)/, \"\$1client-js\$2\" );</script>\n<script>
(window.RLQ=window.RLQ||[]).push(function(){mw.config.set({\"wgCanonicalNamespace\":\"\",\"wgCanonicalSpecia
lPageName\":false,\"wgNamespaceNumber\":0,\"wgPageName\":\"Julia_(programming_language)\",\"wgTitle\":\"J"
```

Sure enough, using Chrome's view page source will reveal the same HTML:

```
1  <!DOCTYPE html>
2  <html class="client-nojs" lang="en" dir="ltr">
3  <head>
4  <meta charset="UTF-8"/>
5  <title>Julia (programming language) - Wikipedia</title>
6  <script>document.documentElement.className =
   document.documentElement.className.replace( /(^|\s)client-nojs(\s|$)/,
   "$1client-js$2" );</script>
7  <script>(window.RLQ=window.RLQ||[]).push(function()
   {mw.config.set({"wgCanonicalNamespace":"","wgCanonicalSpecialPageName":false
   ,"wgNamespaceNumber":0,"wgPageName":"Julia_(programming_language)","wgTitle"
   :"Julia (programming
```

It's confirmed—we just took our first successful step toward building our web crawler!

Learning about pairs

While looking at the response header, you might've noticed that its type is an `Array` of `Pair` objects:

```
julia> resp.headers
25-element Array{Pair{SubString{String},SubString{String}},1}
```

A `Pair` represents a Julia data structure—and the corresponding type. The `Pair` contains a couple of values that are generally used to reference key-value relationships. The types of the two elements determine the concrete type of the `Pair`.

For example, we can construct a `Pair` with the following:

```
julia> Pair(:foo, "bar")
:foo => "bar"
```

If we check its type we'll see that it's a `Pair` of `Symbol` and `String`:

```
julia> typeof(Pair(:foo, "bar"))
Pair{Symbol,String}
```

We can also create `Pairs` by using the `x => y` literal notation:

```
julia> 3 => 'C'
3 => 'C'

julia> typeof(3 => 'C')
Pair{Int64,Char}
```

The `=>` double arrow should look familiar. It's what we saw in the response header, for example:

```
"Content-Type" => "text/html; charset=UTF-8"
```

Obviously, once created, it is possible to access the values stored in a `Pair`. One way to do it is by indexing into it:

```
julia> p = "one" => 1
"one" => 1

julia> p[1]
"one"

julia> p[2]
1
```

We can also access the `first` and `second` fields in order to get to the `first` and `second` values, respectively:

```
julia> p.first
"one"

julia> p.second
1
```

Just like the tuples, the `Pairs` are immutable, so this won't work:

```
julia> p.first = "two"
ERROR: type Pair is immutable

julia> p[1] = "two"
ERROR: MethodError: no method matching setindex!(::Pair{String,Int64}
```

`Pairs` are one of the building blocks of Julia and can be used, among other things, for creating dictionaries, one of the most important types and data structures.

Dictionaries

The dictionary, called `Dict`, is one of Julia's most powerful and versatile data structures. It's an associative collection—it *associates* keys with values. You can think of a `Dict` as a look-up table implementation—given a single piece of information, the key, it will return the corresponding value.

Constructing dictionaries

Creating an empty instance of a `Dict` is as simple as the following:

```
julia> d = Dict()
Dict{Any,Any} with 0 entries
```

The information between the curly brackets, `{Any,Any}`, represents the types of keys and values of the `Dict`. Thus, the concrete type of a `Dict` itself is defined by the type of its keys and values. The compiler will do its best to infer the type of the collection from the types of its parts. In this case, since the dictionary was empty, no information could be inferred, so Julia defaulted to `Any` and `Any`.

An `{Any,Any}` type of `Dict` allows us to add any kind of data, indiscriminately. We can use the `setindex!` method to add a new key-value pair to the collection:

```
julia> setindex!(d, "World", "Hello")
Dict{Any,Any} with 1 entry:
  "Hello" => "World"
```

However, adding values to a `Dict` is routinely done using the square bracket notation (which is similar to indexing into it, while also performing an assignment):

```
julia> d["Hola"] = "Mundo"
"Mundo"
```

Till now, we've only added `Strings`—but like I said, because our `Dict` accepts any kind of keys and value, there aren't any constraints:

```
julia> d[:speed] = 6.4
6.4
```

Here is our `Dict` now:

```
julia> d
Dict{Any,Any} with 3 entries:
  "Hello"  => "World"
  :speed   => 6.4
  "Hola"   => "Mundo"
```

Note that the key => value pairs are not in the order in which we added them. `Dicts` are not ordered collections in Julia. We'll talk more about this in a few paragraphs.

If the key already exists, the corresponding value will be updated, returning the new value:

```
julia> d["Hello"] = "Earth" "Earth"
```

Here's our updated `Dict`. Note that `"Hello"` now points to `"Earth"` and not `"World"`:

```
julia> d
Dict{Any,Any} with 3 entries:
  "Hello"  => "Earth"
  :speed   => 6.4
  "Hola"   => "Mundo"
```

If we provide some initial data when instantiating the Dict, the compiler will be able to do better at identifying the types:

```
julia> dt = Dict("age" => 12)
Dict{String,Int64} with 1 entry:
  "age" => 12
```

We can see that the type of the Dict is now constraining the keys to be String, and the values to be Int—which are the types of the Pair we used to instantiate the Dict. Now, if a different type is passed for a key or a value, Julia will attempt to convert it—if that fails, an error will occur:

```
julia> dt[:price] = 9.99
MethodError: Cannot `convert` an object of type Symbol to an object of type
String
```

In some instances, the automatic conversion works:

```
julia> dx = Dict(1 => 11)
Dict{Int64,Int64} with 1 entry:
  1 => 11
julia> dx[2.0] = 12
12
```

Julia has silently converted 2.0 to the corresponding Int value:

```
julia> dx
Dict{Int64,Int64} with 2 entries:
  2 => 12
  1 => 11
```

But that won't always work:

```
julia> dx[2.4] = 12
InexactError: Int64(Int64, 2.4)
```

We can store randomly complex data in a Dict and its type will be correctly inferred by Julia:

```
julia> clients_purchases = Dict(
        "John Roche" => ["soap", "wine", "apples", "bread"],
        "Merry Lou"  => ["bottled water", "apples", "cereals", "milk"]
        )
Dict{String,Array{String,1}} with 2 entries:
  "John Roche" => ["soap", "wine", "apples", "bread"]
  "Merry Lou"  => ["bottled water", "apples", "cereals", "milk"]
```

You can also specify and constrain the type of `Dict` upon constructing it, instead of leaving it up to Julia:

```
julia> dd = Dict{String,Int}("" => 2.0)
Dict{String,Int64} with 1 entry:
  "x" => 2
```

Here, we can see how the type definition overruled the type of the 2.0 value, which is a `Float64` (of course, as in the previous example, Julia has converted 2.0 to its integer counterpart).

We can also use `Pairs` to create a `Dict`:

```
julia> p1 = "a" => 1
"a"=>1
julia> p2 = Pair("b", 2)
"b"=>2
julia> Dict(p1, p2)
Dict{String,Int64} with 2 entries:
  "b" => 2
  "a" => 1
```

We can also use an `Array` of `Pair`:

```
julia> Dict([p1, p2])
Dict{String,Int64} with 2 entries:
  "b" => 2
  "a" => 1
```

We can do the same with arrays of tuples:

```
julia> Dict([("a", 5), ("b", 10)])
Dict{String,Int64} with 2 entries:
  "b" => 10
  "a" => 5
```

Finally, a `Dict` can be constructed using comprehensions:

```
julia> using Dates
julia> Dict([x => Dates.dayname(x) for x = (1:7)])
Dict{Int64,String} with 7 entries:
  7 => "Sunday"
  4 => "Thursday"
  2 => "Tuesday"
  3 => "Wednesday"
  5 => "Friday"
  6 => "Saturday"
  1 => "Monday"
```

Your output will be different as it's likely that the keys won't be ordered from 1 to 7. That's a very important point—as already mentioned, in Julia, the `Dict` is not ordered.

Ordered dictionaries

If you ever need your dictionaries to stay ordered, you can use the `OrderedCollections` package (https://github.com/JuliaCollections/OrderedCollections.jl), specifically the `OrderedDict`:

```
pkg> add OrderedCollections
julia> using OrderedCollections, Dates
julia> OrderedDict(x => Dates.monthname(x) for x = (1:12))
DataStructures.OrderedDict{Any,Any} with 12 entries:
   1  => "January"
   2  => "February"
   3  => "March"
   4  => "April"
   5  => "May"
   6  => "June"
   7  => "July"
   8  => "August"
   9  => "September"
  10  => "October"
  11  => "November"
  12  => "December"
```

Now the elements are stored in the order in which they are added to the collection (from 1 to 12).

Working with dictionaries

As we've already seen, we can index into a `Dict` using the square bracket notation:

```
julia> d = Dict(:foo => 1, :bar => 2)
Dict{Symbol,Int64} with 2 entries:
  :bar => 2
  :foo => 1

julia> d[:bar]
2
```

Attempting to access a key that has not been defined will result in a `KeyError`, as follows:

```
julia> d[:baz]
ERROR: KeyError: key :baz not found
```

To avoid such situations, we can check if the key exists in the first place:

```
julia> haskey(d, :baz)
false
```

As an alternative, if we want to also get a default value when the key does not exist, we can use the following:

```
julia> get(d, :baz, 0)
0
```

The `get` function has a more powerful twin, `get!`, which also stores the searched key into the `Dict`, using the default value:

```
julia> d
Dict{Symbol,Int64} with 2 entries:
  :bar => 2
  :foo => 1

julia> get!(d, :baz, 100)
100

julia> d
Dict{Symbol,Int64} with 3 entries:
  :baz => 100
  :bar => 2
  :foo => 1

julia> haskey(d, :baz)
true
```

In case you're wondering, the exclamation mark at the end of the function name is valid—and denotes an important Julia naming convention. It should be taken as a warning that using the function will modify its arguments' data. In this case, the `get!` function will add the `:baz = 100` `Pair` to the d `Dict`.

Removing a key-value `Pair` is just a matter of invoking `delete!` (note the presence of the exclamation mark here too):

```
julia> delete!(d, :baz)
Dict{Symbol,Int64} with 2 entries:
  :bar => 2
  :foo => 1

julia> haskey(d, :baz)
false
```

As requested, the :baz key and its corresponding value have vanished.

We can ask for the collections of keys and values using the aptly named functions keys and values. They will return iterators over their underlying collections:

```julia
julia> keys(d)
Base.KeySet for a Dict{Symbol,Int64} with 2 entries. Keys:
  :bar
  :foo

julia> values(d)
Base.ValueIterator for a Dict{Symbol,Int64} with 2 entries. Values:
  2
  1
```

Use collect to retrieve the corresponding arrays:

```julia
julia> collect(keys(d))
2-element Array{Symbol,1}:
 :bar
 :foo

julia> collect(values(d))
2-element Array{Int64,1}:
 2
 1
```

We can combine a Dict with another Dict:

```julia
julia> d2 = Dict(:baz => 3)
Dict{Symbol,Int64} with 1 entry:
  :baz => 3

julia> d3 = merge(d, d2)
Dict{Symbol,Int64} with 3 entries:
  :baz => 3
  :bar => 2
  :foo => 1
```

If some of the keys are present in multiple dictionaries, the values from the last collection will be preserved:

```julia
julia> merge(d3, Dict(:baz => 10))
Dict{Symbol,Int64} with 3 entries:
  :baz => 10
  :bar => 2
  :foo => 1
```

Using the HTTP response

Armed with a good understanding of Julia's dictionary data structure, we can now take a closer look at the headers property of resp, our HTTP response object.

To make it easier to access the various headers, first let's convert the array of Pair to a Dict:

```
julia> headers = Dict(resp.headers)
Dict{SubString{String},SubString{String}} with 23 entries:
"Connection"      => "keep-alive"
  "Via"           => "1.1 varnish (Varnish/5.1), 1.1 varnish (Varni...
  "X-Analytics"   => "ns=0;page_id=38455554;https=1;nocookies=1"
#... output truncated... #
```

We can check the Content-Length value to determine whether or not we have a response body. If it's larger than 0, that means we got back a HTML message:

```
julia> headers["Content-Length"]
"193324"
```

It's important to remember that all the values in the headers dictionary are strings, so we can't go comparing them straight away:

```
julia> headers["Content-Length"] > 0
ERROR: MethodError: no method matching isless(::Int64, ::String)
```

We'll need to parse it into an integer first:

```
julia> parse(Int, headers["Content-Length"]) > 0
true
```

Manipulating the response body

Earlier, we read the response body into a String and stored it into the resp_body variable. It's a long HTML string and, in theory, we could use Regex and other string-processing functions to find and extract the data that we need. However, such an approach would be extremely complicated and error-prone. The best way to search for content in a HTML document is via HTML and CSS selectors. The only problem is that these selectors don't operate on strings—they only work against a **Document Object Model** (**DOM**).

Building a DOM representation of the page

The DOM represents an in-memory structure of an HTML document. It is a data structure that allows us to programmatically manipulate the underlying HTML elements. The DOM represents a document as a logical tree, and we can use selectors to traverse and query this hierarchy.

Parsing HTML with Gumbo

Julia's `Pkg` ecosystem provides access to `Gumbo`, a HTML parser library. Provided with a HTML string, `Gumbo` will parse it into a document and its corresponding DOM. This package is an important tool for web scraping with Julia, so let's add it.

As usual, install using the following:

```
pkg> add Gumbo
julia> using Gumbo
```

We're now ready to parse the HTML string into a DOM as follows:

```
julia> dom = parsehtml(resp_body)
 HTML Document
```

The `dom` variable now references a `Gumbo.HTMLDocument`, an in-memory Julia representation of the web page. It's a simple object that has only two fields:

```
julia> fieldnames(typeof(dom))
(:doctype, :root)
```

The `doctype` represents the HTML `<!DOCTYPE html>` element, which is what the Wikipedia page uses:

```
julia> dom.doctype
"html"
```

Now, let's focus on the `root` property. This is effectively the outermost element of the HTML page—the `<html>` tag containing the rest of the elements. It provides us with an entry point into the DOM. We can ask `Gumbo` about its attributes:

```
julia> dom.root.attributes
Dict{AbstractString,AbstractString} with 3 entries:
  "class" => "client-nojs"
  "lang"  => "en"
  "dir"   => "ltr"
```

It's a `Dict`, the keys representing HTML attributes and the values—the attributes' values. And sure enough, they match the page's HTML:

```
1  <!DOCTYPE html>
2  <html class="client-nojs" lang="en" dir="ltr">
```

There's also a similar `attrs` method, which serves the same purpose:

```
julia> attrs(dom.root)
Dict{AbstractString,AbstractString} with 3 entries:
  "class" => "client-nojs"
  "lang"  => "en"
  "dir"   => "ltr"
```

When in doubt, we can just ask about the name of an element using the `tag` method:

```
julia> tag(dom.root)
:HTML
```

Gumbo exposes a `children` method which returns an array containing all the nested `HTMLElement`. If you just go ahead and execute `julia> children(dom.root)`, the REPL output will be hard to follow. The REPL representation of an `HTMLElement` is its HTML code, which, for top-level elements with many children, will fill up many Terminal screens. Let's use a `for` loop to iterate over the children and show just their tags:

```
julia> for c in children(dom.root)
            @show tag(c)
       end
tag(c) = :head
tag(c) = :body
```

Much better!

Since the children are part of a collection, we can index into them:

```
julia> body = children(dom.root)[2];
```

Please note the closing semicolon (;). When used in the REPL at the end of an expression, it will suppress the output (so we won't see the very long HTML code of the <body> that would otherwise be output). The body variable will now reference an instance of HTMLElement{:body}:

```
HTMLElement{:body}:
<body class="mediawiki ltr sitedir-ltr mw-hide-empty-elt ns-0 ns-subject
page-Julia_programming_language rootpage-Julia_programming_language skin-
vector action-view">
# ... output truncated ...
```

The last method that we'll need is getattr, which returns the value of an attribute name. If the attribute is not defined for the element, it raises a KeyError:

```
julia> getattr(dom.root, "class")
"client-nojs"

julia> getattr(dom.root, "href") # oops!
ERROR: KeyError: key "href" not found
```

Asking about the href attribute of a <html> tag doesn't make any sense. And sure enough, we promptly got a KeyError, since href was not an attribute of this HTMLElement.

Coding defensively

An error like the previous one, when part of a larger script, has the potential to completely alter a program's execution, leading to undesired and potentially costly results. In general, when something unexpected occurs during the execution of a program, it may leave the software in an erroneous state, making it impossible to return a correct value. In such cases, rather than pushing on and potentially propagating the problem throughout the whole execution stack, it's preferable to explicitly notify the calling code about the situation by throwing an Exception.

Many functions, both in Julia's core and within third-party packages, make good use of the error-throwing mechanism. It's good practice to check the docs for the functions you use and to see what kinds of errors they throw. An error is called an exception in programming lingo.

As in the case of `getattr`, the author of the `Gumbo` package warned us that attempting to read an attribute that was not defined would result in a `KeyError` exception. We'll learn soon how to handle exceptions by capturing them in our code, getting info about the problem, and stopping or allowing the exception to propagate further up the call stack. Sometimes it's the best approach, but it's not a technique we want to abuse since handling errors this way can be resource-intensive. Dealing with exceptions is considerably slower than performing simple data integrity checks and branching.

For our project, the first line of defense is to simply check if the attribute is in fact defined in the element. We can do this by retrieving the keys of the attributes `Dict` and checking if the one we want is part of the collection. It's a one-liner:

```julia
julia> in("href", collect(keys(attrs(dom.root))))
false
```

Clearly, `href` is not an attribute of the `<html>` tag.

Using this approach, we can easily write logic to check for the existence of an attribute before we attempt to look up its value.

The pipe operator

Reading multiple nested functions can be taxing on the brain. The previous example, `collect(keys(attrs(dom.root)))`, can be rewritten to improve readability using Julia's pipe operator, `|>`.

For example, the following snippet nests three function calls, each inner function becoming the argument of the outermost one:

```julia
julia> collect(keys(attrs(dom.root)))
3-element Array{AbstractString,1}:
 "class"
 "lang"
 "dir"
```

This can be rewritten for improved readability as a chain of functions using the pipe operator. This code produces the exact same result:

```julia
julia> dom.root |> attrs |> keys |> collect
3-element Array{AbstractString,1}:
 "class"
 "lang"
 "dir"
```

What the |> operator does is that it takes the output of the first value and *pipes* it as the argument of the next function. So dom.root |> attrs is identical to attrs(dom.root). Unfortunately, the pipe operator works only for one-argument functions. But it's still very useful for decluttering code, massively improving readability.

> For more advanced piping functionality you can check out the Lazy
> package, specifically @> and @>> at
> https://github.com/MikeInnes/Lazy.jl#macros.

Handling errors like a pro

Sometimes, coding defensively won't be the solution. Maybe a key part of your program requires reading a file on the network or accessing a database. If the resource can't be accessed due to a temporary network failure, there's really not much you can do in the absence of the data.

The try...catch statements

If you identify parts of your code where you think the execution can go off the rails due to conditions that are out of your control (that is, *exceptional* conditions—hence the name *exception*), you can use Julia's try...catch statements. This is exactly what it sounds like—you instruct the compiler to *try* a piece of code and if, as a result of a problem, an exception is *thrown*, to *catch* it. The fact that an exception is *caught* implies that it won't propagate throughout the whole application.

Let's see it in action:

```
julia> try
    getattr(dom.root, "href")
catch
    println("The $(tag(dom.root)) tag doesn't have a 'href' attribute.")
end
The HTML tag doesn't have a 'href' attribute.
```

In this example, once an error is encountered, the execution of the code in the try branch is stopped exactly at that point, and the execution flow continues right away, in the catch branch.

It becomes clearer if we modify the snippet as follows:

```julia
julia> try
    getattr(dom.root, "href")
    println("I'm here too")
catch
    println("The $(tag(dom.root)) tag doesn't have a 'href' attribute.")
end
The HTML tag doesn't have a 'href' attribute.
```

The newly added line, `println("I'm here too")`, is not executed, as demonstrated by the fact that the message is not output.

Of course, things change if no exception is thrown:

```julia
julia> try
getattr(dom.root, "class")
    println("I'm here too")
catch
    println("The $(tag(dom.root)) tag doesn't have a 'href' attribute.")
end
I'm here too
```

The `catch` construct takes an optional argument, the `Exception` object that's been thrown by the `try` block. This allows us to inspect the exception and branch our code depending on its properties.

In our example, the `KeyError` exception is built into Julia. It is thrown when we attempt to access or delete a non-existent element (such as a key in a `Dict` or an attribute of a `HTMLElement`). All instances of `KeyError` have a key property, which provides information about the missing data. Thus, we can make our code more generic:

```julia
julia> try
    getattr(dom.root, "href")
catch ex
    if isa(ex, KeyError)
            println("The $(tag(dom.root)) tag doesn't have a '$(ex.key)'
attribute.")
    else
            println("Some other exception has occurred")
    end
end
The HTML tag doesn't have a 'href' attribute.
```

Here, we pass the exception into the `catch` block as the `ex` variable. We then check if we're dealing with a `KeyError` exception—if we are, we use this information to display a custom error by accessing the `ex.key` field to retrieve the missing key. If it's a different type of exception, we show a generic error message:

```
julia> try
    error("Oh my!")
catch ex
    if isa(ex, KeyError)
        println("The $(tag(dom.root)) tag doesn't have a '$(ex.key)'
attribute.")
    else
        println("Some exception has occurred")
    end
end
Some exception has occurred
```

The finally clause

In code that performs state changes or uses resources such as files or databases, there is typically some clean-up work (such as closing files or database connections) that needs to be done when the code is finished. This code would normally go into the `try` branch—but what happens if an exception is thrown?

In such cases, the `finally` clause comes into play. This can be added after a `try` or after a `catch` branch. The code within the `finally` block is *guaranteed* to be executed, regardless of whether exceptions are thrown or not:

```
julia> try
    getattr(dom.root, "href")
catch ex
    println("The $(tag(dom.root)) tag doesn't have a '$(ex.key)'
attribute.")
finally
    println("I always get called")
end
The HTML tag doesn't have a 'href' attribute.
I always get called
```

It is illegal to have a `try` without a `catch` or a `finally`:

```
julia> try getattr(dom.root, "href") end syntax: try without catch or
finally
```

We need to provide either a `catch` or a `finally` block (or both).

The `try/catch/finally` blocks will return the last expression evaluated, so we can capture it in a variable:

```julia
julia> result = try
            error("Oh no!")
       catch ex
           "Everything is under control"
         end
"Everything is under control"

julia> result
"Everything is under control"
```

Throwing exceptions on errors

As developers, we too have the option to create and throw exceptions when our code encounters a problem and shouldn't continue. Julia provides a long list of built-in exceptions that cover a multitude of use cases. You can read about them at `https://docs.julialang.org/en/stable/manual/control-flow/#Built-in-Exceptions-1`.

In order to throw an exception, we use the aptly named `throw` function. For example, if we want to replicate the error raised by Gumbo's `getattr` method, all we have to do is call the following:

```julia
julia> throw(KeyError("href"))
ERROR: KeyError: key "href" not found
```

If the built-in exceptions provided by Julia aren't relevant enough for your situation, the language provides a generic error type, the `ErrorException`. It takes an additional `msg` argument which should offer more details about the nature of the error:

```julia
julia> ex = ErrorException("To err is human, but to really foul things up
you need a computer.")
ErrorException("To err is human, but to really foul things up you need a
computer.")

julia> throw(ex)
ERROR: To err is human, but to really foul things up you need a computer.

julia> ex.msg
"To err is human, but to really foul things up you need a computer."
```

Julia provides a shortcut for throwing `ErrorException`, the `error` function:

```
julia> error("To err is human - to blame it on a computer is even more
so.")
ERROR: To err is human - to blame it on a computer is even more so.
```

Rethrowing exceptions

But what do we do if we realize that the exception we've caught cannot (or should not) be handled by our code? For example, say we were expecting to catch a possible missing attribute, but it turned out we got a `Gumbo` parsing exception instead. Such an issue would have to be handled higher up the execution stack, maybe by trying to fetch the web page again and reparsing it, or by logging an error message for the admin.

If we `throw` the exception ourselves, the origin (the `stacktrace`) of the initial error would be lost. For such cases, Julia provides the `rethrow` function, which can be used as follows:

```
julia> try
            Dict()[:foo]
        catch ex
            "nothing to see here"
        end
"nothing to see here"
```

If we simply throw the exception ourselves, this is what happens:

```
julia> try
            Dict()[:foo]
        catch ex
            throw(ex)
        end
ERROR: KeyError: key :foo not found
Stacktrace:
 [1] top-level scope at REPL
```

We throw the `KeyError` exception, but the origin of the exception is lost; it appears as if it originates in our code in the `catch` block. Contrast this with the following example, where we use `rethrow`:

```
julia> try
            Dict()[:foo]
        catch ex
             rethrow(ex)
        end
ERROR: KeyError: key :foo not found
```

```
Stacktrace:
 [1] getindex(::Dict{Any,Any}, ::Symbol) at ./dict.jl:474
 [2] top-level scope at REPL[140]
```

The original exception is being rethrown, without changing the stacktrace. Now we can see that the exception originated within the dict.jl file.

Learning about functions

Before we get to write our first full-fledged Julia program, the web crawler, we need to take yet another important detour. It's the last one, I promise.

As our code becomes more and more complex, we should start using functions. The REPL is great for exploratory programming due to its quick input-output feedback loop, but for any non-trivial piece of software, using functions is the way to go. Functions are an integral part of Julia, promoting readability, code reuse, and performance.

In Julia, a function is an object that takes a tuple of values as an argument and returns a value:

```
julia> function add(x, y)
           x + y
       end
add (generic function with 1 method)
```

There's also a compact *assignment form* for function declaration:

```
julia> add(x, y) = x + y
add (generic function with 1 method)
```

This second form is great for simple one-line functions.

Invoking a function is simply a matter of calling its name and passing it the required arguments:

```
julia> add(1, 2)
3
```

The return keyword

If you have previous programming experience, you might be surprised to see that invoking the add function correctly returns the expected value, despite the fact that we didn't put any explicit return statement in the function's body. In Julia, a function automatically returns the result of the last expression that was evaluated. This is usually the last expression in the body of the function.

An explicit return keyword is also available. Using it will cause the function to exit immediately, with the value passed to the return statement:

```
julia> function add(x, y)
           return "I don't feel like doing math today"
           x + y
       end
add (generic function with 1 method)

julia> add(1, 2)
"I don't feel like doing math today"
```

Returning multiple values

Although Julia does not support returning multiple values, it does offer a neat trick that's very close to the actual thing. Any function can return a tuple. And because constructing and destructing tuples is very flexible, this approach is very powerful and readable:

```
julia> function addremove(x, y)
           x+y, x-y
       end
addremove (generic function with 1 method)

julia> a, b = addremove(10, 5)
(15, 5)

julia> a
15

julia> b
5
```

Here we defined a function, addremove, which returns a tuple of two integers. We can extract the values within the tuple by simply assigning a variable corresponding to each of its elements.

Optional arguments

Function arguments can have sensible defaults. For such situations, Julia allows defining default values. When they are provided, the corresponding arguments no longer have to be passed explicitly on every call:

```
julia> function addremove(x=100, y=10)
          x+y, x-y
       end
addremove (generic function with 3 methods)
```

This function has default values for both x and y. We can invoke it without passing any of the arguments:

```
julia> addremove()
(110, 90)
```

This snippet demonstrates how Julia uses the default values when they are not provided upon function invocation.

We can pass the first argument only—and for the second one, the default value will be used:

```
julia> addremove(5)
(15, -5)
```

Finally, we can pass both arguments; all the defaults will be overwritten:

```
julia> addremove(5, 1)
(6, 4)
```

Keyword arguments

The functions that require a long list of arguments can be hard to use, as the programmer has to remember the order and the types of the expected values. For such cases, we can define functions that accept labeled arguments instead. These are called **keyword arguments**.

In order to define functions that accept keyword arguments, we need to add a semicolon after the function's list of unlabeled arguments and follow it with one or more keyword=value pairs. We actually encountered such functions in Chapter 11, *Creating Our First Julia App*, when we used Gadfly to plot the Iris flower dataset:

```
plot(iris, x=:SepalLength, y=:PetalLength, color=:Species)
```

In this example, x, y, and `color` are all keyword arguments.

The definition of a function with keyword arguments looks like this:

```
function thermal_confort(temperature, humidity; scale = :celsius, age = 35)
```

Here, we define a new function, `thermal_confort`, which has two required arguments, `temperature` and `humidity`. The function also accepts two keyword arguments, `scale` and `age`, which have the default values of `:celsius` and 35, respectively. It is necessary for all the keyword arguments to have default values.

Invoking such a function implies using the positional as well as the keyword arguments:

```
thermal_confort(27, 56, age = 72, scale = :fahrenheit)
```

If the values for the keyword arguments are not supplied, the default values are used.

Keyword argument default values are evaluated left to right, which means that default expressions may refer to prior keyword arguments:

```
function thermal_confort(temperature, humidity; scale = :celsius, age = 35,
health_risk = age/100)
```

Note that we reference the keyword argument `age` in the default value of `health_risk`.

Documenting functions

Julia comes out of the box with powerful code-documenting features. The usage is straightforward—any string appearing at the top level, right before an object, will be interpreted as documentation (it's called a **docstring**). The docstring is interpreted as markdown, so we can use markup for rich formatting.

The documentation for the `thermal_confort` function could be as follow:

```
"""
        thermal_confort(temperature, humidity; <keyword arguments>)
Compute the thermal comfort index based on temperature and humidity. It can
optionally take into account the age of the patient. Works for both Celsius
and Fahrenheit.
# Examples:
```julia-repl
julia> thermal_confort(32, 78)
12
```

Arguments
```

```
    - temperature: the current air temperature
    - humidity: the current air humidity
    - scale: whether :celsius or :fahrenheit, defaults to :celsius
    - age: the age of the patient
    """
    function thermal_confort(temperature, humidity; scale = :celsius, age = 35)
```

Now we can access the documentation of our function by using the REPL's help mode:

```
help?> thermal_confort
```

The output is as follows:

```
help?> thermal_confort
search: thermal_confort

        thermal_confort(temperature, humidity; <keyword arguments>)

  Compute the thermal comfort index based on temperature and humidity. It can optionally take int
o account the age of the patient. Works for both Celsius and
  Fahrenheit.

  Examples:
  ≡≡≡≡≡≡≡≡≡≡≡

  julia> thermal_confort(32, 78)
  12


  Arguments
  ≡≡≡≡≡≡≡≡≡≡≡

    •  temperature: the current air temperature

    •  humidity: the current air humidity

    •  scale: whether :celsius or :fahrenheit, defaults to :celsius

    •  age: the age of the patient
```

Pretty useful, isn't it? Docstrings can also be used to generate complete documentation for your Julia projects, with the help of external packages which build full API docs as standalone websites, markdown documents, PDF documents, etcetera.

Writing a basic web crawler – take one

We're now ready to write our first fully-fledged Julia program—a simple web crawler. This first iteration will make a request for Julia's Wikipedia page, will parse it and extract all the internal URLs, storing them in an `Array`.

Setting up our project

The first thing we need to do is to set up a dedicated project. This is done by using `Pkg`. It is a very important step as it allows us to efficiently manage and version the packages on which our program depends.

For starters, we need a folder for our software. Create one—let's call it `WebCrawler`. I'll use Julia to make it, but you do it however you like:

```
julia> mkdir("WebCrawler")
"WebCrawler"

julia> cd("WebCrawler/")
```

Now we can use `Pkg` to add the dependencies. When we start a new project, we need to initialise it. This is achieved with the following:

```
pkg> activate .
```

This tells `Pkg` that we want to manage dependencies in the current project as opposed to doing it globally. You will notice that the cursor has changed, indicating the name of the active project, `WebCrawler`:

```
(WebCrawler) pkg>
```

All the other packages we installed up until this point were in the global environment, which was indicated by the (`v1.0`) cursor:

```
(v1.0) pkg>
```

(`v1.0`) is the global environment, labeled with the currently installed Julia version. If you try the examples on a different Julia version, you'll get a different label.

If we check the status, we'll see that no packages were installed yet in the project's environment:

```
(WebCrawler) pkg> st
    Status `Project.toml`
```

Our software will have two dependencies—HTTP and Gumbo. It's time to add them:

```
(WebCrawler) pkg> add HTTP
(WebCrawler) pkg> add Gumbo
```

Now we can create a new file to host our code. Let's call it webcrawler.jl. It can be created using Julia:

```
julia> touch("webcrawler.jl")
"webcrawler.jl"
```

Writing a Julia program

Unlike our previous work in the REPL and IJulia notebooks, this will be a standalone program: all the logic will go inside this webcrawler.jl file, and when ready, we'll use the julia binary to execute it.

Julia files are parsed top to bottom, so we need to provide all the necessary instructions in the right order (using statements, variables initialization, function definitions, etcetera). We'll pretty much condense all the steps we took so far in this chapter to build this small program.

To make things simpler, it's best to use a full-fledged Julia editor. Open webcrawler.jl in Atom/Juno or Visual Studio Code (or whatever your favorite editor is).

The first thing we want to do is to inform Julia that we plan on using the HTTP and Gumbo packages. We can write a single using statement and list multiple dependencies, separated by a comma:

```
using HTTP, Gumbo
```

Also, we decided that we wanted to use Julia's Wikipedia page to test our crawler. The link is https://en.wikipedia.org/wiki/Julia_(programming_language). It's good practice to store such configuration-like values in constants, rather than spreading *magic strings* throughout the whole code base:

```
const PAGE_URL =
"https://en.wikipedia.org/wiki/Julia_(programming_language)"
```

We also said that we wanted to store all the links in an `Array`—let's set that up too. Remember that constants in Julia are concerned mostly with types, so there is no problem if we push values into the array after it's declared:

```
const LINKS = String[]
```

Here, we initialize the `LINKS` constant as an empty `Array` of `String`. The notation `String[]` produces the same result as `Array{String,1}()` and `Vector{String}()`. It basically represents the empty `Array` literal `[]` plus the `Type` constraint `String`—creating a `Vector` of `String` values.

The next steps are—fetch the page, look for a successful response (status `200`), and then check the headers to see if we received a message body (`Content-Length` greater than zero). In this first iteration, we only have to do this one time. But thinking ahead, for the final version of our game, we'll have to repeat this process up to six times per game session (because there will be up to Six Degrees of Wikipedia, so we'll have to crawl up to six pages). The best thing we can do is to write a generic function which takes a page URL as its only parameter, fetches the page, performs the necessary checks, and returns the message body if available. Let's call this function `fetchpage`:

```
function fetchpage(url)
    response = HTTP.get(url)
    if response.status == 200 && parse(Int,
Dict(response.headers)["Content-Length"]) > 0
        String(response.body)
    else
        ""
    end
end
```

First, we call `HTTP.get(url)`, storing the `HTTP.Messages.Response` object in the `response` variable. Then we check if the response status is `200` and if the `Content-Length` header is greater than `0`. If they are, we read the message body into a string. If not, we return an empty string, `""`, to represent the empty body. That's a lot of *ifs*—looks like it's time we take a closer look at the conditional `if`/`else` statements, as they're really important.

Conditional evaluation of if, elseif, and else statements

All, except maybe the most basic, programs must be able to evaluate variables and execute different logical branches depending on their current values. Conditional evaluation allows portions of the code to be executed (or not) depending on the value of a Boolean expression. Julia provides the `if`, `elseif`, and `else` statements for writing conditional expressions. They work like this:

```
julia> x = 5
5

julia> if x < 0
           println("x is a negative number")
       elseif x > 0
           println("x is a positive number greater than 0")
       else
           println("x is 0")
       end
x is a positive number greater than 0
```

If the condition `x < 0` is true, then its underlying block is evaluated. If not, the expression `x > 0` is evaluated, as part of the `elseif` branch. If it is true, its corresponding block is evaluated. If neither expression is true, the `else` block is evaluated.

The `elseif` and `else` blocks are optional, and we can use as many `elseif` blocks as we want. The conditions in the `if`,`elseif` and `else` construct are evaluated until the first one returns `true`. Then the associated block is evaluated and its last computed value is returned, exiting the conditional evaluation. Thus, conditional statements in Julia also return a value—the last executed statement in the branch that was chosen. The following code shows this:

```
julia> status = if x < 0
                    "x is a negative number"
               elseif x > 0
                    "x is a positive number greater than 0"
               else
                    "x is 0"
               end
"x is a positive number greater than 0"

julia> status
"x is a positive number greater than 0"
```

Finally, it's very important to keep in mind that `if` blocks do not introduce local scope. That is, variables defined within them will be accessible after the block is exited (of course, provided that the respective branch has been evaluated):

```julia
julia> status = if x < 0
           "x is a negative number"
       elseif x > 0
           y = 20
           "x is a positive number greater than 0"
       else
           "x is 0"
       end
"x is a positive number greater than 0"

julia> y
20
```

We can see here that the `y` variable, initialized within the `elseif` block, is still accessible outside the conditional expression.

This can be avoided if we declare the variable to be `local`:

```julia
julia> status = if x < 0
           "x is a negative number"
       elseif x > 0
           local z = 20
           "x is a positive number greater than 0"
       else
           "x is 0"
       end
"x is a positive number greater than 0"

julia> z
UndefVarError: z not defined
```

When declared `local`, the variable no longer *leaks* outside the `if` block.

The ternary operator

An `if`,`then` and `else` type of condition can be expressed using the ternary operator `?` `:`. Its syntax is as follows:

```
x ? y : z
```

If x is true, the expression y is evaluated—otherwise, z gets evaluated instead. For instance, consider the following code:

```
julia> x = 10
10

julia> x < 0 ? "negative" : "positive"
"positive"
```

Short-circuit evaluation

Julia provides an even more concise type of evaluation—short-circuit evaluation. In a series of Boolean expressions connected by && and || operators, only the minimum number of expressions are evaluated—as many as are necessary in order to determine the final Boolean value of the entire chain. We can exploit this to return certain values, depending on what gets to be evaluated. For instance:

```
julia> x = 10
10

julia> x > 5 && "bigger than 5"
"bigger than 5"
```

In an expression A && B, the second expression B is only evaluated if and only if A evaluates to true. In this case, the whole expression has the return value of the sub-expression B, which in the previous example is bigger than 5.

If, on the contrary, A evaluates to false, B does not get evaluated at all. Thus, beware—the whole expression will return a false Boolean (not a string!):

```
julia> x > 15 && "bigger than 15"
false
```

The same logic applies to the logical or operator, ||:

```
julia> x < 5 || "greater than 5"
"greater than 5"
```

In an expression A || B, the second expression B is only evaluated if A evaluates to false. The same logic applies when the first sub-expression is evaluated to true; true will be the return value of the whole expression:

```
julia> x > 5 || "less than 5"
true
```

Beware of operator precedence

Sometimes short-circuit expressions can confuse the compiler, resulting in errors or unexpected results. For example, short-circuit expressions are often used with assignment operations, as follows:

```
julia> x > 15 || message = "That's a lot"
```

This will fail with the `syntax: invalid assignment location "(x > 15) ||
message"` error because the = assignment operator has higher precedence than logical or and ||. It can easily be fixed by using brackets to explicitly control the evaluation order:

```
julia> x > 15 || (message = "That's a lot")
"That's a lot"
```

It's something to keep in mind as it's a common source of errors for beginners.

Carrying on with the crawler's implementation

So far, your code should look like this:

```
using HTTP, Gumbo

const PAGE_URL =
"https://en.wikipedia.org/wiki/Julia_(programming_language)"
const LINKS = String[]

function fetchpage(url)
  response = HTTP.get(url)
  if response.status == 200 && parse(Int, Dict(response.headers)["Content-
Length"]) > 0
    String(response.body)
  else
    ""
  end
end
```

It should be now clear that either the response body or an empty string is returned by the `if`/`else` statement. And since this is the last piece of code evaluated inside the `fetchpage` function, this value also becomes the return value of the whole function.

All good, we can now use the `fetchpage` function to get the HTML content of the Wikipedia page and store it in the `content` variable:

```
content = fetchpage(PAGE_URL)
```

If the fetch operation is successful and the `content` is not an empty string, we can pass the HTML string to `Gumbo` to construct the DOM. Then, we can loop through all the children of this DOM's `root` element and look for links (using the `a` tag selector). For each element, we want to check the `href` attribute and store its value only if it points to another Wikipedia page:

```
if ! isempty(content)
  dom = Gumbo.parsehtml(content)
  extractlinks(dom.root)
end
```

The function for extracting the links is:

```
function extractlinks(elem)
  if  isa(elem, HTMLElement) &&
      tag(elem) == :a && in("href", collect(keys(attrs(elem)))))
        url = getattr(elem, "href")
        startswith(url, "/wiki/") && push!(LINKS, url)
  end

  for child in children(elem)
    extractlinks(child)
  end
end
```

Here, we declare an `extractlinks` function which takes a `Gumbo` element, called `elem`, as its only parameter. We then check if `elem` is a `HTMLElement` and, if it is, we check if it corresponds to a link tag (the `:a` Julia `Symbol` which represents an `<a>` HTML tag). Then we check if the element defines a `href` attribute in order to avoid getting a `KeyError`. If all is good, we get the value of the `href` element. And finally, if the value of the `href` is an internal URL—that is, a URL that starts with `/wiki/`—we add it to our `LINKS` `Array`.

Once we're done checking the element for links, we check if it contains other nested HTML elements. If it does, we want to repeat the same process for each of its children. That's what the final `for` loop does.

The only thing left to do is to display the populated `LINKS` Array, at the very end of our file. Since some of the links might come up in the page more than once, let's make sure we reduce the `Array` to the unique elements only, by using the `unique` function:

```
display(unique(LINKS))
```

Now we can execute this script by opening a terminal in the folder where the file is stored. And then run—$ `julia webcrawler.jl`.

There's plenty of links, so the output will be quite long. Here's the top of the list:

```
$ julia webcrawler.jl
440-element Array{String,1}:
 "/wiki/Programming_paradigm"
 "/wiki/Multi-paradigm_programming_language"
 "/wiki/Multiple_dispatch"
 "/wiki/Object-oriented_programming"
 "/wiki/Procedural_programming"
# ... output truncated ...
```

By looking at the output, we'll notice that in the first optimization some links point to special Wikipedia pages—the ones containing parts such as `/File:`, `/Category:`, `/Help:`, `/Special:`, and so on. So we can just go ahead and skip all the URLs that contain a column, `:`, since these are not articles and are not useful for our game.

To do this, look for the line that reads:

```
startswith(url, "/wiki/") && push!(LINKS, url)
```

Replace the preceding line with the following:

```
startswith(url, "/wiki/") && ! occursin(":", url) && push!(LINKS, url)
```

If you run the program now, you should see a list of all the URLs from Julia's Wikipedia page that link to other Wikipedia articles.

This is the full code:

```
using HTTP, Gumbo

const PAGE_URL =
"https://en.wikipedia.org/wiki/Julia_(programming_language)"
const LINKS = String[]

function fetchpage(url)
  response = HTTP.get(url)
  if response.status == 200 && parse(Int, Dict(response.headers)["Content-
```

```
    Length"]) > 0
        String(response.body)
      else
        ""
      end
    end


    function extractlinks(elem)
      if  isa(elem, HTMLElement) && tag(elem) == :a && in("href",
    collect(keys(attrs(elem)))))
            url = getattr(elem, "href")
            startswith(url, "/wiki/") && ! occursin(":", url) && push!(LINKS,
    url)
      end

      for child in children(elem)
        extractlinks(child)
      end
    end
    content = fetchpage(PAGE_URL)

    if ! isempty(content)
      dom = Gumbo.parsehtml(content)
      extractlinks(dom.root)
    end

    display(unique(LINKS))
```

Summary

Web scraping is a key component of data mining and Julia provides a powerful toolbox for handling these tasks. In this chapter, we addressed the fundamentals of building a web crawler. We learned how to request web pages with a Julia web client and how to read the responses, how to work with Julia's powerful `Dict` data structure to read HTTP information, how to make our software more resilient by handling errors, how to better organize our code by writing functions and documenting them, and how to use conditional logic to make decisions.

Armed with this knowledge, we built the first version of our web crawler. In the next chapter, we will improve it and will use it to extract the data for our upcoming Wiki game. In the process, we'll dive deeper into the language, learning about types, methods and modules, and how to interact with relational databases.

13
Building the Wiki Game Web Crawler

Wow, `Chapter 12`, *Setting Up the Wiki Game*, was quite a ride! Laying the foundation of our Wikipedia game took us on a real learning *tour-de-force*. After the quick refresher on how the web and web pages work, we dived deeper into the key parts of the language, studying the dictionary data structure and its corresponding data type, conditional expressions, functions, exception handling, and even the very handy piping operator (`|>`). In the process, we built a short script that uses a couple of powerful third-party packages, `HTTP` and `Gumbo`, to request a web page from Wikipedia, parse it as an HTML DOM, and extract all internal links from within the page. Our script is part of a proper Julia project, which employs `Pkg` to efficiently manage dependencies.

In this chapter, we'll continue the development of our game, implementing the complete workflow and the gameplay. Even if you are not a seasoned developer, it's easy to imagine that even a simple game like this will end up with multiple logical parts. We could maybe have a module for the Wikipedia page crawler, one for the gameplay itself, and one for the UI (the web app that we'll create in the next chapter). Breaking down a problem into smaller parts always makes for a simpler solution. And, that's especially true when writing code—having small, specialized functions, grouped by responsibility, makes the software easier to reason about, develop, extend, and maintain. In this chapter, we'll dig deeper into Julia's constructs for structuring the code, and we'll revisit a few more key elements of the language: the type system, constructors, methods, and multiple dispatch.

In this chapter, we'll cover the following topics:

- *Six Degrees of Wikipedia*, the gameplay
- Organizing our code using modules and loading code from multiple files (the so-called **mixin behavior**)
- Types and the type system, which are key to Julia's flexibility and performance

- Constructors, special functions which allow us to create new instances of our types
- Methods and multiple dispatch, some of the most important aspects of the language
- Interacting with relational databases (specifically, MySQL)

I hope you are ready to dive in.

Technical requirements

The Julia package ecosystem is under continuous development and new package versions are released on a daily basis. Most of the times this is great news, as new releases bring new features and bug fixes. However, since many of the packages are still in beta (version 0.x), any new release can introduce breaking changes. As a result, the code presented in the book can stop working. In order to ensure that your code will produce the same results as described in the book, it is recommended to use the same package versions. Here are the external packages used in this chapter and their specific versions:

```
Cascadia@v0.4.0
Gumbo@v0.5.1
HTTP@v0.7.1
IJulia@v1.14.1
JSON@v0.20.0
MySQL@v0.7.0
```

In order to install a specific version of a package you need to run:

```
pkg> add PackageName@vX.Y.Z
```

For example:

```
pkg> add IJulia@v1.14.1
```

Alternatively you can install all the used packages by downloading the Project.toml file provided with the chapter and using `pkg>` instantiate as follows:

```
julia>
download("https://github.com/TrainingByPackt/Julia-1-Programming-Complete-Reference-Guide/tree/master/Chapter13/Project.toml", "Project.toml")
pkg> activate .
pkg> instantiate
```

Six Degrees of Wikipedia, the gameplay

As we've seen in the previous chapter, the **Six Degrees of Wikipedia game** is a play on the concept of the *six degrees of separation* theory—the idea that all living things (and pretty much everything in the world) are six or fewer steps away from each other. For example, a chain of *a friend of a friend* can be made to connect any two people in a maximum of six steps.

For our own game, the goal of the player is to link any two given Wikipedia articles, passing through six or fewer other Wikipedia pages. In order to make sure that the problem has a solution (the *six degrees of separation* theory has not been demonstrated) and that indeed there is a path from our starting article to the end article, we'll pre-crawl the full path. That is, we'll begin with a random Wikipedia page, which will be our starting point, and we'll link through a number of pages toward our destination, the end article. The algorithm for picking the next linked page will be the simplest—we'll just pick any random internal link.

To make things more interesting, we will also offer a difficulty setting—easy, medium, or hard. This will affect how far apart the start page and the end page will be. For an easy game, they will be two pages away, for medium, four, and for hard, six. Of course, this logic in not super rigorous. Yes, intuitively, we can say that two articles that are further apart will be less related and harder to link. But, it's also possible that the player will find a shorter path. We won't worry about that, though.

The game will also allow the players to go back if they can't find the solution in the maximum number of steps.

Finally, if the player gives up, we'll add an option to show the solution—the path we found from the start article to the destination.

This sounds exciting—let's write some code!

Some additional requirements

In order to follow through this chapter, you will need the following:

- A working Julia installation
- An internet connection
- A text editor

Organizing our code

Up to this point, we've been mostly coding at the REPL. Recently, in the previous chapter, we've started to rely more on the IDE to whip up short Julia files.

But, as our skillset grows and we develop more and more ambitious projects, so will grow the complexity of our programs. This, in turn, will lead to more lines of code, more logic, and more files—and more difficulties in maintaining and understanding all these down the line. As the famous coding axiom goes, the code is read many more times than it is written—so we need to plan accordingly.

Each language comes with its own philosophy and toolset when it comes to code organization. In Julia, we have files, modules, and packages. We'll learn about all of these next.

Using modules to tame our code

Modules group together related functions, variables, and other definitions. But, they are not just organizational units—they are language constructs that can be understood as variable workspaces. They allow us to define variables and functions without worrying about name conflicts. Julia's `Module` is one of the cornerstones of the language—a key structural and logical entity that helps make code easier to develop, understand, and maintain. We'll make good use of modules by architecting our game around them.

A module is defined using the `module <<name>>...end` construct:

```
module MyModule
# code here
end
```

Let's start a new REPL session and look at a few examples.

Say we want to write a function that retrieves a random Wikipedia page—it's one of our game's features. We could call this function `rand`.

As you may suspect, creating random *things* is a pretty common task, so we're not the first ones to think about it. You can see for yourself. Try this at the REPL:

```
julia> rand
rand (generic function with 56 methods)
```

Turns out, 56 `rand` methods are already defined.

This will make it difficult to add our own variant:

```
julia> function rand()
           # code here
       end
error in method definition: function Base.rand must be explicitly imported
to be extended
```

Our attempt to define a new `rand` method raised an error because it was already defined and loaded.

It's easy to see how this can lead to a nightmare scenario when choosing the names of our functions. If all the defined names would live in the same workspace, we'd get into endless name conflicts as we'd run out of relevant names for our functions and variables.

Julia's module allows us to define separate workspaces, providing a level of encapsulation that separates our variables and functions from everybody else's. By using modules, name conflicts are eliminated.

Modules are defined within `module...end` language constructs. Try this example (at the REPL), where we define our `rand` function within a module called `MyModule`:

```
julia> module MyModule

       function rand()
           println("I'll get a random Wikipedia page")
       end

       end
Main.MyModule
```

This snippet defines a module called `MyModule`—and within it, a function called `rand`. Here, `MyModule` effectively encapsulates the `rand` function, which no longer clashes with Julia's `Base.rand`.

As you can see from its full name, `Main.MyModule`, our newly created module, is actually added within another existing module called `Main`. This module, `Main`, is the default module within which code executed at the REPL is evaluated.

In order to access our newly defined function, we need to reference it within MyModule, by *dotting in*:

```
julia> MyModule.rand()
I'll get a random wikipedia page
```

Defining modules

Since modules are designed to be used with larger code bases, they're not REPL-friendly. Because once they are defined, we cannot extend them with extra definitions and we're forced to retype and redefine the whole module, and it's best to use a full-fledged editor.

Let's create a new folder to host our code. Within it, we'll want to create a new folder called modules/. Then, within the modules/ folder, add three files—Letters.jl, Numbers.jl, and module_name.jl.

Files containing Julia code use, by convention, the .jl file extension.

Productive REPL sessions with Julia

Why not use Julia's file-wrangling powers to set up this file structure? Let's take a look at how to do this, as it will come in handy in our day-to-day work.

Remember, you can type ; into the REPL, at the beginning of the line, to trigger the shell mode. Your cursor will change from julia> to shell> to confirm the change of context. In IJulia/Jupyter, you have to prefix the code in the cell with ; in order to be executed in shell mode.

Now, we can perform the following:

```
shell> mkdir modules # create a new dir called "modules"
shell> cd modules # switch to the "modules" directory
```

Don't forget that Julia's shell mode calls commands as if they run straight into the OS Terminal—so the invoked binaries must exist on that platform. Both `mkdir` and `cd` are supported on all major operating systems, so we're safe here. But, when it comes to creating the files, we're out of luck—the `touch` command is not available on Windows. No problem though—all we need to do in this case is to invoke the Julia function with the same name. This will create the files programmatically, in a platform-agnostic way:

```julia
julia> for f in ["Letters.jl", "Numbers.jl", "module_name.jl"]
           touch(f)
       end
```

If you want to make sure that the files were created, use `readdir`:

```julia
julia> readdir()
3-element Array{String,1}:
 "Letters.jl"
 "Numbers.jl"
 "module_name.jl"
```

Please make sure that you name the files exactly as indicated, respecting the case.

Another handy productivity trick is invoking `edit`, which opens a file or directory in your default Julia editor. The next snippet will open `Letters.jl` in whatever default editor you have configured:

```julia
julia> edit("Letters.jl")
```

If the default editor is not your favorite Julia IDE, you can change it by setting one of the `JULIA_EDITOR`, `VISUAL`, or `EDITOR` environment variables to point to the editor of your choice. For instance, on my Mac, I can ask for the path to the Atom editor with the following:

```
shell> which atom
/usr/local/bin/atom
```

And then, I can set `JULIA_EDITOR` as follows:

```julia
julia> ENV["JULIA_EDITOR"] = "/usr/local/bin/atom"
```

The three variables have slightly different purposes, but in this case, setting any of them will have the same effect—changing the default editor for the current Julia session. Keep in mind, though, that they have different *weights*, with JULIA_EDITOR taking precedence over VISUAL, which takes precedence over EDITOR.

Setting up our modules

Let's start by editing Letters.jl to make it look like this:

```
module Letters

using Random

export randstring

const MY_NAME = "Letters"

function rand()
   Random.rand('A':'Z')
end

function randstring()
   [rand() for _ in 1:10] |> join
end

include("module_name.jl")

end
```

Here, we have defined a module called Letters. In it, we added a rand function that uses Julia's Random.rand to return a random letter between A and Z in the form of a Char. Next, we added a function called Letters.randstring, which returns a String of 10 random characters. This string is generated using a Char[] array comprehension (the _ variable name is perfectly legal in Julia and, by convention, it designates a variable whose value is not used) which is piped into the join function to return the string result.

Please note that this is an over complicated way to generate a random string as Julia provides the Random.randstring function. But, at this point, it's important to exploit every opportunity to practice writing code, and I just didn't want to waste the chance of using Julia's comprehension syntax and the pipe operator. Practice makes perfect!

Switching our focus towards the first lines of code, we declared that we'll be using `Random`—and we instructed the compiler to make `randstring` public via `export randstring`. Finally, we have also declared a constant called `MY_NAME`, which points to the `Letters` string (which is the name of the module itself).

The last line of the module, `include("module_name.jl")`, loads the contents of `module_name.jl` into `Letters`. The `include` function is typically used to load source code interactively, or to combine files in packages that are split into multiple source files—and we'll see how this works soon.

Next, let's edit `Number.jl`. It will have a similar `rand` function that will return a random `Integer` between 1 and `1_000`. It exports `halfrand`, a function that gets a value from `rand` and divides it by 2. We pass the result of the division to the `floor` function, which will convert it to the closest less than or equal value. And, just like `Letters`, it also includes `module_name.jl`:

```
module Numbers

using Random

export halfrand

const MY_NAME = "Numbers"

function rand()
  Random.rand(1:1_000)
end
function halfrand()
  floor(rand() / 2)
end

include("module_name.jl")
end
```

Thus, for both modules, we defined a `MY_NAME` constant. We'll reference it by editing the `module_name.jl` file to make it look like this:

```
function myname()
  MY_NAME
end
```

The code returns the corresponding value of the constant, depending on the actual module where we include the `module_name.jl` file. This illustrates Julia's mixin behavior, where included code acts as if it was written directly into the including file. We'll see how this works next.

Referencing modules

Despite the fact that we are only *now* formally discussing modules, we've been using them all along. The `using` statement which we employed so many times takes as its parameter a module name. It's a key language construct that tells the compiler to bring the module's definitions into the current scope. Referencing functions, variables, and types defined in other modules is a routine part of programming in Julia—accessing the functionality provided by a third-party package, for example, revolves around bringing its main module into scope via `using`. But, `using` is not the only tool in Julia's arsenal. We have a few more commands at our disposal, such as `import`, `include`, and `export`.

The `using` directive allows us to reference functions, variables, types, and so on exported by other modules. This tells Julia to make the module's exported definitions available in the current workspace. If the definitions were exported by the module's author, we can invoke them without having to prefix them with the module's name (prefixing the name of the function with the module name represents the fully qualified name). But, be careful though as this is a double-edged sword—if two used modules export functions with the same name, the functions will still have to be accessed using the fully qualified name—otherwise Julia will throw an exception as it won't know which of the functions we refer to.

As for `import`, it is somewhat similar, in that it also brings definitions from another module into scope. But, it differs in two important aspects. First, calling `import MyModule` would still require prefixing the definitions with the module's name, thereby avoiding potential name clashes. Second, if we want to extend functions defined in other modules with new methods, we *have* to use `import`.

On the other hand, `include` is conceptually different. It is used to evaluate the contents of a file into the current context (that is, into the current module's *global* scope). It's a way to reuse code by providing mixin-like behavior, as we have already seen.

The fact that the included file is evaluated in the module's global scope is a very important point. It means that, even if we include a file within a function's body, the contents of the file will not be evaluated within the function's scope, but within the module's scope. To see this in action, let's create a file called `testinclude.jl` in our `modules/` folder. Edit `testinclude.jl` and append this line of code:

```
somevar = 10
```

Now, if you run the following code in the REPL or in IJulia, you'll see what I mean:

```julia
julia> function testinclude()
              include("testinclude.jl")
              println(somevar)
         end

julia> testinclude()
10
```

Apparently, it all worked fine. The `testinclude.jl` file was included and the `somevar` variable was defined. However, `somevar` was not created within the `testinclude` function, but as a global variable in the `Main` module. We can see that easily, as we can access the `somevar` variable directly:

```julia
julia> somevar
10
```

Keep this behavior in mind as it can lead to hard-to-understand bugs by exposing variables in the global scope.

Finally, `export` is used by a module's author to expose definitions, much like a public interface. As we've seen, exported functions and variables are brought into scope by the module's users via `using`.

Setting up the LOAD_PATH

Let's look at some examples that illustrate scoping rules when working with modules. Please open a new Julia REPL.

We've seen the `using` statement many times throughout the previous chapters, and now we understand its role—to bring another module and its definitions (variables, functions, types) into scope. Let's try it with our newly created modules:

```julia
julia> using Letters
ERROR: ArgumentError: Package Letters not found in current path:
- Run `Pkg.add("Letters")` to install the Letters package.
```

Ouch, an exception! Julia informs us that it doesn't know where to find the `Letters` module and advises us to use `Pkg.add("Letters")` to install it. But, since `Pkg.add` only works with registered packages and we haven't published our modules to Julia's registry, that won't help. Turns out we just need to tell Julia where to find our code.

When asked to bring a module into scope via `using`, Julia checks a series of paths to look up the corresponding files. These lookup paths are stored in a `Vector` called the `LOAD_PATH`—and we can append our `modules/` folder to this collection by using the `push!` function:

```
julia> push!(LOAD_PATH, "modules/")
4-element Array{String,1}:
 "@"
 "@v#.#"
 "@stdlib"
 "modules/"
```

Your output might be different, but what matters is that after calling `push!`, the `LOAD_PATH` collection now has an extra element indicating the path to the `modules/` folder.

In order for Julia to match the name of a module with its corresponding file, *the file must have exactly the same name as the module*, plus the `.jl` extension. It's OK for a file to include more than one module, but Julia will not be able to automatically find the extra ones by filename.

In regard to naming the modules themselves, the convention is to use CamelCase. Thus, we'll end up with a module called `Letters` defined in a `Letters.jl` file, or with a `WebSockets` module in a file named `WebSockets.jl`.

Loading modules with using

Now that we've added our folder to the `LOAD_PATH`, we're ready to use our modules:

```
julia> using Letters
```

At this point, two things have happened:

- All the exported definitions are now directly callable in the REPL, in our case, `randstring`
- The definitions that were not exported are accessible by *dotting into* `Letters`—for example, `Letters.rand()`

Let's try it:

```
julia> randstring() # has been exported and is directly accessible
"TCNXFLUOUU"

julia> myname() # has not been exported so it's not available in the
REPLERROR: UndefVarError: myname not defined
```

```
julia> Letters.myname() # but we can access it under the Letters namespace
"Letters"

julia> Letters.rand() # does not conflict with Base.rand
'L': ASCII/Unicode U+004c (category Lu: Letter, uppercase)
```

We can see what a module exports with the `names` function:

```
julia> names(Letters)
2-element Array{Symbol,1}:
 :Letters
 :randstring
```

If we want to get all the definitions of a module, exported or not, `names` takes a second parameter, `all`, a `Boolean`:

```
julia> names(Letters, all = true)
11-element Array{Symbol,1}:
 # output truncated
 :Letters
 :MY_NAME
 :eval
 :myname
 :rand
 :randstring
```

We can easily recognize the variables and functions we defined.

As we can see, for instance, `myname` was not brought directly into scope, since it wasn't exported in `Letters`. But, it turns out that we can still get the exported-like behavior if we explicitly tell Julia to use the function:

```
julia> using Letters: myname
julia> myname() # we no longer need to "dot into" Letters.myname()
"Letters"
```

If we want to bring multiple definitions from the same module directly into scope, we can pass a comma-separated list of names:

```
julia> using Letters: myname, MY_NAME
```

Loading modules with import

Now, let's look at the effects of the import function, using Numbers:

```
julia> import Numbers
julia> names(Numbers)
2-element Array{Symbol,1}:
 :Numbers
 :halfrand
julia> halfrand()
ERROR: UndefVarError: halfrand not defined
```

We can see here that, unlike using, the import function *does not bring into scope* the exported definitions.

However, explicitly importing a definition itself will bring it directly into scope, disregarding whether it was exported or not:

```
julia> import Numbers.halfrand, Numbers.MY_NAME
```

This snippet is equivalent to the following:

```
julia> import Numbers: halfrand, MY_NAME

julia> halfrand()
271.0
```

Loading modules with include

Manipulating the LOAD_PATH works great when developing standalone apps, like the one we're working on now. However, this approach is not available for a package developer. For such instances—and for all the cases when for one reason or another using the LOAD_PATH is not an option—a common way of loading modules is by including their files.

For example, we can include our Letters module at the REPL, as follows (start a new REPL session):

```
julia> include("modules/Letters.jl")
Main.Letters
```

This will read and evaluate the contents of the `modules/Letters.jl` file in the current scope. And as a result, it will define the `Letters` module within our current module, `Main`. But, this is not enough—at this point, none of the definitions within `Letters` were exported:

```
julia> randstring()
ERROR: UndefVarError: randstring not defined
```

We need to bring them into scope:

```
julia> using Letters
ERROR: ArgumentError: Package Letters not found in current path:
- Run `Pkg.add("Letters")` to install the Letters package.
```

Not again! What just happened? This is an important distinction when using `include` with modules. The `Letters` module, like we just said, is included in the current module, `Main`, so we need to reference it accordingly:

```
julia> using Main.Letters

julia> randstring()
"QUPCDZKSAH"
```

We can also reference this kind of nested module hierarchy by using relative *paths*. For example, a dot, `.`, stands for *current module*. So, the previous `Main.Letters` nesting can be expressed as `.Letters`— it's exactly the same thing:

```
julia> using .Letters
```

Similarly, we could use two dots, `..`, to reference the parent module, three dots for the parent of the parent, and so on.

Nesting modules

As we've just seen, sometimes, the logic of our program will dictate that a module has to be part of another module, effectively nesting them. This is used with predilection when developing our own packages. The best way to organize a package is to expose a top module and include all the other definitions (functions, variables, and other modules) within it (to encapsulate the functionality). An example should help clarify things.

Let's make a change—in the `Letters.jl` file, under the line saying `include("module_name.jl")`, go ahead and add another line—`include("Numbers.jl")`.

With this change, the `Numbers` module will effectively be defined within the `Letters` module. In order to access the functions of the nested module, we *dot into* as deep as necessary:

```julia
julia> using .Letters

julia> Letters.Numbers.halfrand()
432.5
```

Setting up our game's architecture

Let's create a home for our game—make a new folder called `sixdegrees/`. We'll use it to organize our game's files. Each file will contain a module and each module will package related functionality. We'll make use of Julia's auto-loading features, which means that the filename of each module will be the same as the module's name, plus the `.jl` extension.

The first thing we need to do, though, once we go into the `sixdegrees/` folder, is to initialize our project through `Pkg`—so we can use Julia's dependency management features:

```julia
julia> mkdir("sixdegrees")
"sixdegrees"

julia> cd("sixdegrees/")

julia> ] # go into pkg mode

(v1.0) pkg> activate .

(sixdegrees) pkg>
```

We'll be using the `HTTP` and the `Gumbo` packages, so it's a good idea to add them, now that we're dealing with dependencies:

```julia
(sixdegrees) pkg> add HTTP Gumbo
```

The next thing we need is a container for Wikipedia-related code—a module that encapsulates the functionality for requesting an article and extracting the internal URLs. We already have a first iteration of the code in the `webcrawler.jl` file we wrote in Chapter 12, *Setting Up the Wiki Game*. Now, all we need to do is create a `Wikipedia` module and fill it up with the contents of `webcrawler.jl`.

Within the `sixdegrees` folder, create a new file called `Wikipedia.jl`. Set it up with the following code:

```julia
module Wikipedia
using HTTP, Gumbo

const RANDOM_PAGE_URL = "https://en.m.wikipedia.org/wiki/Special:Random"

export fetchrandom, fetchpage, articlelinks

function fetchpage(url)
  response = HTTP.get(url)
  if response.status == 200 && length(response.body) > 0
    String(response.body)
  else
    ""
  end
end

function extractlinks(elem, links = String[])
  if  isa(elem, HTMLElement) && tag(elem) == :a && in("href",
collect(keys(attrs(elem))))
        url = getattr(elem, "href")
        startswith(url, "/wiki/") && ! occursin(":", url) && push!(links,
url)
  end
  for child in children(elem)
    extractlinks(child, links)
  end
  unique(links)
end

function fetchrandom()
  fetchpage(RANDOM_PAGE_URL)
end

function articlelinks(content)
  if ! isempty(content)
    dom = Gumbo.parsehtml(content)

    links = extractlinks(dom.root)
```

```
    end
  end

  end
```

The preceding code should look familiar as it shares much of its logic with
`webcrawler.jl`. But, there are some important changes.

First of all, we wrapped everything into a `module` declaration.

 Please note a very important convention: in Julia, we do not indent the
code within modules as this would cause the whole file to be indented,
which would affect readability.

On the third line, where we used to have the link to Julia's Wikipedia entry, we now define
a `String` constant, `RANDOM_PAGE_URL`, which points to a special Wikipedia URL that
returns a random article. Also, we switched to the mobile version of the Wikipedia website,
as indicated by the `en.m.` subdomains. Using the mobile pages will make our lives easier
as they are simpler and have less markup.

In the `fetchpage` function, we're no longer looking for the `Content-Length` header and
we're instead checking the `length` of the `response.body` property. We're doing this
because requesting the special random Wikipedia page performs a redirect and, in the
process, the `Content-Length` header is dropped.

We have also replaced some of the logic at the bottom of the file. Instead of automatically
fetching Julia's Wikipedia page and dumping the list of internal links onto the screen, we
now define two more functions: `fetchrandom` and `articlelinks`. These functions will be
the public interface of the `Wikipedia` module, and they are exposed using the `export`
statement. The `fetchrandom` function does exactly what the name says—it calls the
`fetchpage` function passing in the `RANDOM_PAGE_URL` const, effectively fetching a random
Wikipedia page. `articlelinks` returns an array of strings representing the linked articles.

Finally, we removed the `LINKS` constant—global variables should be avoided. The
`extractlinks` function has been refactored accordingly, now accepting a second
parameter, `links`, a `Vector` of `String`, which is used to maintain state during recursion.

Checking our code

Let's make sure that, after this refactoring, our code still works as expected, by manually running the code and inspecting the output.

We'll add a new file inside the `sixdegrees/` folder, called `six_degrees.jl`. Looking at its name, you can guess that it will be a plain Julia file and not a module. We'll use it to orchestrate the loading of our game:

```
using Pkg
pkg"activate ."

include("Wikipedia.jl")
using .Wikipedia

fetchrandom() |> articlelinks |> display
```

The code is straightforward and minimalistic—we use `Pkg` to activate the current project. Then, we include the `Wikipedia.jl` file in the current module, and then we ask the compiler to bring the `Wikipedia` module into scope. Finally, we use the previously discussed `fetchrandom` and `articlelinks` to retrieve the list of articles URLs from a random Wikipedia page and display it.

Time to run our code! In the REPL, make sure that you `cd` into the `sixdegrees` folder and execute:

```
julia> include("six_degrees.jl")
21-element Array{String,1}:
 "/wiki/Main_Page"
 "/wiki/Arena"
 "/wiki/Saskatoon,_Saskatchewan"
 "/wiki/South_Saskatchewan_River"
 "/wiki/New_York_Rangers"
# ... output omitted ... #
```

Since we're pulling a random Wikipedia article each time we run our code, your output will be different than in this snippet. The important thing is that you get a non-empty `Array{String,1}` with entries that start with `/wiki/`.

Alternatively, you can use the run code or run file option in Visual Studio Code and Atom. Here's Atom running the `six_degrees.jl` file:

Building our Wikipedia crawler - take two

Our code runs as expected, refactored and neatly packed into a module. However, there's one more thing I'd like us to refactor before moving on. I'm not especially fond of our `extractlinks` function.

First of all, it naively iterates over all the HTML elements. For example, say that we also want to extract the title of the page—every time we want to process something that's not a link, we'll have to iterate over the whole document again. That's going to be resource-hungry and slow to run.

Secondly, we're reinventing the wheel. In `Chapter 12`, *Setting Up the Wiki Game*, we said that CSS selectors are the *lingua franca* of DOM parsing. We'd benefit massively from using the concise syntax of CSS selectors with the underlying optimizations provided by specialized libraries.

Fortunately, we don't need to look too far for this kind of functionality. Julia's `Pkg` system provides access to `Cascadia`, a native CSS selector library. And, the great thing about it is that it works hand in hand with `Gumbo`.

In order to use Cascadia, we need to add it to our project's list of dependencies:

```
(sixdegrees) pkg> add Cascadia
```

Next, tell Julia we'll be using it—modify `Wikipedia.jl` so that the third line reads as follows:

```
using HTTP, Gumbo, Cascadia
```

With the help of `Cascadia`, we can now refactor the `extractlinks` function, as follows:

```
function extractlinks(elem)
  map(eachmatch(Selector("a[href^='/wiki/']:not(a[href*=':'])"), elem)) do
e
    e.attributes["href"]
  end |> unique
end
```

Let's take a closer look at all that happens here. The first thing that stands out is the `Selector` function. This is provided by `Cascadia` and constructs a new CSS selector object. The string that is passed to it as its only parameter is a CSS selector that reads as—all `<a>` elements that have a `href` attribute whose value starts with `'/wiki/'` and does not contain a column (`:`).

`Cascadia` also exports the `eachmatch` method. More accurately, it *extends* the existing `Base.eachmatch` method that we've seen previously with regular expressions. This provides a familiar interface—and we'll see how to extend methods later in this chapter, in the *Methods* section. The `Cascadia.eachmatch` function returns a `Vector` of elements that match the selector.

Once we retrieve the collection of matched elements, we pass it to the map function. The map function is one of the most used tools in the functional programming toolbox. It takes as its arguments a function, f, and a collection, c—and it transforms the collection, c, by applying f to each element, returning the modified collection as the result. Its definition is as follows:

```
map(f, c...) -> collection
```

So then, what's with the strange-looking do e ... end part in the previous snippet? That doesn't look like invoking the previous map function, it's true. But it is, in fact, the exact same function invocation, except with a more readable syntax, provided by Julia's blocks.

Using blocks

Because, in Julia, functions are first-class language constructs, they can be referenced and manipulated like any other type of variable. They can be passed as arguments to other functions or can be returned as the result of other function calls. The functions that take another function as their argument or return another function as their result are called **higher-order functions**.

Let's look at a simple example using map. We'll take a Vector of Int, and we'll apply to each element of its collection a function that doubles the value. You can follow along in a new REPL session (or in the accompanying IJulia notebook):

```
julia> double(x) = x*2
double (generic function with 1 method)

julia> map(double, [1, 2, 3, 5, 8, 13])
6-element Array{Int64,1}:
  2
  4
  6
 10
 16
 26
```

In this snippet, you can see how we passed the reference to the double function as the argument of the higher-order function map. As a result, we got back the Vector, which was passed as the second argument, but with all the elements doubled.

That's all good, but having to define a function just to use it as a one-off argument for another function is inconvenient and a bit wasteful. For this reason, the programming languages that support functional features, including Julia, usually support *anonymous functions*. An anonymous function, or a *lambda*, is a function definition that is not bound to an identifier.

We can rewrite the preceding `map` invocation to use an anonymous function, which is defined on the spot by using the arrow `->` syntax:

```
julia> map(x -> x*2, [1, 2, 3, 5, 8, 13])
6-element Array{Int64,1}:
  2
  4
  6
 10
 16
 26
```

In the definition, x -> x*2, the x at the left of the arrow represents the argument that is passed into the function, while x*2 represents the body of the function.

Great! We have achieved the same end result without having to separately define `double`. But, what if we need to use a more complex function? For instance, note the following:

```
julia> map(x ->
            if x % 2 == 0
                x * 2
            elseif x % 3 == 0
                x * 3
            elseif x % 5 == 0
                x * 5
            else
                x
            end,
        [1, 2, 3, 5, 8, 13])
```

That's pretty hard to follow! Because Julia allows us to indent our code, we can enhance the readability of this example to make it more palatable, but the result is still far from great.

Because these situations occur often, Julia provides the block syntax for defining anonymous functions. All the functions that take another function as their *first* argument can be used with the block syntax. Support for this kind of invocation is baked into the language, so you don't need to do anything—your functions will support it as well, out of the box, as long as the function is the first positional argument. In order to use it, we skip passing in the first argument when invoking the higher-order function—and instead, at the end of the arguments list, outside of the arguments tuple, we add a do...end block. Within this block, we define our lambda.

So, we can rewrite the previous example as follows:

```
map([1, 2, 3, 5, 8, 13]) do x
        if x % 2 == 0
                x * 2
        elseif x % 3 == 0
                x * 3
        elseif x % 5 == 0
                x * 5
        else
                x
        end
end
```

Much more readable!

Implementing the gameplay

Our Wikipedia parser is pretty robust now, and the addition of Cascadia greatly simplifies the code. It's time to think about the actual gameplay.

The most important thing, the core of the game, is to create the riddle—asking the player to find a path from the initial article to the end article. We previously decided that in order to be sure that a path between two articles really exists, we will pre-crawl all the pages, from the first to the last. In order to navigate from one page to the next, we'll simply randomly pick one of the internal URLs.

We also mentioned including difficulty settings. We will use the common-sense assumption that the more links there are between the start article and the end article, the less related their subjects will be; and thus, the more difficult to identify the path between them, resulting in a more challenging level.

All right, time to get coding! For starters, create a new file inside the sixdegrees/ folder. Name it Gameplay.jl and copy and paste the following:

```
module Gameplay

using ..Wikipedia

export newgame

const DIFFICULTY_EASY = 2
const DIFFICULTY_MEDIUM = 4
const DIFFICULTY_HARD = 6

function newgame(difficulty = DIFFICULTY_HARD)
  articles = []

  for i in 1:difficulty
    article = if i == 1
      fetchrandom()
    else
      rand(articles[i-1][:links]) |> Wikipedia.fetchpage
    end

article_data = Dict(:content => article,
  :links => articlelinks(article))
    push!(articles, article_data)
  end

  articles
end

end
```

Gamplay.jl defines a new module and brings Wikipedia into scope. Here, you can see how we reference the Wikipedia module in the parent scope by using ... It then defines three constants that map the difficulty settings to degrees of separation (named DIFFICULTY_EASY, DIFFICULTY_MEDIUM, and DIFFICULTY_HARD).

It then defines a function, newgame, which accepts a difficulty argument, by default set to hard. In the body of the function, we loop for a number of times equal to the difficulty value. On each iteration, we check the current degree of separation—if it's the first article, we call fetchrandom to start off the crawling process. If it's not the first article, we pick a random link from the list of links of the previously crawled article (rand(articles[i-1][:links])). We then pass this URL to fetchpage. When discussing conditionals, we learned that in Julia if/else statements return the value of the last-evaluated expression. We can see it put to good use here, with the result of the evaluation being stored in the article variable.

Once we've fetched the article, we store its content and its links within a Dict called article_data. And, article_data is in turn added to the articles array. On its last line, the newgame function returns the articles vector that now contains all the steps, from first to last. This function is also exported.

That wasn't too hard! But, there's a small glitch. If you try to run the code now, it will fail. The reason is that the article links are *relative*. This means that they are not fully qualified URLs; they look like /wiki/Some_Article_Title. When HTTP.jl makes a request, it needs the full link, protocol, and domain name included. But don't worry, that's easy to fix in Wikipedia.jl. Please switch your editor to the Wikipedia module and replace the const RANDOM_PAGE_URL line with the following three lines:

```
const PROTOCOL = "https://"
const DOMAIN_NAME = "en.m.wikipedia.org"
const RANDOM_PAGE_URL = PROTOCOL * DOMAIN_NAME * "/wiki/Special:Random"
```

We broke the random page URL into its components—the protocol, the domain name, and the rest of the relative path.

We'll use a similar approach to turn relative URLs into absolute URLs when fetching articles. For this, change the body of fetchpage and add this as its first line of code:

```
url = startswith(url, "/") ? PROTOCOL * DOMAIN_NAME * url : url
```

Here, we check the url argument—if it starts with "/", it means it's a relative URL so we need to turn it into its absolute counterpart. We used the ternary operator, as you can tell.

Our code should work just fine now, but spreading this PROTOCOL * DOMAIN_NAME * url throughout our game is a bit of a code smell. Let's abstract this away into a function:

```
function buildurl(article_url)
    PROTOCOL * DOMAIN_NAME * article_url
end
```

A *code smell* in programming parlance refers to a practice that violates
fundamental design principles and negatively impacts quality. It is not a
bug per se, but indicates weakness in design that may increase the risk of
bugs or failures in the future.

The `Wikipedia.jl` file should now look like this:

```julia
module Wikipedia

using HTTP, Gumbo, Cascadia

const PROTOCOL = "https://"
const DOMAIN_NAME = "en.m.wikipedia.org"
const RANDOM_PAGE_URL = PROTOCOL * DOMAIN_NAME * "/wiki/Special:Random"

export fetchrandom, fetchpage, articlelinks

function fetchpage(url)
  url = startswith(url, "/") ? buildurl(url) : url
  response = HTTP.get(url)

  if response.status == 200 && length(response.body) > 0
    String(response.body)
  else
    ""
  end
end

function extractlinks(elem)
  map(eachmatch(Selector("a[href^='/wiki/']:not(a[href*=':'])"), elem)) do
e
    e.attributes["href"]
  end |> unique
end

function fetchrandom()
  fetchpage(RANDOM_PAGE_URL)
end

function articlelinks(content)
  if ! isempty(content)
    dom = Gumbo.parsehtml(content)
    links = extractlinks(dom.root)
  end
end

function buildurl(article_url)
```

```
      PROTOCOL * DOMAIN_NAME * article_url
   end

   end
```

Finishing touches

Our gameplay evolves nicely. Only a few pieces left. Thinking about our game's UI, we'll want to show the game's progression, indicating the articles the player has navigated through. For this, we'll need the titles of the articles. If we could also include an image, that would make our game much prettier.

Fortunately, we are now using CSS selectors, so extracting the missing data should be a piece of cake. All we need to do is add the following to the `Wikipedia` module:

```
import Cascadia: matchFirst

function extracttitle(elem)
  matchFirst(Selector("#section_0"), elem) |> nodeText
end

function extractimage(elem)
  e = matchFirst(Selector(".content a.image img"), elem)
  isa(e, Void) ? "" : e.attributes["src"]
end
```

The `extracttitle` and `extractimage` functions will retrieve the corresponding content from our article pages. In both cases, since we only want to select a single element, the main page heading and the first image respectively, we use `Cascadia.matchFirst`. The `matchFirst` function is not publicly exposed by `Cascadia`—but since it's quite useful, we `import` it.

The `#section_0` selector identifies the main page heading, a `<h1>` element. And, because we need to extract the text between its `<h1>`...`</h1>` tags, we invoke the `nodeText` method provided by `Cascadia`.

You can see in the following screenshot, which shows the main heading of a Wikipedia page in Safari's inspector, how to identify the desired HTML elements and how to pick their CSS selectors by inspecting the source of the page and the corresponding DOM element. The HTML property, `id="section_0"`, corresponds to the `#section_0` CSS selector:

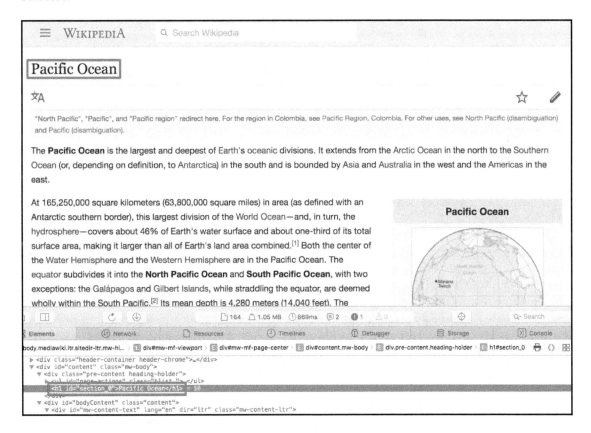

As for `extractimage`, we look for the main article image, represented by the `".content a.image img"` selector. Since not all the pages have it, we check if we do indeed get a valid element. If the page does not have an image, we'll get an instance of `Nothing`, called `nothing`. This is an important construct—`nothing` is the singleton instance of `Nothing`, indicating the absence of an object, corresponding to `NULL` in other languages. If we do get an `img` element, we extract the value of its `src` attribute, which is the URL of the image.

Here is another Wikipedia screenshot, in which I marked the image element that we're targeting. The flag is the first image on Wikipedia's **Australia** page—a perfect match:

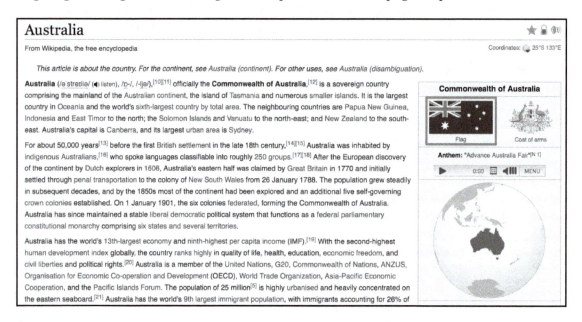

Next, we could extend the `Gameplay.newgame` function, to handle the new functions and values. But by now, this doesn't feel right—too much of the logic of `Wikipedia` would leak into the `Gameplay` module, coupling them; a dangerous anti-pattern. Instead, let's make the extraction of the data and setting up of the article, `Dict`, the full responsibility of `Wikipedia`, completely encapsulating the logic. Make the `Gameplay.newgame` function looks as shown in the following code:

```
function newgame(difficulty = DIFFICULTY_HARD)
  articles = []
  for i in 1:difficulty
    article = if i == 1
                fetchrandom()
              else
                rand(articles[i-1][:links]) |> Wikipedia.fetchpage
              end
    push!(articles, articleinfo(article))
  end

  articles
end
```

Then, update the `Wikipedia` module to read as follows:

```
module Wikipedia

using HTTP, Gumbo, Cascadia
import Cascadia: matchFirst

const PROTOCOL = "https://"
const DOMAIN_NAME = "en.m.wikipedia.org"
const RANDOM_PAGE_URL = PROTOCOL * DOMAIN_NAME * "/wiki/Special:Random"

export fetchrandom, fetchpage, articleinfo

function fetchpage(url)
  url = startswith(url, "/") ? buildurl(url) : url

  response = HTTP.get(url)

  if response.status == 200 && length(response.body) > 0
    String(response.body)
  else
    ""
  end
end

function extractlinks(elem)
  map(eachmatch(Selector("a[href^='/wiki/']:not(a[href*=':'])"), elem)) do
e
    e.attributes["href"]
  end |> unique
end

function extracttitle(elem)
  matchFirst(Selector("#section_0"), elem) |> nodeText
end

function extractimage(elem)
  e = matchFirst(Selector(".content a.image img"), elem)
  isa(e, Nothing) ? "" : e.attributes["src"]
end

function fetchrandom()
  fetchpage(RANDOM_PAGE_URL)
end

function articledom(content)
  if ! isempty(content)
    return Gumbo.parsehtml(content)
```

```
    end

    error("Article content can not be parsed into DOM")
  end

  function articleinfo(content)
    dom = articledom(content)

    Dict( :content => content,
          :links => extractlinks(dom.root),
          :title => extracttitle(dom.root),
          :image => extractimage(dom.root)
    )
  end

  function buildurl(article_url)
    PROTOCOL * DOMAIN_NAME * article_url
  end

end
```

The file has a few important changes. We've removed the `articlelinks` function and instead added `articleinfo` and `articledom`. The new `articledom` function parses the HTML using Gumbo and generates the DOM, which, very importantly, is only parsed once. We don't want to parse the HTML into a DOM every time we extract a type of element, as would've been the case if we kept the previous `articlelinks` function. As for `articleinfo`, it is responsible for setting up an article, `Dict`, with all the relevant information—content, links, title, and image.

We can do a test run of our code, by modifying the `six_degrees.jl` file, as follows:

```
using Pkg
pkg"activate ."

include("Wikipedia.jl")
include("Gameplay.jl")

using .Wikipedia, .Gameplay

for article in newgame(Gameplay.DIFFICULTY_EASY)
  println(article[:title])
end
```

We start a new game, which goes through two articles (`Gameplay.DIFFICULTY_EASY`) and for each article we display its title. We can see it in action by either running it in a REPL session via `julia> include("six_degrees.jl")`, or by simply running the file in Visual Studio Code or Atom. Here it is in the REPL:

```
julia> include("six_degrees.jl")
Miracle Bell
Indie pop
```

One more thing

Our test run shows that our difficulty settings have a small glitch. We should crawl a certain number of articles *after* the starting point. Our initial article should not count. This is super easy to fix. In `Gameplay.newgame`, we need to replace `for i in 1:difficulty` with `for i in 1:difficulty+1` (note the +1 at the end). Now, if we try again, it works as intended:

```
julia> include("six_degrees.jl")
John O'Brien (Australian politician)
Harlaxton, Queensland
Ballard, Queensland
```

Learning about Julia's type system

Our game works like a charm, but there is one thing we can improve—storing our article info as a `Dict`. Julia's dictionaries are very flexible and powerful, but they are not a good fit in every case. The `Dict` is a generic data structure that is optimized for search, delete, and insert operations. None of these are needed here—our articles have a fixed structure and contain data that doesn't change once created. It's a perfect use case for objects and **object-oriented programming** (**OOP**). Looks like it's time we revisit types.

Julia's type system is the bread and butter of the language—it is all-pervasive, defining the language's syntax and being the driving force behind Julia's performance and flexibility. Julia's type system is dynamic, meaning that nothing is known about types until runtime, when the actual values manipulated by the program are available. However, we can benefit from the advantages of static typing by using type annotations—indicating that certain values are of specific types. This can greatly improve the performance of the code and also enhance readability and simplify debugging.

It's impossible to talk about Julia and not talk about types. And sure enough, we've seen many primitive types so far—`Integer`, `Float64`, `Boolean`, `Char`, and so on. We've also been exposed to types while learning about the various data structures, such as `Array`, `Dict`, or tuple. These are all built into the language, but it turns out that Julia makes it very easy to create our own.

Defining our own types

Julia supports two categories of type—primitive and composite. A primitive type is a concrete type whose data consists of plain old bits. A composite type is a collection of named fields, an instance of which can be treated as a single value. In many languages, composite types are the only kind of user-definable type, but Julia lets us declare our own primitive types as well, rather than providing only a fixed set of built-in ones.

 We won't talk about defining primitive types here, but you can read more about them in the official documentation at
https://docs.julialang.org/en/v1/manual/types/.

In order to represent our articles, we're best served by an immutable composite type. Once our article object is created, its data won't change. Immutable composite types are introduced by the `struct` keyword followed by a block of field names:

```
struct Article
    content
    links
    title
    image
end
```

Since we provide no type information for the fields—that is, we don't tell Julia what type we want each field to be—they will default to any, allowing to hold any type of value. But, since we already know what data we want to store, we would greatly benefit from constraining the type of each field. The `::` operator can be used to attach type annotations to expressions and variables. It can be read as *is an instance of*. Thus, we define the `Article` type as follows:

```
struct Article
    content::String
    links::Vector{String}
    title::String
    image::String
end
```

All the fields are of `String` type, with the exception of `links`, which is a one-dimensional `Array` of `String`, also called a `Vector{String}`.

Type annotations can provide important performance benefits—while also eliminating a whole class of type-related bugs.

Constructing types

New objects of `Article` type are created by applying the `Article` type name like a function. The arguments are the values for its fields:

```
julia> julia = Article(
           "Julia is a high-level dynamic programming language",
           ["/wiki/Jeff_Bezanson", "/wiki/Stefan_Karpinski",
            "/wiki/Viral_B._Shah", "/wiki/Alan_Edelman"],
           "Julia (programming language)",
           "/220px-Julia_prog_language.svg.png"
       )
Article("Julia is a high-level dynamic programming language",
["/wiki/Jeff_Bezanson", "/wiki/Stefan_Karpinski", "/wiki/Viral_B._Shah",
"/wiki/Alan_Edelman"], "Julia (programming language)", "/220px-
Julia_prog_language.svg.png")
```

The fields of the newly created object can be accessed using the standard *dot notation*:

```
julia> julia.title
"Julia (programming language)"
```

Because we declared our type to be immutable, the values are read-only, so they can't be changed:

```
julia> julia.title = "The best programming language, period"
ERROR: type Article is immutable
```

Our `Article` type definition won't allow us to change the `julia.title` property. But, immutability should not be dismissed as it does come with considerable advantages, per the official Julia documentation:

- It can be more efficient. Some structs can be packed efficiently into arrays, and in some cases, the compiler is able to avoid allocating immutable objects entirely.
- It is not possible to violate the invariants provided by the type's constructors.
- Code using immutable objects can be easier to reason about.

But, that's not the whole story. An immutable object can have fields that reference mutable objects, such as, for instance, `links`, which points to an `Array{String, 1}`. This array is still mutable:

```
julia> push!(julia.links, "/wiki/Multiple_dispatch")
5-element Array{String,1}:
 "/wiki/Jeff_Bezanson"
 "/wiki/Stefan_Karpinski"
 "/wiki/Viral_B._Shah"
 "/wiki/Alan_Edelman"
 "/wiki/Multiple_dispatch"
```

We can see that there is no error when trying to alter the `links` property, by pushing one more URL to the underlying collection. If a property points to a mutable type, that type can be mutated, as long as its type stays the same:

```
julia> julia.links = [1, 2, 3]
MethodError: Cannot `convert` an object of type Int64 to an object of type
String
```

We are not allowed to change the type of the `links` field—Julia tries to accommodate and attempts to convert the values we provided from `Int` to `String`, but fails.

Mutable composite types

It is also possible (and equally easy) to construct mutable composite types. The only thing we need to do is to use the `mutable struct` statement, instead of just `struct`:

```
julia> mutable struct Player
           username::String
           score::Int
       end
```

Our `Player` object should be mutable, as we'll need to update the `score` property after each game:

```
julia> me = Player("adrian", 0)
Player("adrian", 0)

julia> me.score += 10
10

julia> me
Player("adrian", 10)
```

Type hierarchy and inheritance

Like all programming languages that implement OOP features, Julia allows developers to define rich and expressive type hierarchies. However, unlike most OOP languages, there is a very important difference—*only the final (upper) type in the hierarchy can be instantiated in Julia*. All its parents are just nodes in the type graph, and we can't create instances of them. They are *abstract types* and are defined using the abstract type keywords:

```
julia> abstract type Person end
```

We can use the <: operator to indicate that a type is a subtype of an existing *parent*:

```
julia> abstract type Mammal end
julia> abstract type Person <: Mammal end
julia> mutable struct Player <: Person
           username::String
           score::Int
       end
```

Or, in another example, this is Julia's numerical types hierarchy:

```
abstract type Number end
abstract type Real       <: Number end
abstract type AbstractFloat <: Real end
abstract type Integer  <: Real end
abstract type Signed   <: Integer end
abstract type Unsigned <: Integer end
```

The fact that super-types can't be instantiated can seem limiting, but they have a very powerful role. We can define functions that take a super-type as their argument, in effect accepting all its subtypes:

```
julia> struct User <: Person
           username::String
           password::String
       end

julia> sam = User("sam", "password")
User("sam", "password")

julia> function getusername(p::Person)
           p.username
       end

julia> getusername(me)
"adrian"
```

```
julia> getusername(sam)
"sam"

julia> getusername(julia)
ERROR: MethodError: no method matching getusername(::Article)
Closest candidates are:
  getusername(::Person) at REPL[25]:2
```

Here, we can see how we defined a `getusername` function, which accepts an argument of (abstract) type, `Person`. As both `User` and `Player` are subtypes of `Person`, their instances are accepted as arguments.

Type unions

Sometimes, we might want to allow a function to accept a set of types that are not necessarily part of the same type hierarchy. We could, of course, allow the function to accept any type, but depending on the use case, it could be desirable to strictly limit the arguments to a well-defined subset of types. For such cases, Julia provides *type unions*.

A type union is a special abstract type that includes as objects all instances of any of its argument types, constructed using the special `Union` function:

```
julia> GameEntity = Union{Person,Article}
Union{Article, Person}
```

Here, we have defined a new type union, `GameEntity`, which includes two types—`Person` and `Article`. Now, we can define functions that know how to handle `GameEntities`:

```
julia> function entityname(e::GameEntity)
           isa(e, Person) ? e.username : e.title
       end
entityname (generic function with 1 method)

julia> entityname(julia)
"Julia (programming language)"

julia> entityname(me)
"adrian"
```

Using article types

We can refactor our code to eliminate the generic `Dict` data structure and represent our articles with specialized `Article` composite types.

Let's create a new file in our `sixdegrees/` work folder, and name it `Articles.jl`. Edit the file by typing in the corresponding `module` declaration. Then, add the definition of our type and `export` it:

```
module Articles

export Article

struct Article
  content::String
  links::Vector{String}
  title::String
  image::String
end

end
```

We could've added the `Article` type definition to the `Wikipedia.jl` file, but chances are this will grow and it's better to keep them separated instead.

Another thing to note is that both the `module` and the `type` are Julia entities that are loaded in the same scope. For this reason, we can't use the name `Article` for both the `module` and the `type`—we'd end up with a name clash. However, the pluralized name `Articles` is a good name for the module, since it will encapsulate the logic for dealing with *articles* in general, while the `Article` type represents an *article* entity—hence the singular form.

However, since conceptually an `Article` object references a Wikipedia page, it should be part of the `Wikipedia` namespace. That's easy, we just need to include it into the `Wikipedia` module. Add this after the `import Cascadia: matchFirst` line:

```
include("Articles.jl")
using .Articles
```

We're including the `Articles` module file and bringing it into scope.

Next, in the same `Wikipedia.jl` file, we need to modify the `articleinfo` function. Please make sure it reads as follows:

```
function articleinfo(content)
  dom = articledom(content)
  Article(content,
          extractlinks(dom.root),
          extracttitle(dom.root),
          extractimage(dom.root))
end
```

Instead of creating a generic `Dict` object, we're now instantiating an instance of `Article`.

We also need to make a few changes to `Gameplay.jl` to use the `Article` types instead of `Dict`. It should now look like this:

```
module Gameplay

using ..Wikipedia, ..Wikipedia.Articles

export newgame

const DIFFICULTY_EASY = 2
const DIFFICULTY_MEDIUM = 4
const DIFFICULTY_HARD = 6

function newgame(difficulty = DIFFICULTY_HARD)
  articles = Article[]
  for i in 1:difficulty+1
    article = if i == 1
                fetchrandom()
              else
                rand(articles[i-1].links) |> fetchpage
              end
    push!(articles, articleinfo(article))
  end

  articles
end

end
```

Note that on the third line we bring `Wikipedia.Articles` into scope. Then, in the `newgame` function, we initiate the `articles` array to be of `Vector{Article}` type. And then, we update the code in the `for` loop to deal with `Article` objects—`rand(articles[i-1].links)`.

The last change is in `six_degrees.jl`. Since `newgame` now returns a vector of `Article` objects instead of a `Dict`, we print the title by accessing the `title` field:

```
using Pkg
pkg"activate ."

include("Wikipedia.jl")
include("Gameplay.jl")

using .Wikipedia, .Gameplay

articles = newgame(Gameplay.DIFFICULTY_EASY)

for article in articles
  println(article.title)
end
```

A new test run should confirm that all works as expected (your output will be different since, remember, we're pulling random articles):

```
julia> include("six_degrees.jl")
Sonpur Bazari
Bengali language
Diacritic
```

Inner constructors

The external constructor (where we invoke the `type` as a function) is a default constructor where we provide the values for all the fields, in the right order—and get back an instance of the corresponding type. But, what if we want to provide additional constructors, that maybe impose certain constraints, perform validations, or are simply more user-friendly? For this purpose, Julia provides *internal constructors*. I've got a good use case for them.

I'm not especially fond of our `Article` constructor—it takes too many arguments that need to be passed in the exact right order. It's hard to remember how to instantiate it. We've learned earlier about keyword arguments—and it would be awesome to provide an alternative constructor that takes keyword arguments. Inner constructors are what we need.

Inner constructors are very much like the outer constructors, but with two major differences:

- They are declared inside the block of a type declaration, rather than outside of it like normal methods.
- They have access to a special locally existent function called `new` that creates objects of the same type.

On the other hand, external constructors have a clear limitation (by design)—we can create as many as we want, but they can only instantiate objects by invoking the existing internal constructors (they do not have access to the `new` function). This way, if we define internal constructors that implement some business logic constraints, *Julia guarantees that the external constructors cannot go around them.*

Our inner constructor with keyword arguments will look like this:

```
Article(; content = "", links = String[], title = "", image = "") =
new(content, links, title, image)
```

Note the use of `;`, which separates the empty list of positional arguments from the list of keyword arguments.

This constructor allows us to instantiate `Article` objects using keyword arguments, which we can provide in any order:

```
julia = Article(
        title = "Julia (programming language)",
        content = "Julia is a high-level dynamic programming language",
        links = ["/wiki/Jeff_Bezanson", "/wiki/Stefan_Karpinski",
                "/wiki/Viral_B._Shah", "/wiki/Alan_Edelman"],
        image = "/220px-Julia_prog_language.svg.png"
        )
```

However, there's a small problem. When we don't provide any internal constructor, Julia provides the default one. But, if any inner constructor is defined, no default constructor method is provided anymore—it is presumed that we have supplied ourselves all the necessary inner constructors. In this case, if we want to get back the default constructor with the positional arguments, we'll have to also define it ourselves as an internal one:

```
Article(content, links, title, image) = new(content, links, title, image)
```

The final version of the `Articles.jl` file should now be the following, with the two internal constructors:

```
module Articles

export Article

struct Article
  content::String
  links::Vector{String}
  title::String
  image::String

  Article(; content = "", links = String[], title = "", image = "") =
new(content, links, title, image)
  Article(content, links, title, image) = new(content, links, title, image)
end

end
```

> It is worth pointing out that, in this case, our keyword constructor could've been equally added as an external constructor and defined outside the `struct...end` body. What kind of constructor you use is an architectural decision that has to be taken on a case-by-case basis, taking into account the differences between the internal and the external constructors.

Methods

If you come from an OOP background, you may have noticed a very interesting aspect throughout our discussion of types. Unlike other languages, objects in Julia do not define behavior. That is, Julia's types only define fields (properties) but do not encapsulate functions.

The reason is Julia's implementation of *multiple dispatch*, a distinctive feature of the language.

Multiple dispatch is explained in the official documentation as follows:

> *"The choice of which method to execute when a function is applied is called dispatch. Julia allows the dispatch process to choose which of a function's methods to call based on the number of arguments given, and on the types of all of the function's arguments. This is different than traditional object-oriented languages, where dispatch occurs based only on the first argument [. . .]. Using all of a function's arguments to choose which method should be invoked, rather than just the first, is known as multiple dispatch. Multiple dispatch is particularly useful for mathematical code, where it makes little sense to artificially deem the operations to belong to one argument more than any of the others."*

Julia allows us to define functions that provide specific behavior for certain combinations of argument types. A definition of one possible behavior for a function is called a **method**. The signatures of method definitions can be annotated to indicate the types of arguments, in addition to their number, and more than a single method definition may be provided. An example will help.

Let's say we have our previously defined `Player` type, as follows:

```julia
julia> mutable struct Player
           username::String
           score::Int
       end
```

And here, we see a corresponding `getscore` function:

```julia
julia> function getscore(p)
           p.score
       end
getscore (generic function with 1 method)
```

So far, so good. But, as our game grows incredibly successful, we could end up adding an app store to offer in-app purchases. This will lead us to also define a `Customer` type that could have a homonymous `credit_score` field, which stores their credit score:

```julia
julia> mutable struct Customer
           name::String
           total_purchase_value::Float64
           credit_score::Float64
       end
```

Of course, we'd need a corresponding `getscore` function:

```
julia> function getscore(c)
           c.credit_score
       end
getscore (generic function with 1 method)
```

Now, how would Julia know which function to use? It wouldn't. As both functions are defined to accept any type of argument, the last-defined function overwrites the previous one. We need to specialize the two `getscore` declarations on the type of their arguments:

```
julia> function getscore(p::Player)
           p.score
       end
getscore (generic function with 1 method)

julia> function getscore(c::Customer)
           c.credit_score
       end
getscore (generic function with 2 methods)
```

If you look closely at the output for each function declaration, you'll see something interesting. After the definition of `getscore(p::Player)`, it says `getscore (generic function with 1 method)`. But, after defining `getscore(c::Customer)`, it shows `getscore (generic function with 2 methods)`. So now, we have defined two methods for the `getscore` function, each specializing on its argument type.

But, what if we add the following?

```
julia> function getscore(t::Union{Player,Customer})
           isa(t, Player) ? t.score : t.credit_score
       end
getscore (generic function with 3 methods)
```

Or, alternatively, note the following that we might add:

```
julia> function getscore(s)
           if in(:score, fieldnames(typeof(s)))
               s.score
           elseif in(:credit_score, fieldnames(typeof(s)))
               s.credit_score
           else
               error("$(typeof(s)) does not have a score property")
           end
       end
getscore (generic function with 4 methods)
```

Can you guess which methods will be used when invoking `getscore` with a `Player`, a `Customer`, and an `Article` object? I'll give you a hint: when a function is applied to a particular set of arguments, the most specific method applicable to those arguments is invoked.

If we want to see which method is called for a given set of arguments, we can use `@which`:

```
julia> me = Player("adrian", 10)
Player("adrian", 10)

julia> @which getscore(me)
getscore(p::Player) in Main at REPL[58]:2
```

The same goes for `Customer` types:

```
julia> sam = Customer("Sam", 72.95, 100)
Customer("Sam", 72.95, 100.0)

julia> @which getscore(sam)
getscore(c::Customer) in Main at REPL[59]:2
```

We can see how the most specialized method is invoked—`getscore(t::Union{Player,Customer})`, which is more generic, is actually never used.

However, what about the following?

```
julia> @which getscore(julia)
getscore(s) in Main at REPL[61]:2
```

Passing an `Article` type will invoke the last definition of `getscore`, the one accepting `Any` type of argument:

```
julia> getscore(julia)
ERROR: Article does not have a score property
```

Since the `Article` type does not have a `score` or a `credit_score` property, the `ErrorException` we defined is being thrown.

To find out what methods are defined for a function, use `methods()`:

```
julia> methods(getscore)
# 4 methods for generic function "get_score":
getscore(c::Customer) in Main at REPL[59]:2
getscore(p::Player) in Main at REPL[58]:2
getscore(t::Union{Customer, Player}) in Main at REPL[60]:2
getscore(s) in Main at REPL[61]:2
```

Working with relational databases

Our web crawler is quite performant—using CSS selectors is very efficient. But, as it is right now, if we end up with the same Wikipedia article in different game sessions, we'll have to fetch it, parse it, and extract its contents multiple times. This is a time-consuming and resource-expensive operation—and, more importantly, one we can easily eliminate if we just store the article information once we fetch it the first time.

We could use Julia's serialization features, which we've already seen, but since we're building a fairly complex game, we would benefit from adding a database backend. Besides storing articles' data, we could also persist information about players, scores, preferences, and whatnot.

We have already seen how to interact with MongoDB. In this case, though, a relational database is the better choice, as we'll work with a series of related entities: articles, games (referencing articles), players (referencing games), and more.

Julia's package ecosystem provides a good range of options for interacting with relational databases, from generic ODBC and JDBC libraries to dedicated packages for the main backends—MySQL/MariaDB, SQLite, and Postgres, to name just a few. For our game, we'll use MySQL. If you don't already have MySQL installed on your system, please follow the instructions at `https://dev.mysql.com/downloads/mysql/`. Alternatively, if you're using Docker, you can get the official MySQL Docker image from `https://hub.docker.com/r/library/mysql/`.

On Julia's side, `(sixdegrees) pkg>add MySQL` is all we need in order to add support for MySQL. Make sure you're within the `sixdegrees/` project before adding MySQL. You can confirm this by looking at the prefix of the `pkg>` cursor; it should look like this: `(sixdegrees) pkg>`. If that is not the case, just execute `pkg> activate .` while making sure that you're within the `sixdegrees/` folder.

Adding MySQL support

When working with SQL databases, it's a good practice to abstract away the DB-related logic and to avoid littering all the codebase with SQL strings and database-specific commands. It will make our code more predictable and manageable and will provide a safe level of abstraction if we ever need to change or upgrade the database system. I'm a big fan of using ORM systems, but in this case, as a learning device, we'll be adding this functionality ourselves.

Connecting to the database

For starters, let's instruct our application to connect to and disconnect from our MySQL database. Let's extend our game by adding a new `Database` module within its corresponding file:

```
module Database

using MySQL

const HOST = "localhost"
const USER = "root"
const PASS = ""
const DB = "six_degrees"

const CONN = MySQL.connect(HOST, USER, PASS, db = DB)

export CONN

disconnect() = MySQL.disconnect(CONN)

atexit(disconnect)

end
```

Your `Database.jl` file should look like the snippet—with the exception maybe of the actual connection data. Please set up the `HOST`, `USER`, and `PASS` constants with your correct MySQL connection info. Also, please don't forget to create a new, empty database called `six_degrees`—otherwise the connection will fail. I suggest using `utf8` for the encoding and `utf8_general_ci` for the collation, in order to accommodate all the possible characters we might get from Wikipedia.

Calling `MySQL.connect` returns a connection object. We'll need it in order to interact with the database, so we'll reference it via the `CONN` constant:

```
julia> Main.Database.CONN
MySQL Connection
------------
Host: localhost
Port: 3306
User: root
DB:   six_degrees
```

Since various parts of our code will access this connection object in order to perform queries against the database, we `export` it. Equally importantly, we need to set up some cleanup mechanism, to automatically disconnect from the database when we're done. We've defined a `disconnect` function that can be manually called. But, it's safer if we make sure that the cleanup function is automatically invoked. Julia provides an `atexit` function, which registers a zero-argument function `f` to be called at process exit. The `atexit` hooks are called in **last-in-first-out** (**LIFO**) order.

Setting up our Article module

The next step is to add a few more functions to the `Article` module to enable database persistence and retrieval functionality. Since it will need access to our DB connection object, let's give it access to the `Database` module. We'll also want to use `MySQL` functions. So, under the `export Article` line, add `using..Database, MySQL`.

Next, we'll add a `createtable` method. This will be a one-off function that will create the corresponding database table. We use this instead of just typing `CREATE TABLE` queries in the MySQL client, in order to have a consistent and reproducible way of (re)creating the table. In general, I prefer the use of a fully fledged database migration library, but for now, better to keep things simple (you can read about schema migrations at `https://en.wikipedia.org/wiki/Schema_migration`).

Without further ado, here's our function:

```
function createtable()
  sql = """
    CREATE TABLE `articles` (
      `title` varchar(1000),
      `content` text,
      `links` text,
      `image` varchar(500),
      `url` varchar(500),
      UNIQUE KEY `url` (`url`)
    ) ENGINE=InnoDB DEFAULT CHARSET=utf8
  """

  MySQL.execute!(CONN, sql)
end
```

Here, we define an `sql` variable, which references the MySQL `CREATE TABLE` query, in the form of a `String`. The table will have four columns corresponding to the four fields of our `Article` type. Then, there's a fifth column, `url`, which will store the article's Wikipedia URL. We'll identify articles by URL—and for this reason, we add a unique index on the `url` column.

At the end of the function, we pass the query string to `MySQL.execute!` to be run against the DB connection. Please append the `createtable` definition to the end of the `Articles` module (within the module, above the closing `end`).

Now, let's see it in action. Open a new REPL session in the `sixdegrees/` folder and run the following:

```
julia> using Pkg
julia> pkg"activate ."
julia> include("Database.jl")
julia> include("Articles.jl")
julia> using .Articles
julia> Articles.createtable()
```

That's it, our table is ready!

The workflow should be pretty clear—we made sure we're loading our project's dependencies, we included the `Database.jl` and `Articles.jl` files, we brought `Articles` into scope, and then invoked its `createtable` method.

Adding the persistence and retrieval methods

We said that when an article is fetched and parsed, we want to store its data in the database. Thus, before fetching an article, we'll first want to check our database. If the article was previously persisted, we'll retrieve it. If not, we'll perform the original fetch-and-parse workflow. We use the `url` property to uniquely identify articles.

Let's start by adding the `Articles.save(a::Article)` method for persisting an article object:

```
function save(a::Article)
  sql = "INSERT IGNORE INTO articles (title, content, links, image, url)
VALUES (?, ?, ?, ?, ?)"
  stmt = MySQL.Stmt(CONN, sql)
  result = MySQL.execute!(stmt, [a.title, a.content, JSON.json(a.links),
a.image, a.url])
end
```

Here, we use `MySQL.Stmt` to create a MySQL prepared statement. The query itself is very simple, using MySQL's `INSERT IGNORE` statement, which makes sure that the `INSERT` operation is performed only if there is no article with the same `url`. If there is already an article with the same `url`, the query is ignored.

The prepared statement accepts a specially formatted query string, in which the actual values are replaced with placeholders, designated by question marks—?. We can then execute the prepared statement by passing it to `MySQL.execute!`, together with an array of corresponding values. The values are passed directly from the `article` object, with the exception of `links`. Since this represents a more complex data structure, a `Vector{String}`, we'll first serialize it using `JSON` and store it in MySQL as a string. To access functions from the `JSON` package, we'll have to add it to our project, so please execute `(sixdegrees) pkg> add JSON` in the REPL.

Prepared statements provide a safe way to execute queries because the values are automatically escaped, eliminating a common source of MySQL injection attacks. In our case, MySQL injections are less of a worry since we're not accepting user-generated input. But, the approach is still valuable, avoiding insert errors caused by improper escaping.

Next, we need a retrieval method. We'll call it `find`. As its only attribute, it will take an article URL in the form of a `String`. It will return an `Array` of `Article` objects. By convention, if no corresponding article is found, the array will be empty:

```
function find(url) :: Vector{Article}
  articles = Article[]

  result = MySQL.query(CONN, "SELECT * FROM `articles` WHERE url = '$url'")

  isempty(result.url) && return articles

  for i in eachindex(result.url)
    push!(articles, Article(result.content[i], JSON.parse(result.links[i]),
result.title[i],
                            result.image[i], result.url[i]))
  end

  articles
end
```

In this function's declaration, we can see another Julia feature: return value types. After the regular function declaration, `function find(url)`, we appended `:: Vector{Article}`. This constrains the return value of `find` to an array of `Article`. If our function won't return that, an error will be thrown.

The rest of the code, although very compact, has quite a lot of functionality. First, we create `articles`, a vector of `Article` objects, which will be the return value of our function. Then, we execute a `SELECT` query against the MySQL database through the `MySQL.query` method, attempting to find rows that match the `url`. The result of the query is stored in the `result` variable, which is a `NamedTuple` (each field in the `result NamedTuple` references an array of values corresponding to the database column of the same name). Next, we peek into our query `result` to see if we got anything—we chose to sample the `result.url` field—if it's empty, it means our query didn't find anything and we can just exit the function, returning an empty `articles` vector.

On the other hand, if `result.url` does contain entries, it means our query brought at least one row; so we iterate over the `result.url` array using `eachindex`, and for each iteration we construct an `Article` object with the corresponding values. Finally, we `push!` this new `Article` object into the `articles` vector which is returned, at the end of the loop.

Putting it all together

The last thing we need to do is update the rest of the code to work with the changes we've made so far.

First of all, we need to update the `Article` type to add the extra `url` field. We need it in the list of fields and in the two constructors. Here is the final version of `Articles.jl`:

```
module Articles

export Article, save, find

using ...Database, MySQL, JSON

struct Article
  content::String
  links::Vector{String}
  title::String
  image::String
  url::String

  Article(; content = "", links = String[], title = "", image = "", url =
  "") =
```

```
        new(content, links, title, image, url)
   Article(content, links, title, image, url) = new(content, links, title,
image, url)
end

function find(url) :: Vector{Article}
   articles = Article[]
   result = MySQL.query(CONN, "SELECT * FROM `articles` WHERE url = '$url'")

   isempty(result.url) && return articles

   for i in eachindex(result.url)
     push!(articles, Article(result.content[i], JSON.parse(result.links[i]),
result.title[i],
                             result.image[i], result.url[i]))
   end

   articles
end

function save(a::Article)
   sql = "INSERT IGNORE INTO articles (title, content, links, image, url)
VALUES (?, ?, ?, ?, ?)"
   stmt = MySQL.Stmt(CONN, sql)
   result = MySQL.execute!(stmt, [ a.title, a.content, JSON.json(a.links),
a.image, a.url])
end

function createtable()
   sql = """
     CREATE TABLE `articles` (
       `title` varchar(1000),
       `content` text,
       `links` text,
       `image` varchar(500),
       `url` varchar(500),
       UNIQUE KEY `url` (`url`)
     ) ENGINE=InnoDB DEFAULT CHARSET=utf8
   """

   MySQL.execute!(CONN, sql)
end

end
```

We also need to make a few important changes to `Wikipedia.jl`. First, we'll remove `Article` instantiation from `Wikipedia.articleinfo` since creating `Article` objects should now also take into account database persistence and retrieval. Instead, we'll return a tuple representing the article data:

```
function articleinfo(content)
  dom = articledom(content)
  (content, extractlinks(dom.root), extracttitle(dom.root),
extractimage(dom.root))
end
```

We can now add a new function, `persistedarticle`, which will accept as arguments the article content plus the article URL. It will instantiate a new `Article` object, save it to the database, and return it. In a way, `persistedarticle` can be considered a database-backed constructor, hence the name:

```
function persistedarticle(article_content, url)
  article = Article(articleinfo(article_content)..., url)
  save(article)

  article
end
```

Here, you can see the *splat* operator . . . in action—it decomposes the `articleinfo` result `Tuple` into its corresponding elements so they can be passed into the `Article` constructor as individual arguments.

Also, we have to deal with a minor complication. When we start a new game and call the `/wiki/Special:Random` URL, Wikipedia automatically performs a redirect to a random article. When we fetch the page, we get the redirected page content—but we don't have its URL.

So, we need to do two things. Firstly, we need to check if our request has been redirected and, if so, get the redirection URL. In order to do this, we can check the `request.parent` field of the `response` object. In the case of a redirect, the `response.request.parent` object will be set and will present a `headers` collection. The collection will include a `"Location"` item—and that's what we're after.

Secondly, we also need to return the URL together with the HTML content of the page. This is easy—we'll return a tuple.

Here is the updated `fetchpage` function:

```
function fetchpage(url)
  url = startswith(url, "/") ? buildurl(url) : url
  response = HTTP.get(url)
  content = if response.status == 200 && length(response.body) > 0
              String(response.body)
            else
              ""
            end
  relative_url = collect(eachmatch(r"/wiki/(.*)$",
(response.request.parent == nothing ? url :
Dict(response.request.parent.headers)["Location"])))[1].match

    content, relative_url
end
```

Note that we also use `eachmatch` to extract the part corresponding to the relative URL out of the absolute URL.

Here is the whole `Wikipedia.jl` file:

```
module Wikipedia
using HTTP, Gumbo, Cascadia
import Cascadia: matchFirst

include("Articles.jl")
using .Articles

const PROTOCOL = "https://"
const DOMAIN_NAME = "en.m.wikipedia.org"
const RANDOM_PAGE_URL = PROTOCOL * DOMAIN_NAME * "/wiki/Special:Random"

export fetchrandom, fetchpage, articleinfo, persistedarticle

function fetchpage(url)
  url = startswith(url, "/") ? buildurl(url) : url
  response = HTTP.get(url)
  content = if response.status == 200 && length(response.body) > 0
              String(response.body)
            else
              ""
            end
  relative_url = collect(eachmatch(r"/wiki/(.*)$", (response.request.parent
== nothing ? url :
Dict(response.request.parent.headers)["Location"])))[1].match

    content, relative_url
```

```
end

function extractlinks(elem)
  map(eachmatch(Selector("a[href^='/wiki/']:not(a[href*=':'])"), elem)) do
e
    e.attributes["href"]
  end |> unique
end

function extracttitle(elem)
  matchFirst(Selector("#section_0"), elem) |> nodeText
end

function extractimage(elem)
  e = matchFirst(Selector(".content a.image img"), elem)
  isa(e, Nothing) ? "" : e.attributes["src"]
end

function fetchrandom()
  fetchpage(RANDOM_PAGE_URL)
end

function articledom(content)
  if ! isempty(content)
    return Gumbo.parsehtml(content)
  end

  error("Article content can not be parsed into DOM")
end

function articleinfo(content)
  dom = articledom(content)
  (content, extractlinks(dom.root), extracttitle(dom.root),
extractimage(dom.root))
end

function persistedarticle(article_content, url)
  article = Article(articleinfo(article_content)..., url)
  save(article)

  article
end

function buildurl(article_url)
  PROTOCOL * DOMAIN_NAME * article_url
end

end
```

Now, let's focus on `Gameplay.jl`. We need to update the `newgame` function to take advantage of the newly available methods from the `Wikipedia` module:

```
module Gameplay

using ..Wikipedia, ..Wikipedia.Articles

export newgame

const DIFFICULTY_EASY = 2
const DIFFICULTY_MEDIUM = 4
const DIFFICULTY_HARD = 6

function newgame(difficulty = DIFFICULTY_HARD)
  articles = Article[]

  for i in 1:difficulty+1
    article = if i == 1
                article = persistedarticle(fetchrandom()...)
              else
                url = rand(articles[i-1].links)
                existing_articles = Articles.find(url)

                article = isempty(existing_articles) ?
persistedarticle(fetchpage(url)...) : existing_articles[1]
              end

    push!(articles, article)
  end

  articles
end

end
```

If it's the first article, we fetch a random page and persist its data. Otherwise, we pick a random URL from the previously crawled page and check if a corresponding article already exists. If not, we fetch the page, making sure it's also persisted to the DB.

Lastly, our point of entry into the app, the `six_degrees.jl` file, needs to look like this:

```
using Pkg
pkg"activate ."

include("Database.jl")
include("Wikipedia.jl")
include("Gameplay.jl")
```

```
using .Wikipedia, .Gameplay

articles = newgame(Gameplay.DIFFICULTY_EASY)

for article in articles
  println(article.title)
end
```

A final test run should confirm that all is good:

```
$ julia six_degrees.jl
Hillary Maritim
Athletics at the 2000 Summer Olympics - Men's 400 metres hurdles
Zahr-el-Din El-Najem
```

Running the `six_degrees.jl` file with the `julia` binary in a terminal will output three Wikipedia article titles. And we can check the database to confirm that the data has been saved:

The data for the three previously crawled pages has been safely persisted.

Summary

Congratulations, this was quite a journey! We've applied three key Julia concepts—modules, types and their constructors, and methods to develop the backend of our *Six Degrees of Wikipedia* game, and in the process we've seen how to interact with MySQL databases, persisting and retrieving our `Article` objects.

At the end of the next chapter, we'll get the chance to enjoy the fruits of our hard work: after we add a web UI to our *Six degrees of Wikipedia* backend, we'll relax by playing a few rounds. Let's see if you can beat my best score!

14
Adding a Web UI for the Wiki Game

Developing the backend of our game was quite a learning experience. This strong foundation will serve us well—the modular approach will allow us to easily convert the **read-eval-print loop (REPL)** app into a web app, while our understanding of types will prove to be priceless when dealing with Julia's web stack and its rich taxonomy.

We're now entering the last stage of our game development journey—building a web user interface for the *Six Degrees of Wikipedia*. Since building a full-featured web app is no simple feat, this last part will be dedicated to this task alone. In the process, we will learn about the following topics:

- Julia's web stack; namely, the `HTTP` package and its main components—`Server`, `Router`, `HandlerFunction`, and `Response`
- Architecting a web app to take advantage of `HTTP` and integrate it with existing Julia modules
- Exposing features on the web by defining routes that map URLs to Julia functions
- Spawning a web server to handle user requests and send back proper responses to the clients

The end of this chapter comes with a cool reward—our game will be ready and we'll play a few rounds of *Six Degrees of Wikipedia*!

Technical requirements

The Julia package ecosystem is under continuous development and new package versions are released on a daily basis. Most of the times this is great news, as new releases bring new features and bug fixes. However, since many of the packages are still in beta (version 0.x), any new release can introduce breaking changes. As a result, the code presented in the book can stop working. In order to ensure that your code will produce the same results as described in the book, it is recommended to use the same package versions. Here are the external packages used in this chapter and their specific versions:

```
Cascadia@v0.4.0
Gumbo@v0.5.1
HTTP@v0.7.1
IJulia@v1.14.1
```

In order to install a specific version of a package you need to run:

```
pkg> add PackageName@vX.Y.Z
```

For example:

```
pkg> add IJulia@v1.14.1
```

Alternatively you can install all the used packages by downloading the `Project.toml` file provided with the chapter and using `pkg>` instantiate as follows:

```
julia>
download("https://github.com/TrainingByPackt/Julia-1-Programming-Complete-R
eference-Guide/tree/master/Chapter14/Project.toml", "Project.toml")
pkg> activate .
pkg> instantiate
```

The game plan

We're onto the last stage of our project—the web UI. Let's start by discussing the spec; we need to lay out the blueprint before we can proceed with the implementation.

The player will start on the landing page. This will display the rules and will provide options for launching a new game, allowing the user to choose a difficulty level. Following this starting point, the player will be redirected to the new game page. Here, taking into account the selected difficulty level, we'll bootstrap a new game session by fetching the articles with the algorithm we wrote in the previous chapter. Once we pick the articles that represent the *Six Degrees of Wikipedia*, we will display a heading with the game's objective—the titles of the start and end articles. We'll also display the content of the first article, thus kickstarting the game. When the player clicks on a link in this article, we have to respond accordingly by checking if the player has found the end article and won the game. If not, render the new article and increment the number of steps taken.

We'll also need an area to display the progress of the game—the articles that were viewed in the current session, how many steps have been taken in total, and a form of navigation to allow the players to go back and rethink their choices if they find themselves on the wrong track. Therefore, we'll need to store the player's navigation history. Finally, it would be nice to provide an option to solve the puzzle—of course, as a result, the player will lose the game.

A very important piece of the spec is that between the stateless browser requests and the server responses, while navigating through the Wikipedia articles, we need some sort of mechanism to allow us to maintain the state of the game, that is, to retrieve a game with its corresponding data—difficulty, path (articles) and progress, navigation history, number of steps taken, and so on. This will be achieved by creating a unique game identifier at the beginning of each play session and passing it with every request as a part of the URL.

Learning about Julia's web stack

Julia's package ecosystem has long provided a variety of libraries for building web apps. Some of the most mature are `HttpServer`, `Mux`, `WebSockets`, and `JuliaWebAPI` (to name just a few; this list is not exhaustive). But as the ecosystem settled with Julia version 1, a lot of community effort has been put into a newer package, simply known as `HTTP`. It provides a web server, an HTTP client (which we already used in the previous chapters to fetch the web pages from Wikipedia), as well as various utilities for making web development simpler. We'll learn about key `HTTP` modules ,such as `Server`, `Router`, `Request`, `Response`, and `HandlerFunction`, and we'll put them to good use.

Beginning with a simple example – Hello World

Let's take a look at a simple example of employing the HTTP server stack. This will help us understand the foundational building blocks before we dive into the more complex issue of exposing our game on the web.

If you followed the previous chapter, you should already have the HTTP package installed. If not, you know the drill—run pkg> add HTTP in Julia's REPL.

Now, somewhere on your computer, create a new file called hello.jl. Since this will be a simple piece of software contained in just one file, there's no need to define a module. Here is the full code, the whole eight lines, in all their glory. We'll go over them next:

```julia
using HTTP, Sockets
const HOST = ip"0.0.0.0"
const PORT = 9999
router = HTTP.Router()
server = HTTP.Server(router)
HTTP.register!(router, "/", HTTP.HandlerFunction(req ->
HTTP.Messages.Response(200, "Hello World")))
HTTP.register!(router, "/bye", HTTP.HandlerFunction(req ->
HTTP.Messages.Response(200, "Bye")))
HTTP.register!(router, "*", HTTP.HandlerFunction(req ->
HTTP.Messages.Response(404, "Not found")))
HTTP.serve(server, HOST, PORT)
```

The workflow for handling web requests with HTTP requires four entities—Server, Router, HandlerFunction, and Response.

Beginning our analysis of the code with the simplest part, on the last line, we start our server by calling HTTP.serve. The serve function takes a server, an object of type Server, plus the HOST information (an IP string) and the PORT (an integer) that are used to attach to and listen to requests as arguments. We have defined HOST and PORT at the top of the file as constants. The value of HOST is defined using the non-standard ip"" string literal. We learned about non-standard string literals when we discussed the String type. In this regard, the ip"..." notation is similar to regular expressions (r"..."), version strings (v"..."), or Pkg commands (pkg"...").

Instantiating a new `Server` requires a `Router` object, which we will name `router`. The job of the `Router` is to register a list of mappings (called **routes**) between the links (URIs) that are exposed by our app on the internet and our Julia functions (called `HandlerFunctions`), which provide the response. We have set up the routes using the `register!` function, passing the `router` object, the URI structures (like `/` or `/bye`) and the corresponding `HandlerFunction` objects as arguments.

Now, if you look at the body of the `HandlerFunction`, you'll see that the root page `/` will display the string `"Hello World"`; the `/bye` URL will display the string `"Bye"`; and finally, every other URI, expressed by the star symbol `*`, will return a `"Not found"` text, accompanied by the correct `404 Not Found` header.

I'm sure you can now recognize the arrow `->` operator, hinting to the use of lambdas. Each `HandlerFunction` constructor takes an anonymous function. This function is responsible for processing the request and generating the appropriate `Response`. As its argument, it accepts the `Request` object (named `req`), and it is expected to return an instance of `Response`.

In our example code, we constructed three `Response` objects using two of the available HTTP status codes (`200` for `OK` and `404` for page not found), plus some strings for the body of the responses (the simple strings `"Hello World"`, `"Bye"`, and `"Not found"`, respectively).

To conclude, when the server receives a request, it delegates it to the router, which matches the URI of the request to the most appropriately mapped URI pattern and invokes the corresponding `HandlerFunction`, passing in the `Request` as the argument. The handler function returns a `Response` object, which is sent by the server back to the client.

Let's see it in action. You can use the `Run` functionality in your editor or you can execute `$ julia hello.jl` in the Terminal. Alternatively, you can run the code in this chapter's accompanying IJulia notebook:

```
REPL — ~/Dropbox/Projects/Julia v1.0 By Example/Julia v1.0 By Example/_v1_/Chapter 5

hello.jl
    using HTTP, Sockets

    const HOST = ip"0.0.0.0"
    const PORT = 9999

    router = HTTP.Router()
    server = HTTP.Server(router)

    HTTP.register!(router, "/", HTTP.HandlerFunction(req -> HTTP.Messages.Response(200, "Hello World")))
    HTTP.register!(router, "/bye", HTTP.HandlerFunction(req -> HTTP.Messages.Response(200, "Bye")))
    HTTP.register!(router, "*", HTTP.HandlerFunction(req -> HTTP.Messages.Response(404, "Not found")))

≡ REPL

[ Info: Listening on: Sockets.InetAddr{IPv4}(ip"0.0.0.0", 0x270f)
[ Warning: throttling 127.0.0.1
[    @ HTTP.Servers ~/.julia/packages/HTTP/mwR9J/src/Servers.jl:121
[ Info: Accept (0):  🔓  0↑    0↓    1s 0.0.0.0:9999:9999 ▪16
[ Info: HTTP.Messages.Request:
"""
GET / HTTP/1.1
Host: localhost:9999
Accept: text/html,application/xhtml+xml,application/xml;q=0.9,*/*;q=0.8
Upgrade-Insecure-Requests: 1
Cookie: username-localhost-8888="2|1:0|10:1537888896|23:username-localhost-8888|44:NTE2YTE0MGFjNmY2NDQ3Mzg0NjYxMmUxYjI1NWZl
M2M=|6b8616077698475a8ac1991f4c2031016db8e4f5ae4b250b86a74e37074d83fa"; _xsrf=2|33374d45|c2394d36332967dba67bbc5a521aa5ba|153
7611108
User-Agent: Mozilla/5.0 (Macintosh; Intel Mac OS X 10_13_6) AppleWebKit/605.1.15 (KHTML, like Gecko) Version/12.0 Safari/60
5.1.15
Accept-Language: en-us
Accept-Encoding: gzip, deflate
Connection: keep-alive

                                                                          REPL                                    Main  0 files
```

The preceding screenshot shows the `hello.jl` file running in Juno. The REPL pane displays debugging information from the web server as requests are received and handled.

As soon as the server is ready, you'll get a log message saying that the server is listening on the indicated socket. At this point, you can open a web browser and navigate to `http://localhost:9999`. You'll be greeted by the (in)famous **Hello World** message, as follows:

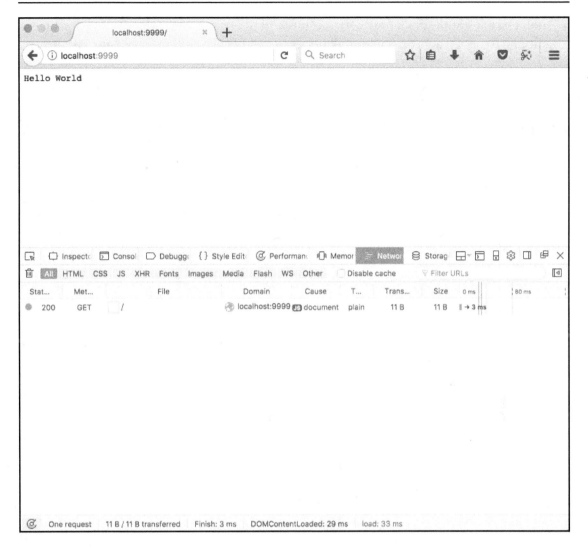

Congratulations—we've just developed our first web app with Julia!

No bonus points for guessing what happens when navigating to
`http://localhost:9999/bye`.

Finally, you can confirm that any other request will result in a `404 Not Found` page by attempting to navigate to any other link under `http://localhost:9999`—for instance, `http://localhost:9999/oh/no`:

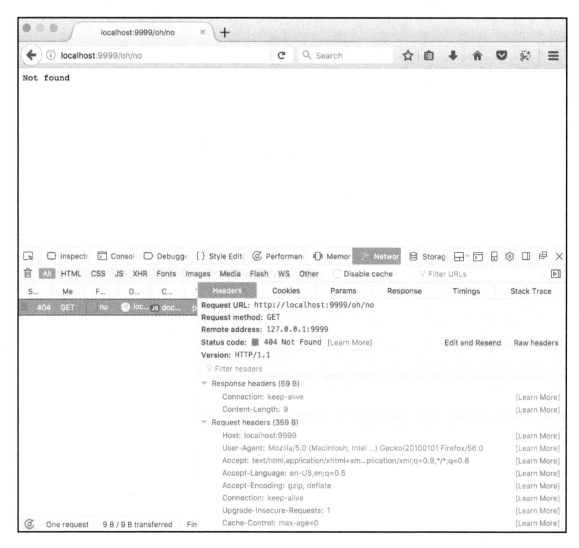

Here is the **Not Found** page, correctly returning the `404` status code.

Developing the game's web UI

Please start your favorite Julia editor and open the `sixdegrees/` folder we used in the previous chapter. It should contain all the files that we've worked on already—`six_degrees.jl`, plus the `Articles`, `Database`, `Gameplay`, and `Wikipedia` modules.

 If you haven't followed through the code up to this point, you can download this chapter's accompanying support files, which are available at `https://github.com/TrainingByPackt/Julia-1-Programming-Complete-Reference-Guide/tree/master/Chapter14`.

Add a new file for our web app. Since the code will be more complex this time and should integrate with the rest of our modules, let's define a `WebApp` module within a new `WebApp.jl` file. Then, we can add these first few lines of code:

```
module WebApp

using HTTP, Sockets

const HOST = ip"0.0.0.0"
const PORT = 8888
const ROUTER = HTTP.Router()
const SERVER = HTTP.Server(ROUTER)

HTTP.serve(SERVER, HOST, PORT)

end
```

No surprises here—similar to the previous example, we define constants for `HOST` and `PORT`, and then instantiate a `Router` and a `Server` and start listening for requests. The code should work just fine, but it's not worth running it yet as it won't do anything useful. We need to define and register our routes, and then set up the handler functions for generating the game's pages.

Defining our routes

By reviewing the high-level spec that we defined at the beginning of the chapter, we can identify the following pages:

- **Landing page**: The starting place of our web app and the home page, where the player can begin a new game and choose the difficulty.
- **New game page**: Bootstraps a new game, taking into account the difficulty settings.
- **Wiki article page**: This will display the Wikipedia article corresponding to a link in the chain and will update the game's stats. Here, we'll also check if the current article is the goal (the end) article, which is to finish the game as a winner. If not, we'll check if the maximum number of articles has been reached, and if so finish the game as a loser.
- **Back page**: This will allow the player to go back up the chain if the solution wasn't found. We'll display the corresponding Wikipedia article while correctly updating the game's stats.
- **Solution page**: If the player gives up, this page will display the last article in the chain, together with the path to it. The game is ended as a loss.
- Any other page should end up as Not Found.

Taking into account that the route handlers will be fairly complex, it's best if we *don't* define them inline with the route definitions. Instead, we'll use separately defined functions. Our route's definitions will look like this—please add them to the WebApp module, as follows:

```
HTTP.register!(ROUTER, "/", landingpage) # root page
HTTP.register!(ROUTER, "/new/*", newgamepage) # /new/$difficulty_level --
new game
HTTP.register!(ROUTER, "/*/wiki/*", articlepage) #
/$session_id/wiki/$wikipedia_article_url -- article page
HTTP.register!(ROUTER, "/*/back/*", backpage) #
/$session_id/back/$number_of_steps -- go back the navigation history
HTTP.register!(ROUTER, "/*/solution", solutionpage) # /$session_id/solution
-- display the solution
HTTP.register!(ROUTER, "*", notfoundpage) # everything else -- not found
```

You might be wondering what's with the extra * in front of the URI patterns. We stated that we'll need a way to identify a running game session between the otherwise stateless web requests. The articlepage, backpage, and solutionpage functions will all require an existing game session. We'll pass this session ID as the first part of the URL. Effectively, their paths are to be interpreted as /$session_id/wiki/*, /$session_id/back/*, and /$session_id/solution, where the $session_id variable represents the unique game identifier. As for the trailing *, it represents different things for different routes—in the case of new, it's the difficulty level of the game; for articlepage, it's the actual Wikipedia URL, which is also our article identifier; and for the backpage, it represents the index in the navigation stack. Similar to regular expressions, for route matching as well, the * will match anything. If this sounds complicated, don't worry—seeing and running the code will make things clear.

Let's add placeholder definitions for each handler function—please add these *before* the list of routes:

```
const landingpage = HTTP.HandlerFunction() do req
end
const newgamepage = HTTP.HandlerFunction() do req
end
const articlepage = HTTP.HandlerFunction() do req
end
const backpage = HTTP.HandlerFunction() do req
end
const solutionpage = HTTP.HandlerFunction() do req
end
const notfoundpage = HTTP.HandlerFunction() do req
end
```

Preparing the landing page

Straight away, we can address the landing page handler. All it needs to do is display some static content describing the game's rules, as well as provide a way to start a new game with various levels of difficulty. Remember that the difficulty of the game determines the length of the article chain, and we need this information when we start a new game. We can pass it to the new game page as part of the URL, under the format /new/$difficulty_level. The difficulty levels are already defined in the Gameplay module, so don't forget to declare that we're using Gameplay.

Taking this into account, we'll end up with the following code for our `WebApp` module. We're putting everything together and we're also adding the `landingpage` `HandlerFunction`. This works in correlation with the first route—`HTTP.register!(ROUTER, "/", landingpage)`. What this means is that when we access the / route in the browser, the `landingpage HandlerFunction` will be executed and its output will be returned as the response. In this case, we're simply returning a bunch of HTML code. If you're not familiar with HTML, here's what the markup does—we include the Twitter Bootstrap CSS theme to make our page prettier, we display a few paragraphs of text explaining the rules of the game, and we display three buttons for starting a new game—one button for each level of difficulty.

Here is the code:

```
module WebApp

using HTTP, Sockets
using ..Gameplay

# Configuration
const HOST = ip"0.0.0.0"
const PORT = 8888
const ROUTER = HTTP.Router()
const SERVER = HTTP.Server(ROUTER)

# Routes handlers
const landingpage = HTTP.HandlerFunction() do req
  html = """
  <!DOCTYPE html>
  <html>
  <head>
    <meta charset="utf-8" />
    <link rel="stylesheet"
href="https://stackpath.bootstrapcdn.com/bootstrap/4.1.3/css/bootstrap.min.
css" integrity="sha384-
MCw98/SFnGE8fJT3GXwEOngsV7Zt27NXFoaoApmYm81iuXoPkFOJwJ8ERdknLPMO"
crossorigin="anonymous">
    <title>6 Degrees of Wikipedia</title>
  </head>

  <body>
    <div class="jumbotron">
      <h1>Six degrees of Wikipedia</h1>
      <p>
        The goal of the game is to find the shortest path between two
random Wikipedia articles.<br/>
        Depending on the difficulty level you choose, the Wiki pages will
```

be further apart and less related.
     If you can't find the solution, you can always go back up the articles chain, but you need to find the solution within the maximum number of steps, otherwise you lose.
     If you get stuck, you can always check the solution, but you'll lose.
     Good luck and enjoy!
    </p>

    <hr class="my-4">

    <div>
      <h4>New game</h4>
        <a href="/new/$(Gameplay.DIFFICULTY_EASY)" class="btn btn-primary btn-lg">Easy ($(Gameplay.DIFFICULTY_EASY) links away)</a> |
        <a href="/new/$(Gameplay.DIFFICULTY_MEDIUM)" class="btn btn-primary btn-lg">Medium ($(Gameplay.DIFFICULTY_MEDIUM) links away)</a> |
        <a href="/new/$(Gameplay.DIFFICULTY_HARD)" class="btn btn-primary btn-lg">Hard ($(Gameplay.DIFFICULTY_HARD) links away)</a>
      </div>
    </div>
  </body>
  </html>
  """

```julia
  HTTP.Messages.Response(200, html)
end

const newgamepage = HTTP.HandlerFunction() do req
end

const articlepage = HTTP.HandlerFunction() do req
end

const backpage = HTTP.HandlerFunction() do req
end

const solutionpage = HTTP.HandlerFunction() do req
end

const notfoundpage = HTTP.HandlerFunction() do req
end

# Routes definitions
HTTP.register!(ROUTER, "/", landingpage) # root page
HTTP.register!(ROUTER, "/new/*", newgamepage) # /new/$difficulty_level --
new game
HTTP.register!(ROUTER, "/*/wiki/*", articlepage) #
```

```
/$session_id/wiki/$wikipedia_article_url -- article page
HTTP.register!(ROUTER, "/*/back/*", backpage) #
/$session_id/back/$number_of_steps -- go back the navigation history
HTTP.register!(ROUTER, "/*/solution", solutionpage) # /$session_id/solution
-- display the solution
HTTP.register!(ROUTER, "*", notfoundpage) # everything else -- not found

# Start server
HTTP.serve(SERVER, HOST, PORT)

end
```

Let's update the `six_degrees.jl` file to bootstrap our web app. Please make sure that it now reads as follows:

```
using Pkg
pkg"activate ."

include("Database.jl")
include("Wikipedia.jl")
include("Gameplay.jl")
include("WebApp.jl")

using .Wikipedia, .Gameplay, .WebApp
```

Run `six_degrees.jl` using your preferred approach, either in the editor or the Terminal (`$ julia six_degrees.jl`). Look for the message `Info: Listening on:...`, which notifies us that the web server has been started. Visit `http://localhost:8888/` in your browser and feast your eyes on our landing page! I'm sure you'll notice the effect of including the Twitter Bootstrap CSS file—adding just a few CSS classes to our code makes for a great visual impact!

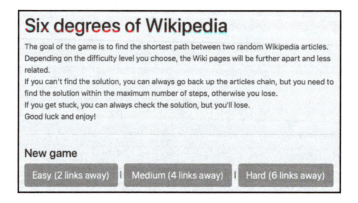

The preceding screenshot is of our game's landing page running on localhost at port `8888`.

Starting a new game

Excellent! Now, let's focus on the functionality for starting a new game. Here, we need to implement the following steps:

1. Extract the difficulty settings from the URL.
2. Start a new game. This game should have an ID, which will be our `session id`. Plus, it should keep track of the list of articles, progress, navigation history, the total number of steps taken, and the difficulty.
3. Render the first Wikipedia article.
4. Set up in-article navigation. We need to make sure that the links within the Wikipedia article will properly link back into our app, and not the Wikipedia website itself.
5. Display information about the game session, such as the objective (start and end articles), number of steps taken, and so on.

We'll look at all of these steps next.

Extracting the difficulty settings from the page URL

This is the very first step. Remember that within our `HandlerFunction`, we have access to the `Request` object, `req`. All the `Request` objects expose a field called `target` that references the URL of the request. The `target` does not include the protocol or the domain name, so it will be of the form `/new/$difficulty_level`. A quick way to extract the value of `$difficulty_level` is to simply replace the first part of the URI with an empty string, `""`, effectively removing it. The result will be used in a function, `newgamesession`, to create a new game of the indicated difficulty. Put into code, it will look like this:

```
game = parse(UInt8, (replace(req.target, "/new/"=>""))) |> newgamesession
```

Since we represent difficulty levels as integers (number of articles), we parse the string into an integer (specifically of type `UInt8`) before using it.

Starting a new game session

Starting a new game session is the second step. The game session manager, which should include the preceding `newgamesession` function, is missing entirely, so it's time we added it. We'll represent a game session as an instance of a corresponding type. Let's pack the `type` definition and the methods for manipulating it into a dedicated module. We can name the module `GameSession`, and the type `Game`. Please create the `GameSession.jl` file within the `"sixdegrees/"` folder.

Our `Game` type will need a custom constructor. We'll provide the difficulty level, and the constructor will take care of setting all of the internals—it will fetch the right number of Wikipedia articles using the previously created `Gameplay.newgame` function; it will create a unique game ID (which will be our session ID); and it'll initialize the rest of the fields with default values.

A first attempt will look like this:

```
module GameSession

using ..Gameplay, ..Wikipedia, ..Wikipedia.Articles
using Random

mutable struct Game
  id::String
  articles::Vector{Article}
  history::Vector{Article}
  steps_taken::UInt8
  difficulty::UInt8

  Game(game_difficulty) =
    new(randstring(), newgame(game_difficulty), Article[], 0,
game_difficulty)
end

const GAMES = Dict{String,Game}()

end
```

The `Random.randstring` function creates a random string. This is our game's and our session's ID.

We've also defined a `GAMES` dictionary, which will store all the active games and will allow us to look them up by their `id` field. Remember, our game is exposed on the web, so we'll have multiple game sessions running in parallel.

We can now add the rest of the functions. Add the following definitions before the module's closing `end`, as follows:

```
export newgamesession, gamesession, destroygamesession

function newgamesession(difficulty)
  game = Game(difficulty)
  GAMES[game.id] = game
  game
end

function gamesession(id)
  GAMES[id]
end

function destroygamesession(id)
  delete!(GAMES, id)
end
```

This is very straightforward. The snippet defines the `newgamesession` function, which creates a new `Game` of the indicated difficulty and stores it into the `GAMES` dict data structure. There's also a `getter` function, `gamesession`, which retrieves a `Game` by `id`. Finally, we add a `destructor` function, which removes the corresponding `Game` from the `GAMES` dict, effectively making it unavailable on the frontend and leaving it up for garbage collection. All of these functions are exported.

It's worth noting that storing our games in memory is fine for the purpose of this learning project, but in production, with a lot of players, you'd risk running out of memory quickly. For production use, we'd be better off persisting each `Game` to the database and retrieving it as necessary.

Rendering the first Wikipedia article from the chain

This is the third step. Going back to our `WebApp` module (in `WebApp.jl`), let's continue with the logic for the `newgamepage` handler. The implementation will look like this:

```
using ..GameSession, ..Wikipedia, ..Wikipedia.Articles

const newgamepage = HTTP.HandlerFunction() do req
  game = parse(UInt8, (replace(req.target, "/new/"=>""))) |> newgamesession
  article = game.articles[1]
  push!(game.history, article)
```

```
      HTTP.Messages.Response(200, wikiarticle(article))
    end
```

Once we create a new game, we need to reference its first article. We add the starting article to the game's history and then we render it as HTML using the following `wikiarticle` function:

```
function wikiarticle(article)
  html = """
  <!DOCTYPE html>
  <html>
  <head>
    <meta charset="utf-8" />
    <link rel="stylesheet"
href="https://stackpath.bootstrapcdn.com/bootstrap/4.1.3/css/bootstrap.min.
css" integrity="sha384-
MCw98/SFnGE8fJT3GXwEOngsV7Zt27NXFoaoApmYm81iuXoPkFOJwJ8ERdknLPMO"
crossorigin="anonymous">
    <title>6 Degrees of Wikipedia</title>
  </head>

  <body>
    <h1>$(article.title)</h1>
    <div id="wiki-article">
      $(article.content)
    </div>
  </body>
  </html>
  """
end
```

We simply display the title of the Wikipedia article as the main heading, and then the content.

Finally, don't forget to load `GameSession` into our app by adding it to `"six_degrees.jl"`. Beware that it needs to be loaded before `WebApp` to be available for `WebApp`. The full `"six_degrees.jl"` file should now look like this:

```
using Pkg pkg"activate ." include("Database.jl") include("Wikipedia.jl")
include("Gameplay.jl") include("GameSession.jl") include("WebApp.jl") using
.Wikipedia, .Gameplay, .GameSession, .WebApp
```

If you rerun our code and navigate to `http://localhost:8888/new/2`, you'll see our app rendering a random Wikipedia article:

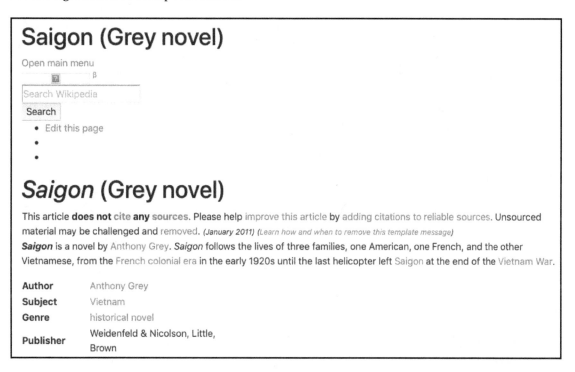

It's a good start, but there are some problems. First, we were a bit too greedy when fetching the content from Wikipedia. It includes the full page HTML, which contains things we don't really need, like the invisible `<head>` section and the all-too visible Wikipedia content from above the article's text (the search form, the menu, and so on). This is easy to fix—all we need to do is be a bit more specific about the content we want by using a better-defined CSS selector. A bit of playing around with the browser's inspector will reveal that the desired selector is `#bodyContent`.

Armed with this knowledge, we need to update the `Wikipedia` module. Please replace the existing `articleinfo` function with this one:

```
function articleinfo(content)
  dom = articledom(content)
  (extractcontent(dom.root), extractlinks(dom.root),
extracttitle(dom.root), extractimage(dom.root))
end
```

Instead of using the whole HTML, we will now extract just the content of the desired CSS selector:

```
function extractcontent(elem)
  matchFirst(Selector("#bodyContent"), elem) |> string
end
```

Please add the definition of `extractcontent` to the `Wikipedia.jl` file, under the `extractimage` function.

By revisiting our page at `http://localhost:8888/new/2`, we will see our efforts rewarded with a much better-looking replacement:

Millwall F.C.–West Ham United F.C. rivalry

The **rivalry between Millwall and West Ham United** is one of the longest-standing and most bitter in English football. The two teams, then known as Millwall Athletic and Thames Ironworks, both originated in the East End of London, and were located under three miles apart. They first played each other in the 1899–1900 FA Cup. The match was historically known as the **Dockers derby**, as both sets of supporters were predominantly dockers at shipyards on either side of the River Thames. Consequently, each set of fans worked for rival firms who were competing for the same business; this intensified the tension between the teams. In 1910, Millwall moved south of the River Thames to New Cross and the teams were no longer East London neighbours. Both sides have relocated since, but remain just under four miles apart. Millwall moved to The Den in Bermondsey in 1993 and West Ham to the London Stadium in Stratford in 2016.

The last derby at Upton Park.

(4 February 2012)

Locale	London (East and South)
Teams	Millwall and West Ham United

Setting up in-article navigation

All right, that wasn't so hard! But the next issue is more difficult. The fourth step is all about the setup. We established that we need to capture all the internal Wikipedia links so that when the player clicks on a link, they are taken to our app instead of going to the original Wikipedia article. Half of this work is done by Wikipedia's content itself because it uses relative URLs. That is, instead of using absolute URLs in the form of `https://en.wikipedia.org/wiki/Wikipedia:Six_degrees_of_Wikipedia`, it uses the relative form `/wiki/Wikipedia:Six_degrees_of_Wikipedia`. This means that when rendered in the browser, these links will inherit the domain name (or the *base URL*) of the current host. That is, when rendering the content of a Wikipedia article at `http://localhost:8888/`, its relative URLs will be interpreted as `http://localhost:8888/wiki/Wikipedia:Six_degrees_of_Wikipedia`. Therefore, they'll automatically point back to our web app. That's great, but one big piece of the puzzle is missing: we said that we want to maintain the state of our game by passing the session ID as part of the URL. Thus, our URLs should be of the form `http://localhost:8888/ABCDEF/wiki/Wikipedia:Six_degrees_of_Wikipedia`, where `ABCDEF` represents the game (or session) ID. The simplest solution is to replace `/wiki/` with `/ABCDEF/wiki/` when rendering the content—of course, using the actual game ID instead of `ABCDEF`.

In the definition of the `WebApp.wikiarticle` function, please look for this:

```
<div id="wiki-article">
    $(article.content)
</div>
```

Replace it with the following:

```
<div id="wiki-article">
    $(replace(article.content, "/wiki/"=>"/$(game.id)/wiki/"))
</div>
```

Because we now need the `game` object, we must make sure that we pass it into the function, so its declaration should become the following:

```
function wikiarticle(game, article)
```

This means that we also need to update the `newgamepage` route handler to correctly invoke the updated `wikiarticle` function. The last line of the `WebApp.newgamepage` function should now be as follows:

```
HTTP.Messages.Response(200, wikiarticle(game, article))
```

If you execute `six_degrees.jl` and take your browser to `http://localhost:8888/new/2`, you should see a nice rendering of a Wikipedia article with all the internal links containing the game ID:

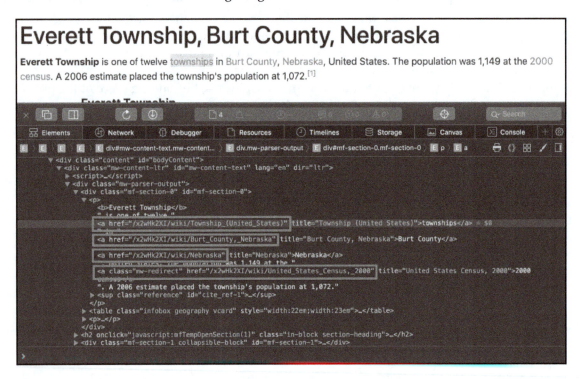

In the preceding screenshot, we can see that all the URLs start with `/x2wHk2XI`—our game ID.

Displaying information about the game session

For the fifth and very last part of our spec, we need to display information about the game and provide a way to navigate back to the previous articles. We'll define the following functions:

```
function objective(game)
    """
    <h3>
      Go from <i>$(game.articles[1].title)</i>
      to <i>$(game.articles[end].title)</i>
    </h3>
    <h5>
      Progress: $(size(game.history, 1) - 1)
      out of maximum $(size(game.articles, 1) - 1) links
      in $(game.steps_taken) steps
    </h5>
    <h6>
      <a href="/$(game.id)/solution">Solution?</a> |
      <a href="/">New game</a>
    </h6>"""
end
```

The `objective` function informs the player about the start and end articles and about the current progress. It also provides a small menu so that you can view the solution or start a new game.

For navigating back, we need to generate the game history links:

```
function history(game)
    html = "<ol>"
    iter = 0
    for a in game.history
      html *= """
      <li><a href="/$(game.id)/back/$(iter + 1)">$(a.title)</a></li>
      """
      iter += 1
    end
    html * "</ol>"
end
```

Finally, we need a bit of extra logic to check if the game was won or lost:

```
function puzzlesolved(game, article)
  article.url == game.articles[end].url
end
```

We have a winner if the URL of the current article is the same as the URL of the last article in the game.

The game is lost if the player runs out of moves:

```
function losinggame(game)
  game.steps_taken >= Gameplay.MAX_NUMBER_OF_STEPS
end
```

The complete code, so far, should look like this:

```
module WebApp

using HTTP, Sockets
using ..Gameplay, ..GameSession, ..Wikipedia, ..Wikipedia.Articles

# Configuration
const HOST = ip"0.0.0.0"
const PORT = 8888
const ROUTER = HTTP.Router()
const SERVER = HTTP.Server(ROUTER)

# Functions
function wikiarticle(game, article)
  html = """
  <!DOCTYPE html>
  <html>
  $(head())

  <body>
    $(objective(game))
    $(history(game))
    <hr/>
    $(
      if losinggame(game)
        "<h1>You Lost :( </h1>"
      else
        puzzlesolved(game, article) ? "<h1>You Won!</h1>" : ""
      end
    )

    <h1>$(article.title)</h1>
```

```
      <div id="wiki-article">
        $(replace(article.content, "/wiki/"=>"/$(game.id)/wiki/"))
      </div>
    </body>
    </html>
    """
end

function history(game)
  html = "<ol>"
  iter = 0
  for a in game.history
    html *= """
    <li><a href="/$(game.id)/back/$(iter + 1)">$(a.title)</a></li>
    """
    iter += 1
  end

  html * "</ol>"
end

function objective(game)
  """
  <h3>
    Go from <i>$(game.articles[1].title)</i>
    to <i>$(game.articles[end].title)</i>
  </h3>
  <h5>
    Progress: $(size(game.history, 1) - 1)
    out of maximum $(size(game.articles, 1) - 1) links
    in $(game.steps_taken) steps
  </h5>
  <h6>
    <a href="/$(game.id)/solution">Solution?</a> |
    <a href="/">New game</a>
  </h6>"""
end

function head()
  """
  <head>
    <meta charset="utf-8" />
    <link rel="stylesheet"
href="https://stackpath.bootstrapcdn.com/bootstrap/4.1.3/css/bootstrap.min.
css" integrity="sha384-
MCw98/SFnGE8fJT3GXwEOngsV7Zt27NXFoaoApmYm81iuXoPkFOJwJ8ERdknLPMO"
crossorigin="anonymous">
    <title>6 Degrees of Wikipedia</title>
```

```
        </head>
        """
end

function puzzlesolved(game, article)
  article.url == game.articles[end].url
end

function losinggame(game)
  game.steps_taken >= Gameplay.MAX_NUMBER_OF_STEPS
end

# Routes handlers
const landingpage = HTTP.HandlerFunction() do req
  html = """
  <!DOCTYPE html>
  <html>
  $(head())

  <body>
    <div class="jumbotron">
      <h1>Six degrees of Wikipedia</h1>
      <p>
        The goal of the game is to find the shortest path between two
random Wikipedia articles.<br/>
        Depending on the difficulty level you choose, the Wiki pages will
be further apart and less related.<br/>
        If you can't find the solution, you can always go back up the
articles chain, but you need to find the solution within the maximum number
of steps, otherwise you lose.<br/>
        If you get stuck, you can always check the solution, but you'll
lose.<br/>
        Good luck and enjoy!
      </p>

      <hr class="my-4">

      <div>
        <h4>New game</h4>
          <a href="/new/$(Gameplay.DIFFICULTY_EASY)" class="btn btn-primary
btn-lg">Easy ($(Gameplay.DIFFICULTY_EASY) links away)</a> |
          <a href="/new/$(Gameplay.DIFFICULTY_MEDIUM)" class="btn btn-
primary btn-lg">Medium ($(Gameplay.DIFFICULTY_MEDIUM) links away)</a> |
          <a href="/new/$(Gameplay.DIFFICULTY_HARD)" class="btn btn-primary
btn-lg">Hard ($(Gameplay.DIFFICULTY_HARD) links away)</a>
        </div>
    </div>
  </body>
```

```
        </html>
        """

    HTTP.Messages.Response(200, html)
end

const newgamepage = HTTP.HandlerFunction() do req
    game = parse(UInt8, (replace(req.target, "/new/"=>""))) |> newgamesession
    article = game.articles[1]
    push!(game.history, article)

    HTTP.Messages.Response(200, wikiarticle(game, article))
end

const articlepage = HTTP.HandlerFunction() do req
end

const backpage = HTTP.HandlerFunction() do req
end

const solutionpage = HTTP.HandlerFunction() do req
end

const notfoundpage = HTTP.HandlerFunction() do req
end


# Routes definitions
HTTP.register!(ROUTER, "/", landingpage) # root page
HTTP.register!(ROUTER, "/new/*", newgamepage) # /new/$difficulty_level --
new game
HTTP.register!(ROUTER, "/*/wiki/*", articlepage) #
/$session_id/wiki/$wikipedia_article_url -- article page
HTTP.register!(ROUTER, "/*/back/*", backpage) #
/$session_id/back/$number_of_steps -- go back the navigation history
HTTP.register!(ROUTER, "/*/solution", solutionpage) # /$session_id/solution
-- display the solution HTTP.register!(ROUTER, "*", notfoundpage) #
everything else -- not found # Start server HTTP.serve(SERVER, HOST, PORT)

end
```

Please note that we've also refactored the <head> of the pages, abstracting it away into the head function, which is used by both landingpage and wikiarticle. This way, we keep our code DRY, avoiding the repetition of the same <head> HTML element.

Now, let's make sure that we add `Gameplay.MAX_NUMBER_OF_STEPS` to `Gameplay.jl`. Add it at the top, under the difficulty constants:

```
const MAX_NUMBER_OF_STEPS = 10
```

Displaying a Wikipedia article page

The player has read the starting article and clicked on a link within the content. We need to add the logic for rendering the linked article. We'll have to fetch the article (or read it from the database if it was already fetched), display it, and update the game's state.

Here is the code:

```
const articlepage = HTTP.HandlerFunction() do req
  uri_parts = parseuri(req.target)
  game = gamesession(uri_parts[1])
  article_uri = "/wiki/$(uri_parts[end])"
  existing_articles = Articles.find(article_uri)
  article = isempty(existing_articles) ?
    persistedarticle(fetchpage(article_uri)...) :
    existing_articles[1]
  push!(game.history, article)
  game.steps_taken += 1
  puzzlesolved(game, article) && destroygamesession(game.id)
  HTTP.Messages.Response(200, wikiarticle(game, article))
end
```

We start by parsing the `Request` URI to extract all the values sent via GET. It is a string with the format `/$session_id/wiki/$article_name`, for example, `/c701b1b0b1/wiki/Buenos_Aires`. We want to break it into its parts. Since this is an operation that we'll need to perform more than once, we will abstract this functionality into the `parseuri` function:

```
function parseuri(uri)
  map(x -> String(x), split(uri, "/", keepempty = false))
end
```

Here, we use Julia's `split` function to break the URI string into an `Array` of `SubString`, corresponding to the segments between forward slashes `/`. Then, we convert the resulting `Array` of `SubString` to an `Array` of `String`, which is returned and stored in the `uri_parts` variable.

Continuing with the definition of the `articlepage` handler, we use the first element of the `uri_parts` array, which corresponds to the session ID, to retrieve our game object, by invoking `gamesession(uri_parts[1])`. With the last element, we generate the Wikipedia article URL. We then look up the article by URL, and either retrieve it from the database or fetch it from the website.

Once we have the article, we add it to the game's history and increase the `game.steps_taken` counter. Then, we check if we should end the game as a win:

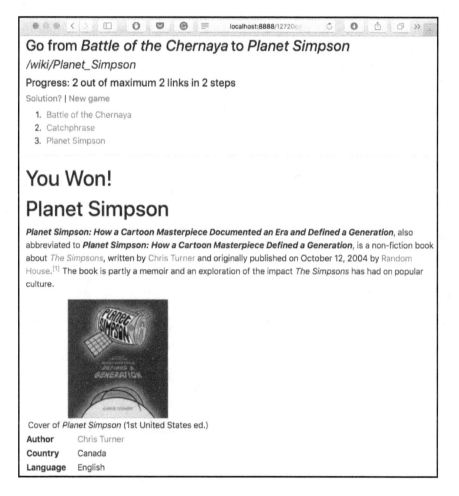

This is a screenshot of the winning article page. The design is not great, but the sweet taste of victory surely is!

Finally, similar to the new game page, we respond by rendering the article and all the game information.

Navigating back up the article chain

Keep in mind that a back navigation URL looks like `/c701b1b0b1/back/1`, where the first part is the session ID and the last part is the index of the item in the history stack. To implement it, the workflow is similar to `articlepage`—we parse the `Request` URI, retrieve the game by session ID, and get the article from the game's history stack. Since we go back in the game's history, everything beyond the current article index is to be removed from the navigation stack. When done, we respond by rendering the corresponding Wikipedia article. The code is short and readable:

```
const backpage = HTTP.HandlerFunction() do req
  uri_parts = parseuri(req.target)
  game = gamesession(uri_parts[1])
  history_index = parse(UInt8, uri_parts[end])

  article = game.history[history_index]
  game.history = game.history[1:history_index]

  HTTP.Messages.Response(200, wikiarticle(game, article))
end
```

Showing the solution

For the solution page, the only thing we need from the `Request` URI is the session ID. Then, we follow the same workflow to get the current `Game` object. Once we have it, we copy the list of articles into the history stack to display the game's solution using the existing rendering logic. We also set the `steps_taken` counter to the maximum because the game is considered a loss. Finally, we display the last article:

```
const solutionpage = HTTP.HandlerFunction() do req
  uri_parts = parseuri(req.target)
  game = gamesession(uri_parts[1])
  game.history = game.articles
  game.steps_taken = Gameplay.MAX_NUMBER_OF_STEPS
  article = game.articles[end]
  HTTP.Messages.Response(200, wikiarticle(game, article))
end
```

The solution page appears as follows, settling the game as a loss:

Handling any other requests

Similar to our `Hello World` example, we'll respond to any other requests with a `404 Not Found` response:

```
const notfoundpage = HTTP.HandlerFunction() do req
  HTTP.Messages.Response(404, "Sorry, this can't be found")
end
```

Wrapping it up

I've added a few more UI tweaks to the `WebApp.jl` file to spice things up a bit. Here are the important parts—please download the full file from `https://github.com/TrainingByPackt/Julia-1-Programming-Complete-Reference-Guide/tree/master/Chapter14/sixdegrees/WebApp.jl`:

```julia
module WebApp

# code truncated #

function history(game)
  html = """<ol class="list-group">"""
  iter = 0
  for a in game.history
    html *= """
      <li class="list-group-item">
        <a href="/$(game.id)/back/$(iter + 1)">$(a.title)</a>
      </li>
    """
    iter += 1
  end

  html * "</ol>"
end

function objective(game)
    """
    <div class="jumbotron">
      <h3>Go from
        <span class="badge badge-info">$(game.articles[1].title)</span>
        to
        <span class="badge badge-info">$(game.articles[end].title)</span>
      </h3>
      <hr/>
      <h5>
        Progress:
        <span class="badge badge-dark">$(size(game.history, 1) - 1)</span>
        out of maximum
        <span class="badge badge-dark">$(size(game.articles, 1) - 1)</span>
        links in
        <span class="badge badge-dark">$(game.steps_taken)</span>
        steps
      </h5>
      $(history(game))
      <hr/>
      <h6>
```

```
      <a href="/$(game.id)/solution" class="btn btn-primary btn-
lg">Solution?</a> |
      <a href="/" class="btn btn-primary btn-lg">New game</a>
    </h6>
  </div>
  """
end

# code truncated #

end
```

You will see that I have reorganized the layout a bit and that I've added a few extra styles to make our UI prettier. Here is our game with its updated look:

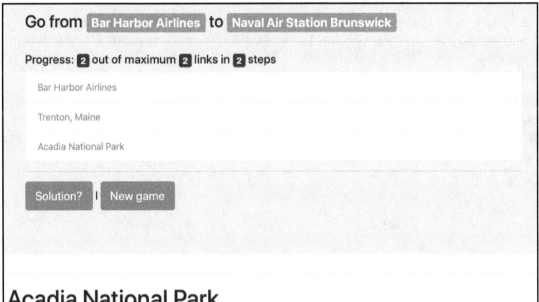

As for the rest of the files, if you need them, they are available for download in this chapter's GitHub repository, which is accessible at `https://github.com/TrainingByPackt/Julia-1-Programming-Complete-Reference-Guide/tree/master/Chapter14/sixdegrees`.

That is all we need to do to run a full game of *Six Degrees of Wikipedia*. Now, it's time to enjoy it!

Summary

Julia focuses on scientific computing and data science. But thanks to its great qualities as a generic programming language, its native parallel computing features, and its performance, we have an excellent use case for Julia in the area of web development.

The package ecosystem provides access to a powerful set of libraries dedicated to web programming. They are relatively low level, but still abstract away most of the complexities of working directly with the network stack. The HTTP package provides a good balance between usability, performance, and flexibility.

The fact that we managed to build a fairly complex (albeit small) web app with so little code is a testimony to the power and expressiveness of the language and to the quality of the third-party libraries. We did a great job with our learning project—it's now time to relax a bit and enjoy a round of *Six Degrees of Wikipedia*, Julia style!

15
Implementing Recommender Systems with Julia

In the previous chapters, we took a deep dive into data mining and web development with Julia. I hope you enjoyed a few relaxing rounds of *Six Degrees of Wikipedia* while discovering some interesting articles. Randomly poking through the millions of Wikipedia articles as part of a game is a really fun way to stumble upon interesting new content. Although I'm sure that, at times, you've noticed that not all the articles are equally good—maybe they're stubs, or subjective, or not so well written, or simply irrelevant to you. If we were able to learn about each player's individual interests, we could filter out certain Wikipedia articles, which would turn each game session into a wonderful journey of discovery.

It turns out that we're not the only ones struggling with this—information discovery is a multibillion-dollar problem, regardless of whether it's articles, news, books, music, movies, hotels, or really any kind of product or service that can be sold over the internet. As consumers, we are exposed to an immense variety of choices, while at the same time, we have less and less time to review them—and our attention span is getting shorter and shorter. Making relevant recommendations instantly is a key feature of all successful online platforms, from Amazon to Booking.com, to Netflix, to Spotify, to Udemy. All of these companies have invested in building powerful recommender systems, literally inventing new business models together with the accompanying data collection and recommendation algorithms.

In this chapter, we'll learn about recommender systems—the most common and successful algorithms that are used in the wild for addressing a wide variety of business needs. We'll look at the following topics:

- What recommender systems are and how are they used
- Content-based versus collaborative filtering recommender systems
- User-based and item-based recommender systems

- More advanced data analysis using `DataFrames` and statistical functions
- How to roll out our own recommender systems using content-based and collaborative filtering algorithms

Technical requirements

The Julia package ecosystem is under continuous development and new package versions are released on a daily basis. Most of the times this is great news, as new releases bring new features and bug fixes. However, since many of the packages are still in beta (version 0.x), any new release can introduce breaking changes. As a result, the code presented in the book can stop working. In order to ensure that your code will produce the same results as described in the book, it is recommended to use the same package versions. Here are the external packages used in this chapter and their specific versions:

```
CSV@v0.4.3
DataFrames@v0.15.2
Distances@v0.7.4
IJulia@v1.14.1
Plots@v0.22.0
StatPlots@v0.8.2
```

In order to install a specific version of a package you need to run:

```
pkg> add PackageName@vX.Y.Z
```

For example:

```
pkg> add IJulia@v1.14.1
```

Alternatively you can install all the used packages by downloading the `Project.toml` file provided with the chapter and using `pkg>` instantiate as follows:

```
julia>
download("https://github.com/TrainingByPackt/Julia-1-Programming-Complete-R
eference-Guide/tree/master/Chapter15/Project.toml", "Project.toml")
pkg> activate .
pkg> instantiate
```

Understanding recommender systems

In its broadest definition, a **recommender system** (**RS**) is a technique that's used for providing suggestions for items that are useful to a person. These suggestions are meant to help in various decision-making processes, usually related to buying or consuming a certain category of products or services. They can be about buying a book, listening to a song, watching a movie, eating out at a certain restaurant, reading a news article, or picking the hotel for your next holiday.

People have relied on recommendations pretty much since the beginning of history. Some RS researchers talk about the first recommendations as being the first orally transmitted information about dangerous plants, animals, or places. Others think that recommendations systems functioned even before language, by simply observing the effects on other humans of consuming plants or unwisely confronting dangerous creatures (that could count as an extreme and possibly violent example of implicit ratings, as we'll see in the following paragraphs).

But we don't have to go that far into human history. In more recent (and less dangerous) times, we can find some great examples of highly successful recommender systems, such as librarians suggesting books based on your tastes and interests, the butcher presenting meat products for your Sunday recipe, your friends' opinion of the latest blockbuster, your neighbor's stories about the kindergarten across the street, and even your MD recommending what treatment to follow to alleviate the symptoms and eliminate the cause of your disease. Other recommender systems are more formal, but equally pervasive and familiar, such as the star category ranking of hotels or the blue flags on top beaches around the world.

For a very long time, the experts in various fields played the part of recommenders, using their expertise in combination with their understanding of our tastes and interests, skillfully probing us for details. However, the rise of the internet and online platforms (e-commerce websites, online radios, movie streaming platforms, and social networks) has replaced the traditional models by making a huge catalog of items (products) available to a potentially very large consumer base (now called **users**). Due to considerations like 24-hour availability, language barriers, and sheer volume, personal recommendations were no longer a feasible option (although in the last couple of years, there was a certain recurrence of human-curated recommendations, from music, to books, to luxury products—but that's a different discussion).

This expansion in the number of choices made finding the right product a very difficult task. At that point, software-based recommender systems entered the stage.

Amazon.com is credited as being the first online business that deployed software recommender systems at scale, with extraordinary business benefits. Later on, Netflix became famous for awarding a one million dollar prize to the team that came up with a recommendation algorithm better than theirs. Nowadays, automated recommender systems power all major platforms, from Spotify's *Discover Weekly* playlists to Udemy's recommended courses.

Classifying recommender systems

Different business needs—from suggesting related products after buying your new laptop, to compiling the perfect driving playlist, to helping you reconnect with long lost schoolmates—led to the development of different recommendation algorithms. A key part of rolling out a recommender system is picking the right approach for the problem at hand to fully take advantage of the data available. We'll take a look at the most common and most successful algorithms.

Learning about non-personalized, stereotyped, and personalized recommendations

The simplest types of recommendations, from a technical and algorithmic perspective, are the non-personalized ones. That is, they are not customized to take into account specific user preferences. Such recommendations can include best-selling products, various top 10 songs, blockbuster movies, or the most downloaded apps of the week.

Non-personalized recommendations are less challenging technically, but also considerably less powerful. They can be good approximations in certain cases, especially when the product catalog is not very large (there are not that many Hollywood releases, for example). But for an e-commerce retailer like Amazon, with millions of products available at any given time, the chances of getting it right using generic recommendations are slim.

An improvement in non-personalized recommendations comes from combining them with a classification strategy. By stereotyping, we can make the recommended items more relevant, especially when we can identify significantly different user demographics. A good example of this is app store recommendations, which are broken down by country. Take, for instance, the following list of recommended new games. This is what it looks like if you are a user accessing the app store from the US:

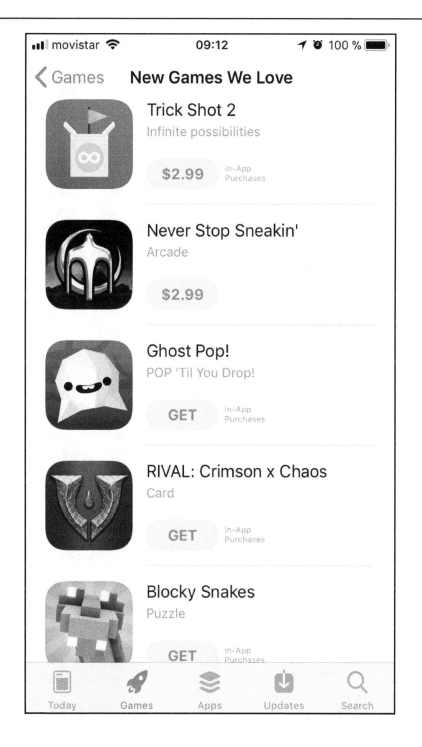

This is what it looks like for a user in Romania, at the exact same time:

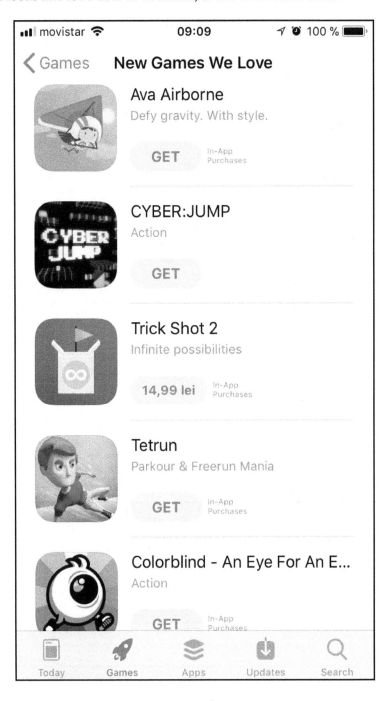

You can easily notice that the top selections vary widely. This is driven by both cultural differences and preferences, but also by availability (copyright and distribution) issues.

We won't focus on non-personalized recommendations in this chapter, since implementing them is quite straightforward. All that is needed for making such recommendations is to identify the relevant metrics and the best performing items, such as the number of downloads for apps, copies sold for a book, volume of streams for a song or movie, and so on. However, non-personalized recommendations, as a business solution, should not be dismissed, as they can be useful when dealing with users that don't present any relevant personal preferences—usually new users.

Understanding personalized recommendations

Both from a business and a technical perspective, the most interesting recommender systems are the ones that take into account the user's preferences (or user's ranking).

Explicit and implicit ratings

When looking for personalization features, we must take into account both explicit data that's willingly provided by the user, as well as relevant information that's generated by their behavior in the app or on the website (or anywhere else where we're tracking user behavior really, since the boundary between the online and physical realms is becoming more blurry, for example, with the introduction of smart cars and autonomous shop checkouts, to name just a few). The explicit rating includes actions such as grading a product or an experience, awarding stars to a movie or purchase, and retweeting or liking a post. On the other hand, not bouncing back to the search results page, sharing a song, or watching a video until the end are all examples of an implicit positive rating, while returning a product, canceling a subscription, or not finishing an online training course or an eBook are instances of negative implicit ranking.

Understanding content-based recommender systems

One of the most common and successful types of recommendations are content-based. The core idea is that if I expressed a preference for a certain set of items, I will most likely be interested in more items that share the same attributes. For example, the fact that I watched `Finding Nemo (2003)` can be used as an indication that I will be interested in other movies from the animation and comedy genres.

Alternatively, watching one of the original *Star Wars* movie can be interpreted as a signal that I like other movies from the franchise, or movies with Harrison Ford, or directed by George Lucas, or science fiction in general. Indeed, Netflix employs such an algorithm, except at a more granular level. Per a recent article, Netflix has a large team that's tasked with watching and tagging movies in detail—later on, matching movie features with users groups. The users themselves are equally carefully classified into thousands of categories.

More advanced content-based recommender systems also take into account the relative weight of the different tags. In the case of the previously mentioned `Finding Nemo (2003)`, the suggestions should be less about movies with fish and sharks and more about the fact that it's a funny, light-hearted family movie, so hopefully, the recommendation will be more `Finding Dory (2016)` and less *Jaws*.

Let's see how we can build a basic movie recommender using a content-based algorithm. To keep things simple, I have set up a table with the top 10 movies of 2016 and their genres. You can find this file in this book's GitHub repository, as `top_10_movies.tsv`, at `https://github.com/TrainingByPackt/Julia-1-Programming-Complete-Reference-Guide/tree/master/Chapter15/top_10_movies.tsv`:

	A	B	C	D	E	F	G	H	I
1	Movie title	Action	Animation	Comedy	Drama	Kids	Mistery	Musical	SF
2	Moonlight (2016)	0	0	0	1	0	0	0	0
3	Zootopia (2016)	1	1	1	0	0	0	0	0
4	Arrival (2016)	0	0	0	1	0	1	0	1
5	Hell or High Water (2016)	0	0	0	1	0	1	0	0
6	La La Land (2016)	0	0	1	1	0	0	1	0
7	The Jungle Book (2016)	1	0	0	0	1	0	0	0
8	Manchester by the Sea (2016)	0	0	0	1	0	0	0	0
9	Finding Dory (2016)	0	1	0	0	0	0	0	0
10	Captain America: Civil War (2016)	1	0	0	0	0	0	0	1
11	Moana (2016)	1	1	0	0	0	0	0	0

In the preceding screenshot, you can see how we use a binary system to represent whether a movie belongs to a genre (encoded by a 1) or not (a 0).

We can easily load such a table from a CSV/TSV file into Julia by using the `readdlm` function, which is available in the `DelimitedFiles` module. This module comes with the default Julia installation, so there's no need to add it:

```
julia> using DelimitedFiles
Julia> movies = readdlm("top_10_movies.tsv", '\t', skipstart=1)
```

In the preceding snippet, `skipstart=1` tells Julia to skip the first line when reading the *Tab* separated `top_10_movies.tsv` file—otherwise, Julia would interpret the header row as a data row as well.

There is also the option of letting `readdlm` know that the first row is the header, passing `header = true`. However, this would change the return type of the function invocation to a tuple of (`data_cells, header_cells`), which is not pretty-printed in interactive environments. At this exploratory phase, we're better off with a table-like representation of the data. The result is a tabular data structure that contains our movie titles and their genres:

```
10×9 Array{Any,2}:
"Moonlight (2016)"                    0  0  0  1  0  0  0  0
"Zootopia (2016)"                     1  1  1  0  0  0  0  0
"Arrival (2016)"                      0  0  0  1  0  1  0  1
"Hell or High Water (2016)"           0  0  0  1  0  1  0  0
"La La Land (2016)"                   0  0  1  1  0  0  1  0
"The Jungle Book (2016)"              1  0  0  0  1  0  0  0
"Manchester by the Sea (2016)"        0  0  0  1  0  0  0  0
"Finding Dory (2016)"                 0  1  0  0  0  0  0  0
"Captain America: Civil War (2016)"   1  0  0  0  0  0  0  1
"Moana (2016)"                        1  1  0  0  0  0  0  0
```

Let's see what movie from the top 10 list we could recommend to a user who watched the aforementioned movie, `Finding Nemo (2003)`. Rotten Tomatoes classifies `Finding Nemo (2003)` under the *Animation, Comedy,* and *Kids* genres. We can encode this as follows:

```
julia> nemo = ["Finding Nemo (2003)", 0, 1, 1, 0, 1, 0, 0, 0] 9-element
Array{Any,1}:
  "Finding Nemo (2003)"
 0
 1
 1
 0
 1
 0
 0
 0
```

To make a movie recommendation based on genre, all we have to do is find the ones that are the most similar, that is, the movies that share the most genres with our `Finding Nemo (2003)`.

There is a multitude of algorithms for computing the similarity (or on the contrary, the distance) between items—in our case, as we're dealing with binary values only, the Hamming distance looks like a good choice. The Hamming distance is a number that's used to denote the difference between two binary strings. This distance is calculated by comparing two binary values and taking into account the number of positions at which the corresponding bits are different. We'll compare each bit in succession and record either 1 or 0, depending on whether or not the bits are different or the same. If they are the same, we record a 0. For different bits, we record a 1. Then, we add all the 1s and 0s in the record to obtain the Hamming distance.

A function for calculating the Hamming distance is available in the Distances package. This is a third-party Julia package that provides access to a multitude of functions for evaluating distances between vectors, including Euclidian, Jaccard, Hemming, Cosine, and many others. All we need to do to access this treasure of functionality is run the following:

```
julia> using Pkg
pkg> add Distances
julia> using Distances
```

Then, we need to iterate over our movies matrix and compute the Hamming distance between each movie and Finding Nemo (2003):

```
julia> distances = Dict{String,Int}()
Dict{String,Int64} with 0 entries

julia> for i in 1:size(movies, 1)
            distances[movies[i,:][1]] = hamming(Int[movies[i,2:end]...],
Int[nemo[2:end]...])
       end
```

In the preceding snippet, we iterated over each movie and calculated the Hamming distance between its genres and the genres of Finding Nemo (2003). To do this, we only extracted the genres (leaving off the name of the movie) and converted the list of values into an array of Int. Finally, we placed the result of the computation into the distances Dict we defined previously, which uses the name of the movie as the key, and the distance as the value.

This is the end result:

```
julia> distances
Dict{String,Int64} with 10 entries:
  "The Jungle Book (2016)"              => 3
  "Hell or High Water (2016)"           => 5
  "Arrival (2016)"                      => 6
  "La La Land (2016)"                   => 4
```

```
"Moana (2016)"                      => 3
"Captain America: Civil War (2016)" => 5
"Moonlight (2016)"                  => 4
"Finding Dory (2016)"               => 2
"Zootopia (2016)"                   => 2
"Manchester by the Sea (2016)"      => 4
```

Since we're computing distances, the most similar movies are the ones within the shortest distance. So, according to our recommender, a user who watched `Finding Nemo (2003)` should next watch `Finding Dory (2016)` or `Zootopia (2016)` (distance 2) and when done, should move on to `The Jungle Book (2016)` and `Moana (2016)` (both at a distance of 3). If you haven't watched all of these recommended movies already, I can tell you that the suggestions are quite appropriate. Similarly, the least recommended movie is `Arrival (2016)`, which although is an excellent science fiction drama, has nothing in common with cute Nemo and forgetful Dory.

Beginning with association-based recommendations

Although content-based recommender systems can produce great results, they do have limitations. For starters, they can't be used to recommend new items. Based on my initial `Finding Nemo (2003)` ranking alone, I would be stuck getting suggestions for animated movies alone and I'd never get the chance to hear about any new documentaries or car or cooking shows that I sometimes enjoy.

Also, it works best for categories of items that can be purchased repeatedly, like books, apps, songs, or movies, to name a few. But if I'm on Amazon and purchase a new dishwasher from the *Home and kitchen* category, it doesn't make a lot of sense to get recommendations about products within the same group, such as a fridge or a washing machine, as chances are I'm not replacing all of the expensive kitchen appliances at the same time. However, I will most likely need the corresponding joints and taps and pipes and whatever else is needed to install the dishwasher, together with the recommended detergent and maybe other accessories. Since the e-commerce platform is selling all of these products as well, it's beneficial to order them together and receive them at the same time, saving on transport too.

These bundles of products can form the foundation of a RS based on product association. These types of recommendations are quite common, and are usually presented as *frequently bought together* on e-commerce platforms. For physical stores, this type of data analysis—also known as **market basket analysis**—is used to place products that are purchased together in close physical proximity. Think, for example, about pasta being side by side with sauces, or shampoo with conditioners.

One of the most popular algorithms used for association based recommendations is the `Apriori` algorithm. It is used to identify items that frequently occur together in different scenarios (shopping baskets, web browsing, adverse drug reactions, and so on). The `Apriori` algorithm helps us identify correlations through data mining by employing association rules.

Space constraints don't allow us to get into the details of building such as system, but if you would like to dive deeper into this topic, there are many free resources to get you started. I recommend beginning with *Movie Recommendation with Market Basket Analysis* (`https://rpubs.com/vitidN/203264`) as it builds a movie recommender that's very similar to ours.

Learning about collaborative filtering

Collaborative filtering (**CF**) is another very successful and widely used recommendation algorithm. It is based on the idea that people with similar preferences will have similar interests. If two customers, let's call them Annie and Bob, give `Finding Nemo (2003)` a good rating and Annie also highly ranks `Finding Dory (2016)`, then chances are that Bob will also like `Finding Dory (2016)`. Of course, comparing two users and two products may not seem like much, but applied to very large datasets representing both users and products, the recommendations become highly relevant.

If you're confused as to what the difference between CF and content filtering is, since both can be used to infer `Finding Dory (2016)` based on `Finding Nemo (2003)`, the key point is that CF does not care about item attributes. Indeed, when using CF, we don't need the movie genre information, nor any other tags. The algorithm is not concerned with the classification of the items. It pretty much states that if, for whatever reason, the items were ranked highly by a subset of users, then other items that are highly ranked by the same subset of users will be relevant for our target user, hence making for a good recommendation.

Understanding user-item CF

This was the basic idea, and with the advent of big data, the CF technique has become quite powerful. As it's been applied to different business needs and usage scenarios, the algorithm was refined to better address the problems it was attempting to solve. As a consequence, a few other approaches emerged, and the original one became known as **user-item CF**.

It's gotten this name because it takes as its input user data (user preferences, rankings) and outputs item data (item recommendations). It's also known as **user-based CF**.

You can see it illustrated in the following diagram:

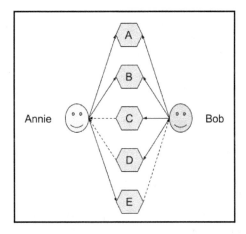

The preceding diagram shows that **Annie** likes **A**, **B**, and **E**, while **Bob** likes **A**, **B**, **C**, and **D**.

The `recommender` algorithm established that, between **Annie** and **Bob**, there's a high degree of similarity because they both like items **A** and **B**. Next, it will assume that **Annie** will also like other items from Bob's list of preferences that she hasn't discovered yet, and the reverse for **Bob**—he'll like items from Annie's list that he hasn't discovered yet. Thus, since Annie also likes item E, we can recommend it to **Bob**, and since Bob's very fond of **C** and **D** and Annie has no knowledge about these yet, we can confidently suggest that she checks them out.

Let's take another very simple example, also from the realm of movie recommendations. Sticking to our previous list of top 10 movies for the year 2016 on Rotten Tomatoes, this time, let's ignore the classification by genre and imagine that we have user ratings data instead:

Movie title	Acton	Annie	Comey	Dean	Kit	Missie	Musk	Sam
Moonlight (2016)		3		10		9	2	
Zootopia (2016)	9	10	7		10		5	
Arrival (2016)	5		6	10		9		10
Hell or High Water (2016)	3		3	10		8		
La La Land (2016)	6		8	9			10	
The Jungle Book (2016)	8	7		2	9		6	
Manchester by the Sea (2016)			2	8				
Finding Dory (2016)	7	8	5	4	10			
Captain America: Civil War (2016)	10		5	6				9
Moana (2016)	8	9			10		7	

The preceding screenshot shows a table of movie titles and users and their corresponding ratings. As it happens in real life, not all of the users have rated all of the moves—the absence of a rating is indicated by an empty cell.

You will notice in the preceding screenshot that by a strange twist of faith, the user's names provide a hint as to what kind of movies they prefer. Acton is very much into action movies, while Annie loves animations. Comey's favorites are the comedies, while Dean enjoys good dramas. Kit's highest rankings went to kids movies, Missie loves mystery movies, while musical's are Musk reasons for binge watching. Finally, Sam is a science fiction fan.

The dataset is provided in this chapter's files under the name `top_10_movies_user_rankings.csv`. Please download it from https://github.com/TrainingByPackt/Julia-1-Programming-Complete-Reference-Guide/blob/master/Chapter15/top_10_movies_user_rankings.csv and place it somewhere on your hard drive where you can easily access it from Julia's REPL.

We can load it into memory using the same `readdlm` Julia function as before:

```
movies = readdlm("/path/to/top_10_movies_user_rankings.csv", ';')
```

This file uses the ; char as the column separator, so we need to pass that into the `readdlm` function call. Remember that in Julia, ";" is different from ':'. The first is a `String` of length one, while the second is a `Char`.

This is the result of the `.csv` file being read—a matrix containing movies on rows and people on columns, with each person's rating at the corresponding intersection between rows and columns:

```
11×9 Array{Any,2}:
 "Movie title"                      "Acton"   "Annie"  …   "Dean"   "Kit"   "Missie"   "Musk"   "Sam"
 "Moonlight (2016)"                 ""        3            10       ""      9          2        ""
 "Zootopia (2016)"                  9         10           ""       10      ""         5        ""
 "Arrival (2016)"                   5         ""           10       ""      9          ""       10
 "Hell or High Water (2016)"        3         ""           10       ""      8          ""       ""
 "La La Land (2016)"                6         ""       …   9        ""      ""         10       ""
 "The Jungle Book (2016)"           8         7            2        9       ""         6        ""
 "Manchester by the Sea (2016)"     ""        ""           8        ""      ""         ""       ""
 "Finding Dory (2016)"              7         8            4        10      ""         ""       ""
 "Captain America: Civil War (2016)" 10       ""           6        ""      ""         ""       9
 "Moana (2016)"                     8         9        …   ""       10      ""         7        ""
```

It works, but the data doesn't look too good. As usually happens with data in real life, we don't always have ratings from all the users. The `missing` values were imported as empty strings `""`, and the headers were interpreted as entries in the matrix. Julia's `readdlm` is great for quick data imports, but for more advanced data wrangling, we can benefit considerably from using Julia's powerful `DataFrames` package.

`DataFrames` is a third-party Julia package that exposes a rich set of functions for manipulating tabular data. You should remember it from our Using DataFrames in Chapter 8, *I/O, Networking, and Parallel Computing*—if not, please take a few minutes to review that part. The rest of our discussion will assume that you have a basic understanding of `DataFrames` so that we can now focus on the more advanced features and use cases.

If, for some reason, you no longer have the `DataFrames` package, `pkg> add DataFrames` is all we need. While we're at it, let's also install the `CSV` package—it's a powerful utility library for handling delimited text files. We can add both in one step:

```
pkg> add DataFrames CSV
```

We'll use `CSV` to load the comma-separated file and produce a `DataFrame`:

```
julia> movies = CSV.read("top_10_movies_user_rankings.csv", delim = ';')
```

The resulting `DataFrame` should look like this:

```
10×9 DataFrame
 Row │ Movie title                         Acton    Annie    Comey    Dean     Kit      Missie   Musk     Sam
     │ Union{Missing, String}              Int64⍰   Int64⍰   Int64⍰   Int64⍰   Int64⍰   Int64⍰   Int64⍰   Int64⍰
─────┼────────────────────────────────────────────────────────────────────────────────────────────────────────
   1 │ Moonlight (2016)                    missing  3        missing  10       missing  9        2        missing
   2 │ Zootopia (2016)                     9        10       7        missing  10       missing  5        missing
   3 │ Arrival (2016)                      5        missing  6        10       missing  9        missing  10
   4 │ Hell or High Water (2016)           3        missing  3        10       missing  8        missing  missing
   5 │ La La Land (2016)                   6        missing  8        9        missing  missing  10       missing
   6 │ The Jungle Book (2016)              8        7        missing  2        9        missing  6        missing
   7 │ Manchester by the Sea (2016)        missing  missing  2        8        missing  missing  missing  missing
   8 │ Finding Dory (2016)                 7        8        5        4        10       missing  missing  missing
   9 │ Captain America: Civil War (2016)   10       missing  5        6        missing  missing  missing  9
  10 │ Moana (2016)                        8        9        missing  missing  10       missing  7        missing
```

We get a beautifully rendered tabular data structure, with the missing ratings correctly represented as `missing` data.

We can get a quick summary of our data by using the `describe` function:

```julia
julia> describe(movies)
```

The output for this is as follows:

```
9×8 DataFrame
 Row │ variable     mean      min              median   max              nunique   nmissing   eltype
     │ Symbol       Union…    Any              Union…   Any              Union…    Int64      DataType
─────┼────────────────────────────────────────────────────────────────────────────────────────────────
   1 │ Movie title            Arrival (2016)            Zootopia (2016)  10        0          String
   2 │ Acton        7.0       3                7.5      10                         2          Int64
   3 │ Annie        7.4       3                8.0      10                         5          Int64
   4 │ Comey        5.14286   2                5.0      8                          3          Int64
   5 │ Dean         7.375     2                8.5      10                         2          Int64
   6 │ Kit          9.75      9                10.0     10                         6          Int64
   7 │ Missie       8.66667   8                9.0      9                          7          Int64
   8 │ Musk         6.0       2                6.0      10                         5          Int64
   9 │ Sam          9.5       9                9.5      10                         8          Int64
```

Multiple columns have `missing` values. A `missing` value represents a value that is absent in the dataset. It is defined in the `Missings` package (`https://github.com/JuliaData/Missings.jl`), and it's the singleton instance of the `Missing` type. If you're familiar with `NULL` in SQL or `NA` in R, `missing` is the same in Julia.

Missing values are problematic when working with real-life datasets as they can affect the accuracy of the computations. For this reason, common operations that involve `missing` values usually propagate `missing`. For example, `1 + missing` and `cos(missing)` will both return `missing`.

We can check if a value is missing by using the `ismissing` function:

```julia
julia> movies[1,2]
missing

julia> ismissing(movies[1, 2])
true
```

In many cases, `missing` values will have to be skipped or replaced with a valid value. What value is appropriate for replacing `missing` will depend from case to case, as dictated by the business logic. In our case, for the missing ratings, we can use the value 0. By convention, we can agree that valid ratings range from 1 to 10, and that a rating of 0 corresponds to no rating at all.

One way to do the replacement is to iterate over each column except `Movie title` and then over each cell, and if the corresponding value is missing, replace it with 0. Here is the code:

```julia
julia> for c in names(movies)[2:end]
           movies[ismissing.(movies[c]), c] = 0
       end
```

We're all done—our data is now clean, with zeroes replacing all the previously missing values:

10×9 DataFrame

| Row | Movie title | Acton | Annie | Comey | Dean | Kit | Missie | Musk | Sam |
	Union{Missing, String}	Int64⍰	Int64⍰	Int64⍰	Int64⍰	Int64⍰	Int64⍰	Int64⍰	Int64⍰
1	Moonlight (2016)	0	3	0	10	0	9	2	0
2	Zootopia (2016)	9	10	7	0	10	0	5	0
3	Arrival (2016)	5	0	6	10	0	9	0	10
4	Hell or High Water (2016)	3	0	3	10	0	8	0	0
5	La La Land (2016)	6	0	8	9	0	0	10	0
6	The Jungle Book (2016)	8	7	0	2	9	0	6	0
7	Manchester by the Sea (2016)	0	0	2	8	0	0	0	0
8	Finding Dory (2016)	7	8	5	4	10	0	0	0
9	Captain America: Civil War (2016)	10	0	5	6	0	0	0	9
10	Moana (2016)	8	9	0	0	10	0	7	0

It would help if you saved this clean version of our data as a *Tab* separated file, for future reference, with the following code:

```julia
julia> CSV.write("top_10_movies_user_rankings.tsv", movies, delim='\t')
```

Now that we have our ratings loaded into Julia, the next step is to compute the similarity between the various users. The Hamming distance, the formula that we used when computing content based recommendations, would not be a good choice for numerical data. A much better alternative is Pearson's correlation coefficient. This coefficient, also known as ***Pearson's r or bivariate correlation***, is a measure of the linear correlation between two variables. It has a value between +1 and −1. A value of 1 indicates total positive linear correlation (both values increase together), while −1 represents total negative linear correlation (one value decreases while the other increases). The value 0 means that there's no linear correlation.

Here are a few examples of scatter diagrams with different visualizations of the correlation coefficient (By Kiatdd—Own work, CC BY-SA 3.0, `https://commons.wikimedia.org/w/index.php?curid=37108966`):

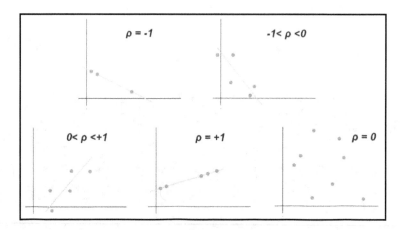

Let's see how we would calculate the similarity between Acton and Annie, based on the movie ratings they provided. Let's make things simpler and focus strictly on their data by extracting the Movie title column, together with the Acton and Annie columns:

```julia
julia> acton_and_annie = movies[:, 1:3]
```

The output is as follows:

```
10×3 DataFrame
 Row │ Movie title                          Acton   Annie
     │ Union{Missing, String}               Int64m  Int64m
─────┼──────────────────────────────────────────────────────
  1  │ Moonlight (2016)                     0       3
  2  │ Zootopia (2016)                      9       10
  3  │ Arrival (2016)                       5       0
  4  │ Hell or High Water (2016)            3       0
  5  │ La La Land (2016)                    6       0
  6  │ The Jungle Book (2016)               8       7
  7  │ Manchester by the Sea (2016)         0       0
  8  │ Finding Dory (2016)                  7       8
  9  │ Captain America: Civil War (2016)    10      0
  10 │ Moana (2016)                         8       9
```

This returns another `DataFrame`, referenced as `acton_and_annie`, which corresponds to the columns one to three of the `movies` `DataFrame`, representing Acton's and Annie's ratings for each of the movies.

This is good, but we're only interested in the movies that were rated by both users. If you remember from our discussion of `DataFrame` in `Chapter 8`, *I/O, Networking, and Parallel Computing,* we can select rows (and columns) by passing a Boolean value—`true` to select it, `false` to skip it. We can use this in combination with the dot syntax for element-wise operations to check if the values in the `:Acton` and `:Annie` columns are greater than 0. The code will look like this:

```julia
julia> acton_and_annie_in_common = acton_and_annie[(acton_and_annie[:Acton]
.> 0) .& (acton_and_annie[:Annie] .> 0), :]
```

Although it might look a bit intimidating, the snippet should be easy to follow: we use the `(acton_and_annie[:Acton] .> 0) .& (acton_and_annie[:Annie] .> 0)` expression to check element-wise if the values in the `Acton` and `Annie` columns are greater than 0. Each comparison will return an array of `true`/`false` values—more exactly two `10-element` `BitArrays`, as follows:

```julia
julia> acton_and_annie[:Acton] .> 0
10-element BitArray{1}:
 false
  true
  true
  true
  true
  true
 false
```

```
     true
     true
     true

julia> acton_and_annie[:Annie] .> 0
10-element BitArray{1}:
   true
   true
  false
  false
  false
   true
  false
   true
  false
   true
```

Next, we apply the bitwise & operator, which is also element-wise, to the resulting arrays:

```
julia> (acton_and_annie[:Acton] .> 0) .& (acton_and_annie[:Annie] .> 0)
10-element BitArray{1}:
  false
   true
  false
  false
  false
   true
  false
   true
  false
   true
```

Finally, this array of true/false values is passed into the DataFrame to filter the rows. The preceding snippet will produce the following output, a new DataFrame that contains only the movies that have been rated by both Acton and Annie:

The output is as follows:

4×3 DataFrame			
Row	Movie title Union{Missing, String}	Acton Int64⬚	Annie Int64⬚
1	Zootopia (2016)	9	10
2	The Jungle Book (2016)	8	7
3	Finding Dory (2016)	7	8
4	Moana (2016)	8	9

To quickly visualize our data, let's use the appropriately named Plots library that we saw in Chapter 10, *The Standard Library and Packages*.

Plots is designed as a higher-level interface to other plotting libraries (named *backends* in Plots language), such as GR or PyPlot. It basically unifies multiple lower-level plotting packages (backends) under a common API.

As always, start with pkg> add Plots and continue with using Plots.

We're now ready to generate the visualization:

```julia
julia> plot(acton_and_annie_in_common[:,2], acton_and_annie_in_common[:,3],
seriestype=:scatter, xticks=0:10, yticks=0:10, lims=(0,11), label="")
```

In the preceding snippet, we invoke the plot function, passing it Acton's and Annie's ratings. As options, we ask it to produce a scatter plot. We also want to make sure that the axes start at **0** and end at 11 (so that value **10** is fully visible), with ticks at each unit. We'll end up with the following plot:

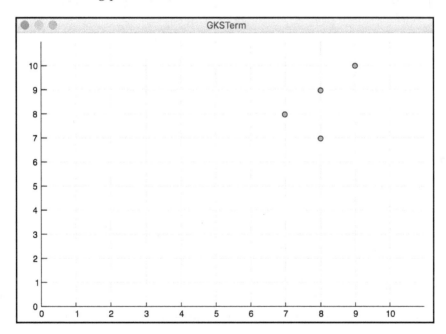

By the looks of it, there is a good correlation between the user's movie preferences. But we can do even better.

Julia's ecosystem provides access to yet another powerful package that combines both plotting and statistical features. It's called StatPlots and actually works on top of the Plots package, providing statistical plotting recipes for Plots. It also supports DataFrame visualizations out of the box, so it's a perfect match for our needs.

Let's add it with pkg> add StatPlots and bring it into scope (using StatPlots). We can now use the @df macro that's exposed by StatPlots to generate a scatter plot of our data:

```
julia> @df acton_and_annie_in_common scatter([:Acton], [:Annie], smooth =
true, line = :red, linewidth = 2, title = "Acton and Annie", legend =
false, xlimits = (5, 11), ylimits = (5, 11))
```

The preceding code will produce the following visualization:

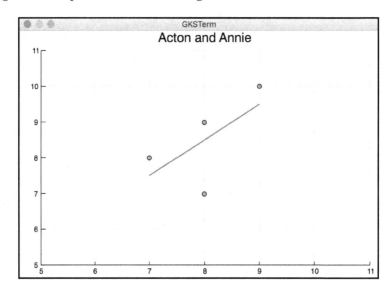

This new plot shows the correlation between the movies, despite the outlier.

Let's compute the Pearson correlation between Acton's and Annie's ratings:

```
julia> using Statistics
julia> cor(acton_and_annie_in_common[:Acton],
acton_and_annie_in_common[:Annie])

0.6324555320336759
```

Pretty much any value over 0.6 indicates a good similarity, so it looks like we're onto something.

Now, we can recommend to Annie some of Acton's favorites that she hasn't seen, as follows:

```julia
julia> annies_recommendations = acton_and_annie[(acton_and_annie[:Annie]
.== 0) .&  (acton_and_annie[:Acton] .> 0), :]
```

This snippet should be easy to understand since it's a slight variation of the common rating formula. From the `acton_and_annie DataFrame`, we only select the rows where Annie's score is 0 (she hasn't rated the movie) and Acton's is greater than 0 (he has rated the movie).

We'll get a `DataFrame` with four rows:

4×3 DataFrame			
Row	Movie title Union{Missing, String}	Acton Int64⍰	Annie Int64⍰
1	Arrival (2016)	5	0
2	Hell or High Water (2016)	3	0
3	La La Land (2016)	6	0
4	Captain America: Civil War (2016)	10	0

However, there's a small glitch. We assumed that all the ratings indicate a strong preference, but in this case, many of Acton's ratings are rather an indication of a dislike. With the exception of `Captain America: Civil War (2016)`, all the possible recommendations have bad ratings. Luckily, that is easy to fix—we just need to recommend movies that have a high rating, let's say, of at least 7:

```julia
julia> annies_recommendations = acton_and_annie[(acton_and_annie[:Annie]
.== 0) .&(acton_and_annie[:Acton] .>= 7 ), :]
```

This leaves us with only one movie, `Captain America: Civil War (2016)`:

1×3 DataFrame			
Row	Movie title Union{Missing, String}	Acton Int64⍰	Annie Int64⍰
1	Captain America: Civil War (2016)	10	0

Now that we understand the logic of user-based recommender systems, let's put all of these steps together to create a simple recommender script.

We'll analyze our users' rating matrix in a script that will take advantage of all the available data to generate recommendations for all of our users.

Here's a possible implementation—please create a `user_based_movie_recommendations.jl` file with the following code. Do make sure that the `top_10_movies_user_rankings.tsv` file is in the same folder (or update the path in the code to match your location). Here's the code:

```julia
using CSV, DataFrames, Statistics

const minimum_similarity = 0.8
const movies = CSV.read("top_10_movies_user_rankings.tsv", delim = '\t')

function user_similarity(target_user)
    similarity = Dict{Symbol,Float64}()
    for user in names(movies[:, 2:end])
        user == target_user && continue
        ratings = movies[:, [user, target_user]]
        common_movies = ratings[(ratings[user] .> 0) .&
(ratings[target_user] .> 0), :]
        correlation = try
            cor(common_movies[user], common_movies[target_user])
        catch
            0.0
        end
        similarity[user] = correlation
    end
    similarity
end

function recommendations(target_user)
    recommended = Dict{String,Float64}()
    for (user,similarity) in user_similarity(target_user)
        similarity > minimum_similarity || continue
        ratings = movies[:, [Symbol("Movie title"), user, target_user]]
        recommended_movies = ratings[(ratings[user] .>= 7) .&
(ratings[target_user] .== 0), :]
        for movie in eachrow(recommended_movies)
            recommended[movie[Symbol("Movie title")]] = movie[user] *
similarity
        end
    end
    recommended
end
```

```
for user in names(movies)[2:end]
    println("Recommendations for $user: $(recommendations(user))")
end
```

In the preceding snippet, we define two functions, `user_similarity` and `recommendations`. They both take, as their single argument, a user's name in the form of a Symbol. This argument matches the column name in our `movies DataFrame`.

The `user_similarity` function computes the similarity of our target user (the one passed into the function as the argument) with all the other users and returns a dictionary of the form:

```
Dict(
    :Comey => 1.0,
    :Dean => 0.907841,
    :Missie => NaN,
    :Kit => 0.774597,
    :Musk => 0.797512,
    :Sam => 0.0,
    :Acton => 0.632456
)
```

The `dict` represents Annie's similarity with all the other users.

We use the similarities in the recommendations function to pick the relevant users and make recommendations based on their favorite movies, which were not already rated by our target user.

I've also added a little twist to make the recommendations more relevant—a weight factor. This is computed by multiplying the user's rating with the user's similarity. If, say, `Comey` gives a movie an 8 and is 100% similar to `Missie` (correlation coefficient equals 1), the weight of the recommendation will also be *8 (8 * 1)*. But if Comey is only 50% similar to Musk (0.5 correlation coefficient), then the weight of the recommendation (corresponding to the estimated rating) will be just *4 (8 * 0.5)*.

At the end of the file, we bootstrap the whole process by looping through an array of all the users, and we produce and print the movie recommendations for each of them.

Running this will output movie recommendations, together with their weights for each of our users:

```
Recommendations for Acton: Dict("Moonlight (2016)"=>9.0)
Recommendations for Annie: Dict("La La Land (2016)"=>8.0)
Recommendations for Comey: Dict("The Jungle Book (2016)"=>7.0,"Moana
(2016)"=>7.0,"Moonlight (2016)"=>9.0)
Recommendations for Dean: Dict("Moana (2016)"=>10.0,"Zootopia
```

```
(2016)"=>10.0)
Recommendations for Kit: Dict("Hell or High Water (2016)"=>10.0,"Arrival
(2016)"=>10.0,"La La Land (2016)"=>9.0,"Moonlight (2016)"=>10.0,"Manchester
by the Sea (2016)"=>8.0)
Recommendations for Missie: Dict("The Jungle Book (2016)"=>8.0,
"Moana (2016)"=>8.0, "La La Land (2016)"=>8.0,"Captain America: Civil War
(2016)"=>10.0,"Finding Dory (2016)"=>7.0,"Zootopia (2016)"=>9.0)
Recommendations for Musk: Dict{String,Float64}()
Recommendations for Sam: Dict("Hell or High Water (2016)"=>10.0,
"La La Land (2016)"=>9.0,"Moonlight (2016)"=>10.0,"Zootopia
(2016)"=>7.0,"Manchester by the Sea (2016)"=>8.0)
```

The data looks quite good, considering that this is a toy example. A production quality recommender system should be based on millions of such ratings.

However, if you look closely, you might notice that something's not quite right—the `Recommendations for Kit`. Kit likes kids movies—light-hearted animated comedies. Our system recommends him, with quite a lot of weight, a lot of dramas! What gives? If we look at the similarity data for Kit, we'll see that he's very well correlated with Dean and Dean likes drama. That might sound weird, but it's actually correct if we check the data:

```julia
julia> movies[:, [Symbol("Movie title"), :Dean, :Kit]]
```

The output is as follows:

Row	Movie title Union{Missing, String}	Dean Int64⍰	Kit Int64⍰
1	Moonlight (2016)	10	0
2	Zootopia (2016)	0	10
3	Arrival (2016)	10	0
4	Hell or High Water (2016)	10	0
5	La La Land (2016)	9	0
6	The Jungle Book (2016)	2	9
7	Manchester by the Sea (2016)	8	0
8	Finding Dory (2016)	4	10
9	Captain America: Civil War (2016)	6	0
10	Moana (2016)	0	10

10×3 DataFrame

Notice how the only movies they both watched are `The Jungle Book (2016)` and `Finding Dory (2016)`, and how the ratings are correlated since both give higher ratings to `Finding Dory (2016)`. Therefore, there is a strong positive correlation between Dean and Kit. But what our algorithm doesn't take into account is that even if Dean likes `Finding Dory (2016)` more than `The Jungle Book (2016)`, he still doesn't really like either, as indicated by the low ratings of 4 and 2, respectively.

The solution is quite simple, though—we just need to remove ratings that don't indicate a strong positive preference. Again, we can use a rating equal to or larger than 7 to count as a like. So, in the `user_similarity` function, please look for the following line:

```
common_movies = ratings[(ratings[user] .> 0) .& (ratings[target_user] .>
0), :]
```

Replace `ratings[user] .> 0` with `ratings[user] .> 7` so that the whole line now reads as follows:

```
common_movies = ratings[Array(ratings[user] .> 7) .&
Array(ratings[target_user] .> 0), :]
```

What this does is now compute similarity only based on favorites. As a result, `Kit` is no longer similar to `Dean` (the correlation coefficient is 0).

Another consequence of the fact that our recommendations are more targeted is that we no longer have recommendations for all the users—but this is, again, caused by the fact that we're working with a very small example dataset. Here are the final recommendations:

```
Recommendations for Acton: Dict("Moonlight (2016)"=>9.0)
Recommendations for Annie: Dict{String,Float64}()
Recommendations for Comey: Dict(
"Moana (2016)"=>9.0,
"Moonlight (2016)"=>9.0)
Recommendations for Dean: Dict(
"Moana (2016)"=>8.0,
"Zootopia (2016)"=>9.0)
Recommendations for Kit: Dict{String,Float64}()
Recommendations for Missie: Dict{String,Float64}()
Recommendations for Musk: Dict{String,Float64}()
Recommendations for Sam: Dict{String,Float64}()
```

We only have suggestions for Acton, Comey, and Dean, but they are now much more accurate.

Item-item CF

User-based CF works quite well and is widely used in production in the wild, but it does have a few considerable downsides. First, it's difficult to get enough preference information from users, leaving many of them without a solid base for relevant recommendations. Second, as the platform and the underlying business grows, the number of users will grow much faster than the number of items. Netflix, for example, to keep the discussion in the familiar area of movies, grows its user base massively by expanding into new countries, while the production of movies stays pretty much the same on a yearly basis. Finally, the user's data does change quite a lot, so the rating matrix would have to be updated often, which is a resource-intensive and time-consuming process.

These problems became painfully obvious at Amazon, some 10 years ago. They realized that since the number of products grows at a much slower rate than the number of users, instead of computing user similarity, they could compute item similarity and make recommendations stemming from the list of related items.

The following diagram should help you understand the difference between item-based (or item-item) and user-based (or user-item) CF:

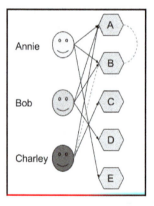

The preceding diagram shows that **Annie** purchased **A**, **B**, and **E**, **Bob** purchased **A**, **B**, and **D**, and **Charley** purchased **A** and **C**. The purchasing behavior of **Annie** and **Bob** will indicate a correlation between **A** and **B**, and since **Charley** already purchased **A** but not **B**, we can recommend **Charley** to take a look at **B**.

From an implementation perspective, there are similarities to user-item CF, but it is more involved as it includes an extra layer of analysis. Let's try this out with our imaginary movie rankings. Let's create a new file called `item_based_recommendations.jl` to host our code.

Here is the complete implementation:

```julia
using CSV, DataFrames, DelimitedFiles, Statistics

const minimum_similarity = 0.8

function setup_data()
    movies = readdlm("top_10_movies_user_rankings.tsv", '\t')
    movies = permutedims(movies, (2,1))
    movies = convert(DataFrame, movies)
    names = convert(Array, movies[1, :])[1,:]
    names!(movies, [Symbol(name) for name in names])
    deleterows!(movies, 1)
    rename!(movies, [Symbol("Movie title") => :User])
end

function movie_similarity(target_movie)
    similarity = Dict{Symbol,Float64}()
    for movie in names(movies[:, 2:end])
        movie == target_movie && continue
        ratings = movies[:, [movie, target_movie]]
        common_users = ratings[(ratings[movie] .>= 0) .&
(ratings[target_movie] .> 0), :]
        correlation = try
            cor(common_users[movie], common_users[target_movie])
        catch
            0.0
        end

        similarity[movie] = correlation
    end

    # println("The movie $target_movie is similar to $similarity")
    similarity
end

function recommendations(target_movie)
    recommended = Dict{String,Vector{Tuple{String,Float64}}}()
    # @show target_movie
    # @show movie_similarity(target_movie)

    for (movie, similarity) in movie_similarity(target_movie)
        movie == target_movie && continue
        similarity > minimum_similarity || continue
        # println("Checking to which users we can recommend $movie")
        recommended["$movie"] = Vector{Tuple{String,Float64}}()

        for user_row in eachrow(movies)
```

```
                if user_row[target_movie] >= 5
                    # println("$(user_row[:User]) has watched $target_movie so
we can recommend similar movies")
                    if user_row[movie] == 0
                        # println("$(user_row[:User]) has not watched $movie so
we can recommend it")
                        # println("Recommending $(user_row[:User]) the movie
$movie")
                        push!(recommended["$movie"], (user_row[:User],
user_row[target_movie] * similarity))
                    end
                end
            end
        end

        recommended
end

const movies = setup_data()
println("Recommendations for users that watched Finding Dory (2016):
$(recommendations(Symbol("Finding Dory (2016)")))")
```

To keep the code simpler, we're only generating recommendations for a single movie—but it should be relatively simple to extend it to come up with recommendations for each movie in our list (you can try this as an exercise). We'll only suggest similar movies to the users that have watched `Finding Dory (2016)`.

Let's take it apart and see how the script works.

 As you can see, I've added some `println` and `@show` calls that output extra debug information—they're commented out, but feel free to uncomment them when running the file to help you better understand what each section does and what the workflow of the code is.

Setting up our data matrix is more difficult now. We need to transpose our initial dataset, that is, rotate it. The `setup_data` function is dedicated to this task alone—loading the data file, transposing the matrix, and setting up the data into a `DataFrame`. It's a proper **extract, transform, load (ETL)** process in just a few lines of code, which is pretty cool! Let's look at this closely—it's quite a common day-to-day data science task.

In the first line of the function, we load the data into a Julia matrix. The `readdlm` function is not as powerful as `DataFrames`, so it has no knowledge of headers, gobbling everything into an `Array`:

```
julia> movies = readdlm("top_10_movies_user_rankings.tsv", '\t')
```

We'll end up with the following matrix:

```
11×9 Array{Any,2}:
 "Movie title"                          "Acton"   "Annie"   "Comey"   "Dean"   "Kit"   "Missie"   "Musk"   "Sam"
 "Moonlight (2016)"                      0         3         0         10       0       9          2        0
 "Zootopia (2016)"                       9         10        7         0        10      0          5        0
 "Arrival (2016)"                        5         0         6         10       0       9          0        10
 "Hell or High Water (2016)"             3         0         3         10       0       8          0        0
 "La La Land (2016)"                     6         0         8         9        0       0          10       0
 "The Jungle Book (2016)"                8         7         0         2        9       0          6        0
 "Manchester by the Sea (2016)"          0         0         2         8        0       0          0        0
 "Finding Dory (2016)"                   7         8         5         4        10      0          0        0
 "Captain America: Civil War (2016)"     10        0         5         6        0       0          0        9
 "Moana (2016)"                          8         9         0         0        10      0          7        0
```

As we can see, the headings are mixed with the actual data.

Now, we need to transpose the matrix. Unfortunately, transposing doesn't work smoothly for all kinds of matrices in Julia yet, and the recommended way is to do this via `permutedims`:

```julia
julia> movies = permutedims(movies, (2,1))
```

The output is as follows:

```
9×11 Array{Any,2}:
 "Movie title"   "Moonlight (2016)"     "Zootopia (2016)"      "Arrival (2016)"   …   "Moana (2016)"
 "Acton"         0                      9                      5                      8
 "Annie"         3                      10                     0                      9
 "Comey"         0                      7                      6                      0
 "Dean"          10                     0                      10                     0
 "Kit"           0                      10                     0                  …   10
 "Missie"        9                      0                      9                      0
 "Musk"          2                      5                      0                      7
 "Sam"           0                      0                      10                     0
```

We're getting closer!

Next, we convert it into a `DataFrame`:

```julia
julia> movies = convert(DataFrame, movies)
```

The output is as follows:

```
9×11 DataFrame
```

Row	x1 Any	x2 Any	x3 Any	x4 Any	x5 Any
1	Movie title	Moonlight (2016)	Zootopia (2016)	Arrival (2016)	Hell or High Water (2016)
2	Acton	0	9	5	3
3	Annie	3	10	0	0
4	Comey	0	7	6	3
5	Dean	10	0	10	10
6	Kit	0	10	0	0
7	Missie	9	0	9	8
8	Musk	2	5	0	0
9	Sam	0	0	10	0

Row	x6 Any	x7 Any	x8 Any
1	La La Land (2016)	The Jungle Book (2016)	Manchester by the Sea (2016)
2	6	8	0
3	0	7	0
4	8	0	2
5	9	2	8
6	0	9	0
7	0	0	0
8	10	6	0
9	0	0	0

Row	x9 Any	x10 Any	x11 Any
1	Finding Dory (2016)	Captain America: Civil War (2016)	Moana (2016)
2	7	10	8
3	8	0	9
4	5	5	0
5	4	6	0
6	10	0	10
7	0	0	0
8	0	0	7
9	0	9	0

TIP

If you run the previous code yourself, you might notice that the REPL will omit some of the `DataFrame` columns, since the output is too wide. To get Julia to display all the columns, like in this snippet, you can use the `showall` function, as in `showall(movies)`.

It looks good, but we need to give the columns proper names, using the data that is now on the first row. Let's extract all the columns names into a `Vector`:

```julia
julia> movie_names = convert(Array, movies[1, :])[1,:]
11-element Array{Any,1}:
 "Movie title"
 "Moonlight (2016)"
```

```
"Zootopia (2016)"
"Arrival (2016)"
"Hell or High Water (2016)"
"La La Land (2016)"
"The Jungle Book (2016)"
"Manchester by the Sea (2016)"
"Finding Dory (2016)"
"Captain America: Civil War (2016)"
"Moana (2016)"
```

Now, we can use it to name the columns:

```
julia> names!(movies, [Symbol(name) for name in movie_names])
```

The output is as follows:

9×11 DataFrame

Row	Movie title	Moonlight (2016)	Zootopia (2016)	Arrival (2016)	Hell or High Water (2016)
	Any	Any	Any	Any	Any
1	Movie title	Moonlight (2016)	Zootopia (2016)	Arrival (2016)	Hell or High Water (2016)
2	Acton	0	9	5	3
3	Annie	3	10	0	0
4	Comey	0	7	6	3
5	Dean	10	0	10	10
6	Kit	0	10	0	0
7	Missie	9	0	9	8
8	Musk	2	5	0	0
9	Sam	0	0	10	0

Row	La La Land (2016)	The Jungle Book (2016)	Manchester by the Sea (2016)
	Any	Any	Any
1	La La Land (2016)	The Jungle Book (2016)	Manchester by the Sea (2016)
2	6	8	0
3	0	7	0
4	8	0	2
5	9	2	8
6	0	9	0
7	0	0	0
8	10	6	0
9	0	0	0

Row	Finding Dory (2016)	Captain America: Civil War (2016)	Moana (2016)
	Any	Any	Any
1	Finding Dory (2016)	Captain America: Civil War (2016)	Moana (2016)
2	7	10	8
3	8	0	9
4	5	5	0
5	4	6	0
6	10	0	10
7	0	0	0
8	0	0	7
9	0	9	0

Our `DataFrame` looks better already. The only things left to do are to remove the extra row with the headers and change the `Movie title` header to `User`:

```julia
julia> deleterows!(movies, 1) julia> rename!(movies, Symbol("Movie title")
=> :User)
```

The output is as follows:

8×11 DataFrame

Row	User	Moonlight (2016)	Zootopia (2016)	Arrival (2016)	Hell or High Water (2016)
	Any	Any	Any	Any	Any
1	Acton	0	9	5	3
2	Annie	3	10	0	0
3	Comey	0	7	6	3
4	Dean	10	0	10	10
5	Kit	0	10	0	0
6	Missie	9	0	9	8
7	Musk	2	5	0	0
8	Sam	0	0	10	0

Row	La La Land (2016)	The Jungle Book (2016)	Manchester by the Sea (2016)
	Any	Any	Any
1	6	8	0
2	0	7	0
3	8	0	2
4	9	2	8
5	0	9	0
6	0	0	0
7	10	6	0
8	0	0	0

Row	Finding Dory (2016)	Captain America: Civil War (2016)	Moana (2016)
	Any	Any	Any
1	7	10	8
2	8	0	9
3	5	5	0
4	4	6	0
5	10	0	10
6	0	0	0
7	0	0	7
8	0	9	0

All done—our ETL process is complete!

We start our recommender by invoking the `recommendations` function, passing in the name of the movie, `Finding Dory (2016)`, as a `Symbol`. The first thing this function does is invoke the `movie_similarity` function, which computes which other movies are similar to `Finding Dory (2016)` based on the users' ratings. For our target movie, we'll get the following results:

```
Dict(
Symbol("La La Land (2016)")=>-0.927374,
Symbol("Captain America: Civil War (2016)")=>-0.584176,
Symbol("The Jungle Book (2016)")=>0.877386,
Symbol("Manchester by the Sea (2016)")=>-0.785933,
Symbol("Arrival (2016)")=>-0.927809,
Symbol("Zootopia (2016)")=>0.826331,
Symbol("Moonlight (2016)")=>-0.589269,
Symbol("Hell or High Water (2016)")=>-0.840462,
Symbol("Moana (2016)")=>0.933598
)
```

We can see here that there's an almost perfect negative correlation with `La La Land (2016)` (so users that like `La La Land (2016)` do not like `Finding Dory (2016)`). There is also a very strong positive correlation with `The Jungle Book (2016)`, `Zootopia (2016)`, and `Moana (2016)`, which makes sense, since they're all animations.

Here is where the logic gets a bit more complicated. Now, we have a list of movies that are similar to `Finding Dory (2016)`. To make recommendations, we want to look at all the users that have watched `Finding Dory (2016)` (and gave it a good enough rating), and suggest similar movies that they haven't watched yet (movies that have a rating of 0). This time, we'll be using a minimum rating of 5 instead of the previous 7, since given our very limited dataset, 7 would be too restrictive and would yield no recommendations. We'll compute the weight of the suggestions as the product between the user's rating of `Finding Dory (2016)` and the correlation coefficient between `Finding Dory (2016)` and the recommended movie. Makes sense? Let's see it in action!

If we run the script, we get the following output:

```
Recommendations for users that watched Finding Dory (2016):
Dict(
    "The Jungle Book (2016)"=> Tuple{String,Float64}[("Comey", 4.38693)],
    "Moana (2016)"=> Tuple{String,Float64}[("Comey", 4.66799)],
    "Zootopia (2016)"=> Tuple{String,Float64}[]
)
```

The only user that would be (kind of) interested in watching movies similar to `Finding Dory (2016)` in our small dataset is `Comey`—but the recommendations won't be great. The algorithm estimates a weight (and thus, a rating) of `4.38693` for `The Jungle Book (2016)` and `4.66799` for `Moana (2016)`.

Summary

This concludes the first part of our journey into recommender systems. They are an extremely important part of today's online business models and their usefulness is ever-growing, in direct relation to the exponential growth of data generated by our connected software and hardware. Recommender systems are a very efficient solution to the information overload problem—or rather, an information filter problem. Recommenders provide a level of filtering that's appropriate for each user, turning information, yet again, into a vector of customer empowerment.

Although it's critical to understand how the various types of recommender systems work, in order to be able to choose the right algorithm for the types of problems you'll solve in your work as a data scientist, implementing production-grade systems by hand is not something most people do. As with almost everything in the realm of software development, it's best to use stable, powerful, and mature existing libraries when they're available.

In the next chapter, we'll learn how to build a more powerful recommender system using existing Julia libraries. We'll generate recommendations for a dating site, taking advantage of publicly available and anonymized dating data. In the process, we'll learn about yet another type of recommender system, called model-based (as a side note, all of the algorithms that were discussed in this chapter were memory-based, but don't worry—I'll explain everything in a minute).

16
Machine Learning for Recommender Systems

I hope that you are now excited about the amazing possibilities offered by the recommender systems that we've built. The techniques we've learned will provide you with a tremendous amount of data-taming prowess and practical abilities that you can already apply in your projects.

However, there is more to recommendation systems than that. Due to their large-scale applications in recent years, as an efficient solution to the information overload caused by the abundance of offerings on online platforms, recommenders have received a lot of attention, with new algorithms being developed at a rapid pace. In fact, all the algorithms that we studied in the previous chapter are part of a single category, called **memory-based recommenders**. Besides these, there's another very important class or recommender, which is known as **model-based**.

In this chapter, we'll learn about them. We will discuss the following topics:

- Memory-based versus model-based recommendation systems
- Data processing for training a model-based recommender
- Building a model-based recommender
- Hybrid recommendation systems

Technical requirements

The Julia package ecosystem is under continuous development and new package versions are released on a daily basis. Most of the times this is great news, as new releases bring new features and bug fixes. However, since many of the packages are still in beta (version 0.x), any new release can introduce breaking changes. As a result, the code presented in the book can stop working. In order to ensure that your code will produce the same results as described in the book, it is recommended to use the same package versions. Here are the external packages used in this chapter and their specific versions:

```
CSV@v.0.4.3
DataFrames@v0.15.2
Gadfly@v1.0.1
IJulia@v1.14.1
Recommendation@v0.1.0+
```

In order to install a specific version of a package you need to run:

```
pkg> add PackageName@vX.Y.Z
```

For example:

```
pkg> add IJulia@v1.14.1
```

Alternatively you can install all the used packages by downloading the `Project.toml` file provided with the chapter and using `pkg>` instantiate as follows:

```
julia>
download("https://github.com/TrainingByPackt/Julia-1-Programming-Complete-R
eference-Guide/tree/master/Chapter16/Project.toml", "Project.toml")
pkg> activate .
pkg> instantiate
```

Comparing the memory-based versus model-based recommenders

It is important to understand the strengths and weaknesses of both memory-based and model-based recommenders so that we can make the right choice according to the available data and the business requirements. As we saw in the previous chapter, we can classify recommender systems according to the data they are using and the algorithms that are employed.

First, we can talk about non-personalized versus personalized recommenders. Non-personalized recommenders do not take into account user preferences, but that doesn't make them less useful. They are successfully employed when the relevant data is missing, for example, for a user that is new to the system or just not logged in. Such recommendations can include the best apps of the week on the Apple App Store, trending movies on Netflix, songs of the day on Spotify, NY Times bestsellers, Billboard Top 10, and so on.

Moving on to personalized recommender systems, these can be further split into content-based and collaborative system. A content-based system makes recommendations by matching an item, specifications. A famous example of this category is Pandora and its Music Genome Project. The Music Genome Project, which powers Pandora, is the most comprehensive analysis of music ever undertaken. They worked with trained musicologists who listened to music across all genres and decades, studying and collecting musical details on every track—450 musical attributes altogether. Pandora makes recommendations by picking other songs from its catalog that closely match the features (*features* is data-science language for attributes, properties, or tags) of the tracks that the user previously liked.

As for collaborative filtering, the idea behind it is that we can identify a metric that correctly reflects a user's tastes and then exploit it in combination with a dataset of other users, whose preferences were already collected. The underlying supposition is that if we have a pool of users that enjoy many of the same things, we can recommend to one of them some items from another's user list, which were not yet discovered by the targeted user. Any item in the list of options that is not part of the targeted user's list can readily be offered as a recommendation because similar preferences will lead to other similar choices.

This specific type of collaborative filtering was named user-based since the primary focus of the algorithm is the similarity between the target user and other users.

Another variation of the collaborative algorithm is **item-based filtering**. The main difference between this and user-based filtering is that the focus is on similar items. Which approach is the best depends on the specific use case—item-based recommendations are more efficient when the product catalog is considerably smaller and changes less often than the number of users and their preferences.

The last of the commonly accepted typologies divides the recommender systems into memory-based and model-based. *Memory-based* refers to the fact that the system requires the whole dataset to be loaded into working memory (the RAM). The algorithms rely on mapping to and from memory to consequently calculate the similarity between two users or items, and produce a prediction for the user by taking the weighted average of all the ratings. A few ways of computing the correlation can be used, such as *Pearson's r*. There are certain advantages to this approach, like the simplicity of the implementation, the easy facilitation of new data, or the fact that the results can be easily explained. But, unsurprisingly, it does come with significant performance downsides, creating problems when the data is sparse and the datasets are large.

Because of the limitations of the memory-based recommender systems, alternative solutions were needed, mainly driven by the continuous growth of online businesses and their underlying data. These were characterized by large volumes of users and an increasing number of products. The most famous example is Netflix's one million dollar competition—in 2006, Netflix offered a one million dollar prize to the individual or team that could improve their existing recommendations algorithm, called **Cinematch**, by at least 10%. It took three years for this feat to be achieved, and it was done by a joint team of initial competitors, who ultimately decided to join forces to grab the prize.

Learning about the model-based approach

This innovative approach to recommender systems was named *model-based*, and it made extensive use of matrix factorization techniques. In this approach, models are developed using different machine learning algorithms to predict a user's ratings. In a way, the model-based approach can be seen as a complementary technique to improve memory-based recommendations. They address the matrix sparsity problem by guessing how much a user will like a new item. Machine learning algorithms are used to train on the existing vector of ratings of a specific user, and then build a model that can predict the user's score for an item that the user hasn't tried yet. Popular model-based techniques are Bayesian Networks, **singular value decomposition** (**SVD**), and **Probabilistic Latent Semantic Analysis** (**PLSA**) or **Probabilistic Latent Semantic Indexing** (**PLSI**).

There are a number of popular approaches for building the models:

- **Probability**: Making a recommendation is framed as a problem of predicting the probability of a rating being of a particular value. Bayesian networks are often used with this implementation.

- **Enhanced memory-based**: This uses a model to represent the similarities between users or items and then predicts the ratings. The Netflix prize-winning ALS-WR algorithm represents this type of implementation.
- **Linear algebra**: Finally, recommendations can be made by performing linear algebra operations on the matrices of users and ratings. A commonly used algorithm is SVD.

In the following sections, we'll implement a model-based recommender. We'll use a third-party Julia package and code our business logic around it.

Understanding our data

To get conclusive results from our **Machine Learning** (**ML**) models, we need data—and plenty of it. There are many open source datasets available online. Kaggle, for example, provides a large collection of high quality and anonymized data dumps that can be used for training and experimenting, and is available for download at `https://www.kaggle.com/datasets`. Another famous data repository is provided by FiveThirtyEight, at `https://github.com/fivethirtyeight/data`. Buzzfeed also makes a large treasure of data public at `https://github.com/BuzzFeedNews`.

For our project, we'll create a book recommendation system. We'll use the *Book-Crossing Dataset*, which is available for download at `http://www2.informatik.uni-freiburg.de/~cziegler/BX/`. This data was collected during the months of August and September 2004, under permission, from the Book-Crossing community (`https://www.bookcrossing.com/`). It includes over 1.1 million book ratings, for more than 270,000 books, from 278,000 users. The user data is anonymized, but still includes demographic information (location and age, where available). We'll use this data to train our recommendation system and then ask it for interesting new books for our users.

A first look at the data

The dataset is composed of three tables—one for users, one for books, and one for ratings. The `BX-Users` table contains the users' data. The `User-ID` is a sequential integer value, as the original user ID has been anonymized. The `Location` and `Age` columns contain the corresponding demographic information. This is not available for all the users and in these cases, we'll encounter the `NULL` value (as the `NULL` string).

The BX-Books table stores the information about the books. For the unique identifier, we have the standard ISBN book code. Besides this, we are also provided with the book's title (the Book-Title column), author (Book-Author), publishing year (Year-of-Publication), and the publisher (Publisher). URLs of thumbnail cover images are also provided, corresponding to three sizes—small (Image-URL-S), medium (Image-URL-M), and large (Image-URL-L).

Finally, the BX-Book-Ratings table contains the actual ratings. The table has a simple structure, with three columns—User-ID, for the user making the rating; the ISBN of the book; and Book-Rating, which is the score. The ratings are expressed on a scale from 1 to 10, where higher is better. The value 0 signifies an implicit rating.

This dataset is available in SQL and CSV formats, packaged as ZIP archives. Please download the CSV version from
http://www2.informatik.uni-freiburg.de/~cziegler/BX/BX-CSV-Dump.zip.

Unzip the file somewhere on your computer.

Loading the data

Loading this dataset is going to be a bit more challenging, as we have to work with three distinct files, and due to the particularities of the data itself. Here is the head of the BX-Users.csv file, in a plain text editor:

```
"User-ID";"Location";"Age"
"1";"nyc, new york, usa";NULL
"2";"stockton, california, usa";"18"
"3";"moscow, yukon territory, russia";NULL
"4";"porto, v.n.gaia, portugal";"17"
"5";"farnborough, hants, united kingdom";NULL
"6";"santa monica, california, usa";"61"
```

We have to explicitly handle the following formatting particularities, which will otherwise cause the import to fail:

- The columns are separated by ; instead of the more customary comma or *Tab*
- Missing values are represented by the string NULL
- The first row is the header, representing the column names
- The data is enclosed in double quotes " ", and double quotes within the data itself are escaped by backslashes, for example, "1273";"valladolid, \"n/a\", spain";"27"

Fortunately, the CSV package provides additional options for passing in all of this information when reading in the file:

```
julia> users = CSV.read("BX-Users.csv", header = 1, delim = ';',
missingstring = "NULL", escapechar = '\\')
```

It might take a bit of time to load the table, but eventually, we'll get the sweet taste of success—278858 rows loaded into memory!

```
278858×3 DataFrames.DataFrame
 Row │ User-ID │ Location                                       │ Age
     │ Int64⍰  │ Union{Missing, String}                         │ Int64⍰

 1   │ 1       │ nyc, new york, usa                             │ missing
 2   │ 2       │ stockton, california, usa                      │ 18
 3   │ 3       │ moscow, yukon territory, russia                │ missing
 4   │ 4       │ porto, v.n.gaia, portugal                      │ 17
 5   │ 5       │ farnborough, hants, united kingdom             │ missing
 6   │ 6       │ santa monica, california, usa                  │ 61
```

We'll use the same approach to load the books and rankings tables:

```
julia> books = CSV.read("BX-Books.csv", header = 1, delim = ';',
missingstring = "NULL", escapechar = '\\')
271379×8 DataFrames.DataFrame
# output omitted #

julia> books_ratings = CSV.read("BX-Book-Ratings.csv", header = 1, delim =
';', missingstring = "NULL", escapechar = '\\')
1149780×3 DataFrames.DataFrame
# output omitted #
```

Excellent! We now have all three tables loaded into memory as `DataFrames`.

Handling missing data

In data science, missing values occur when no data value is stored for a field in a record—in other words, when we don't have a value for a column in a row. It is a common scenario, but nonetheless, it can have a significant negative effect on the usefulness of the data, so it needs to be explicitly handled.

The approach in `DataFrames` is to mark the missing value by using the `Missing` type. The default behavior is the propagation of the missing values, thus *poisoning* the data operations that involve `missing`—that is, operations involving valid input, and `missing` will return `missing` or `fail`. Hence, in most cases, the missing values need to be addressed in the data-cleaning phase.

The most common techniques for handling missing values are as follows:

- **Deletion**: The rows containing the missing variables are deleted (also called **listwise deletion**). The downside of this approach is that it leads to loss of information. However, if we have plenty of data and not many incomplete records (say, under 10%), this is the simplest approach and the most commonly used.
- **Imputation**: The `missing` values are inferred using some technique, usually `mean`, `median`, or `mode`. However, you need to be careful, as this artificially reduces the variation of the dataset. As an alternative, a predictive model could be used to infer the missing value by applying statistical methods.

 You can read more about Julia's treatment of missing values in the documentation at `https://docs.julialang.org/en/v1.0/manual/missing/`, while a more advanced discussion of the theoretical aspects of handling missing data can be found at `https://datascience.ibm.com/blog/missing-data-conundrum-exploration-and-imputation-techniques/`.

Data analysis and preparation

Let's get a feel of the data, starting with the users:

```julia
julia> using DataFrames
julia> describe(users, stats = [:min, :max, :nmissing, :nunique, :eltype])
```

The output is as follows:

3×6 DataFrame

Row	variable Symbol	min Any	max Any	nmissing Int64	nunique Union…	eltype DataType
1	User-ID	1	278858	0		Int64
2	Location	"alexandria"., "alexandria"., egypt	\xfdzm\xfdr, n/a, turkey	0	57339	String
3	Age	0	244	110762		Int64

We chose a few key stats—the minimum and maximum values, the number of missing and unique values, and the type of data. Unsurprisingly, the `User-ID` column, which is the table's primary key, starts at 1 and goes all the way up to 278858 with no missing values. However, the `Age` column shows a clear sign of data errors—the maximum age is 244 years! Let's see what we have there by plotting the data with `Gadfly`:

```julia
julia> using Gadfly
julia> plot(users, x = :Age, Geom.histogram(bincount = 15))
```

The output is as follows:

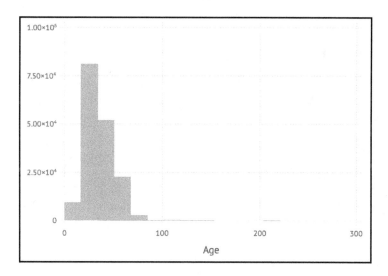

We rendered a histogram of the ages, splitting the data into 15 intervals. We have some outliers indicating incorrect ages, but most of the data is distributed within the expected range, up to 80-90 years old. Since anything after **100** years old is highly unlikely to be correct, let's get rid of it. The simplest way is to filter out all the rows where the age is greater than **100**:

```julia
julia> users = users[users[:Age] .< 100, :]
ERROR: ArgumentError: unable to check bounds for indices of type Missing
```

Oops! Our `Age` column has `missing` values that cannot be compared. We could remove these as well, but in this case, the missing age seems to be more of a symptom of the user not disclosing the information, rather than a data error. Therefore, I'm more inclined to keep the rows while replacing the missing data with valid values. The question is, what values? Imputation using the `mean` seems like a good option. Let's compute it:

```julia
julia> using Statistics
```

```
julia> mean(skipmissing(users[:Age]))
34.75143370454978
```

We used the `skipmissing` function to iterate over all the non-missing `Age` values and compute the `mean`. Now, we can use this in conjunction with `coalesce` to replace the missing values:

```
julia> users[:Age] = coalesce.(users[:Age], mean(skipmissing(users[:Age])))
278858-element Array{Real,1}:
 34.75143370454978
 18
 34.75143370454978
 17
 34.75143370454978
# output omitted #
```

We are effectively replacing the `Age` column of the `users` `DataFrame` with a new array, resulting from the application of `coalesce` to the same `Age` column. Please notice the dot in the invocation of `coalesce`, indicating that it is applied element-wise.

Great—finally, we need to get rid of those erroneous ages:

```
julia> users = users[users[:Age] .< 100, :]
278485×3 DataFrame
# output omitted #

julia> head(users)
```

The output is as follows:

```
6×3 DataFrame
 Row │ User-ID │ Location                           │ Age
     │ Int64m  │ Union{Missing, String}             │ Real
─────┼─────────┼────────────────────────────────────┼─────────
 1   │ 1       │ nyc, new york, usa                  │ 34.7514
 2   │ 2       │ stockton, california, usa           │ 18
 3   │ 3       │ moscow, yukon territory, russia     │ 34.7514
 4   │ 4       │ porto, v.n.gaia, portugal           │ 17
 5   │ 5       │ farnborough, hants, united kingdom  │ 34.7514
 6   │ 6       │ santa monica, california, usa       │ 61
```

Looking good!

We're done with the users, so let's move on to the books data:

```julia
julia> describe(books, stats = [:nmissing, :nunique, :eltype])
```

The output is as follows:

```
8×4 DataFrame
 Row │ variable            nmissing  nunique  eltype
     │ Symbol              Int64     Union…   DataType

   1 │ ISBN                0         271379   String
   2 │ Book-Title          0         242154   String
   3 │ Book-Author         0         102028   String
   4 │ Year-Of-Publication 0                  Int64
   5 │ Publisher           0         16807    String
   6 │ Image-URL-S         0         271063   String
   7 │ Image-URL-M         0         271063   String
   8 │ Image-URL-L         0         271063   String
```

The data looks much cleaner—first of all, there's no missing values. Then, looking at the counts for `nunique`, we can tell that some of the books have identical titles and that there's a considerable amount of authors that have published more than one book. Finally, the books come from almost 17,000 publishers.

So far, so good, but let's take a look at the `Year-Of-Publication`:

```julia
julia> maximum(skipmissing(books[Symbol("Year-Of-Publication")]))
2050

julia> minimum(skipmissing(books[Symbol("Year-Of-Publication")]))
0
```

Something's not right here—we have some publishing years that don't make sense. Some are too far in the past, while others are way in the future. I wonder what the distribution looks like. Let's render another histogram:

```julia
julia> plot(books, x = Symbol("Year-Of-Publication"), Geom.histogram)
```

The output is as follows:

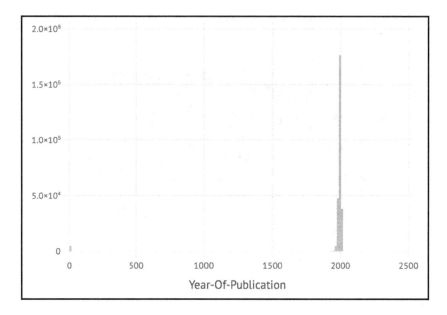

Most of the data seems to be correct, but there are some faulty outliers. We can take a look at the values:

```julia
julia> unique(books[Symbol("Year-Of-Publication")]) |> sort
116-element Array{Union{Missing, Int64},1}:
      0
   1376
   1378
# output omitted #
   2037
   2038
   2050
```

At first sight, we can get rid of the rows that have the publishing year equal to 0. We can also safely assume that all the rows where the publishing date is greater than the year when the data was collected (2004) are also wrong, and so they can be removed. It's difficult to say what to do about the rest, but still, it's hard to believe that people have ranked books that were published in the Middle Ages. Let's just keep the books that were published between 1970 and 2004:

```julia
julia> books = books[books[Symbol("Year-Of-Publication")] .>= 1970, :]
264071×8 DataFrame
# output omitted #
```

```
julia> books = books[books[Symbol("Year-Of-Publication")] .<= 2004, :]
263999×8 DataFrame
# output omitted #

julia> plot(books, x = Symbol("Year-Of-Publication"), Geom.histogram)
```

The output is as follows:

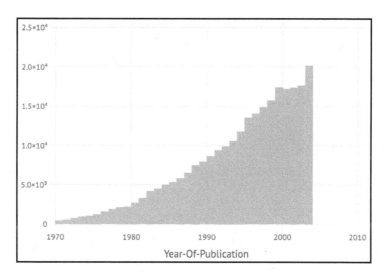

This is much better and entirely plausible.

Finally, let's check the ratings:

```
julia> describe(books_ratings)
```

The output is as follows:

3×8 DataFrame

| Row | variable | mean | min | median | max | nunique | nmissing | eltype |
	Symbol	Union…	Any	Union…	Any	Union…	Int64	DataType
1	User-ID	1.40386e5	2	141010.0	278854		0	Int64
2	ISBN		0330299891		lucrosoft	340556	0	String
3	Book-Rating	2.86695	0	0.0	10		0	Int64

There's no missing values, which is great. The `Book-Rating` values are between 0 (implicit rating) and 10, where 1 to 10 represent explicit ratings. The median of 0.0 is a bit of a concern though, so let's take a look:

```julia
julia> plot(books_ratings, x = Symbol("Book-Rating"), Geom.histogram)
```

The output is as follows:

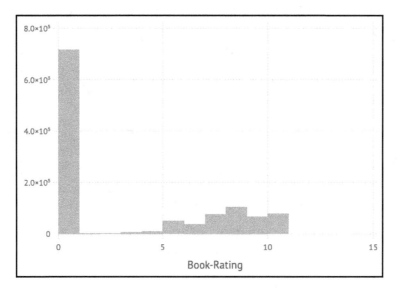

It turns out that most of the ratings are implicit, thus set to 0. These are not relevant to our recommender, so let's get rid of them:

```julia
julia> books_ratings = books_ratings[books_ratings[Symbol("Book-Rating")]
.> 0, :]
433671×3 DataFrame
# output omitted #

julia> plot(books_ratings, x = Symbol("Book-Rating"), Geom.histogram)
```

Here is the output:

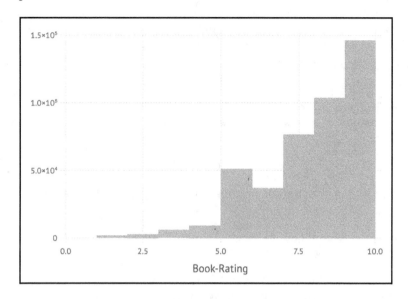

We're doing great! There's one more step in our **extract, transform, load (ETL)** process—let's put the three DataFrames together by joining them on the matching columns, thus removing the various orphan entries (the ones that don't have corresponding rows in all the other tables).

First, we'll join book ratings and books:

```julia
julia> books_ratings_books = join(books_ratings, books, on = :ISBN, kind =
:inner)
374896×10 DataFrame
# output omitted #
```

We're using the join method, indicating the two DataFrames we want to join, plus the join column and the kind of join we want. An inner join requires that the result contains rows for values of the key that exist in both the first and second DataFrame.

Now, let's join with the user's data:

```julia
julia> books_ratings_books_users = join(books_ratings_books, users, on =
Symbol("User-ID"), kind = :inner)
374120×12 DataFrame
# output omitted #
```

Our dataset now contains only the valid data, nicely packed in a single DataFrame.

As our ratings are on a scale between 1 and 10, not all of these ratings can be considered an endorsement for the book. It's true that the vast majority of the rankings are above 5, but a 5 is still not good enough for a useful recommendation. Let's simplify our data a bit to make the computations faster by assuming that any ranking starting with 8 represents a positive review and would make for a strong recommendation. Therefore, we'll keep only these rows and discard the rest:

```julia
julia> top_ratings =
books_ratings_books_users[books_ratings_books_users[Symbol("Book-Rating")]
.>= 8, :]
217991x12 DataFrame
# output omitted #
```

This is looking good, but it will look even better with just a small tweak to make the column names more Julia-friendly:

```julia
julia> for n in names(top_ratings) rename!(top_ratings, n =>
Symbol(replace(string(n), "-"=>""))) end
```

We will iterate over each column name and remove the dashes. This way, we'll be able to use the names without having to explicitly use the `Symbol` constructor every time. We'll end up with the following names:

```julia
julia> names(top_ratings)
12-element Array{Symbol,1}:
 :UserID
 :ISBN
 :BookRating
 :BookTitle
 :BookAuthor
 :YearOfPublication
 :Publisher
 :ImageURLS
 :ImageURLM
 :ImageURLL
 :Location
 :Age
```

We're getting closer—the last step in our data processing workflow is to check the number of reviews per user. The more reviews we have from a user, the better the preference profile we can create, leading to more relevant and better quality recommendations. Basically, we want to get a count of ratings, per user, and then get a count of each count (that is, how many rating of ones, twos, threes, and so on, up to ten ratings we have):

```julia
julia> ratings_count = by(top_ratings, :UserID, df -> size(df[:UserID])[1])
```

Here, we group the `top_ratings` data by `UserID` and use the `size` function as our `aggregation` function, which returns a tuple of dimensions—out of which we retrieve just its first dimension. We'll get the following result, where the `x1` column contains the number of ratings provided by the corresponding user:

The output is as follows:

46106×2 DataFrame		
Row	UserID Int64▥	x1 Int64
1	276747	3
2	276751	1
3	276754	1
4	276762	1
5	276772	2
6	276774	1

Wondering what this data will reveal? Let's find out:

```julia
julia> describe(ratings_count)
```

Here is the output:

2×8 DataFrame								
Row	variable Symbol	mean Float64	min Int64	median Float64	max Int64	nunique Nothing	nmissing Union…	eltype DataType
1	UserID	1.39098e5	12	1.38387e5	278854		0	Int64
2	x1	4.72804	1	1.0	5491			Int64

The minimum number of ratings is 1, while the most productive user has provided no less than 5491, with a mean of around 5 reviews per user. Considering that the recommendations for a user with less than 5 reviews would be pretty weak anyway, we're better off removing the users without enough data:

```julia
julia> ratings_count = ratings_count[ratings_count[:x1] .>= 5, :]
7296×2 DataFrame
# output omitted #
```

We're only keeping the users that have at least 5 ratings. Let's see how the number of ratings is distributed now:

```julia
julia> plot(ratings_count, x = :x1, Geom.histogram(maxbincount = 6))
```

The output is as follows:

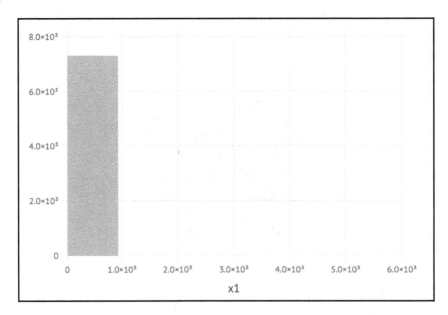

Looks like the vast majority of users have up to 1000 ratings. What about the outliers with lots of reviews?

```julia
julia> ratings_count[ratings_count[:x1] .> 1000, :]
```

The output is as follows:

3×2 DataFrame		
Row	UserID Int64⍰	x1 Int64
1	11676	3639
2	98391	5491
3	153662	1579

There's only 3 users. We'd better remove them so that they don't skew our results:

```julia
julia> ratings_count = ratings_count[ratings_count[:x1] .<= 1000, :]
7293×2 DataFrame
# output omitted #
```

Now that we have the list of final users, the next step is to remove all the others from the `top_ratings` DataFrame. Again, let's use an inner join—it's pretty straightforward:

```
julia> top_ratings = join(top_ratings, ratings_count, on = :UserID, kind =
:inner)
150888x13 DataFrame
# output omitted #
```

That's it, our data is ready. Great job!

If you want, you can save this data to file by using `CSV.write`:

```
julia> CSV.write("top_ratings.csv", top_ratings)
```

 If you've had problems following along, don't worry. In a few paragraphs, I'll explain how you can load a ready-made dataset, which is provided in this chapter's support files.

Training our data models

Machine learning can be divided into four main types, depending on the methodology and the type of data that is used:

- Supervised
- Unsupervised
- Semi-supervised
- Reinforcement

In supervised learning, we start with a dataset that contains training (or teaching) data, where each record is labeled, representing both input (let's call it X), and output values (named Y). Then, the algorithm's job is to identify a function f from input to output, so that $Y = f(X)$. Once this function is identified, it can be used on new data (that is, new inputs that are not labeled) to predict the output. Depending on the type of output that needs to be computed, if the output has to be assigned to a certain class of entities (as in, it represents categorical data), then a classification algorithm will be used. Alternatively, if the type of output is a numeric value, we'll be dealing with a regression problem.

With unsupervised machine learning, we have the inputs, but not the outputs. In such a scenario, once we use the learning dataset to train our system, the main goal will be data clustering, that is, generating different clusters of inputs and being able to assign new data to the most appropriate cluster.

Semi-supervised, as the name suggests, represents a mixture of the two previously described approaches, both of which are applicable when our data contains both labeled and unlabeled records.

In reinforcement learning, the algorithm is informed about the success of its previous decisions. Based on this, the algorithm modifies its strategy in order to maximize the outcome.

Depending on the learning style and the specific problem that's meant to be solved, there are a multitude of algorithms that can be applied. For supervised learning, we can use regression (linear or logistic), decision trees, or neural networks, to name just a few. With unsupervised learning, we could choose k-means clustering or `Apriori` algorithms.

Since our data is tagged (we have the rating for each user), we are dealing with a supervised machine learning problem. For our test case, since our data is represented as a matrix, we'll employ an algorithm called **Matrix Factorization** (**MF**).

You can read more about the various types of ML algorithms and how to choose them at the following links:
`https://docs.microsoft.com/en-us/azure/machine-learning/studio/a`
`lgorithm-choice`
`https://blog.statsbot.co/machine-learning-algorithms-183cc73197c`
`https://elitedatascience.com/machine-learning-algorithms`
`https://machinelearningmastery.com/a-tour-of-machine-learning-al`
`gorithms/`

Scaling down our dataset

Training machine learning models at scale usually requires (lots of) powerful computers and plenty of time. If you have neither of these while reading this book, I have prepared a smaller dataset so that you can go through our project.

Training the recommender on the full `top_ratings` data took over 24 hours on my quad-core, 16 GB RAM laptop. If you're so inclined, feel free to try it. It is also available for download at `https://github.com/TrainingByPackt/Julia-1-Programming-Complete-Reference-Guide/blob/master/Chapter16/data/large/top_ratings.csv.zip?raw=true`.

However, if you'd like to follow through the code while reading this chapter, please download the `top_ratings.csv` file that's provided with this chapter's support files at `https://github.com/TrainingByPackt/Julia-1-Programming-Complete-Reference-Guide/tree/master/Chapter16/data/top_ratings.csv`. I will be using the data from this smaller file for the remainder of this chapter.

Once you've downloaded the file, you can load its content into the `top_ratings` variable by using the `CSV.read` function:

```
julia> top_ratings = CSV.read("top_ratings.csv")
11061x13 DataFrame
# output omitted #
```

Training versus testing data

A common strategy in machine learning implementations is to split the data into training (some 80-90%) and testing (the remaining 10-20%) datasets. First, we'll initialize two empty `DataFrames` to store this data:

```
julia> training_data = DataFrame(UserID = Int[], ISBN = String[], Rating =
Int[])
0x3 DataFrame

julia> test_data = DataFrame(UserID = Int[], ISBN = String[], Rating =
Int[])
0x3 DataFrame
```

Next, we'll iterate through our `top_ratings` and put the contents into the corresponding `DataFrame`. We'll go with 10% of data for testing—so with each iteration, we'll generate a random integer between 1 and 10. The chances of getting a 10 are, obviously, one in ten, so when we get it, we put the corresponding row into the test dataset. Otherwise, it goes into the training one, as follows:

```
julia> for row in eachrow(top_ratings)
  rand(1:10) == 10 ?
  push!(test_data, convert(Array, row[[:UserID, :ISBN, :BookRating]])) :
  push!(training_data, convert(Array, row[[:UserID, :ISBN, :BookRating]]))
  end
```

There's no canonical way for pushing a `DataFrameRow` onto another `DataFrame`, so we're using one of the recommended approaches, which is to convert the row into an `Array` and `push!` it to the `DataFrame`. Our training and testing datasets are now ready.

For me, they look like this, but since the data was generated randomly, it will be different for you:

```
julia> test_data
1056x3 DataFrame
 # output omitted #

julia> training_data
```

```
10005×3 DataFrame
# output omitted #
```

If you prefer for us to work with the same datasets, you can download the data dump from this chapter's support files (available at `https://github.com/TrainingByPackt/Julia-1-Programming-Complete-Reference-Guide/tree/master/Chapter16/data/training_data.csv` and `https://github.com/TrainingByPackt/Julia-1-Programming-Complete-Reference-Guide/tree/master/Chapter16/data/test_data.csv`, respectively) and read them in as follows:

```
julia> test_data = CSV.read("data/test_data.csv")
julia> training_data = CSV.read("data/training_data.csv")
```

Machine learning-based recommendations

Julia's ecosystem provides access to `Recommendation.jl`, a package that implements a multitude of algorithms for both personalized and non-personalized recommendations. For model-based recommenders, it has support for SVD, MF, and content-based recommendations using TF-IDF scoring algorithms.

There's also another very good alternative—the `ScikitLearn.jl` package (`https://github.com/cstjean/ScikitLearn.jl`). This implements Python's very popular scikit-learn interface and algorithms in Julia, supporting both models from the Julia ecosystem and those of the scikit-learn library (via `PyCall.jl`). The Scikit website and documentation can be found at `http://scikit-learn.org/stable/`. It is very powerful and definitely worth keeping in mind, especially for building highly efficient recommenders for production usage. For learning purposes, we'll stick to `Recommendation`, as it provides for a simpler implementation.

Making recommendations with Recommendation

For our learning example, we'll use `Recommendation`. It is the simplest of the available options, and it's a good teaching device, as it will allow us to further experiment with its plug-and-play algorithms and configurable model generators.

Before we can do anything interesting, though, we need to make sure that we have the package installed:

```
pkg> add Recommendation#master
julia> using Recommendation
```

Please note that I'm using the `#master` version, because the tagged version, at the time of writing this book, was not yet fully updated for Julia 1.0.

The workflow for setting up a recommender with `Recommendation` involves three steps:

1. Setting up the training data

2. Instantiating and training a recommender using one of the available algorithms

3. Once the training is complete, asking for recommendations

Let's implement these steps.

Setting up the training data

`Recommendation` uses a `DataAccessor` object to set up the training data. This can be instantiated with a set of `Event` objects. A `Recommendation.Event` is an object that represents a user-item interaction. It is defined like this:

```
struct Event
    user::Int
    item::Int
    value::Float64
end
```

In our case, the `user` field will represent the `UserID`, the `item` field will map to the ISBN, and the `value` field will store the `Rating`. However, a bit more work is needed to bring our data in the format required by `Recommendation`:

1. First of all, our ISBN data is stored as a string and not as an integer.
2. Second, internally, `Recommendation` builds a sparse matrix of `user * item` and stores the corresponding values, setting up the matrix using sequential IDs. However, our actual user IDs are large numbers, and `Recommendation` will set up a very large, sparse matrix, going all the way from the minimum to the maximum user IDs.

What this means is that, for example, we only have 69 users in our dataset (as confirmed by `unique(training_data[:UserID]) |> size`), with the largest ID being 277,427, while for books we have 9,055 unique ISBNs. If we go with this, `Recommendation` will create a 277,427 x 9,055 matrix instead of a 69 x 9,055 matrix. This matrix would be very large, sparse, and inefficient.

Therefore, we'll need to do a bit more data processing to map the original user IDs and the ISBNs to sequential integer IDs, starting from 1.

We'll use two `Dict` objects that will store the mappings from the `UserID` and `ISBN` columns to the recommender's sequential user and book IDs. Each entry will be of the form `dict[original_id] = sequential_id`:

```julia
julia> user_mappings, book_mappings = Dict{Int,Int}(), Dict{String,Int}()
```

We'll also need two counters to keep track of, and increment, the sequential IDs:

```julia
julia> user_counter, book_counter = 0, 0
```

We can now prepare the `Event` objects for our training data:

```julia
julia> events = Event[]
julia> for row in eachrow(training_data)
 global user_counter, book_counter user_id, book_id, rating = row[:UserID],
row[:ISBN], row[:Rating] haskey(user_mappings, user_id) ||
(user_mappings[user_id] = (user_counter += 1)) haskey(book_mappings,
book_id) || (book_mappings[book_id] = (book_counter += 1)) push!(events,
Event(user_mappings[user_id], book_mappings[book_id], rating)) end
```

This will fill up the events array with instances of `Recommendation.Event`, which represent a unique `UserID`, `ISBN`, and `Rating` combination. To give you an idea, it will look like this:

```julia
julia> events
10005-element Array{Event,1}:
 Event(1, 1, 10.0)
 Event(1, 2, 8.0)
 Event(1, 3, 9.0)
 Event(1, 4, 8.0)
 Event(1, 5, 8.0)
 # output omitted #
```

Please remember this very important aspect—in Julia, the `for` loop defines a new scope. This means that variables defined outside the `for` loop are not accessible inside it. To make them visible within the loop's body, we need to declare them as `global`.

Now, we are ready to set up our `DataAccessor`:

```julia
julia> da = DataAccessor(events, user_counter, book_counter)
```

Building and training the recommender

At this point, we have all that we need to instantiate our recommender. A very efficient and common implementation uses MF—unsurprisingly, this is one of the options provided by the `Recommendation` package, so we'll use it.

Matrix Factorization

The idea behind MF is that, if we're starting with a large sparse matrix like the one used to represent *user x profile* ratings, then we can represent it as the product of multiple smaller and denser matrices. The challenge is to find these smaller matrices so that their product is as close to our original matrix as possible. Once we have these, we can fill in the blanks in the original matrix so that the predicted values will be consistent with the existing ratings in the matrix:

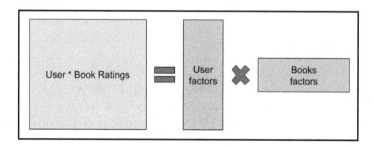

Our *user x books* rating matrix can be represented as the product between smaller and denser users and books matrices.

To perform the matrix factorization, we can use a couple of algorithms, among which the most popular are SVD and **Stochastic Gradient Descent (SGD)**. `Recommendation` uses SGD to perform matrix factorization.

The code for this looks as follows:

```julia
julia> recommender = MF(da)
julia> build(recommender)
```

We instantiate a new MF recommender and then we build it—that is, train it. The build step might take a while (a few minutes on a high-end computer using the small dataset that's provided in this chapter's support files).

If we want to tweak the training process, since SGD implements an iterative approach for matrix factorization, we can pass a `max_iter` argument to the build function, asking it for a maximum number of iterations. The more iterations we do, in theory, the better the recommendations—but the longer it will take to train the model. If you want to speed things up, you can invoke the build function with a `max_iter` of 30 or less—`build(recommender, max_iter = 30)`.

We can pass another optional argument for the learning rate, for example, `build` `(recommender, learning_rate=15e-4, max_iter=100)`. The learning rate specifies how aggressively the optimization technique should vary between each iteration. If the learning rate is too small, the optimization will need to be run a lot of times. If it's too big, then the optimization might fail, generating worse results than the previous iterations.

Making recommendations

Now that we have successfully built and trained our model, we can ask it for recommendations. These are provided by the `recommend` function, which takes an instance of a recommender, a user ID (from the ones available in the training matrix), the number of recommendations, and an array of books ID from which to make recommendations as its arguments:

```julia
julia> recommend(recommender, 1, 20, [1:book_counter...])
```

With this line of code, we retrieve the recommendations for the user with the recommender ID 1, which corresponds to the `UserID` 277427 in the original dataset. We're asking for up to 20 recommendations that have been picked from all the available books.

We get back an array of a `Pair` of book IDs and recommendation scores:

```
20-element Array{Pair{Int64,Float64},1}:
 5081 => 19.1974
 5079 => 19.1948
 5078 => 19.1946
 5077 => 17.1253
 5080 => 17.1246
 # output omitted #
```

Testing the recommendations

Finally, our machine learning-based recommender system is ready. It will provide a significant boost in user experience for any bookshop, for sure. But before we start advertising it, we should make sure that it's reliable. Remember that we put aside 10% of our dataset for testing purposes. The idea is to compare the recommendations with actual ratings from the test data to see what degree of similarity exists between the two; that is, how many of the actual ratings from the dataset were in fact recommended. Depending on the data that's used for the training, you may want to test that both correct recommendations are made, but also that bad recommendations are not included (that is, the recommender does not suggest items that got low ratings, indicating a dislike). Since we only used ratings of 8, 9, and 10, we won't check if low-ranked recommendations were provided. We'll just focus on checking how many of the recommendations are actually part of the user's data.

Because the test data uses the original user and profile IDs, and our recommender uses the normalized, sequential IDs, we'll need a way to convert the data between the two. We already have the `user_mappings` and `book_mappings` dictionaries, which map from the original IDs to recommender IDs. However, we'll also need the reverse. So, let's start by defining a helper function for reversing a dictionary:

```
julia> function reverse_dict(d) Dict(value => key for (key, value) in d)
end
```

This is simple, but very useful—we can now use this function to look up the original IDs based on the recommender IDs. For instance, if we want to test the recommendations for user `1`, we'll need to retrieve this user's actual ratings, so we'll need the original ID. We can easily get it with the following code:

```
julia> reverse_dict(user_mappings)[1]
277427
```

The same applies to the books mappings—for instance, the recommendation with ID `5081` corresponds to ISBN `981013004X` from the original dataset:

```
julia> reverse_dict(book_mappings)[5081]
"981013004X"
```

All right, let's check the test data that we put aside for `UserID` `277427` (recommender user 1):

```
julia> user_testing_data = test_data[test_data[:UserID] .==
reverse_dict(user_mappings)[1], :]
8×3 DataFrame
```

The output is as follows:

Row	UserID Int64m	ISBN Stringm	Rating Int64m
1	277427	0060006641	10
2	277427	0441627404	10
3	277427	0446600415	10
4	277427	0671727079	9
5	277427	0671740504	8
6	277427	0671749897	8
7	277427	0836218817	10
8	277427	0842370668	10

The snippet filters the `testing_data` `DataFrame` by doing an element-wise comparison—for each row, it checks if the `UserID` column equals `277427` (which is the ID returned by `reverse_dict(user_mappings)[1]`, remember?). If yes, then the whole row is added to `user_testing_data`.

To check for recommended versus actually rated profiles, the easiest approach is to intersect the vector of recommendations with the vector of ratings. So, the first thing to do is put the test ratings into a vector, out of the `DataFrame`:

```
julia> test_profile_ids = user_testing_data[:, :ISBN]
8-element Array{Union{Missing, String},1}:
 "0060006641"
 "0441627404"
 "0446600415"
 "0671727079"
 "0671740504"
 "0671749897"
 "0836218817"
 "0842370668"
```

We just select the ISBN column data, for all the rows, as an `Array`.

Doing the same for the recommendations is a bit more involved. Also, since I expect we'll want to test with various recommender settings and with different numbers of recommendations, it's best to define a function that converts the recommendations to a vector of ISBNs, so that we can easily reuse the code:

```julia
julia> function recommendations_to_books(recommendations)
           [reverse_dict(book_mappings)[r[1]] for r in recommendations]
       end
```

The `recommendations_to_books` function takes the vector of `id => score` pairs generated by the recommender as its only argument and converts it into a vector of original ISBNs:

```julia
julia> recommendations_to_books(recommend(recommender, 1, 20,
[1:book_counter...]))
20-element Array{String,1}:
 "981013004X"
 "1856972097"
 "1853263656"
 "1853263133"
 "1857231791"
 # output omitted #
```

The `recommendations_to_books` function outputs the ISBNs for the 20 recommended books.

Now, we have all of the pieces to check recommendations versus ratings:

```julia
julia> intersect(test_profile_ids,
recommendations_to_books(recommend(recommender, 1, 500,
[1:book_counter...])))
1-element Array{Union{Missing, String},1}:
 "0441627404"
```

We use the intersect function to check what elements from the first vector—the list of books we put away for testing—also show up in the second vector, that is, the recommendations. We had to ask for 500 recommendations as the chances of hitting one of the eight test books in a pool of 9,055 books were very slim. This is due to the fact that we worked with very little data, but in a production environment and potentially billions of rows, we would get a lot more overlapping data.

Let's see what the top five recommendations were:

```
julia> for i in recommendations_to_books(recommend(recommender, 1, 20,
[1:book_counter...])) top_ratings[top_ratings.ISBN .== i, :BookTitle] |>
println end

Union{Missing, String}["Fun With Chinese Characters Volume 1"]
Union{Missing, String}["Fantasy Stories (Story Library)"]
Union{Missing, String}["The Wordsworth Complete Guide to Heraldry
(Wordsworth Reference)"]
Union{Missing, String}["The Savoy Operas (Wordsworth Collection)"]
Union{Missing, String}["Against a Dark Background"]
```

In an IJulia Notebook, we can even look at the covers, thus rendering a small piece of HTML using the cover's URLs:

```
thumbs = DataFrame(Thumb = String[])

for i in recommendations_to_profiles(recommend(recommender, 1, 20,
[1:book_counter...]))
    push!(thumbs, top_ratings[top_ratings.ISBN .== i, :ImageURLL])
end

for img in thumbs[:, :Thumb]
    HTML("""<img src="$(img)">""") |> display
end
```

The output will be as follows:

Excellent! We did a great job. We tamed a very complex dataset, performed advanced analysis, and then we optimized it for usage in our recommender. We then successfully trained our recommender and used it to generate book recommendations for our users.

Deploying and working with the `Recommendation` package is very straightforward, as I'm sure you've come to appreciate. Again, as in most data science projects, the ETL step was the most involved.

Learning about hybrid recommender systems

There are some clear advantages when using model-based recommenders. As mentioned already, scalability is one of the most important. Usually, the models are much smaller than the initial dataset, so that even for very large data samples, the models are small enough to allow efficient usage. Another benefit is the speed. The time required to query the model, as opposed to querying the whole dataset, is usually considerably smaller.

These advantages stem from the fact that the models are generally prepared offline, allowing for almost instantaneous recommendations. But since there's no such thing as free performance, this approach also comes with a few significant negatives—on one hand, it is less flexible, because building the models takes considerable time and resources, making the updates difficult and costly; on the other hand, because it does not use the whole dataset, the predictions can be less accurate.

As with everything, there's no silver bullet, and the best approach depends on the data you have at hand and the problem you need to solve. However, it doesn't always have to be memory-based versus model-based. Even more, it doesn't have to be just one recommender system. It turns out that multiple algorithms and approaches can be efficiently combined to compensate for the limitations of one type of recommender. Such architectures are called **hybrid**. Due to space limitations, we won't cover any implementations of hybrid recommender systems, but I want to give you an idea of the possible approaches. I'm just going to refer you to Robin Burke's classification from *Chapter 12* of *The Adaptive Web*, entitled *Hybrid Web Recommender Systems*. The whole chapter is available online for free at `https://www.researchgate.net/publication/200121024_Hybrid_Web_Recommender_Sy stems`. If you're interested in this topic, I highly recommended it.

Summary

Recommender systems represent a very active and dynamic field of study. They started initially as a marginal application of machine learning algorithms and techniques, but due to their practical business value, they have become mainstream in recent years. These days, almost all major programming languages provide powerful recommendations systems libraries—and all major online businesses employ recommenders in one form or another.

Julia is a great language for building recommenders due to its excellent performance. Despite the fact that the language is still young, we already have a couple of interesting packages to choose from.

Now, you have a solid understanding of the model-based recommendation systems and of their implementation workflow—both on a theoretical and practical level. Plus, throughout our journey, we've also been exposed to more advanced data wrangling using `DataFrames`, an invaluable tool in Julia's data science arsenal.

We hope that this whirlwind overview of Julia has shown you why Julia is a rising star in the world of scientific computing and (big) data applications. You are now prepared—and we hope eager—to use Julia in your projects. So, instead of Goodbye, we'd like to say—*Welcome to the wonderful world of Julia programming*!

Other Books You May Enjoy

If you enjoyed this book, you may be interested in these other books by Packt:

Julia 1.0 Programming Cookbook
Bogumił Kamiński, Przemysław Szufel

ISBN: 9781788998369

- Boost your code's performance using Julia's unique features
- Organize data in to fundamental types of collections: arrays and dictionaries
- Organize data science processes within Julia and solve related problems
- Scale Julia computations with cloud computing
- Write data to IO streams with Julia and handle web transfer
- Define your own immutable and mutable types
- Speed up the development process using metaprogramming

Hands-On Computer Vision with Julia
Dmitrijs Cudihins

ISBN: 978-1-78899-879-6

- Analyze image metadata and identify critical data using JuliaImages
- Apply filters and improve image quality and color schemes
- Extract 2D features for image comparison using JuliaFeatures
- Cluster and classify images with KNN/SVM machine learning algorithms
- Recognize text in an image using the Tesseract library

Leave a review - let other readers know what you think

Please share your thoughts on this book with others by leaving a review on the site that you bought it from. If you purchased the book from Amazon, please leave us an honest review on this book's Amazon page. This is vital so that other potential readers can see and use your unbiased opinion to make purchasing decisions, we can understand what our customers think about our products, and our authors can see your feedback on the title that they have worked with Packt to create. It will only take a few minutes of your time, but is valuable to other potential customers, our authors, and Packt. Thank you!

Index

just in time (JIT) compiler 11

K

Kaggle
  reference 413
keyword arguments 54, 55, 268, 269

L

landing page
  preparing 349, 352
last-in-first-out (LIFO) 329
libraries 115
link
  structure 240
Lisp 121
list comprehensions 60, 61
listwise deletion 416
local scope 76
low-level communications
  using 153, 154, 155

M

Machine Learning (ML) models 413
machine learning-based recommendations
  about 430
  creating 434
  recommendations, creating 430
  recommender, building 433
  recommender, training 433
  testing 435, 436, 437, 438, 439
  training data, setting up 431, 432, 433
macros
  defining 125, 126, 127
  versus functions 126
map 60, 61
market basket analysis 384
matrices 83, 84, 85, 86, 87, 88, 89
Matrix Factorization (MF) 428, 433, 434
memory-based recommenders
  versus model-based recommenders 410, 411, 412
method 62
methods
  about 323
  defining 324, 325, 326

missing values
  handling 416
  handling, via deletion 416
  handling, via imputation 416
  reference 416
Missings package
  reference 388
mixin behavior 281
ML algorithms
  reference 428
model-based approach
  enhanced memory-based 413
  linear algebra 413
  probability 412
model-based recommenders
  about 412
  data 413
  data analysis 416, 417, 419, 420, 422, 423, 424, 425, 426
  data models, training 427, 428
  data preparation 416, 417, 419, 420, 422, 423, 424, 425, 426
  data, preprocessing 413
  dataset, loading 414, 415
  dataset, scaling down 428
  missing data, handling 415
  testing data, versus training data 429
modules, Six Degrees of Wikipedia game
  defining 286
  LOAD_PATH, setting up 291, 292
  loading 292, 293
  loading, with import function 294
  loading, with include 294, 295
  nesting 295
  productive REPL sessions 286, 288
  setting up 288, 289
  using 284, 285, 286
multiple dispatch 62, 63, 323
mutable composite types 316
MySQL Docker image
  reference 327
MySQL
  adding 327
  connecting to 328, 329
  reference 327

N

naming conventions 26, 27, 28
new game
  difficulty settings, extracting from page URL 353
  in-article navigation, setting up 359, 360
  information, displaying 361, 362, 365
  session, starting 354, 355
  starting 353
  Wikipedia article, rendering from chain 355, 356, 357
non-standard string literals 191
numbers
  about 194
  integers 195

O

object-oriented (OO) languages 62
object-oriented programming (OOP) 313
Open Database Connectivity (ODBC) 148
operator precedence 277
operators 57
optional arguments 268
optional positional arguments 54, 55
ordered dictionaries 253
overloading 62

P

package
  about 16
  adding 16, 17
pairs 248
parallel computing
  about 150
  low-level communications, using 153, 154, 155
  processes, creating 151, 152
parallel operations 150
parametric type 33, 113, 114
Pearson's r correlation 390
performance tips, Julia
  reference 169
personalized recommendations
  about 379
  explicit ratings 379
  implicit ratings 379

pipe operator 260, 261
Plots
  using, on data 176
primitive type 314
Probabilistic Latent Semantic Analysis (PLSA) 412
Probabilistic Latent Semantic Indexing (PLSI) 412
profiler tool
  about 169
  reference 169
Python
  calling 166

Q

quote 122

R

ranges 39, 40, 41
rational numbers 32, 33
raw string literals 194
Read Evaluate Print Loop (REPL) 9
read-eval-print loop (REPL) 233
recommender systems
  about 375
  association-based 383
  classifying 376
  content-based 379
  non-personalized 376
  personalized 376, 379
  stereotyped 376
recommender
  building 433
  Matrix Factorization (MF) 433, 434
  training 433
reflection
  capabilities 131, 132
regular expressions 37, 38, 39
  about 191, 192
  reference 193
relational databases
  Article model, setting up 329, 330
  MySQL support, adding 327
  working with 327
repeated evaluation
  about 69
  break statement 71, 72